Introducing World Christianity

To Katherine, with love

Introducing World Christianity

Edited by Charles E. Farhadian

WILEY-BLACKWELL

A John Wiley & Sons, Ltd., Publication

This edition first published 2012
© Blackwell Publishing Ltd.

Blackwell Publishing was acquired by John Wiley & Sons in February 2007. Blackwell's publishing program has been merged with Wiley's global Scientific, Technical, and Medical business to form Wiley-Blackwell.

Registered Office
John Wiley & Sons Ltd, The Atrium, Southern Gate, Chichester, West Sussex, PO19 8SQ, UK

Editorial Offices
350 Main Street, Malden, MA 02148-5020, USA
9600 Garsington Road, Oxford, OX4 2DQ, UK
The Atrium, Southern Gate, Chichester, West Sussex, PO19 8SQ, UK

For details of our global editorial offices, for customer services, and for information about how to apply for permission to reuse the copyright material in this book please see our website at www.wiley.com/wiley-blackwell.

The right of Charles E. Farhadian to be identified as the author of the editorial material in this work has been asserted in accordance with the UK Copyright, Designs and Patents Act 1988.

Library of Congress Cataloging-in-Publication Data

Introducing world Christianity / edited by Charles E. Farhadian.
      p. cm.
   Includes bibliographical references and index.
    ISBN 978-1-4051-8249-2 (hardback) – ISBN 978-1-4051-8248-5 (paperback)
  1. Christianity. I. Farhadian, Charles E., 1964–
  BR121.3.I58 2012
  230–dc23   2011033060

A catalogue record for this book is available from the British Library.

This book is published in the following electronic formats: ePDFs ISBN 9781444344547; ePub ISBN 9781444344554; mobi ISBN 9781444344561

Set in 10/12pt, Bembo by Thomson Digital, Noida, India

Printed in Singapore by Ho Printing Singapore Pte Ltd

1 2012

Contents

List of Illustrations vii

List of Contributors viii

Foreword ix
Robert W. Hefner

Acknowledgments xi

Map 0.1 Percentage majority religion by province, 2010 xii

Introduction 1
Charles E. Farhadian

Part I: Africa 5

1 Middle Eastern and North African Christianity: Persisting in the Lands of Islam 7
   Heather J. Sharkey

2 Christian Belongings in East Africa: Flocking to the Churches 21
   Ben Knighton

3 West African Christianity: Padres, Pastors, Prophets, and Pentecostals 36
   Ogbu Kalu

4 Christianity in Southern Africa: The Aesthetics of Well-Being 51
   Frederick Klaits

Part II: Europe 63

5 Christianity in Western Europe: Mission Fields, Old and New? 65
   Simon Coleman

6 Christianity in Eastern Europe: A Story of Pain, Glory, Persecution, and Freedom 77
   Peter Kuzmic

Part III: Asia 91

7 Christianity in South Asia: Negotiating Religious Pluralism 93
   Arun Jones

8 Christianity in Southeast Asia: Similarity and Difference in a Culturally Diverse Region 108
   Barbara Watson Andaya

9 Christianity in East Asia: Evangelicalism and the March First Independence Movement in Korea   122
   Timothy S. Lee

Part IV: Americas   **137**

10 Christianity in North America: Changes and Challenges in a Land of Promise   139
    Kevin J. Christiano

11 Central America and the Caribbean: Christianity on the Periphery   154
    Virginia Garrard-Burnett

12 Christianity in Latin America: Changing Churches in a Changing Continent   171
    Samuel Escobar

13 Brazilian Charisma: Pentecostalized Christianity in Latin America's Largest Nation   186
    R. Andrew Chesnut

Part V: The Pacific   **201**

14 Christianity in Australia and New Zealand: Faith and Politics in Secular Soil   203
    Marion Maddox

15 Christianity in Polynesia: Transforming the Islands   218
    Ian Breward

16 Christianity in Micronesia: The Interplay between Church and Culture   230
    Francis X. Hezel

17 Christianity in Melanesia: Transforming the Warrior Spirit   244
    Garry W. Trompf

Conclusion: World Christianity – Its History, Spread, and Social Influence   259
Robert D. Woodberry

Index   272

List of Illustrations

Maps

0.1 Percentage majority religion by province, 2010   xii
1.1 Middle East and North Africa   8
2.1 East Africa   22
3.1 West Africa   37
4.1 Southern Africa   52
5.1 Western Europe   66
6.1 Eastern Europe   78
7.1 South Asia   94
8.1 Southeast Asia   109
9.1 East Asia   123
10.1 North America   140
11.1 Central America and the Caribbean   155
12.1 Latin America   172
13.1 Brazil   187
14.1 Australia and New Zealand   204
15.1 Polynesia   219
16.1 Micronesia   231
17.1 Melanesia   245

Figures

1.1 Martyrology of Coptic Saints   12
1.2 Christian Woman in Itsa, Fayoum Governorate, Egypt.   15
2.1 Anglican Bishops blessing a school bus at the consecration of the first Bishop of Kitale   24
2.2 Scott Memorial Church, Thogoto   26
3.1 Life of Olaudah   40
4.1 Women members of an Apostolic church in Botswana dressed in uniforms   57
4.2 A burial service in Botswana   60
5.1 Jesus House Ministry in Brent Cross, Northwest London   73
5.2 A women's conference in London   74
6.1 Evangelical Pentecostal Church "Radosne Vijesti"   84

6.2 St Andrew's Orthodox Church in Kyiv, Ukraine   88
7.1 A Syrian Orthodox Church in Kerala   98
7.2 A Khrist Panthi worshiping Jesus   102
8.1 Our Lady of Antipolo   111
8.2 Cathedral, Vigan, the Philippines   113
8.3 Good Friday procession in Larantuka, Flores, Indonesia   114
8.4 Tomb of a Toba Batak Christian, Sumatra, Indonesia   120
9.1 Women's Bible study group in Chemulp'o (Incheon)   126
9.2 Prayer meeting in Pyongyang   128
10.1 A community of Trappist monks   144
10.2 Richard M. Nixon joins the famed Christian evangelist Billy Graham   148
11.1 Cathedral Of Santo Domingo   158
12.1 Iglesia Sarhua, Peru   173
12.2 La Paz, Bolivia   175
13.1 Deliverance from Demons   193
13.2 Brazilian Export: The Universal Church of the Kingdom of God   194
14.1 Rev. John Dunmore Lang, D.D., A.M.   207
14.2 Armed Constabulary Field Force, Parihaka   212
15.1 Papeiha - Cook Islands missionary   220
15.2 "King George of Tonga"   222
16.1 Fr. Edwin McManus with students   235
16.2 Women dressed in uniform for presentation of songs at the Christmas celebration   238
17.1 Catholic Church, Ambunti, Sepik River region   250

Tables

2.1 Religious adherence in East African countries   29
10.1 The 10 largest religious affiliations – United States (2008)   143
10.2 The 10 largest religious affiliations – Canada (2001)   143

List of Contributors

Barbara Watson Andaya is Professor of Asian Studies and the Director of the Center for Southeast Asian Studies at the University of Hawai'i.

Ian Breward is Senior Fellow in the School of Historical and Philosophical Studies, University of Melbourne, and Emeritus Professor of Church History in the Uniting Church's Theological Hall, Ormond College, Melbourne.

Virginia Garrard-Burnett is Professor of History and Religious Studies at the University of Texas at Austin, Texas.

R. Andrew Chesnut is the Bishop Walter Sullivan Chair of Catholic Studies and Professor of Religious Studies at Virginia Commonwealth University, Richmond, Virginia.

Kevin J. Christiano is Associate Professor of Sociology at the University of Notre Dame, Notre Dame, Indiana.

Simon Coleman is Jackman Professor at the Centre for the Study of Religion, University of Toronto, Canada.

Samuel Escobar is Professor Emeritus at Palmer Theological Seminary in Wynnewood, Pennsylvania, and President Emeritus of the Latin American Theological Fraternity.

Charles E. Farhadian is Associate Professor of World Religions and Christian Mission at Westmont College, Santa Barbara, California.

Francis X. Hezel, SJ is a Jesuit priest who has worked in Micronesia since 1963, serving as the Director of Xavier High School in Chuuk, the Regional Superior of the Jesuits in Micronesia, and Director of Micronesian Seminar, Pohnpei, Micronesia.

Arun Jones is Dan and Lillian Hankey Associate Professor of World Evangelism, Candler School of Theology, Emory University, Atlanta, Georgia.

Ogbu Kalu was Luce Professor of World Christianity and Mission at McCormick Theological Seminary, Chicago, Illinois, until his death in 2009.

Frederick Klaits, a cultural anthropologist, is Assistant Professor of Anthropology at Northern Kentucky University, Highland Heights, Kentucky.

Ben Knighton is Dean of the Research Programme at Oxford Centre for Mission Studies (OCMS), Oxford, England.

Peter Kuzmic is the Eva B. and Paul E. Toms Distinguished Professor of Missions and European Studies at Gordon-Conwell Theological Seminary, South Hamilton, Massachusetts.

Timothy S. Lee is Associate Professor of the History of Christianity and Director of Asian Church Studies at Brite Divinity School, Forth Worth, Texas.

Marion Maddox is Director of the Centre for Research on Social Inclusion at Macquarie University, Sydney.

Heather J. Sharkey is an Associate Professor in the Department of Near Eastern Languages and Civilizations at the University of Pennsylvania, Philadelphia, Pennsylvania.

Garry W. Trompf is Emeritus Professor in the History of Ideas and Adjunct Professor at the Centre for Peace and Conflict Studies, University of Sydney.

Robert D. Woodberry is Assistant Professor of Sociology at the University of Texas at Austin, Texas.

Foreword

Robert W. Hefner

When Western social theorists in the mid-twentieth century assessed the forces reshaping the modern world, few regarded religion as of much importance. Capitalism, the nation-state, education, science, and technology – these were the locomotives propelling modernity's forward surge. The major question for these thinkers was not whether religion was still vital, but whether the forces of modernization would consign religion to the private sphere – or do away with it entirely.

Few forecasts in modern social thought have proved more massively mistaken than this one. As we move into the second decade of the twenty-first century, one of the most striking characteristics of the age is the near-global resurgence of religion. One is obliged to say "near-global" because, with the notable exception of its pious immigrants, Western Europe – once thought the model for all modernizing societies – appears to be the great exception to the late-modern religious rule. But whereas scholars of modernity and religion once regarded Western Europe as a window into the soon-to-be-global, today the continent's stark secularity seems, well, simply exceptional.

What makes the public revitalization of religion all the more intriguing is that it is not just taking place in one tradition, but in most of the world's great religions. Whether it is Islam in the Middle East, Africa, and Asia, Hinduism in India and the global Indian diaspora, Buddhism in East and Southeast Asia, Christianity in America and the global South, or any number of other faiths, the late-modern surge of religion is powerful and pervasive.

In sheer demographic and sociological terms, however, two of today's religious revitalizations are particularly notable: Islam and Christianity. Although it is sometimes mistakenly equated with radical Islamism, the Islamic resurgence is not first of all radical but piety-minded. Unlike its militant offshoots, which have a strong presence only in select portions of the world, the resurgence in Islamic observance and sociability has been felt in virtually all corners of the globe, wherever the world's 1.8 billion Muslims reside. Two striking sociological features of the Islamic resurgence are, first, that its leadership is overwhelmingly middle class and well educated, and, second, that notwithstanding the fact that most of its participants reject radicalism, the resurgence has been marked by a heightened interest in bringing religion into politics, enterprise, and the public sphere.

As the essays in this fine volume make compellingly clear, the global vitalization of Christianity differs in several ways from that of its Muslim counterpart. The most striking difference is that whereas the Islamic resurgence has had its most powerful impact on already established populations, Christianity's late-modern surge has been marked by the diffusion of the faith to new lands. As the chapters in this book demonstrate, the diffusion has brought a genuine world Christianity into being. A world Christianity is a faith no longer overwhelmingly concentrated in the West, but one rooted socially and demographically in the global South. In the twentieth and twenty-first centuries, Christianity has returned to a global standing that had been lost for half a millennium after its catastrophic collapse in the Middle East and western Asia during the late Middle Ages.

Seen from the perspective of the new ecumene's media, finances, and, for mainline denominations, centers of ecclesiastical authority, Westerners still enjoy an influence in world Christianity disproportionate to their numbers as a whole. But the growing phenomenon of missionaries being dispatched from Africa, Latin America, and East Asia to the West and other lands reminds us that it is only a matter of time before the intellectual weight of the Christian South matches its demographic girth. It is the phenomenon of a Christianity becoming truly global, with all that means for the social and theological plurality of the faith, to which the essays in this volume bear witness.

This book's essays also remind us of another difference between the Islamic resurgence and world Christianity. Although the leadership of the Islamic resurgence is educated and middle class, evangelical and, especially, Pentecostal Christianity in the global South tends to have a poorer and less educated profile. In the 1970s and 1980s, some Western observers saw the relative deprivation of the global South's new Christians as proof that the main agents for the evangelical spread were North Americans. It is true that a significant portion of the funding and worship styles of Protestantism in the global South at first showed the influence of American ministries. However, as the contributors to this volume demonstrate so clearly, Christianity in the global South has long since developed an organizational dynamism of its own. In fact, it was only after evangelical and Pentecostal congregations declared their independence from their North American supporters that the new communities acquired the evangelical momentum that they now have.

As several chapters in this volume also indicate, the ascent of Southern Christianity may have a theolog-ically conservative influence, not least of all on questions of gender and sexuality. However, the broader political impact of this self-confident Southern Christianity will almost certainly be varied – as it has been, for example, in Brazil, where evangelical voters are no more conservative than their Catholic counterparts. The variation is a sign of the fact that the center of gravity for most of the new Christian communities is not agreement on or commitment to a particular model of the state, but a concern for personal salvation, social healing, and divinely given dignity.

A distinguished scholar of world Christianity with whom I have had the great pleasure to work over the years, Charles Farhadian has brought together an outstanding team of specialists of world Christianity for this volume. Their scholarship sheds new light on just how this world Christianity came into being, and where it is going. No less important, the authors show us how it is that contrary to the secularist forecasts of the mid-twentieth century, the Christian message of otherworldy transcendence and inner-worldly optimism is as resonant and meaningful as ever for hundreds of millions of people.

Robert W. Hefner
Director, Institute on Culture, Religion, and World
Affairs, Boston University

Acknowledgments

This volume would be impossible without the authors who contributed chapters contained within it. So I begin by thanking each author for his or her contribution. Our authors span the globe and thus are in a superb position to provide scholarly reflection on their region. Gratitude goes to my teachers and other scholars who have shaped my thinking about the complexities of world Christianity: Miriam Adeney, Stephen Bevans, Peter Berger, Benny Giay, Robert Hefner, Lewis Rambo, Dana Robert, Lamin Sanneh, and Andrew Walls. A special thanks goes to Darrell Whiteman, with whom I share areal interests, for his helpful comments on the Introduction. As a faculty member, I thank the administration and my colleagues at Westmont College for their support and the faculty development grants that have enabled me to complete this project, especially Bruce Fisk, Maurice Lee, Tremper Longman III, Chandra Mallampalli, William Nelson, Richard Pointer, Caryn Reeder, Helen Rhee, Warren Rogers, Curt Whiteman, and Telford Work. The book has come into existence due to the guidance and perseverance of the editorial team at Wiley-Blackwell: Isobel Bainton, Lucy Boon, Helen Gray, Rebecca Harkin, Andrew Humphries, and Bridget Jennings. Most importantly, I want to express my love and appreciation to my wife, Katherine, and sons Gabriel and Gideon, who allowed me time away from the family to complete this book.

Charles Farhadian
Santa Barbara, California

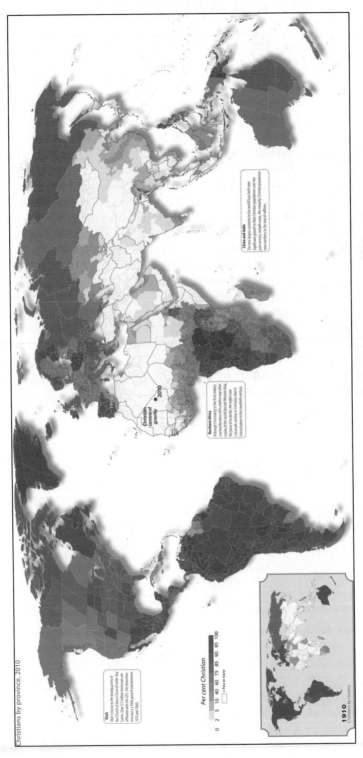

Christians by province, 2010

Utah
Utah is home to the headquarters of the Church of Jesus Christ of Latter-day Saints. Over 57 million Americans are affiliated with the LDS. The Mormons have had a 2.5% growth rate between 1910 and 2000.

Per cent Christian

0 2 5 10 40 60 75 85 90 95 100

☐ = Few or none

Northern Africa
Although Christianity in the first century reached Northern Africa, before any other region of the world (except Western Asia, the place of its birth), the region has a dramatic decline in Christians due to Islamicisation in the twentieth century.

1910   2010

Christian centre of gravity

China and India
The two largest countries in the world have both seen significant growth in their Christian populations over the past century. In both cases, the minority Christian population now numbers in the tens of millions.

1910
Christianity by country

Map 0.1 Percentage majority religion by province, 2010

Introduction

Charles E. Farhadian

An introduction to world Christianity poses several problems that are by no means particular to the discipline of studying religions. My challenge lies in distinguishing this book from the numerous publications of the last two decades. In a nutshell, this book seeks to explore world Christianity through the complexities of global interdependence and globalization by investigating the dynamic nature of social, cultural, political, and religious encounters with Christianity. World Christianity consists of the diverse forms of indigenous Christianity unified worldwide not by political, economic, cultural, linguistic, or geographic commonalities, but by communities of faith responsive to God's forgiveness through Jesus Christ, attentive to being individually and corporately shaped by the Bible, and animated by the Holy Spirit to be witnesses to the Gospel across cultural and linguistic boundaries. Christianity, then, is inherently missionary in its approach to the world, seeking to be enacted within cultures and societies worldwide. Until recently two major paradigms have dominated the interpretation of world Christianity. This book contributes to a third paradigm.

The first paradigm, surfacing in the late nineteenth and early twentieth centuries, sought to map Christianity's presence on the world stage. In the words of American historian Kenneth Scott Latourette (1884–1968), "One of the most striking facts of our time is the global extension of Christianity." This interpretation of world Christianity stressed the Western-initiated Christian mission movement propelled by Western powers in introducing Christianity to "pagans," also frequently emphasizing the "national mission" of the expansion of North American and European civilization (including democracy, individual rights, individual conscience, voluntary associations, and social and economic free enterprise).[1] Many American scholars upheld the perspective that exporting American civilization was quite benign, and, in fact, the national mission of Western nations at times coalesced quite conveniently with Christian missions, being stimulated partly by Enlightenment assurances of progress and development.

The second paradigm, appearing in the last few decades of the twentieth century, interpreted world Christianity as polycentric in nature, where each center possessed equivalent yet independent authority. This interpretative paradigm sought to avoid privileging a single command center (e.g., the West) that navigated the global flow of Christian movements and discourse.[2] Moving past colonial interpretations in order to illustrate local agency even in the face of colonial domination, these scholars underscored the results of Christianity as nation-making, increasing literacy rates, introducing modern education and healthcare, the heightening of cultural confidence, and the burgeoning of historical agency in postcolonial contexts. Christianity, scholars noted, gave those colonized the confidence to overturn colonial regimes – because Christianity contained a message of human liberation and reconciliation with God. Researchers employing this paradigm highlighted the demographic shift of Christianity to the global South that gave rise to innovative theologies and new Christian discourses – a "new Christendom," in Philip Jenkins's words, that challenged and enlivened Christianity in the global North by Southern Christianity's more conservative biblical hermeneutics and original theological thinking emerging from contexts of suffering and poverty. Biblical translation into indigenous languages and the contextualization of Christian theology provided the combustible energy that propelled Christianity around the world, making the faith meaningful in all kinds of contexts. This approach added significantly to our understanding of world Christianity, particularly in terms of how it demonstrated the powerful and unpredictable ways that the biblical message transformed people and nations.

This book contributes to a third paradigm, which builds on the contributions of earlier approaches. Given that earlier paradigms in the study of world Christianity were heavily historical, this book widens our interpretative scope by drawing connections between social, cultural, political, religious, and historical forces and their uneven relationships with Christianity. Along the way, authors keep a watchful eye on the emergent styles of citizenship, mobilization, and subjectivities as a result of Christianity, since the adoption of Christianity appears to have led to the transformation of individual and corporate identities, enabling love for one another and for God. Such changes have immense social, cultural, and political consequences. Anthropologist Kenelm Burridge, referring to transformations brought by Christianity, suggested that this "new consciousness requires a new world in which to realize itself. And if that new world is not there, the new consciousness seeks to create it."[3] The social, cultural, and political results of this transformation of consciousness warrant our attention.

Scholars have used several metaphors to communicate the dynamic growth of Christianity across cultural and linguistic frontiers, with the most popular being Christianity as *movement* (e.g., "the world Christian movement"). For two decades media researchers, geographers, demographers, and economists have used

an additional metaphor – that of *flows* – to speak about how ideas, people, and technologies migrate across spatial frontiers.[4] When researchers use the metaphor of movement to describe Christianity, they recognize that Christianity too exhibits a kind of flow – since Christian missionaries, discourses, and institutions *embody* the message of Christianity, especially when traveling across cultural and linguistic spaces. Naturally, the communication of Christianity is not through disembodied voices (except, I guess, through the medium of radio or Internet); communicators of the faith are themselves carriers of ideas, technologies, institutions, and preferences which recipients have (mis)understood as part and parcel of the communication of the Gospel. Bible translators, too, are embodied subjects who communicate messages about Christianity both discursively and non-discursively, even while they work to translate the Bible into vernacular languages. Their physical presence matters and carries with it an embodiment of Christian faith. As Bishop Lesslie Newbigin has pointed out, there is no pure, decontextualized Gospel. So our task here is to investigate the historical, cultural, social, and political forces that in part serve as carriers of the tradition.

Christianity is movement – a flow, a traveling religion, at home yet never completely domesticated in any particular location. Yet there is more, since the flow of Christianity is characterized by varying *rates of change*, moments of acceleration and deceleration that partly account for the changing nature of world Christianity itself. In our analyses, it is critical to capture the processes and speed of the flows of these global itineraries of Christianity, paying attention to what Ulf Hannerz calls "the multicentricity of flows, to crisscrossing flows, and to counterflows."[5] Under conditions of globalization, cultural and religious flows over wide distances have become commonplace, such as when denominational boards or ecumenical bodies make decisions that affect churches located far from those centers of decision-making. As you read these chapters, keep an eye on the directions of those flows. By underscoring the polycentric nature of the Christian ecumene, as though world Christianity consists of equally authoritative centers spread out around the globe, one might overlook the fact that some forms of Christianity (e.g., North American Christianity) still exhibit immense influence on the rest of world

Christianity, not the least in terms of economics, worship styles, and theological and biblical standardization through its publishing houses.[6]

Christian transformations of cultures and societies that occurred as a result of the circulation of people, ideas, technologies, and institutions marked boundaries. While marking boundaries, this circulation also helped to establish means of transport for all kinds of personal and corporate mobilities out of locales, increasing communication between distant (and transnational) congregations and lessening ecclesiastical isolation. What is important to recognize is that world Christianity is not only dynamic but relational, with the historical paths observed by historians serving as channels of flows whereby ideas, people, technology, money, and information traveled. Christianity is a traveling religion. And studying world Christianity helps us to appreciate its translocal, interconnected nature.

The investigation of Christianity as "world Christianity" is a recent phenomenon. Sociologist Robert Wuthnow notes that the phrase "world Christianity" first appeared in Francis John McConnell's *Human Needs and World Christianity* (1929).[7] But the term "world Christianity" was popularized through a series of publications beginning most notably with Dana Robert's essay, "Shifting Southward: Global Christianity since 1945" (2000), Philip Jenkins's *The Next Christendom: The Coming of Global Christianity* (2002), and Lamin Sanneh's *Whose Religion is Christianity?: The Gospel Beyond the West* (2003). Since these publications, a proliferation of books and articles have sought to illuminate the implications of the demographic shifts of Christianity worldwide, where since the mid-1980s roughly 60 percent of the world's Christians resided in the global South. That Christianity was the largest world religion was nothing new. What was novel was the identification of Christianity as a worldwide religion linked historically and ontologically as the body of Christ through time and space. The rising numerical predominance of Christianity in the global South compelled Western scholars to take seriously non-Western varieties of Christianity.

This book advances a third interpretative paradigm, which combines both historical breadth and social scientific depth. Why is this approach so important? Too often interpretations of the worldwide Christian movement fixate on analyses of Christianity during the period of European colonial expansion, when Western missionaries often made what Ben Knighton has called "strange and inevitable bedfellows" with colonial powers. Such analyses coupled Christianity with empire-building to demonstrate that their combined efforts led to the erosion of local cultures. There are two problems with such an interpretation of world Christianity. First, this interpretation overlooked the fact that local recipients of Christianity maintained their agency even in the face of the powerful forces of Church and empire. New forms of Christianity emerged, despite the motivations of colonialists or missionaries and the antipathy of Church authorities. Second, an interpretation that investigated only a narrow band of history, namely the period of European colonial Christianity, sidelined centuries of pre-colonial (e.g., patristic and medieval) and postcolonial (e.g., from mid-twentieth-century) historical accounts. Such a truncated historical perspective leaves us with an incomplete picture of the nature of world Christianity because it gives interpretative privilege to only one period of history. Nevertheless, we need more than a broad historical perspective to understand world Christianity. To complement the breadth of historical analysis, we need the depth of what can be unearthed through social scientific investigation, since social scientific perspectives help us see Christianity as events that have transformed cultural, social, religious, and political domains. Thus our approach here has combined historical and social scientific insights.

Driving this book is a simple question: "What difference has Christianity made in the world?" This is a worthwhile question given the fact that adherents to Christianity make up about 33.2 percent of the world's population.[8] Authors begin their chapters with a brief historical overview of a particular region, then launch into an analysis of regional aspects of world Christianity by employing a variety of disciplinary perspectives. Conspicuously absent are the voices of theologians and biblical scholars, not because these perspectives cannot teach us something valuable about the nature of world Christianity, but because our focus is on the social, cultural, and political changes afoot as a result of Christian presence. The temporal focus is late modernity, which witnessed the rise of nation-states, intensification of globalization, increase of the influence of science and technology, and the proliferation of mass media.

4

Notes and References

[1] Daniel H. Bays, "The Foreign Missionary Movement in the 19th and early 20th Centuries," National Humanities Center, available [online] at: <http://nationalhumanitiescenter.org/tserve/nineteen/nkeyinfo/fmmovement.htm>.

[2] Robert Wuthnow, *Boundless Faith: The Global Outreach of American Churches* (Berkeley, CA: University of California Press, 2009), 62–74.

[3] Kenelm Burridge, *In the Way: A Study of Christian Missionary Endeavors* (Vancouver: University of British Columbia Press, 1991), 163.

[4] A helpful theoretical positioning of religion as movement, flow, travel is provided by Thomas A. Tweed, *Crossing and Dwelling: A Theory of Religion* (Cambridge, MA: Harvard University Press, 2006), 57.

[5] Ulf Hannerz, "Flows, Boundaries, and Hybrids: Keywords in Transnational Anthropology" (Plenary Lecture at the Twentieth Biennial Meeting of the Associacao Brasileira de Antropologia at Salvador de Bahia, April 14–17, 1996).

[6] See, for instance, Robert Wuthnow, *Boundless Faith: The Global Outreach of American Churches* (Berkeley, CA: University of California Press, 2009).

[7] Ibid., 34.

[8] Todd M. Johnson and Kenneth R. Ross, *Atlas of Global Christianity* (Edinburgh: Edinburgh University Press, 2009), 6.

Part I

Africa

1

Middle Eastern and North African Christianity
Persisting in the Lands of Islam

Heather J. Sharkey

Historical Introduction

The Middle East and North Africa were cradles of Christianity. Jesus spent his life in the "Holy Land" where Israel and the Palestinian territories exist today. His disciples spread the Christian message into the Roman and Persian empires in Western Asia and Northern Africa. During the next four centuries, Roman North Africa produced some of early Christianity's most brilliant philosophers: men like Athanasius and Cyril of Alexandria (Egypt); Tertullian and Cyprian of Carthage (Tunisia); and Augustine of Hippo (Algeria). However, following the rise of Islam in the early seventh century, and the establishment through conquest of an Islamic empire that stretched, by 711, from what is now Morocco to the India–Pakistan border, Christianity lost ground to Islam. One scholar described Christian history in the Islamic world as a history of "hanging on"; another called it a history of "constrained lives."[1] Perhaps deterred by impressions of chronic strain and attrition, the authors of many recent studies of world Christianity overlook the modern Middle East after sketching the region's early place in Christian history.[2] Nevertheless, vibrant Christian communities remain and take pride in rich histories on which they build. Today, Middle Eastern Christians also offer lively models of ecumenical and interfaith dialogue, while pursuing social service and civic engagement.

How have Christians fared and endured in the Islamic Middle East and North Africa, and why have their numbers declined? Historically, Muslim governments set policies that limited Christian communities. The boundaries encircling Christian communities arose, above all, from Islamic (*shariah*) laws of conversion, marriage, and inheritance. The early Islamic empire, like its successor states, also offered social and economic incentives that encouraged Christians and others to embrace Islam, thereby eliciting large-scale conversions that occurred, in most places and periods, with little or no coercion. Meanwhile, in modern times, three other factors reduced Christian communities: voluntary emigration (especially to the Americas, Western Europe, and later Australia), war-related refugee movements and population transfers, and low birth rates. Historians of the region debate the importance of a fourth factor in this contraction: the impact of contacts with Western Christians of Catholic, Protestant, and Orthodox varieties, from what is now France, Britain, Russia, the United States, and elsewhere. Did Western contacts, in the modern period as earlier (for example, during the Crusades of the twelfth and thirteenth centuries), bolster Middle Eastern Christians or undermine them, by stoking mistrust and resentment among Muslims? Given the current situation in Iraq, where an estimated 600,000 out of some 1.3 million Christians fled the country in the five years following the US invasion of 2003, this last question appears more relevant than ever.[3]

Introducing World Christianity, First Edition. Edited by Charles E. Farhadian.
© 2012 Blackwell Publishing Ltd. Published 2012 by Blackwell Publishing Ltd.

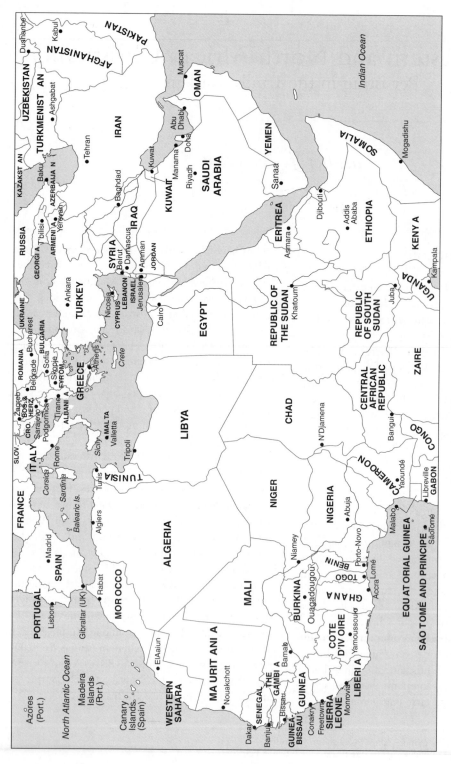

Map 1.1   Middle East and North Africa

Christian Pluralism, Early Islam, and the Terms of *Dhimmi* Life

Surveying such a long and complex history in this short space is impossible, and yet a few points are worth highlighting. By the time Islam emerged in the seventh century, Middle Eastern and North African Christians were already evincing the doctrinal and communal pluralism, or sectarianism, that became one of world Christianity's defining features. Arising initially from debates about the divine and human nature(s) of Jesus, sectarian differences coalesced in the period stretching from the fifth through the seventh or eighth centuries. In the long run, communities reinforced sectarian distinctions by using particular languages (e.g., Greek, Armenian, Syriac, or Coptic) for their church liturgies and literatures. In some cases, church-centered cultures evolved to produce, by the modern era, what scholars have described as nationalist identities. Consider, for example, the adherents of the Church of the East (sometimes called, by outsiders, the Nestorian Church). By the early twentieth century, in what is now Northern Iraq, Southeast Turkey, and Northwest Iran, members of this community called themselves Assyrians and evinced a nationalist consciousness that drew strength, first, from a literary history rooted in the Classical Syriac literature of their Church, and second, from a budding print culture in the neo-Aramaic language (which American Presbyterian missionaries helped to promote).

After the Council of Chalcedon in 451 (where bitter theological disputes arose over the nature of Christ), Byzantine Christian authorities in Constantinople began to persecute Egyptians who belonged to what became known as the Coptic Orthodox Church. Historians point to such persecution to explain the lack of Christian solidarity that prevailed when Muslim Arabs expanded beyond Arabia into the Byzantine imperial territories of the Levant and North Africa, and into the Sassanian (Persian) imperial territories of Iraq and Iran. Thus, for example, when Muslim armies reached Egypt in 640, local Coptic Christians greeted the invaders with more of a welcome than a show of resistance and looked for relief from persecution. One scholar suggests, "The advent of Islam may have helped to establish firm doctrinal differences [among

Eastern Christians] for the first time," if only because Islamic rule "freed Christians from the pressure of Byzantine conformity."[4] Muslim rulers did not generally care about the sects to which Christians belonged, and this proved liberating to some Christians, even in the modern period when Catholic and Protestant missionaries were active.

In accordance with the Qur'an, which Muslims regarded as a message that Muhammad had conveyed from God to humankind, the early Muslim invaders recognized Christians and Jews as "People of the Book," meaning monotheists having scriptural traditions. To People of the Book who surrendered, the Muslims guaranteed freedom of worship and livelihood, provided that they remained loyal to the Muslim state and paid a poll tax, called the *jizya*, to support Muslim armies. Thus, by the mid-seventh century, in the emerging Islamic empire, Christians, Jews, and also Zoroastrians became *dhimmis*, meaning people who lived under the Muslim state's pact of protection. Meanwhile, from the mid-seventh century through the twentieth, Muslim governments appointed Christian and Jewish professionals to their bureaucracies, where they served as doctors, accountants, translators, and advisers. In this way Christians, like Jews, contributed to the making of Islamic civilization. Within a few centuries many Christians also made the Arabic language into their own, while Christian scholars produced a rich Arabic literature of Church philosophy.

Over generations, however, some provisions of the early conquest agreements calcified and thus marginalized Christians, while reinforcing their subordination to Muslims. By the terms of the "Pact of Umar" (as a form of the early Muslim compact with *dhimmis* was eventually remembered), Christians could not build or repair churches without acquiring permission from Muslim rulers; nor could they bear arms or serve in Islamic armies. (Note that these provisions inform laws in many Islamic countries even today.) Meanwhile, the obligations of *jizya*-paying gave Christians an incentive to join Islam as a way of easing taxes. In Egypt, especially, conversions to Islam gained momentum among Christian farmers, who faced a land tax as well. "As conversions proceeded," two demographic historians observed, "the decline in the number of taypayers liable to pay the *jizya* resulted in an increase in the amount due per capita."[5] Those who remained Christian bore a heavier load. Islamic inheritance law offered further incentives for conversion: it stipulated that non-Muslims could not inherit from Muslims. Thus Christian wives of Muslim men, or Christian relatives of recent converts to Islam, lost rights of inheritance unless they, too, joined the Muslim community.

Islamic laws of conversion posed the steepest obstacles to Christian societies. Islamic law held that anyone could join Islam, but that no one could leave it once converted or born to the faith. Leaving Islam amounted to apostasy, a crime punishable by death. While Christians and Jews could join Islam, *dhimmi*s could not convert to other religions; thus Jews could not become Christians, just as Christians could not become Jews. Furthermore, Islamic law deemed children of Muslim fathers to be Muslim, regardless of their mothers' religions. As specified in the Qur'an, Muslim men could marry Christian or Jewish women (on the grounds that such women were believers in God); Christian and Jewish men, however, could not marry Muslim women. Islamic law recognized slavery and concubinage, and regarded it as licit for Muslim men to have sexual relations with slaves whom they owned; the children of female slaves and free Muslim fathers were born into Islam (and freedom) as well. In the early Islamic period of imperial expansion through conquest, when "intermarriage" with Christians was common (to use the euphemistic term favored by scholars when describing Muslim men's relationships with females who may have been technically wives, slaves, or war captives), paternity offered an important route to Islamization.

Islamic laws about conversion and Muslim status are not historical abstractions; they inform the legal systems of many states even today, and determine such things as who can marry whom, who can inherit, even who can gain child custody after divorces. In the modern era, slavery or the slave trade was officially abolished in all Muslim states, even though the Qur'an recognizes slavery, and even though residual forms of the practice sometimes persisted. (For example, Egypt abolished the slave trade in the mid-nineteenth century, while Saudi Arabia abolished slavery in 1962.) But laws barring Muslims from leaving or renouncing Islam (whether for Christianity or otherwise) remain in force today in nearly all Muslim-majority states.

In practice, since the late nineteenth century, many Islamic states have merely made it impossible for converts from Islam to register their changed faith, or have subjected converts to sustained harassment, often including assault or imprisonment. Other states, such as Sudan, Saudi Arabia, and Iran, retain laws declaring apostasy from Islam a capital crime.[6]

Historically, Christian communities under Islamic rule could only grow in two ways: through natural increase, or at each other's expense. Missionary-sponsored Catholic and Protestant churches eventually did the latter, by drawing members from Eastern Orthodox communities. Christians could not evangelize among Muslims, for whom apostasy, in any case, offered grounds for a death sentence. Nor could Christians easily assert themselves by building churches, for indeed, church permits were hard to secure.[7] These challenges to Christians have persisted, sometimes taking new forms. Consider, for example, how in the late twentieth and early twenty-first centuries, the Gulf States (which lack indigenous Christian minorities) have kept church building and even church staffing to a minimum, despite the presence of large Christian expatriate or guest worker populations, including Filipinos, South Indians, and others. Thus two writers noted in 2003, "In Dubai, one of the seven United Arab Emirates, eighty thousand Catholics are associated with a single parish where only a few priests are allowed work permits." The situation in the Emirates was, at least, better than in Saudi Arabia, where non-Muslims were prohibited from organizing worship.[8]

Christian Attrition in the World of Islam: Rates and Reasons

Christian communities hemorrhaged members to Islam after the early Islamic conquests of the seventh century, and yet the losses were neither automatic nor total. In some regions substantial rates of Islamization occurred in a generation or two; in other places, the diminution occurred over several centuries. Studying these patterns of Islamization is worthwhile because it helps to make sense of modern Christian demography, by showing where in the Middle East and North Africa Christianity withered, and where it stayed rooted.

In Egypt, judging by the evidence of *jizya* revenues from non-Muslims, more than half the Coptic Christian population appear to have converted to Islam within 40 years of the Muslim conquest; in Iraq, more than two thirds of the population appear to have converted within 50 years of the conquest. By contrast, conversion to Islam was much slower in Syria: there, it seems, a Christian majority persisted for nearly three centuries.[9] In Iran, another scholar suggests, only 10 percent of the population had become Muslim by 743 (the year 125 in the Islamic calendar (AH)), though by 888 (275 AH), some 90 percent of the Iranian population were Muslim.[10]

In North Africa west of Egypt, "dechristianization" was more dramatic. Consider Carthage, now in Tunisia, which had once been a vital center for Christian philosophy. Muslims seized Carthage in 698. Some Christian presence persisted for nearly four centuries, judging from a letter written by the Roman Pope to a Carthaginian bishop in 1076. But by the time the crusading Louis IX of France (St Louis) died near Tunis in 1270, indigenous Christianity was long gone.[11] Christianity also disappeared in Nubia, now Northern Sudan, where Christian kings had been ruling since the sixth century. In 1315, a Muslim claimed the throne of Nubia; two years later, Muslims converted the "cathedral" of Dongola into a mosque. Nubian Christianity soon became extinct.[12]

Viewing history over a long duration, one can identify four other developments that affected the diminution of Christian populations. Together these "deepen[ed] the introversion of Christian communities under *dhimmi* status," and strengthened bonds between churches and communal identities.[13]

First, there was the continued erosion of the Byzantine Empire, which survived in what is now Greece and Turkey after the Muslim Arab conquests of the seventh century. In the eleventh century, Turkish Muslim horse nomads moved into Anatolia, where they raided Greek- and Armenian-speaking Christian communities, displacing them, absorbing them through "intermarriage," or subjecting them to Muslim rule. In 1071, Seljuk Turks defeated Byzantine imperial armies at the Battle of Manzikert; thenceforth Turkish immigration into Anatolia occurred unhindered, allowing for the long-term ethnic and religious transformation of the Anatolian plateau. The final collapse of the Byzantine Empire occurred when Constantinople fell to the Ottoman Turks in 1453. The Ottoman sultan, Mehmet II ("Mehmet the Conqueror"), signaled the change of imperial religion from Orthodox Christianity to Sunni Islam by immediately ordering the conversion of the church of Hagia Sophia into a mosque. Meanwhile, Islam continued to spread, especially in places such as Cyprus and Crete, where Ottomans kept garrisons and where conversion to Islam offered new opportunities in the military.

Second, there came the Crusades, which were disastrous by many counts. The Roman Pope, Urban II, started these wars in 1096 when he answered the Byzantine emperor's plea for help against Turkish incursions by sending armies. Crusaders slaughtered indiscriminately, and undermined the already fragile Byzantine Empire by laying waste to Byzantine territories. Their actions soured Orthodox–Catholic relations for almost a millennium. The Crusades also stoked anti-Christian violence among Muslims, who suspected local Christians of sympathizing with the Crusaders. This was particularly true in Egypt, where the Mamluk dynasty rose to power in 1250 and, within 25 years, uprooted the last Crusader kingdom from Jerusalem. Coptic chroniclers described the Mamluk period as an age of persecution and martyrs, when Muslim mobs destroyed churches, killed Copts, and created an atmosphere of fear in which many Christians converted to Islam. By the time the Mamluk era ended in 1517, Christians accounted for perhaps 7 percent of Egypt's population – about the same proportion as in the late twentieth century.[14]

The third development, which affected the region corresponding to Iraq, Iran, Turkey, and Syria, came from the thirteenth-century Mongol conquests, which devastated urban and rural areas and felled the Abbasid Empire, centered in Baghdad, in 1258. In the fourteenth century, the conqueror Tamerlane (1336–1405) ravaged many of the same lands. Tamerlane was technically a Muslim, but like the Crusaders, slaughtered people and waged wars without regard to religious identities. Consider that at the height of the Abbasid era (*c.*1000) the Church of the East had sent missionaries from Baghdad to China and India and had developed a "supra-ethnic and multi-lingual identity." After the Mongols, Tamerlane, and some waves of forced conversions, this Church was so shrunken, and so geographically curtailed within Iran and Iraq, that it was becoming less of a "World Church" than an (ethnic) Aramaic-speaking entity, with adherents taking refuge in isolated mountainous regions.[15]

The fourth development consisted of a series of plague outbreaks that ravaged the Middle East and North Africa and left Christian monasteries, important centers of Church scholarship, as "conspicuous casualties." The worst of these outbreaks was the Black Death, which killed a quarter to a third of the region's population in the 1340s; another bad outbreak occurred less than a century later, in 1429. Whereas in the desert of Wadi al-Natrun in Egypt there had been about a hundred monasteries before the Black Death struck in 1347–48, there were only seven left by the early 1400s. Monasteries in Palestine, including ones in Nazareth and Hebron, also vanished.[16]

Once consolidated, the Ottoman Empire (which stretched at its peak in the sixteenth century from Algeria to Iraq) brought stability to its domains. The Ottomans recognized Christians and Jews as belonging to *millets*, meaning religious communities. Ottoman authorities mediated civil administration (e.g., tax collection) through the religious leaders of these *millets*, and allowed communities to manage their internal affairs. The chief Christian liaison in this system was the Orthodox patriarch in Istanbul, whose relationship with Ottoman authorities enhanced the prestige of the Greek-speaking Orthodox community relative to other Christians. By dividing society into religious segments, the Ottoman *millet* system may have helped Christians to retain communal coherence. Division aided survival, since when "populations tended to live in greater separation from one another, even within the same town ... there was less occasion for meeting and thus much less intermarriage [with Muslims]."[17]

Figure 1.1   Martyrology of Coptic Saints (Arabic, n.d. [circa 14th century]). Courtesy of the Library at the Herbert D. Katz Center for Advanced Judaic Studies, University of Pennsylvania.

Meanwhile, for Arabic-speaking Christians who lived along the Eastern Mediterranean coast, Ottoman stability, together with new economic opportunities for coastal trade with Europeans, translated into greater prosperity. Prosperity, in turn, led to greater education and better health among Christians. The result, some scholars argue, was that between the sixteenth and nineteenth centuries, Christian Arabic-speaking communities rebounded in the Eastern Mediterranean, reaching perhaps 20 percent of the population in some areas.[18]

The Modern Period: New Opportunities, New Strains

The very conditions that enabled Christians to prosper in the Ottoman era made them, by the nineteenth century, more vulnerable vis-à-vis Muslim society. By some accounts, in nineteenth-century Syria and Palestine, local Muslim–Christian relations grew strained as some Christian merchants flaunted wealth and behaved without the discretion expected of *dhimmis*. In this period, when the Ottoman state's power was waning relative to the rest of Europe, "Local Christians [began to] serve for some Muslims ... as convenient surrogates for the anger that could only rarely be expressed directly against the Europeans."[19]

Muslim anger was mounting for three reasons. First, European Christians, and increasingly their local Christian protégés, were benefiting from the Capitulations, a series of fiscal and legal privileges granted by treaty. Second, European powers were asserting special relations with local Christians in ways that challenged the jurisdiction of Ottoman Muslim authorities. (Thus, in 1740, France secured the right by treaty to protect Catholics in the Ottoman Empire, and above all, the Maronites of Lebanon who had recognized Vatican authority during the Crusades; in 1774, Russia claimed kindred rights vis-à-vis Orthodox Christians.[20]) Third, European powers were encroaching on Ottoman territories and were also whittling away at other parts of the Muslim world, such as Iran (under the Qajar dynasty) and the Mughal Empire of India. For example, in 1804, 30 years after seizing the Ottoman Crimea (now in Ukraine), Russia ex-

propriated Georgia and part of Azerbaijan from Iran. In 1830, France conquered Algeria and developed it as a settler colony; in 1881, France also occupied Tunisia. In 1839, Britain annexed Aden, in Yemen, which held a strategic position on maritime routes to India. In 1878, Britain persuaded the Ottomans to grant Cyprus as a naval base. In 1882, Britain invaded and occupied Egypt. Beginning in the late nineteenth century, European speculators also secured monopolies over Middle Eastern commodities and services, ranging from Caspian Sea caviar to toll-paying traffic through the Suez Canal. These conditions left many Muslims feeling beleaguered, and prompted some intellectuals to articulate ideologies of pan-Islamic solidarity that inspired modern Islamist movements while harkening back to the era of Muhammad (*c.*570–632) and his early successors.

In the nineteenth century, the Ottoman Empire was also losing ground to nationalist secession movements. In the 1820s, Greek nationalists waged a successful war for independence that drew British, French, and Russian support. Fearing that nationalism would "infect" other large Christian communities (who accounted for approximately 24 percent of the Ottoman Empire's population in 1876[21]) and eager to maintain British support against Russian expansion, the Ottoman sultan issued an edict called the *Hatt-i Humayun* in 1856. This edict declared equality between Muslims, Christians, and Jews in the empire, abolished *dhimmi* status and the *millet* system, and promised that Christians in the Ottoman Empire could serve in the military and freely secure church-building permits in proportion to their numbers. In practice, however, popular assumptions about the place of Christians relative to Muslims persisted, while the edict, to the extent that it was advertised, may have only aggravated tensions between the religious communities.

In the long run, Ottoman attempts to generate a sense of empire-wide identity failed to win the hearts of the Armenians, who claimed a Christian history going back to the conversion of King Trdat around the year 300, and who, in an age of growing nationalism, recalled a history of independent Armenian Christian statehood. From 1894 to 1896, Ottoman authorities responded to a series of Armenian revolts in Eastern Anatolia by massacring untold thousands. Armenians faced more violence after 1908, when a group of

Turkish nationalist military men called the "Young Turks" seized power in Istanbul. In 1915, amidst World War I, Ottoman soldiers and Kurdish mercenaries perpetrated massacres that were so severe that Armenians today call them genocide, meaning a concerted attempt at annihilation. The massacres of 1915 killed an estimated 1–1.5 million Armenians (or one third to one half of all Armenian people), while survivors dispersed widely, to Syria and the Nile Valley, and further afield to North America.[22] Debates over what happened persist. The government of Turkey, which succeeded the Ottoman state in Anatolia and Thrace, has continued to deny that mass killings or a genocide occurred and has described the massacres as a response to Armenian disloyalty and complicity with Russia during the war. Turkey has tried to stifle citizens who question this official version of history. In 2005, for example, it prosecuted the Turkish novelist (and later Nobel laureate), Orhan Pamuk, for "insulting the nation" by mentioning the deaths of a million Armenians.

During World War I, the Assyrian Christians of Southeastern Turkey faced a similar trauma at the hands of Ottoman Turkish and Kurdish soldiers, leading some to describe these killings as genocide too. In the long run, the institutional dislocation of Assyrian Christian culture was dramatic, insofar as the high leadership of the Church of the East eventually packed up and left. "The Church of the East," notes one historian, "is the only church whose patriarchal see is no longer in the Middle East but in the diaspora. After years of exile in Cyprus and Great Britain, Mar Shim'un XXIII Eshay (1920–75) settled in the United States, around 1961." Claiming a venerable history in the Tigris-Euphrates basin that stretches back to the dawning years of Christianity, the Church of the East now has its patriarchal headquarters in Chicago.[23]

At its best, the Ottoman Empire was a multicultural empire in which Sunni Muslim authorities maintained an atmosphere of stability and relative tolerance vis-à-vis Christians and Jews. However, the Turkish Republic that succeeded the Ottoman Empire was not – and did not want to be –multicultural. The Armenians of the future Turkish republic were either destroyed or dispersed, while a population exchange in 1922 – according to which Greece and Turkey swapped Christian "Greeks" in Turkey for Muslim

"Turks" in Greece – eliminated Turkey's Greek-speaking Orthodox Christians almost entirely, while also ensuring greater cultural homogeneity for Greece. In 2008, Turkey's population was 99.8 percent Muslim. Proportionally speaking, neighboring Syria had a much larger Christian population (estimated at 16 percent of the total population), as did Egypt (10 percent) and Jordan (6 percent). Iran's Christian population was less than 2 percent.[24]

In the nineteenth and twentieth centuries, some Lebanese Christians were also uprooted. In 1860, civil war broke out in Mount Lebanon, dividing people not only by religion but also, and perhaps more importantly, by class (landowners versus peasants).[25] This war sharpened sectarian lines and in the long run helped to shape what analysts have called Lebanon's "confessional politics." After 1860, sectarian and social tensions in Lebanese society propelled both Christians and Muslims to seek opportunities abroad, particularly in the Americas. More than a century later, in 1975, another civil war broke out in Lebanon, prompting further dispersions of Christians. Although reliable population data is lacking, analysts now assume that Christians are no longer the largest religious cluster within Lebanese society. That distinction goes to Shi'a Muslims, who are believed to outnumber Lebanon's Sunni Muslim and Druze populations too.

No discussion of Middle Eastern diasporas is complete without reference to Palestinian Arabs. In 1900, Christians accounted for some 16 percent of the population of Palestine.[26] Following the declaration of Israel as a Jewish state in 1948, Christians were among the Arabs who fled amid war or were pushed out by Jewish armies. Their numbers also shrank as a result of voluntary emigration. Today, minute Christian populations (less than 2 percent) are found in Israel, the West Bank, and Gaza.

In the twentieth century, another factor appears to have led to the diminution of Christian communities, relative to Muslim majorities: Christians had smaller families. This situation may have correlated to Christians' higher rates of education, later marriage ages among females, and wider access to contraception. In Egypt, for example, a local Protestant organization known as the Coptic Evangelical Organization of Social Services (CEOSS) began in 1957 to educate villagers about family planning; later, CEOSS

Figure 1.2 Christian Woman in Itsa, Fayoum Governorate, Egypt. Photograph courtesy of Hands along the Nile Development Services, Inc.

cooperated with the Egyptian government in sponsoring family planning clinics and distributing contraception among married Christian and Muslim women. For Christians, smaller families may have functioned as another strategy for survival: parents could spend more on their children's education or on helping to establish their livelihoods when there were fewer mouths to feed.

In the midst of social changes and political upheavals, and in spite of their small numbers relative to Muslims, Christians remained active members of Arab societies. Just as Arabic-speaking Christians developed a thriving intellectual life in the early and middle centuries of the Islamic era, so did many contribute to the *nahda*, meaning the modern Arabic cultural revival.[27] In the twentieth century, Arab Christians also distinguished themselves in film (such as the Egyptian director Youssef Chahine) and popular mu-

sic (such as the Lebanese singer Fairouz). Christians also played active roles in secular Arab nationalist movements in which Muslim identity was not a prerequisite, while a few played controversial roles in Arab politics. Consider Michel Aflaq (1910–89), who was born into a Greek Orthodox family. Aflaq was the ideological founder of the secular pan-Arab Ba'th Party, which drew men like Hafiz al-Asad (ruled Syria 1971–2000) and Saddam Hussein (ruled Iraq 1979–2003) as party members. Consider, too, George Habash (1926–2008), who came from a Palestinian Christian family: after the Six-Day Arab–Israeli War of 1967, he founded the radical Popular Front for the Liberation of Palestine (PFLP). Believing that violence was a legitimate tactic in the Palestinian national struggle, Habash in 1970 orchestrated a series of airplane hijackings that added a new tool to the kit of modern terrorism.

Missionary Legacies, Ecumenism, and Social Activism

In the nineteenth and twentieth centuries, Middle Eastern Christianity became even more diverse than it had historically been. This was largely the result of foreign Catholic and Protestant missions that fostered new churches, while inspiring local Christians to undertake missionary work at the grass roots. Two points are worth noting here. First, studies of the modern missionary movement must reckon with the controversial history of Western imperialism, since Catholic and Protestant missionaries were only able to expand in the Middle East and North Africa to the extent that they did because the British and French empires offered protection. Second, histories of local or "native" Christian missionaries – including pastors, priests, nuns, and lay evangelists, as well as catechists, Bible Women, and colporteurs – are still largely unwritten. Until more research is done, historical accounts of modern missionary activities in the Middle East and North Africa will invariably center on foreigners.

Catholic missions in the Middle East can be traced to the Crusader era, and even included, in 1219, the visit to Egypt of St Francis, who made peaceful overtures to Muslim rulers. In the centuries ahead, Catholic missionaries reached out to Eastern ecclesiastical leaders, prompting some, like the Maronites of Greater Syria, to recognize Vatican authority. Later, some Armenians, Assyrians, Arabic-speaking Greek Orthodox, and Copts identified with Catholicism as well. Catholic missionary activities among Orthodox Christians gained new momentum during the late nineteenth century and resulted in the continued growth of Catholicism in places like Upper Egypt, where some adherents of Coptic Orthodoxy joined Coptic Catholic communities. Today, the Middle Eastern Catholic churches, which preserve non-Latin liturgies and some distinct customs, are known as "Eastern rite" Catholic churches. In the early twenty-first century, Eastern rite Catholic churches were also flourishing in the diaspora, while some – such as the Melkite Greek Catholic Church in the US – were successfully attracting members who were not of Middle Eastern heritage.

In Egypt and Western Asia, as missionary activities burgeoned in the late nineteenth and early twentieth centuries, Catholics concentrated almost completely on Eastern Christians, among whom they established modern schools. The legacy of Catholic education endures today, for example, in the prestigious, Jesuit-founded Université Saint-Joseph of Beirut. By contrast, in Northwest Africa, and especially in the French settler colony of Algeria, some Catholic missionaries initiated missions to Muslims, thereby challenging the traditional Islamic ban on Christian evangelization among non-Christians. For example, in 1868, Cardinal Charles Lavigerie, Archbishop of Algiers, founded a mission popularly called the White Fathers (after the color of the missionaries' robes), which later expanded into sub-Saharan Africa. The White Fathers attracted few Muslim converts, although they did have a substantial cultural impact on some Berber-speaking communities in Algeria's Northern Kabyle region. Likewise, Charles de Foucauld (d. 1916), a former Trappist monk and hermit who inspired the foundation of the Order now known as the Little Brothers of Jesus, undertook a mission to Muslims in the Algerian Sahara. Like many other Catholic and Protestant missionaries of this period, Foucauld made pathbreaking contributions to linguistic analysis – in his case by compiling a Tuareg dictionary and grammar, along with studies of the Tuareg *Tifinagh* writing system.

The Moravian Brethren, who arrived in Egypt in the mid-eighteenth century and worked there for 40 years, were among the first Protestant missionaries to approach the Middle East. Yet sustained Protestant missionary activities only took off in the early nineteenth century, when organizations like the British Anglican Church Missionary Society (CMS), the American Board of Commissioners for Foreign Missions (ABCFM) (a joint Congregationalist-Presbyterian enterprise), and the German Missionary Society (Basel Mission) began work in the Eastern Mediterranean lands of the Ottoman Empire. CMS and American Presbyterian missionaries eventually expanded eastward to Iran, and (together with Italian Catholics) southward into Sudan. Protestants of many other denominations and nationalities arrived too, including Scottish and English Presbyterians (some of whom focused exclusively on missions to Jews), as well as German, Dutch, Swedish, and Danish organizations that operated schools, orphanages, and medical clinics in such places as Jerusalem, the Suez Canal Zone, and Kurdistan. In 1884, American Mormons (Latter-day Saints) also arrived, pursuing mission work first in Anatolia and later in Syria and Palestine. Protestants left some enduring educational legacies, among them the American University of Beirut (AUB) and the American University in Cairo (AUC).

By the time of World War I, American organizations were sending the largest Protestant missionary contingents to the region, and women were outnumbering men on mission rosters – a position that enabled them to provide schools and services for females. American missions were increasingly diverse: by 1914, for example, there were Methodists in Algeria, Pentecostals in Egypt, and Reformed Church of America missionaries in Oman and the Persian Gulf region.[28] Some of the most important Protestant missions were publishing missions (especially the British and Foreign Bible Society and the American Bible Society), which worked with scores of other mission societies to translate, publish, and distribute the Bible. The Nile Mission Press of Cairo shipped books and pamphlets throughout the Middle East and North Africa, but also to places like China, South Africa, and Venezuela, wherever Muslims (including Arab émigrés) were found.

Many Protestant missions focused on Muslim evangelization, although conversions from Islam were rare. By the 1950s, one missionary estimated that there were only about 200 living converts from Islam in Egypt, while another source, from the same period, estimated a similar number in Morocco.[29] Missionaries pointed to Muslim social sanctions against apostasy to explain the lack of converts. Concerns over barriers to conversion from Islam led some missionaries to advocate religious human rights, to press the issue of religious liberty with the League of Nations, and later, to support the promulgation of the United Nations' Universal Declaration of Human Rights (UDHR) in 1948.

In the mid-twentieth century, when the French and British empires began to contract through decolonization, Muslim nationalists throughout the Middle East and North Africa enforced new restrictions on Christian missionary activities. In some cases, postcolonial governments nationalized mission schools and hospitals. In other cases, they expelled particular missions (e.g., the (British) Egypt General Mission, in the wake of the 1956 Suez Crisis) or deported Christian missionaries en masse (as in Sudan, vis-à-vis both Catholic and Protestant missionaries, between 1962 and 1964). In still other places (notably in Libya and Algeria), governments banned the import of Arabic Bibles. Postcolonial governments also reinforced the traditional ban on Christian evangelization among Muslims, interpreting such activity as a challenge to "public order." On such grounds, for example, the (Anglo-American) North Africa Mission lost its legal status in Algeria in 1977. In Israel, meanwhile, Jewish organizations also agitated for restrictions on Christian missionary activities.

The departure of foreign missionaries prompted indigenous churches to assert independence and to cultivate local Christians as church leaders. Meanwhile, foreign Christian organizations looked for new ways to spread their message. Some harnessed radio and later satellite television as transnational broadcast media (using places like Cyprus for their stations), while others initiated work among Muslim diasporas, for example, among North Africans living in France.[30]

In the late twentieth century, Christian communities inside the Middle East also developed social service programs, many of which Catholic and Protestant missionaries had pioneered. In some cases Christian organizations developed partnerships with international, non-faith-based philanthropies. In Egypt in the late 1950s, for example, both Catholic and Protestant organizations secured grants from the Ford Foundation of New York, for agricultural development and job-training programs. Other Christian organizations supported public library projects and micro-credit lending programs that could benefit mixed Muslim-Christian communities. Part of the goal, as one Egyptian Christian leader explained it in 2005, was to develop a culture in which Christians could live with Muslims as neighbors and fellow citizens, not as *dhimmis*, while together addressing the needs of the larger society.[31]

In 2001, one Lebanese Protestant leader looked back on the history of foreign missions with ambivalence, and expressed concern about the challenges of building unity among Middle Eastern Christians in the face of dwindling numbers. "In retrospect," he wrote, "it is impossible to deny the fact that the Protestant presence in the Middle East has played, and continues to play, a divisive role in the church history of the region – exactly as the Roman Catholic presence has and still does."[32] This assessment may be too bleak. For in spite of its internal divisions, Middle Eastern Christianity has in the past century offered impressive models for ecumenical dialogue and cooperation. Consider the evolution of the Near East Christian Council (NECC), which was founded in 1929 as a forum for dialogue and cooperation among the major Protestant missions in the Middle East and North Africa. In the early 1960s, Middle Eastern Christian leaders assumed leadership of this organization and changed its name to the Near East Council of Churches, while retaining the NECC acronym. By this stage, the Orthodox churches were participating actively in NECC discussions. In 1974, the NECC evolved into the Middle East Council of Churches (MECC). The MECC, in turn, reached a milestone in 1990 when the Catholic churches (Maronite, Melkite, Coptic Catholic, etc.) officially joined. Strikingly, the MECC's own website acknowledges the organization's roots in the NECC but harkens back to an even earlier moment of ecumenical overture: namely, 1902, when Yoachim III, the Orthodox Patriarch of Constantinople, issued an encyclical calling for Christian unity and Orthodox reconciliation with Catholics and Protestants.[33]

Regardless of its "true" beginnings, ecumenism in the Middle East has not been a mere discussion piece for NECC or MECC meetings. Since the 1960s (a generation before the Catholic churches formally joined the MECC), ecumenism has grown at the grass roots through programs, such as Egyptian rural literacy campaigns, that have drawn Orthodox, Catholic, and Protestant churches together. Ecumenism has also flourished in academic settings, at places like the University of Balamand in Lebanon. Founded in 1988 under the sponsorship of the Antiochan Orthodox Church, and built on the site of a Cistercian monastery dating to the late twelfth-century Crusader era, the University of Balamand identifies itself as a "private secular institution [aiming] to serve all people without regard to race, religion, gender, and ethnic consideration." Operating trilingually, in Arabic, French, and English, the university also proclaims a goal of promoting "human rights, democratic institutions, and Christian-Muslim understanding," while encouraging research on the history and pluralistic culture of Arab Christianity.[34]

Conclusion: The Future of Middle Eastern Christianity

There is a practical reason for the growth of Middle Eastern ecumenism. With their numbers diminishing, Middle Eastern Christians often describe feeling increasingly vulnerable within Islamic societies, particularly during times of political and economic malaise. Hence Middle Eastern Christians are allowing sectarian differences to recede for the sake of common survival.

As dwindling communities, Middle Eastern Christians are also eager to bolster and retain the goodwill of Muslim friends and neighbors. They welcome dialogue with Muslim organizations like the Royal Institute for Inter-Faith Studies (RIIFS), founded in 1994 by the Jordanian prince El Hassan bin Talal. Based in Amman, this institute sponsors local and international conferences, and describes itself as a "venue in the Arab world for the interdisciplinary study and rational discussion of religion and religious issues, with particular reference to Christianity in Arab and Islamic society."[35] More recently, the institute has broadened its focus to study Muslims in predominantly Christian societies, such as the US. The RIIFS promotes a vision of a diverse but tolerant world in which Christians and Muslims can flourish together.

Today, churches in the Middle East function as vibrant centers of worship and social activity. Yet full of life as they are, the reality is that Christian populations are unlikely to grow or even hold their numbers in coming years. As one observer of Arab Christianity has noted, "Where there is tension within society, and discrimination between religions, and where increased Islamization marginalizes followers of other faiths . . . there is little incentive to stay when family members press invitations to join them overseas and the prospects at home are dim."[36] The future of Christianity in the Middle East and North Africa holds uncertainties.

Many Christians have already left and others are still leaving, with the result that diasporic Middle Eastern churches are now flourishing in cities like Sydney, Los Angeles, and Toronto, as well as in small towns like Södertälje, Sweden, and Teaneck, New Jersey. Consider that the Coptic Orthodox Church alone, which had only seven churches in the diaspora in 1971, was by 1999 claiming almost 80 churches in North America, 26 in Australia, and 30 in Western Europe.[37] By 2000, diasporic churches had become transnational churches or "World Churches," much as the Church of the East had been a millennium ago, when it was sending missionaries from Baghdad to Tibet and India's Malabar Coast.[38] Today's diasporic "World Churches" also have the power to lend financial support and engage in political advocacy on behalf of Christians remaining in the Middle East. However, their intervention may come with a price, if they confirm suspicions among Middle Eastern Muslims regarding the loyalty of local Christians.

During the late nineteenth century, as one historian suggested, local Christians in the Arab provinces of the Ottoman Empire served for some Muslims as "convenient surrogates" for frustrations that Muslims could not vent against Europeans.[39] In the early twenty-first century, when the US and its allies were embroiled in Iraq and Afghanistan, when the Israeli–Palestinian conflict remained unresolved, and when the world was still grappling with fallout from the September 11, 2001, attacks and the resulting American "war on terror," one could say much the same about the vulnerability of Middle Eastern Christians. Between the tug and pull of East and West, Middle Eastern Christians must find ways to survive in the region where Christianity was born.

In sum, Christian peoples have had an illustrious history in the Middle East and North Africa, and have richly contributed to the political, economic, and cultural heritage upon which Islamic civilization has built. Christians have been, and will continue to be, integral members of Middle Eastern societies.

Notes and References

[1] Martin Marty, *The Christian World* (New York: The Modern Library, 2007), 35; Ken Parry, ed., *The Blackwell Companion to Eastern Christianity* (Oxford: Blackwell Publishing, 2007), xvi.

[2] For example, Adrian Hastings, ed., *A World History of Christianity* (Grand Rapids, MI: Eerdmans, 1999); and David Chidester, *Christianity: A Global History* (San Francisco, CA: HarperCollins, 2000).

[3] Andrew E. Kramer, "For Iraqi Christians, Money Brought Survival," *The New York Times*, June 26, 2008. At: <http://www.nytimes.com/2008/06/26/world/middleeast/26christians.html?pagewanted=all>.

[4] David Thomas, "Arab Christianity," in Parry, ed., *The Blackwell Companion to Eastern Christianity*, 10, 16.

[5] Youssef Courbage and Philippe Fargues, *Christians and Jews under Islam*, transl. Judy Mabro (London: I.B. Tauris, 1998), 23.

[6] Ann Elizabeth Mayer, *Islam and Human Rights*, 4th edn (Boulder, CO: Westview Press, 2007).

[7] Consider church-building in modern Egypt: Alastair Hamilton, *The Copts and the West, 1439–1822* (Oxford: Oxford University Press, 2006), 88–9; and Heather J. Sharkey, *American Evangelicals in Egypt* (Princeton, NJ: Princeton University Press, 2008), 24, 31, 53, 58–9, 190, 202–3.

[8] Betty Jane Bailey and J. Martin Bailey, *Who Are the Christians in the Middle East?* (Grand Rapids, MI: Eerdmans, 2003), 182–3.

[9] Courbage and Fargues, 6–20.

[10] Richard Bulliet, *Conversion to Islam in the Medieval Period* (Cambridge, MA: Harvard University Press, 1979), 44 (Graph 5).

[11] Courbage and Fargues, 29–43.

[12] Yusuf Fadl Hasan, *The Arabs and the Sudan* (Edinburgh: Edinburgh University Press, 1967), 126.

[13] Kenneth Cragg, *The Arab Christian* (Louisville, KY: Westminster/John Knox Press, 1991), 18.

[14] Thomas, "Arab Christianity," 19; and M. Martin, "Statistiques chrétiennes d'Égypte," *Travaux et jours* (Beirut), 24 (1967): 65–75.

[15] Heleen Murre-van den Berg, "The Church of the East in the Sixteenth to the Eighteenth Century," in J. J. Van Ginkel et al., *Redefining Christian Identity* (Leuven: Uitgeverij Peeters en Department Oosterse Studies, 2005), 301–20; and Heleen Murre-van den Berg, "Syriac Christianity," in Ken Parry, ed., *The Blackwell Companion to Eastern Christianity* (Oxford: Blackwell Publishing, 2007), 249–68.

[16] Michael W. Dols, *The Black Death in the Middle East* (Princeton, NJ: Princeton University Press, 1977), 167–8, 206.

[17] Thomas, "Arab Christianity," 20.

[18] Ibid.

[19] Bruce Masters, *Christians and Jews in the Ottoman Arab World* (Cambridge: Cambridge University Press, 2001), 7.

[20] Charles D. Smith, *Palestine and the Arab-Israeli Conflict*, 3rd edn (New York: St Martin's Press, 1996), 12–13.

[21] Stanford A. Shaw and Ezel Kural Shaw, *History of the Ottoman Empire and Modern Turkey*, vol. 2 (Cambridge: Cambridge University Press, 1977), 240.

[22] Razmik Panossian, *The Armenians* (New York: Columbia University Press, 2006), 231.

[23] Murre-van den Berg, "Syriac Christianity," 260.

[24] Central Intelligence Agency, *The World Factbook* (July 15, 2008, edition), available [online] at:<https://www.cia.gov/library/publications/the-world-factbook/>; accessed July 24, 2008. Numbers should be approached with caution, since religious demographics are disputed in the Middle East.

[25] Ussama Makdisi, *The Culture of Sectarianism* (Berkeley, CA: University of California Press, 2000).

[26] Smith, *Palestine and the Arab–Israeli Conflict*, 32.

[27] Sidney H. Griffith, *The Church in the Shadow of the Mosque* (Princeton, NJ: Princeton University Press, 2007); Albert Hourani, *Arabic Thought in the Liberal Age, 1798–1939* (Cambridge: Cambridge University Press, 1983).

[28] Mehmet Ali Doğan and Heather J. Sharkey, eds, *American Missionaries in the Middle East* (Salt Lake City: University of Utah Press, 2011).

[29] H. E. Philips, *Blessed Be Egypt My People* (Philadelphia, PA: The Judson Press, 1953), 7; and Bible Society Archives, Cambridge University Library, BSA/E3/3/23/1: Translations Dept. Correspondence, Arabic: North African Colloquial, LRS to WJB [sic], Memo, [1957].

[30] Jos M. Strengholt, *Gospel in the Air* (Zoetermeer, Netherlands: Boekencentrum, 2008).

[31] Conversation with Dr Nabil Abadir, Director of the Coptic Evangelical Organization for Social Services (CEOSS), Cairo, May 26, 2005.

[32] Habib Badr, "The Protestant Evangelical Community in the Middle East," *International Review of Mission*, 89/352 (2001): 67.

[33] Middle East Council of Churches, "History and Character," available [online] at: <http://www.mec-churches.org/about_mecc.htm>; accessed July 23, 2008.

[34] University of Balamand, "Information about the University," available [online] at: <http://www.balamand.edu.lb/english/TheUniversity.asp?id=921&fid=48>; accessed July 24, 2008.

[35] Royal Institute for Inter-Faith Studies, "About RIIFS," available [online] at: <http://www.riifs.org/purpose/purpose.htm>; accessed July 24, 2008.

[36] Thomas, "Arab Christianity," 21.

[37] Otto F. A. Meinardus, *Two Thousand Years of Coptic Christianity* (Cairo: The American University in Cairo Press, 1999), 7.

[38] On this idea of a "World Church," see Murre-van den Berg, "The Church of the East in the Sixteenth to the Eighteenth Century," 301–20.

[39] Masters, *Christians and Jews in the Ottoman Arab World*, 7.

2

Christian Belongings in East Africa
Flocking to the Churches

Ben Knighton

Introduction

Bearing in mind that Christian religion only began to penetrate East Africa from the mid-nineteenth century, the take-up of Christian faith in East Africa has been staggering. The Edinburgh Missionary Conference of 1910 did not expect to see much growth in that part of the world.[1] Kenya had only 5,000 Christians in 1900, 90 percent of whom were first generation, with just 230 baptisms a year.[2] The missionaries saw traditional religions as overwhelming in famine-stricken cultures that lacked even the reassurances of manufactured clothes, literacy, and permanent architecture. In fact these features, accompanying the onset of civilizing mission and imperial expansion, became so attractive to Africans that many young people were prepared to explore new avenues in order to acquire them, primarily Western education found in the mission schools. From 1914, the missions, even some German ones, grew at up to 20 percent a year until World War II, after which they amounted to 32.6 of the Kenyan population. David Barrett found the Christian religion to be expanding "at a meteoric rate" before 1945.[3]

Cultural Penetrations

More than most regions of the world, East Africa had traditional cultures uninfluenced by the West. To be sure, there was local mobility, trade in gold, ivory, slaves, beads, and arms, but unlike North, West, or South Africa, Westerners and their pattern of culture were simply not visible, almost to the last quarter of the nineteenth century. Apart from Arab slave raiders along certain routes in the previous 70 years, East Africa was marked by high degrees of African autonomy with few intermediaries. When direct interaction did come, the cultural distance resulted in shocks on both sides.

Replacement

The predominant missionary approach has been that Christian initiation, salvation, or conversion required a "total break with the past." This was due to both the early predominance of evangelical mission in most of the region, and to missionaries finding that their first enquirers were irascible adults loath to show any outward signs of change. The combination embedded a strong dualism among previously integrated societies. Traditional Africa was demonized by Christians, assumed to be shrouded in relentless darkness and division, superstition and sacrilege, ignorance and imbecility. Against this contrast the light of the Gospel was self-evident, but attempts at communicating the triune God were very rare. A cosmological dualism better fitted the isolation of the mission station as islands in heathenism, surrounded by a multitude of

Introducing World Christianity, First Edition. Edited by Charles E. Farhadian.
© 2012 Blackwell Publishing Ltd. Published 2012 by Blackwell Publishing Ltd.

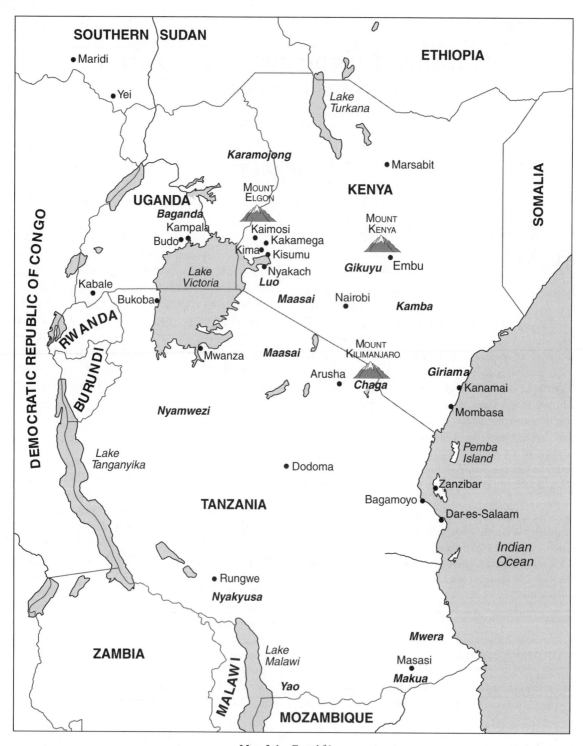

Map 2.1 East Africa

hyperactive evil spirits and life-devouring divinities. That the religious duality also overlapped with old polarities between white and black, civilized and uncivilized, Europe and Africa, was a comfort to missionary senses of superiority. Missionaries themselves have been regarded and remembered with the greatest of ambiguity. At one extreme they robbed the Africans of their soul and connived in the colonial theft of the land, and on the other, many are remembered with great affection, having given Africans knowledge and founded the good institutions of the new states. In the course of a lifetime it would be easy for a church-person to voice both opinions.

Such foundational dualism laid the ground for later counter-cultural movements, whether by African Instituted Churches (AICs), revivalist movements, signally the East African Revival, or Pentecostalism. While many an AIC was formed by schism with a mission church over too rigid a discipline against a small number of customs like polygyny or Female Genital Cutting (FGC), very often they would patrol markers against other traditional, or modern, practices with greater rigor.[4] One catechist answered to his enquiring garden-boy (many initial converts were the product of such a relationship):

> Eleazar explained that being a Christian meant "a real cut with the old life and all it contained," including even the white missionary habit of smoking. His reasons boiled down to experience: "if I now started smoking again I should sooner or later go right back into the old heathen ways and lose the gift of God," and he gave the analogy of a giraffe in a cartwheel trap. Still not satisfied, as an educated man, Lokong again asked, "Why?". "I cannot tell you why," replied Eleazar, resorting to mystery, "All I can say is that I know, as you will know if you follow truly."[5]

While the Protestant missions were emphasizing right beliefs and justification by faith, Africans were exchanging one set of enforced customs for another, though with great effect.

Translation

Protestants emphasized translation of the Bible into the vernacular, so a great deal of missionary energy, which also recruited the more intelligent neophytes, went into "reducing" local languages to writing and to turning out the Scriptures. To begin with, this was seen as an urgent priority, even when surrounded by oral cultures, and later as a task to achieve greater perfection than in any other task of the Church, and finally as an expression of ethnic "coming of age," when "we too have the Bible in our mother-tongue." The emphasis on translation therefore shows no sign of dimming, and the ecumenical supremacy of the United Bible Societies is now challenged by eager competitors from the USA, such as the International Bible Society.

The assumption was that if you could translate the Scriptures, convert a few Africans, and teach them to read the Bibles given them, then the initial work was done. Louise Pirouet's *Black Evangelists*[6] broke a thought paradigm that existed mainly in the minds of mission supporters at home that it was missionary heroes like "Albert Cook of Uganda,"[7] "Carey Francis of Kenya,"[8] or the autobiographical "Doctor of Tanganyika,"[9] who were converting the helpless natives of East Africa. These men were indeed busy, feverishly constructing medical and educational institutions on Western lines, for which there was a demand, and out of which they would seldom be able to escape for long. They knew very well that the best agent in the conversion of an African was another African, so it was the evangelists and catechists who drilled various Christian traditions into East Africa. Thus a translation approach shaded into indigenization.

Indigenization

Often a tradition may have been adapted from the missionaries initially, at the start of its propagation, but thereafter it became entrenched in the denomination and practice of many of those that it spawned: "for ever and ever. Amen" is a popular epithet to describe this tendency in the churches today.[10] Nevertheless, indigenization was taken to be the future solution in the mid-twentieth-century mission churches, which meant ordaining and promoting Africans, not on ability so much as their inclination to remain faithful to the traditions of the mission. Thus Festo Olang, who made havoc in the Anglican Church in western Kenya by retiring elderly Luo clergy and promoting elderly Luyia,[11] was appointed the first bishop and archbishop of the whole country. He was a good Revival brother, and the East African Revival was not designed to reformulate a Western religious tradition, but to allow its African adherents, including women, to use leverage over their European "brethren."

Even indigenization came painfully slowly in East Africa. In Tanzania there was a lack of educated African clergy, and in Kenya the poverty of the mainstream churches meant they were either funded from outside or by settlers, skewing it towards white needs and adding to feelings of African inferiority. In 1984, the organist of All Saints' Cathedral, Nairobi, was blasting out "Land of Hope and Glory" and "Rule Britannia" on St George's Day. Yet the most perplexing case was Uganda, where the energetic Bishop Tucker had set out to organize the Native Anglican Church according to the model of the Church Missionary Society strategist, Henry Venn, so that it should be self-extending, self-governing, and self-supporting. This meant the euthanasia of mission, as

the local church took responsibility for itself in the shortest possible time. Tucker gave the church Bagandan evangelists, education, a constitution for a rapidly expanding church, and left 38 African clergy in 1911. However, the sons of Buganda's aristocracy preferred better-paid jobs in government, while Bishop Willis concentrated power in the center and could not see Africans being ready for responsibility. An African bishop was not consecrated until 1947 and an archbishop not until 1977. With the greater human power of missionary Orders, the Roman Catholic Church was even slower to foster an African priesthood, which from the beginning faced the unprecedented obstacle of lifelong celibacy.

Adaptation

While the Bible and the Gospel needed translating, it was assumed that the social form of the Church could still be modeled on Western institutional forms. The

Figure 2.1 Anglican Bishops blessing a school bus at the consecration of the first Bishop of Kitale before President Moi
Source © 1997 Ben Knighton.

first cathedral at Namirembe was a giant thatched hut, vulnerable to wind or fire, so was replaced by red brick and a dome. This was more moderate than the Moravians' direct collision with African culture among the Nyakyusa in Southern Tanzania.[12] However, East Africa was also the site of a very interesting experiment in mission that tried to mold itself around the life of the people. Bruno Gutmann was a Leipzig missionary among the Chaga on Mount Kilimanjaro, 1902–38, although removed with other German nationals for the years 1920–5.[13] He saw Chaga not as individuals to be saved, almost from society, but bound by "primal ties" to an organic community (*Gemeinschaft*), which contrasted favorably with the merely constructed organization of a society (*Gesellschaft*). In fact, for Gutmann and his opponent, Georg Fritze, European civilization was the great enemy to the African.[14]

Such adaptations were too radical for many a missionary, and more often the supporters at home, who ethnocentrically expected their beliefs and rites to be faithfully reproduced for the salvation of the world. However, to tar all missionaries with the brush of ignorance, so frequently done in East African seminaries and universities today, would be to overlook the learning experience of some.[15] That said, deliberate missionary adaptations to African traditions were the exception and not the rule, being sporadic and arbitrary, as with the two leading cases here. Concessions to African marriage and polygyny were meager at best, leading to great social cost for all, eventually contributing to the spread of HIV as customs broke down in the rural areas.[16] Gutmann[17] and Lucas[18] were aware of the damage that could be done by disrupting traditional society with Western individualism, just to name one consequence, but many missionaries were not. Then again, many African Church people were ready to support missionary decisions in the first place, or invent their own, and then replicate them for many decades.

Inculturation

However, missionaries developed increasing awareness of the unsatisfactory fit of their churches as social institutions in Africa, and after the greater freedom from Western traditions allowed by the Second Vatican Council and the onset of postmodernity, some began to address it. East Africa has a special role to play here, because of a cluster of Roman Catholic missionary theologians, mostly Maryknoll: Eugene Hillmann and Vincent Donovan among the Maasai,[19] Aylward Shorter,[20] and Joseph Healey.[21] These were intellectually responsible for infusing the agenda of the African Synod at Rome in 1994 with inculturation. Yet papal blessing also meant pontifical control and limitation. While a few theologians would have liked to push inculturation so far that African people became responsible for expressing the Gospel in their culture, the Roman Curia has always been careful not to authorize such decentering, to ensure inculturation is always in the control of the Church. Although a two-way process was envisaged of authentic cultural values being intimately transformed by their integration into the form of Christianity implanted into different human cultures, the agent of both has always been the Church – taken into a culture, necessarily as a foreign plant, in order to transform it. The basic concept is remarkably similar to conservative evangelical formulations of the same era of "One Gospel, Many Clothes."[22]

Tribute is paid to the cultural difference so important to African identities and values, but only as a disguise, a wrapping, or packaging of what has been pre-formulated in the West as the one true Church or Gospel. Both versions reflect a defective theology of the incarnation: docetism, or the error of perceiving Jesus while on earth to have been emphatically God, to preserve his unity with the Godhead, and to consider him as only appearing to be human. Although the term "inculturated" was originally (in 1962 before the Second Vatican Council) a French spelling by a Jesuit for enculturated, it well encapsulates the idea of putting newly met culture into the age-old tradition of Rome.[23] At this level the Roman Catholic churches have been most effective in changing the appearance of Catholicism in East Africa. In terms of clerical robes, more communal spaces in the round, language, music, and liturgy, the Roman Catholics are usually streets ahead of other mainstream churches and a good number of African Initiated Churches as well, which has done no harm to its greater numerical allegiance.

Yet the changes are aesthetic rather than cultural; formal rather than substantial. It is still not quite the Church of the people, but rather the Church that looks appropriate for the people, although it does manage to avoid schisms. Again there are missiologists who are dissatisfied with the extent of this step, but Aylward Shorter gave the orthodox Roman Catholic take on inculturation: "The reality of the Roman Catholic Church today may well be that of a universal sub-culture ubiquitously present as a sub-system in the various cultures of humanity."[24] The problem is with the word "universal" rather than "sub-culture," yet even the latter is optimistic. If a social institution claims universality and its own irreducible patrimony, its openness to a particular culture becomes suddenly narrow, so the "Eucharist cannot be reduced to the cultural circumstances of an everyday meal." It was precisely the Eucharistic elements that Bishop Tucker was willing to change, provisionally sanctioning in 1896 the use of "native wine" from banana juice instead of the hardly obtainable Mediterranean beverage. African wines have even entered the canon law of the Church of Uganda, and have been encouraged by the Anglican African "Kanamai Statement" of 1993.[25] However, no East African Anglican or Roman Arch-bishop has publicly advocated the Eucharistic elements of anything other than bread from wheat or wine from grapes. The patrimony of the faith, or rather the cultural vehicle of Christian faith to East Africa, still rules.

Enculturation

While the focus above might appear to emphasize what the missionaries did – and after all, without the modern missionary movement, the Christian religion would not have so shaped the East African states – close historical studies as cited above show that the growth and survival of a church depended on African agency and appropriation. Africans could show supreme in-difference, such as the Tanzanian Maasai and Batemi, the Karamojong, and the Giriama even in their ex-posed position by the Kenyan coast, or if not, they could change various features of the foreign tradition as they negotiated their acceptance. Admittedly, under colonial rule this was a history from below, so the visible forms of mission religion became remarkably persistent, but nevertheless the churches that emerged were seldom those intended, designed, or even wanted by missionaries. Bishop John V. Taylor died without ever having seen his hope of a relatively highly suc-cessful Anglican Church ever coming to terms with the cultures of Uganda in a systematic way.[26]

Enculturation, understood in a socio-cultural way, is an inverse of all the above approaches, because of the locus of agency. In this perspective it is not a question of how the Church makes itself appear more cultural, but how a society or culture corporately absorbs or appropriates a foreign religious tradition. The ways of doing this are manifold, and the outcome unpredict-able in its particulars, because no sovereignty is as-sumed for missionary intentionality. Looked at this way round, the outcomes of Christian mission have been largely disappointing in East Africa; not that a great deal of appropriation has failed to occur. The churches may not have been in thrall to missionary whims for long, but rather they or their leaders, more than society at large, were deeply attracted – if not dazzled – by various features of Western culture. The sights of the churches were seldom aimed at salvation for Africans in common, or, especially, African cul-tures, despite the great commission of Matthew 28:19 enjoining the discipling of $\pi\acute{\alpha}\nu\tau\alpha$ $\tau\grave{\alpha}$ $\acute{\epsilon}\theta\nu\eta$ ("all the ethnic groups"). Mission education and Western cul-tural values operated together in African appropriation to encourage sectional interests and elites, thus dis-locating African cultures rather than redeeming or fulfilling them.[27] It is precisely the duality of mission in East Africa that has strangled attempts to produce theology to integrate the African and the Christian, because the modern is allowed to invalidate the African.[28]

Figure 2.2 Scott Memorial Church, Thogoto, built by the Church of Scotland Mission outside Nairobi. © 2007 Ben Knighton.

With the advent of postmodernity, it was hoped that AICs would provide the answer, and large churches in South Africa, the Congo, and West Africa began to deliver on a less schizophrenic Christian faith, but in East Africa, seldom has one of these forms become a wide movement in a given culture, but instead has proved to be another source of division.[29] These traditions have raised prophets and healers, and spiritual resistance to, or collaboration with, unrepresentative governments, but again sectional or personal interests have been to the fore. In other words, the agents changing the foreign tradition have belonged to a church within a church, forming a sect out of what had, in cultural terms, not been a very vernacular church anyway, while the guardians of African culture – elders, chiefs, religious specialists – were not allowed to reconfigure, let alone shape, the Western tradition that was upending their societies.

Cultural Implications

If culture is taken as the accumulated pattern or framework of military, territorial, legal, jural, political, social, economic, and other forces at any point in time, then it can be seen that changes in the religious aspect of culture will have ripple effects at least on the other aspects. Because these aspects have not been segregated by allowing the state to be emancipated from society, which would be to secularize, religious change in Africa mediates social change powerfully to other areas and the converse.

Social

From the start mission education enabled young men to find alternative and often more lucrative and fashionable livelihoods by cutting short the long process of gerontocratic graduation, which awarded social power and status to the survivor. Thus those who had broken social taboos could find not only a refuge in the Church, but also relatively quick social promotion by government, which levied hut and poll tax on all.[30] A church led or peopled by social delinquents confused ideas of merit or justice, so another way was opened.[31] The churches have continued to be seen and used as a means to further studies, especially those left behind in

the highly competitive education system. Although less valued in Tanzania, education has been considered the route to a gentlemanly or aristocratic life, or to knowledge as display. Among the Gikuyu, whose prophet, Cege wa Kabiru, urged his people to learn from the whites instead of fighting them so that they would go away, it appears now that full salvation lies just beyond the acquisition of a doctorate.

If the move into education is seen as a social movement, the churches were primary providers of it, since there were so few government schools before the 1940s. However, it was the growing demand for schooling by many Africans, and the increasing availability of grants from taxation, which drove the Church in this direction. When missions like the Gospel Missionary Society (GMS) and the Africa Inland Mission (AIM) refused, or were unable, to deliver a full primary education or any secondary schools, these religious groups were abandoned by the Gikuyu. When schools and churches were used as a discipline against girls' initiation and Female Genital Cutting (FGC), their membership was decimated in areas where the missionary took a hard line.[32] In fact a denomination was founded, named African Schools and Churches, as well as two associations of independent schools. In these widespread grievances, and the organized response to them, lay two of the roots of Mau Mau.[33] The Land (ithaka) and Freedom (wiathi) Movement has been categorized as a peasant revolt, of which secret oathing has been a feature elsewhere, but it is better seen as a politico-religious movement since the ritual nature of the oath, drawing on older Gikuyu symbols, the frequent traditional prayers to Mwene Nyaga (the owner of Mount Kenya), and the aping of Christian creeds and hymns (reworded against the ban on FGC, the mission churches, and the government) were the dominant recruiting unifying mechanisms, which a secular socio-political movement could never provide.

After independence, governments were quick to take control of education, leaving the churches in a marginal position regarding their old institutions. In fact the teachers, as centrally trained professionals, have increasingly adopted neo-Pentecostalist allegiances that have enabled them to look down on the slower, less-educated parish churches, despite their own anti-intellectual thrust. Thus the mainstream churches have been trumped in the very education stakes that they set up. Nevertheless, except for highly traditionalist tribes, there are few educated without affiliation to a church or mosque.

Ordinary people and those aspiring to middle-class respectability saw in the Church not only a route to self-improvement, including further studies, but communal improvement. Their village would be on the modern map with a church. A large section of the construction industry since the 1980s has revolved around the erection of church buildings. A place of worship may remain a concrete eyesore for many years, while awaiting fund-raising events for further construction, but in the end it will be finished, because it is there and the new members who have been attracted will build the church, very often before they have a permanent home in which to live themselves.

The question now is whether this kind of commitment is sustainable. There are not many more unevangelized people left, even if there is great competition in proselytization. As offers of salvation become ever grander, but more exclusive, in a situation of high unemployment, with low wages and patchy infrastructure, will the credibility of the churches fall like a house of cards, as it did for Europe in the trenches of Flanders?

Looking at the statistics in table 2.1 and in previous years for religious affiliation across three countries set to hold a population of 144 million in 2025, there are some surprising comparisons between 1970 and Barrett's extrapolations for 2025. Uganda's Christian mission was the latest one to have been started. The colonial government allowed much less freedom to missions other than RC and Anglican, and President Amin tried to privilege Islam, but Uganda has had the highest proportion of Christian allegiance throughout. Tanzania and Kenya experienced early and late violent resistance to colonial rule respectively, and in the former an unpopular colonial government fell, resulting in an increase in Islam, despite being replaced by another Protestant power. Early in the nineteenth century it appeared that the first beneficiaries of colonial rule were Muslims and Asians, because their literacy and labor skills made them eligible for government employment. However, the mission schools quickly allowed Africans to catch up. Therefore, in general, what enabled the most sustainable church growth was an invitation for mission by a monarchical tribal state; peaceful, continuous colonial rule; large, well-organized European-led missions that provided schools, medical care, and wider development, opening opportunities one way or another for leadership to Africans.

The more recent growth has been forged by the neo-Pentecostalists, but typically they attract members of other churches, or rather their youth, instead of converting non-Christians, not even being present in the more rural areas where the ethno-religionists reside, who have been providing the churches with their fresh converts all through. Because of the transfer out of urban youth, the mainstream churches – which have all descended from Western missions – are considered rather *passé*, but they comprise 68 percent of all Christians in Kenya, 91 percent in Tanzania, and a massive 94 percent in Uganda. Future allegiance will be determined by whichever churches have the appropriate form of government and leaders to hold both their biological increase and the "Charismatics."

The fastest growth of the Independents in Kenya, as noted in the research of both Barrett and Welbourn, were the African Initiated Churches (AICs) during the period 1930–65.[34] Yet in recent years this sector has appeared relatively weak, because of its sectarian nature and lack of provision or emphasis in education or development.[35] Denominations that were obvious in a district 40 years ago are hardly recognizable now, such as the Church of Kenya Family in Embu. The neo-Pentecostalists may have more than replaced AICs in the growth and schism of churches, but their relatively unsatisfactory Church government may mean that many will not survive the mainstream churches. Later the multiplication of radically opposed Gospels, far removed from a theology of either Old Testament or New Testament, may result in widespread disillusion. The prosperity Gospel rivals the discourse on socioeconomic development; teaching of political subservience, engagement, and quiescence jostle for position; and some traditions exalt Jesus Christ as though his incarnation were inconceivable, while others are happy to replace or join him with a contemporary African messiah. As yet East Africans still like to be considered religious, but these figures have yet to pick up Muingiki and other reinvented warrior groups, who represent a noticeable, conservative reaction to

Table 2.1 Religious adherence in East African countries

| Religious adherence | Percentage of national population | | | | | | | | |
| Country | Kenya | | | Tanzania | | | Uganda | | |
	1970	mid-2000	mid-2025	1970	mid-2000	mid-2025	1970	mid-2000	mid-2025
Christians	**63.5**	**79.3**	**82**	**36.1**	**50.4**	**56.1**	**69.0**	**88.7**	**92.0**
Unaffiliated	10.6	5.1	2.9	3.7	3.5	2.6	19.0	1.7	0.7
Roman Catholics	16.8	23.3	25.6	20.5	24.7	27.6	34.6	41.9	42.8
Independents	14.3	22.0	24	0.4	1.9	2.9	1.0	3.7	4.7
Protestants	14.5	21.2	24.6	7.8	16.5	18.0	1.1	2.7	3.6
Anglicans	5.1	10.0	10.8	2.8	7.9	9.2	13.2	39.4	41.4
Orthodox	2.2	2.5	3.1	0.1	0.0	0.1	0.1	0.2	0.2
Marginal	0.0	0.1	0.1	0.0	0.1	0.1	0.0	0.0	0.1
Doubly-affiliated	0.0	-4.2	-9.1	0.0	-4.2	-4.3	0.0	-1.0	-1.3
Trans-megabloc groupings									
Evangelicals	14.8	22.4	25.2	5.2	14.5	16.0	6.2	17.9	19.5
Pentecostals/Charismatics	8.9	27.8	30	0.0	10.2	15.0	1.8	23.0	28.0
Great Commission Christians	10.0	12.3	14	21.6	16.8	18.0	11.0	13.9	15.0
Ethno-religionists	**28.1**	**11.5**	**8.4**	**31.8**	**16.1**	**8.9**	**22.0**	**4.4**	**1.6**
Muslims	**6.4**	**7.3**	**7.4**	**31.5**	**31.8**	**32.8**	**6.0**	**5.2**	**4.7**
Baha'is	1.1	1.0	1.3	0.3	0.4	0.4	2.3	0.5	0.1
Hindus	0.3	0.5	0.5	0.1	0.9	1.0	0.7	0.8	0.8
Jains	0.3	0.2	0.2	0.0	0.0	0.0	0.0	0.0	0.0
Non-religious	0.0	0.1	0.1	0.0	0.4	0.5	0.0	1.1	0.7
Sikhs	0.1	0.1	0.2	0.0	0.0	0.0	0.1	0.0	0.0
Jews	0.0	0.0	0.0	0.0	0.0	0.0	0.0	0.0	0.0
Zoroastrians	0.0	0.0	0.0	0.0	0.0	0.0	0.0	0.0	0.0
Buddhists	0.0	0.0	0.0	0.1	0.1	0.2	0.0	0.0	0.0
Country's population	11,498,062	30,080,000	41,756,000	11,693,900	33,517,000	57,918,000	9,806,400	21,778,000	44,435,000

Source: Barrett, *World Christian Encyclopedia*, I, pp. 426, 729, 761

the contemporary churches.[36] In 2010, however, churches constituted locally the most frequently observable social institution in East Africa beyond the family.

Political aspects

Gavin Flood has pointed out that "we need much closer attention to religious texts being read alongside political documents and questions asked concerning the constraints operative upon the text, the pervasiveness of social agency within them, and questions of resistance and compliance."[37] Flood does not tackle the task himself, saying it is best done in a regional study. East Africa has provided a variety of Christian responses to the state and the churches have often been the imaginers of a nation.

When they have had the opportunity, churches have sought an established role close to the state. Anglicans and Roman Catholics fought for it in Mwanga's Buganda. No less than three missions from Berlin and one from Leipzig worked as if they were cooperating with the German colonial state, while white Anglicans in Kenya attempted to represent "native interests" in the state, including grievances of torture and death in the Emergency. After independence, the National Council of Churches of Kenya (NCCK) participated fully in Kenyatta's nation-building project, as did the Roman Catholic churches in Nyerere's Tanzania. In Uganda, the two main political parties were closely identified with the Roman Catholics and the Anglicans respectively, while lately President Museveni has used neo-Pentecostalism, particularly through his wife, Janet, to lend validity for what is at base a long-running military dictatorship, while fending off the demands of traditional religion in Buganda and Karamoja. Having thrown off Moi's personal rule, the Roman Catholics and the Protestants lost their critical distance with President Kibaki, himself a Roman Catholic sympathetic to the churches, but their ethnic divisions opened a gaping wound. In Tanzania, an unusually comfortable accommodation has emerged between Christians and Muslims in the state. The dominant ostensible relationship of churches to the state has erred on the side of being supine, with even reverence for power, especially in Uganda. Although Archbishop Janani Luwum

gained wide fame for his martyrdom at the hands of Amin in 1977, he and the divided Anglican bishops left it far too late to speak out publicly, while the Roman Catholics waited to replace the Church of Uganda as the more established church.

Thus, for a more interesting case study, post-independent Kenya is chosen to show what the churches can do, if they permit just a few of their leaders to oppose the misuse of power. Indeed, I argue that the willingness of the churches to criticize government – for which Kenya has a long history, starting first in its schismatic church movements, such as *Dini ya Msambwa*[38] and the Gikuyu *karinga* churches[39] – makes a great difference in national history. Without the churches volubly entering the public forum to signal what is ethically wrong, there are insufficient resources in a republic to withstand a president who abuses power. If Christian theology prevents political engagement, then unrestrained power will turn round and hit churches as well as other social institutions; hence the much sorrier history of Uganda, despite its political and economic advantages over Kenya on independence.

In Kenya four clergy – Henry Okullu, David Gitari, Timothy Njoya, and Alexander Muge – came to be given regular exposure in the media, as they attacked voting by queuing, the one-party system, election-rigging, land-grabbing, and finally the Kenyan Constitution itself, since its only amendments since the colonial handover were hardly in a democratic direction. While the politicians stalled, some even promoting pre-election ethnic violence in 1992 and 1997, the churches, together with other religious leaders, started the Ufungamano Initiative to initiate a constitutional review.[40] When the politicians eventually took it up, the whole process used much more time and money, and by 2009 a new constitution was further away, despite Kofi Annan putting it on the agenda for governance in his mediations. Yet the churches were seen by the mass of Kenyan people to be pushing events in the right direction by limiting the scope for political manipulation.

In 2002, Gitari retired as Archbishop and to everyone's relief, Moi did not stand again and the ruling party was swept out of power by a coalition under Mwai Kibaki. Then the General Secretary of the NCCK accepted government appointments and resigned to stand for Kibaki in a parliamentary constituency in 2007. The Roman Catholics were pleased to have one of their members as president for the first time. Although Kibaki was a much more liberal, reforming leader, he proved unable to end the impunity for corruption in public life or to reduce the ugly ethnic dimension in politics, which flared up before the 2007 general elections, and especially when the extremely close presidential results were announced after some belated and obvious gerrymandering. Kofi Annan came to Kenya to mediate and looked for a church leader to offer a local solution, but in vain, for all those in position were untested or themselves ethnically compromised. Gitari was dismayed at the sudden dearth of prophecy, and at Kenyan clergymen having to admit "to blessing warriors to engage in violence and inviting politicians to disseminate hate messages."[41] The Church leaders tried to reclaim a prophetic stance by opposing a new constitution in the referendum of 2010, but as this reversed the mainstream churches' position on political reform over two decades, they were widely ignored by Christian voters.

The churches, either because of their compliance with the rulers of the state, or because of their retreat into ethnic solidarities, have yet to supply the nations of East Africa with sufficient unitive imagination for the state to function impartially. It may be of course that the nation-state is the wrong polity for this part of the world, being such a monstrous import from the West, but if so African theologians must gather the courage to envisage a new order in which peace, justice, and freedom – all biblical emphases – may dwell together.

Religious aspects

Interreligious dialogue is not a significantly major concern in East Africa, because of the predominance of the churches. It is most relevant in Tanzania, where nearly a third of the population is Muslim, but the churches there are content mainly to coexist politically while they continue with their agenda of evangelism and development.[42] In Kenya Archbishop Gitari insisted on working with Muslims on constitutional review, despite underhand government attempts to provoke interreligious violence, yet this was followed by a furor over the draft Constitution, which perpetuated the existence of Kadhi's Courts alongside new

Christian ones to balance them.[43] Evangelicals and Pentecostals made strong objections, to no great purpose other than to deny any concession to Islam in law.[44] In Uganda there are ongoing attempts of Christians and Muslims trying to convert one another peacefully, but the main Muslim concern is their minority status in politics.

There is more lip service to cross-cultural mission in East Africa than costly action. The Roman Catholics are more robust in action because they can transfer celibates across tribes, while with the multiplication of Church units within an ethnic paradigm it becomes ever more unlikely that Church leaders might have to minister trans-ethnically. Non-Luyia wives of local clergy were chased by their congregations out of the region in Kenya's post-election violence, and the leaders were little better off themselves. Much may be made of East Africans going to minister in the West, where of course Christian vocations are generally down, especially Roman Catholic ones, but this seldom happens at the expense of East African churches. Churches in all three countries are still perplexed with how to evangelize the traditional and pastoral societies, mostly in the north of each, because it appears a backward step to admit African rites and customs at this stage, and far easier to bemoan the colonialists destroying their own.

Those cities with international airports, above all Nairobi as a regional center, are favorite targets for neo-Pentecostalist evangelism and Christian aid agencies.[45] Branches of churches outside East Africa are soon overwhelmed by local activity, unless they are neo-Pentecostalist and from the West, such as Chrisco, Nairobi Lighthouse Church, and the Potter's House. Nairobi is on the itinerary of all the major tele-evangelists and crusaders as well as missions that want to evangelize Africa. Broadcasting, Bible Schools, and places at North American seminaries abound. What the junior pastors pick up from this milieu is the business of social entrepreneurship, though there is a very thin dividing line with a straight capitalist expansion in religious services. Planting a church is like opening a shop, and ministries are like consultancies. With the name of Jesus, there are the easiest opportunities to bring in hard cash fast, and the registrar of societies in Nairobi has a great backlog of applications to start new churches.[46]

With the focus on charisma rather than theological education, training is optional, while bishoprics and unresearched doctorates are sprinkled like confetti. The great authority of senior pastors, commensurate with their conspicuous consumption, leads to recurrent leadership wrangles, and frequently to a junior pastor splitting off with part of the congregation to start a new church. In smaller towns, church splitting results in congregations with as few as five (but plenty of electronic sound), and exotic, transient names, as each social entrepreneur tries to hit the big time through one or more of several thousand Pentecostal churches in East Africa. For instance, Solomon Male was a minister of the Synagogue Church of All Nations in Kampala, but denounced it as a cult in 1992, and in 1999 founded Arising for Christ Ministries, which by 2008 was said to have a list of 300 believers who accused born-again pastors of extortion, fraud, and sex-slavery.[47] Older Pentecostalist churches that have established themselves among the professional middle classes, such as the Deliverance Church and Christ is the Answer Ministries (CITAM), have become respectable congregational denominations. However, this category is not spared the schismatic tendency, for the Assemblies of God in Tanzania unwillingly spawned the Evangelical Assemblies of God and malcontents of the Swedish Free Mission founded the Pentecostal Association of Tanzania.[48]

A common feature of neo-Pentecostalist churches across East Africa is their antagonism to African traditions, while focusing on the money economy as modern Africans. A Nairobi team reported back to Lighthouse Church on their mission to Yei and Maridi, in Southern Sudan. The people were hungry and thirsty and had not danced for 20–30 years, for it was a stronghold of witchcraft. Maridi was bound by territorial spirits. People were traumatized with drink, while 10 percent of the 50,000 were mad and 20 percent depressed. Dog flesh was a delicacy for the mother-in-law. The team went to work by delivering people from turning into a cat or a dog, a vicar's wife from 28 demons, and many other examples. Pastors were "getting saved," along with a witchdoctor who had planted his medicine around the tent. Harriet testified in an American accent that people "got saved," especially children who were healed in one

hour from malaria. Diane said that they had to teach people to pray, dance, sing, and clap – Pentecostal style, of course. Yet the shouted prayer then offered in the Sunday service was for offerings and "above offerings," interest and income, checks in the mail and in email, finding money, bills paid off, debts paid, multiplication, a new business, increments of salaries: "All for the sake of the Gospel of Christ!"[49]

Conclusion

While the churches are consolidating in outlying rural, agricultural areas as never before, they still have not learned how profoundly the Christian tradition must be reconfigured to be enculturated in nomadic pastoralist cultures; nor do they see how to navigate the swirling currents of the cosmopolitan centers, where Mammon and sex are gods big enough to command the allegiance of some clergy as well as laymen. Mainstream churches are also being led by charismatics, who remove the emphasis of theological education, fail to make a difference in the political scene, and cut their roots with Western churches. All this is destabilizing, will cause identity problems for their members, and make them as social institutions more susceptible to the ethnic and political storms to come. Are we looking at the high watermark of Church and state in East Africa?[50] The future will bring disillusion to one, or both, as Muingiki betokens among the Gikuyu, who were the keenest to Christianize, modernize, and Westernize. The mainstream churches and state institutions will gradually disintegrate as systems of Church or national government are decreasingly able to cross the rising ethnic barriers or else give sense to plurality. African theologians, as others, must think again about finding unity while building on diversity, as well as addressing the current causes of poverty in a sustainably redemptive approach.

Notes and References

[1] There was one African present (Brian Stanley, *The World Missionary Conference, Edinburgh 1910* (Grand Rapids, MI: Eerdmans, 2009), 99.

[2] Kenya is the only country on which there is detailed quantitative research before 1948, because of David Barrett's research there as a CMS mission-partner: see David B. Barrett, "The Expansion of Christianity in Kenya, AD 1900–2000," in David B. Barrett, G. K. Mambo, J. McLoughlin, and Malcolm J. McVeigh, eds, *Kenya Churches Handbook: The Development of Kenyan Christianity, 1498–1893* (Kisumu: Evangel, 1973), 157–91. My analysis of annual average attendance at the Native Anglican Church from Bluebooks, produced by the Protectorate of Uganda, shows that it doubled every 12 years, that is, at a quarter of the rate of Kenya churches, between 1908 and 1926. Tanganyika and Zanzibar's church growth was lower due to Muslim expansion at this time. In 1900, Tanzania already had 92,000 and Uganda 180,000, 2.4 percent and 6.8 percent of the population respectively: see David B. Barrett, et. al., *World Christian Encyclopedia: A Comparative Survey of Churches and Religions in the Modern World* (New York: Oxford University Press, 2001), III, 426, 729, 761.

[3] Barrett, "Expansion," 157.

[4] For instance, the Seventh-day Adventist (SDA) Reformers broke away claiming that the SDA Church had illicitly authorized her members to take part in World War II and her members to partake in beverages with caffeine, such as tea, coffee, and Coca-cola. The True SDA Church claims that the Church logo should not use the sign of the cross, and moreover the SDA Church had introduced women's ministries as a result of associating with the Vatican (Rev. Godwin Lekundayo, personal communication, November 10, 2008).

[5] Eleazar Kyoko, *c.*1925, quoted in Ben Knighton, "Christian Enculturation in Karamoja, Uganda" (PhD thesis, Durham: University of Durham, 1990), I, 403.

[6] Louise Pirouet, *Black Evangelists: The Spread of Christianity in Uganda, 1891–1914* (London: Rex Collings, 1978).

[7] Joyce Reason, *Safety Last: The Story of Albert Cook of Uganda* (London: Highway Press, 1954).

[8] L. B. Greaves, *Carey Francis of Kenya* (London: Rex Collings, 1969).

[9] Paul Hamilton Hume White, *Doctor of Tanganyika* (London: Paternoster, 1952).

[10] Rev. John Madinda confirms the ineluctability of tradition for Tanzania (personal communication June 23, 2008): "anything which was brought in by missionaries and taught by missionaries is what is right and even if there was a mistake, then it should not be talked about, and anything which is initiated locally is wrong."

[11] Frank Welbourn and Bethwell Ogot, *A Place to Feel at Home* (Nairobi: Oxford University Press, 1966), 40; Marko

Kuhn, *Prophetic Christianity in Western Kenya: Political, Cultural, and Theological Aspects of African Independent Churches* (Frankfurt: Peter Lang, 2007), 14.

[12] Even this "rigidly anti-tribal" pietism was complex, however. For a young Moravian missionary, Traugott Bachmann, conversion "implied total rejection of the normal world." Afterwards Jesus would replace their human chief, but Bachman converted "to an extremely pro-African position." Yet he still banned fundamental socio-economic practices, such as ownership of cattle in a kinship structure and bridewealth. See Marcia Wright, *German Mission in Tanganyika, 1891–1941: Lutherans and Moravians in the Southern Highlands* (London: Oxford University Press, 1971), 88–91. In 1899, Moravians took over the pioneering work of (Livingstone's) London Missionary Society begun in 1879.

[13] Klaus Fiedler, *Christianity and African Culture: Conservative German Protestant missionaries in Tanzania, 1900–1940* (Leiden: Brill, 1996), 28–43.

[14] Ibid., 213.

[15] For instance, Prof. Mugambi insists that missionaries only came to Africa to obtain a proper job back in the West; see Jesse N. D. Mugambi, *From Liberation to Reconstruction: African Christian Theology after the Cold War* (Nairobi: East African Educational Publishers, 1995), 208. Although becoming a missionary was a means for some to rise in class before 1940 (but never so much as for African clergy, as in Masasi, and their children), African experience has usually been seen as a disqualification in Western professions.

[16] Hence Kenyatta gave a rather romantic portrayal of the Gikuyu system for courting and marriage in Jomo Kenyatta, *Facing Mount Kenya: The Tribal Life of the Gikuyu* (London: Secker & Warburg, 1938), but one to which the unlettered subscribe today in their memories.

[17] Bruno Gutmann, *Das Dschaggaland und seine Christen* (Leipzig: Verlag der Evangelische-Lutheran Mission, 1925); "The African Standpoint," *Africa* 8/1 (1935): 1–19.

[18] Terence O. Ranger, "Missionary Adaptation of African Religious Institutions: The Masasi Case," in Terence Ranger and Isaria N. Kimambo, eds, *The Historical Study of African Religion* (London: Heinemann, 1972), 221–51.

[19] Eugene Hillman, *Toward an African Christianity: Inculturation Applied* (New York: Paulist Press, 1993); Vincent J. Donovan, *Christianity Rediscovered: An Epistle from the Maasai* (London: Student Christian Movement, 1982).

[20] Aylward Shorter, *Toward a Theology of Inculturation* (London: Geoffrey Chapman, 1988).

[21] Joseph G Healey and Donald Sybertz, *Towards an African Narrative Theology* (Maryknoll, NY: Orbis, 1996).

[22] Christopher Wrightand Christopher Sugden,eds, *One Gospel – Many Clothes: Anglicans and the Decade of Evangelism: Case-studies on Evangelism to Mark the Retirement of John Stott as President of the Evangelical Fellowship in the Anglican Communion* (Oxford: Regnum, 1990).

[23] Aylward Shorter, *Toward a Theology*, 10.

[24] Aylward Shorter, *Toward a Theology*, 64f.

[25] Philip S. Tovey,"Inculturation: The Bread and the Wine at the Eucharist," *Colloquium Journal* 3 (2006). Available at: <http://www.yale.edu/ism/colloq_journal/vol3/tovey1. html >; accessed December 14, 2008. Tovey was a CMS mission-partner in Northern Uganda, and Kanamai is on the Kenyan coast; see David M. Gitari, ed. *Liturgical Inculturation in Africa: The Kanamai Statement with Introduction, Papers from Kanamai and a First Response* (Bramcote, Nottingham: Grove, 1994).

[26] John V. Taylor, *The Primal Vision: Christian Presence amid African Religion* (London: Student Christian Movement, 1963).

[27] King's School, Budo, and the Alliance High School, Anglican and joint Protestant institutions in Uganda and Kenya respectively, were noted producers of the African elite. For the social divisions exacerbated by churches and schools, see John Lonsdale, "The Moral Economy of Mau Mau: Wealth, Poverty and Civic Virtue in Kikuyu Political Thought," in Bruce Berman and John Lonsdale, eds, *Unhappy Valley: Conflict in Kenya and Africa* (London,/ Nairobi,/Athens, OH: James Currey/Heinemann/Ohio University Press, 1992), 265–504; and "Kikuyu Christianities: A History of Intimate Diversity," in David Maxwell with Ingrid Lawrie, eds, *Christianity and the African Imagination: Essays in Honour of Adrian Hastings* (Leiden: Brill, 2002), 157–97.

[28] As Rev. John Madinda put it for Tanzania (personal communication June 23, 2008), "The task of the church has therefore (especially among its leaders) been to live within a tension of recognising and maintaining the global connection within the church and its relation to the local issues."

[29] "The African Christian has suffered from a form of religious schizophrenia," Desmond Tutu, "Whither African Theology?," in Edward W. Fasholé-Luke et al., ed., *Christianity in Independent Africa* (London: Rex Collings, 1978), 364–9.

[30] Christian institutions also released young women from unwanted possession by old men, and gave them opportunity to speak in church and school. See Marjorie Mbilinyi, "Runaway Wives: Forced Labour and Forced Marriage in Colonial Rungwe," *International Journal of Sociology of Law* 16/1 (1988): 1–29; Emily Onyango, "Luo Women's

Negotiation of Mission Education: A Critical Analysis of Anglican Women in Nyanza, Kenya, from 1895" (PhD thesis, Oxford Centre for Mission Studies/University of Wales, 2006).

[31] John Karanja, *Founding an African Faith: Kikuyu Anglican Christianity, 1900–1945* (Nairobi: Uzima, 1999), shows just how the first churches were peopled. Not seeing a hierarchical society, it was easy for missionaries to mistake the social status of a neophyte and to cater for the sundry clients of government-appointed chiefs, who found their power increased, which was hated by the populace.

[32] Jocelyn Murray,"The Kikuyu Female Circumcision Controversy, with special reference to the Church Mission Society's 'sphere of influence'" (PhD dissertation, Berkeley, CA: University of California, 1974).

[33] Mau Mau was a mass Gikuyu politico-religious movement based on an oath to be kept on pain of death, which prompted Emergency Measures in Kenya from 1952 to 1960. The bitterness and cost of the conflict convinced the British government to drop the interests of white settlers. See Ben Knighton, "Mau Mau," in Peter B. Clarke, ed., *Encyclopedia of New Religious Movements* (London: Routledge, 2006), 355f.

[34] Barrett et al., *Kenya Churches*; Frederick Burkewood Welbourn, *East African Rebels: A Study of Two Independent Churches* (London: Student Christian Movement, 1961).

[35] Timothy John Padwick,"Spirit, Desire, and the World: Roho Churches of Western Kenya in the Era of Globalization," PhD thesis, University of Birmingham.

[36] Knighton, Ben, "Muingiki Madness: The Counter-story to Gitari's Modernization by Mainstream Churches" in Ben Knighton,ed., *Religion and Politics in Kenya: Essays in Honor of a Meddlesome Priest* (New York: Palgrave Macmillan, 2009), 223–50.

[37] Gavin Flood, *Beyond Phenomenology: Rethinking the Study of Religion* (London: Cassell 1999), 3.

[38] Robert Buijtenhujs, "Dini ya Msambwa: Rural Rebellion or Counter-Society," in Wim van Binsbergenand Matthew Schoffeleers,eds, *Theoretical Explorations in African Religion*, ed. (London, African Studies Centre, Leiden, 1985), 322–45.

[39] Ben Knighton, "Karinga" in Peter B. Clarke, ed., *Encyclopedia of New Religious Movements* (London: Routledge, 2006), 295f.

[40] The location for meetings was Ufungamano House, a building owned by the NCCK and the Roman Catholics' Kenya Episcopal Conference (KEC), on the way to State House. Ufungamano is an attempt to denote ecumenism in Swahili, since it means the quality of thick forest where the branches of different trees intertwine.

[41] Ben Knighton, "Introduction: Strange but Inevitable Bedfellows," in Ben Knighton,ed., *Religion and Politics in*

Kenya: Essays in Honor of a Meddlesome Priest (New York: Palgrave Macmillan, 2009), 39.

[42] Despite the poverty of its training, the Anglican Church of Tanzania is already approaching 4,000,000 (Rev. John Madinda, personal communication August 9, 2008).

[43] A *khadi* is a judge of *shar'iah* (law), and Kenyan law has always allowed their courts jurisdiction over family and domestic cases, if both parties are willing to be heard by this process.

[44] John Chesworth, "The Church and Islam: Vyama Vyingi (multipartyism) and the Ufangamano Talks," in Ben Knighton,ed., *Religion and Politics in Kenya: Essays in Honor of a Meddlesome Priest* (New York, Palgrave Macmillan, 2009), 155–80.

[45] NGOs provide a diversion: "the heart of the problem becomes allocating the vision, and motives of each player . . . the only thing the church can do is to trail behind and use the secular professionals" (Rev. John Madinda, personal communication, June 23, 2008).

[46] Paul Gifford, "Christianity Co-opted," in Ben Knighton, ed., *Religion and Politics in Kenya: Essays in Honor of a Meddlesome Priest* (New York, Palgrave Macmillan, 2009), 201–21; and *Christianity, Politics and Public Life in Kenya* (London: Hurst, 2009). Both of these represent a rather tendentious view based on Nairobi.

[47] Eunice Rukundo,"Lies, Sex, and Hypocrisy in Pentecostal Churches in Uganda," available [online] at: <http://majimbokenya.com/home/2009/06/01/lies-sex-and-hypocrisy-in-pentecostal-churches-in-uganda/ > ; accessed September 29, 2009; "Uganda Pastors' Love for America," *Sunday Vision*, August 30, 2009.

[48] Frieder Ludwig, *Church and State in Tanzania: Aspects of a Changing Relationship, 1961–1994* (Leiden: Brill 1999), 182–3.

[49] Nairobi Lighthouse Church, Sunday Morning Service at 9.30 a.m., April 7, 2002.

[50] Tanzania with its more socialist history has far fewer ethnic problems, but that may make it more vulnerable to a sudden rise in ethnic identity, which will come as the rigid traditions of the churches are thrown off with growth and dilution. Zimbabwe, Burundi, Rwanda, Uganda, and Kenya sit on ethnic time-bombs already ticking.

Further Reading

Hansen, Hölger Bernt and Michael Twaddle, eds. *Religion and Politics in East Africa* Oxford: James Currey, 1995.

Hansen, Hölger Bernt and Michael Twaddle, eds. *Christian Missionaries & the State* Oxford: James Currey, 2002.

Knighton, Ben. "Christian Enculturation in the Two-Thirds World," in Frans Wijsenand Robert Schreiter, eds, *Global Christianity: Contested Claims*. Amsterdam/New York: Rodopi, 2007, 51–68.

Knighton, Ben, ed. *Religion and Politics in Kenya: Confrontation and Compliance of Church Leaders*. New York: Palgrave Macmillan, 2009.

Ross, Andrew C. *David Livingstone: Mission and Empire*, Edinburgh: Continuum, 2006.

Spear, Thomas. "Toward the History of African Christianity," in Thomas Spearand Isaria S Kimambo, eds, *East African Expressions of Christianity*. Oxford/Dar es Salaam/Nairob/Athens, OH: Currey/Mkuki wa Nyota/East African Educational Publishers/Ohio University Press, 1999, 3–24.

Welbourn, Frederick Burkewood. *East African Rebels: A Study of Two Independent Churches*. London: Student Christian Movement, 1961.

3

West African Christianity
Padres, Pastors, Prophets, and Pentecostals

Ogbu Kalu

The history of Christianity in West Africa has now been continuous for over half a millennium – in Africa at large, of course, it goes back to the age of the Apostles – though for a long time it was a history of many false starts and abandoned initiatives. In its *longue durée*, it may perhaps be compared to a race in which the precious baton of the Gospel has passed on from one runner to another, though with the important difference that the environment of the race has changed at almost every lap. So my account focuses both on who the bearers of the baton were – Portuguese padres, Protestant missionaries and pastors, African prophets, and latterly Pentecostal evangelists of very diverse kinds – and on the changing historical circumstances in which they discharged the "Great Commission." If there is a single key turning point in the whole story, it is the point at which the essential work of evangelism passed from missionaries from outside to Africans themselves, and the process became irrevocably self-sustaining.

Iberian Catholic Beginnings

Although Africa encountered the Gospel during the heyday of the Jesus movement, it did not penetrate south of the Sahara until the Muslims smashed the early Christian presence in the Graeco-Roman world from the seventh century onwards, and overran most of the centers of early Christianity. From that period, the histories of the two religions in Africa became ineluctably intertwined. Islamic insurgence constituted multiple challenges to Western Europe. Politically, Muslims controlled the Iberian Peninsula, as well as (for many centuries) the Mediterranean Sea and the Levant, and so too the trade routes to the Far East. In West Africa, they established a lucrative trade in salt from the Saharan oasis of Taghaza, and in gold from Bambuk and Bure in the Futa-Jallon basin of the Senegambia. Culturally, they developed intellectual centers in Iberia and in Timbuctu (which is considered as the first university in Africa). Its huge library collections are currently being recovered, reassembled, edited, and indexed.

Challenges elicit responses. Europeans first responded with gallantry and futile crusades. The Portuguese Prince Henry the Navigator (1394–1460) experimented with new sails, astrolabe, compass, keel, and many naval projects, and in 1451 finally captured Ceuta on the Moroccan coast. By 1460, his captains had reached Sierra Leone in search of an alternative sea route to the trans-Saharan gold and spices of the Far East. The Crown secured the monopoly of each segment of the shoestring Portuguese Empire with papal bulls and the *padroãado* agreements that left Christian evangelization activities under the ultimate control of the Portuguese Crown, while commercial motives were veiled in Christian rhetoric. In the

Introducing World Christianity, First Edition. Edited by Charles E. Farhadian.
© 2012 Blackwell Publishing Ltd. Published 2012 by Blackwell Publishing Ltd.

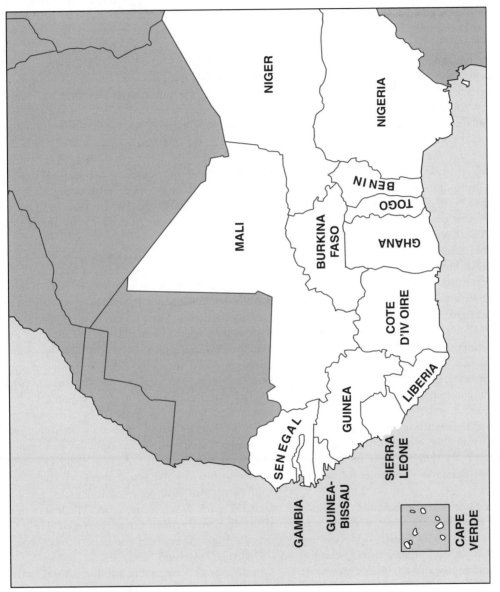

Map 3.1   West Africa

crusading spirit, Prince Henry hoped to reconnect with the mythical empire of Prester John in distant Abyssinia. But the Portuguese cautiously stayed on the islands and forayed only a few miles from the coast in a few places, as in the Gold Coast. The previously uninhabited Cape Verde Islands, which were discovered in 1458, became a little Portugal, while Saõ Tome, further down the coast of Western Africa, served as a major refueling depot. Only in the Kongo-Soyo kingdoms in the north of today's Angola did they succeed in establishing a significant native Christian community. A court alliance bound the monarchy and the elite into a ceremonial Roman Catholic spirituality and immersed the Catholic Church in political intrigues and the slave trade. Portuguese missionary enterprise in West Africa tended to lack consistency and depth of commitment. It is true that there was an active "Catholic" slave trade in Angola and the Kongo, but it was run largely by the Portuguese Crown. The Kongo king Afonso, himself a Catholic, tried but failed to suppress it.[2] Moreover, there is evidence to show that in the Kongo, at least, many Catholic catechists were committed, engaged, and creative, not distant and ineffectual. It is true that there were few Kongolese priests, but Catholic teaching in Central Africa was effective, and people took it seriously.[3] Resistance from local rulers and rivalry from other Europeans added other challenges. When the Portuguese struck a gold coin called the *cruzado,* other Europeans entered the region – Spaniards, Danes, Dutch, English, and French. The seventeenth century ended with the French and the English starting their long-term rivalry for global mastery, and the West African coast was littered with trading forts operated by the chartered companies of several nations.

In the Upper Guinea or Senegambia, stretching from the River Senegal in the north, southwards to Cape Palmas in present-day Liberia and covering Sierra Leone, Gambia, and Guinea Bissau, Portugal set up a commanding base in Saõ Tiago, one of the Cape Verde Islands, in 1533. The goal was to train indigenous priests for evangelistic work. Operational delays followed, but schools were opened in the 1650s to nurture a local elite. Evangelization was fraught with difficulties that could be demonstrated through the eyes of contemporaries. For instance, Father Baltasar

Barreira, who sailed into this region in 1604, left a description of the Guinea coast and a record of his travels (1606). For the first century of Portuguese contact with West Africa from 1440, the gold trade dominated the relationship. Slaves became important later and gradually constituted over 10 percent of Lisbon's own population. According to Barreira, local people stayed loyal to their indigenous religions, and saw little difference between the missionary and the trader. Funding from the state authorities was inadequate, forcing the missionaries into moral compromises: the Jesuits supported themselves through engaging in the slave trade and failed to nurture indigenous priests. By 1600, João Pinto, a Wolof, was the only indigene to be ordained a priest. Many priests were the children and houseboys of traders. Above all, missionaries had such a poor relationship with the Portuguese governors that when Barreira died in 1612, the governor rejoiced that his worst enemy was gone.

The Jesuits were keen to combat Islam, which had originally penetrated into the ancient Mali and Songhay empires through the activities of Arab traders. Barreira described the Jesuit counter-attack that led to the mission entering Sierra Leone. From 1606 to 1608, Barreira developed a court alliance that involved the Temne chiefs, and built a church near Kru Bay. Some chiefs pretended to accept Christianity out of self-interest, but most refused to abandon the ancestral religion that was the basis of their legitimacy. The mission was constantly undermined by its intermittent supply of human power. Barreira's departure was followed by a void until the mid-1600s when a Spanish mission rekindled some fire. An interesting dimension is the role of an African priest, Father Joseph, who was from North America, educated in Britain, and ordained in Spain. When he arrived in 1715, few vestiges of the Iberian Christian presence existed. He built virtually from scratch in the areas that are today known as Granville Town and Kissy.

In the rest of Senegambia, the Iberian missionary presence yielded early fruits in trading centers such as St Louis, Gorée, Rufisque, Portudal, and Joal. Soon local chiefs, who exploited the rivalry between Europeans, blocked the missionaries. Progress came when the French took over Senegambia in the eighteenth century and actively encouraged Catholic missionary activity. They installed a resident Prefect Apostolic from the Holy Ghost Congregation, with the consent of *Propaganda Fidei* in Rome. The missionaries were supported by the state and served as civil servants under the Ministry of Marines. Still, the missionary corps always faced the problem of inadequate manpower supply and the constraints of government control.

São Tome in the Lower Guinea served the same purpose as Cape Verde for the Upper Guinea. It was populated by slaves and prisoners from Portugal, who provided labor in the plantations in São Tomé, Príncipe, and Fernando Po. As the refueling depot and center for training missionary manpower, its history was riddled with chaos. The population staged riots in 1584, 1593, and 1595 against servile working conditions, and the Church clashed with the government. After Bishop Gaspar Cao was tried in 1571 and won against the governor, a rainbow appeared! But for most of the period, the Church was under absentee leadership.

Following his victory, Bishop Cao organized a hinterland mission to Warri in 1574. An earlier mission to Benin had failed. The Portuguese had established a trading station in Benin in 1486. The king, *Oba* Ozolua, wanted guns in exchange for pepper, ivory, and slaves, and deliberately located the church and school within his palace. When the Portuguese found more pepper in India and failed to supply him with guns, the *Oba* lost interest in the mission before his death in 1517. His successor closed the trading depot in 1532 and the fortunes of the mission waned before the last set of priests was expelled in 1651. The Warri mission lasted longer, but as a low-intensity operation limited to a small circle in the palace. Priests accompanied trading ships from São Tomé to stay only during the trading period; the climate was a challenge, and priests survived by trading in slaves. In the 1650s, *Olu* Antonio Domingo invited Spanish missionaries who had difficulties with the Portuguese governors of São Tome, and by the next decade, only a few priests ventured to Warri except for the period 1710–30 when some priests came from Brazil. By the eighteenth century, the only remaining relic of Christianity was a broken statue. The Dutch frequently attacked São Tomé, which exchanged hands many times throughout the period.

Portugal was a small country and could not control such a large empire for long. For instance, in 1482, Diego d'Azambuja established a Portuguese foothold in the Gold Coast at Elmina, named after the castle of St George of Mina. From here missionaries covered a 10 mile radius to Shama, Axim, Efutu, and Komenda. The same factors decimated their initial efforts: shortage of manpower, lack of sustained vision, and insecurity as other nations attacked the Portuguese. The Dutch attacked Elmina in 1607, 1615, 1625, and finally took it in 1637. Shama and Axim fell soon after. Only the syncretistic cult of Nana Antony was left to show that Iberians had preached about saints in West Africa.

Further south from the Slave Coast, the mission to the Kongo/Soyo kingdoms stood out as the major achievement of Iberian Catholicism. But Portuguese involvement in local politics soon caused a conflagration. By the seventeenth century, an African girl, Beatrice Vita Kimpa, whose spiritual journey began with membership in the *ngunza* cult, claimed to be possessed by the spirit of St Antony with a message to mobilize the Christians to stop the violent civil war that ravaged the communities. The people rallied around this apostle of peace, but the Church hanged her as a heretic and snuffed out this brand of popular Catholicism. Iberian Catholicism in Africa collapsed for multiple reasons: the official attack on the Jesuits, European anti-clericalism, the lack of depth bred by depending on court alliances with African rulers, and the increase in slave trading that exacerbated the rivalry among European nations.

As the slave trade intensified, with its disruptive effects on African societies, the Christian presence retreated into chaplaincies located in trading forts. By the eighteenth century, there were about twenty-one forts on the coast of West Africa alone. Not all of these had chaplains, and the few that did tended to treat them with ignominy as dispensable nuisances. Some trading companies used African chaplains who had been trained in Europe. Among Dutch, Danish, or English Protestants, Christian Protten, Philip Quaque, William Amo, and J. E. Capitein all failed out of sheer frustration. Capitein's book, *A Call to the Heathens*, betrays a glowing ardor to save his people with the Gospel, but the fire in him was quenched by the neglect of the trading company that controlled the fort. The trade in human beings hindered the fortunes of the Gospel.

Mission, Abolition, and the Evangelical Revival

My key concern here is to show how the abolitionist impulse of the eighteenth century, linked with the two great waves of evangelical revival, had a crucial impact on missionary enterprise. The forces operating in the home base of missionary enterprise explain much about what happened in the mission field. Abolitionism arose from various sources but soon inspired a network of concerned people in Great Britain, Europe, and North America. Partly, it rose by way of reaction to certain effects of the rise of industrial capitalism in Britain: booming urban populations, with deteriorating conditions of life and work, and the growth of poverty and homelessness alongside the wealth and luxury of the middle and upper classes. Hogarth's paintings reveal the social problems that touched consciences and inspired philanthropy. This sensitivity rubbed off on the growing black population in London that numbered about 15,000 in 1772. Some were free and others still in slavery. The Committee of the Black Poor found it increasingly difficult to sustain such a large number of dependent, unskilled, and unemployed people. Lord Mansfield best expressed the growing, sensitive spirit in his ruling on an abused

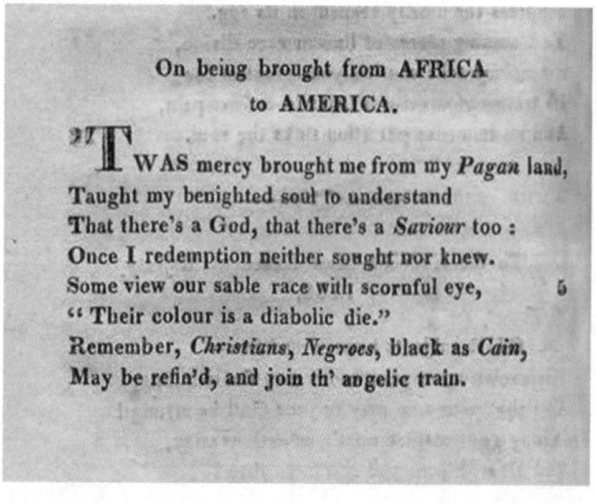

On being brought from AFRICA
to AMERICA.

'T WAS mercy brought me from my *Pagan* land,
Taught my benighted soul to understand
That there's a God, that there's a *Saviour* too:
Once I redemption neither sought nor knew.
Some view our sable race with scornful eye,   5
" Their colour is a diabolic die."
Remember, *Christians*, *Negroes*, black as *Cain*,
May be refin'd, and join th' angelic train.

Figure 3.1 Life of Olaudah; *source*: <http://commons. wikimedia.org/wiki/File:On_being_brought_from_africa_ to_america.jpg>

slave, James Somerset, when he declared that "the air of England has long been too pure for a slave and every man is free who breathes it … let the Negro be discharged." This spirit explains the great interest in the genuine accounts of ex-slaves on the ordeals and evil of human trafficking.

The abolitionist cause was promoted by a variety of constituencies. First were liberated Africans who wrote memoirs of their homeland. In 1787, a Fanti (from today's Ghana) named Ottobah Cuguano wrote a book entitled *Thoughts and Sentiments on Evils of Slavery*. Perhaps he was assisted by Olaudah Equiano (in Igbo language, Ekwuno), who in 1789 wrote an instant best-selling autobiography, *Life of Olaudah Equiano*. He worked hard to redeem himself from slavery and devoted his energy to promoting the anti-slavery cause. A man of muscular Christianity, ironically, his high profile and independence later threatened the work of white philanthropists, even though he was a symbol of the solution to slavery. He networked with groups and individuals in North America at a period when the relationship between Britain and America was in tatters. Second, the question of slavery had a loud hearing between 1770 and 1783. Among the free and educated blacks, many projects were designed to educate blacks and to agitate for the liberation of their race. Societies such as the African Society of Providence sprang up in the 1700s to promote such a cause. Third, some religious groups such as the pacifist Quakers protested against the immorality of slavery; they funded many organizations. But the American Revolution brought matters to a head in 1775, when Lord Dunmore offered to grant freedom to slaves who would desert their masters to join the British forces. Many black loyalists took the offer. The settlement of black British loyalists in Sierra Leone has to be understood in the context of post-revolutionary British politics. After the war, British opinion actively contrasted the abusive character of American slavery with the freedom and liberty that Britain espoused.

Driving this was a new conception of British polity: not as slave owners and slaves, but as a community of free subjects. The Sierra Leone settlement was part of a broader effort to show how freed blacks could contribute to the Commonwealth through their role as producers and consumers. That is to say, there was an active sense of belonging to Britain, which offered blacks a considerably better deal than anything offered by the Americans. The British lost the war, but endeavored to keep their word. Some freed slaves were sent to the West Indies, and others to Nova Scotia, while many joined the bulk of the black poor whose fate aroused philanthropic consciences. Perhaps the principles of the new American Constitution, based on the highest ideals of European polity, inspired the blacks to ask for the same: equality before the law and the opportunity to demonstrate their selfhood through hard work, enterprise, and responsibility. They absorbed the idea of progress and the human potential for social, political, and economic redemption. Though their experience in Nova Scotia belied the rosy promises, it set off agitations for redress. Here the activities of an Egba-Yoruba ex-slave, Thomas Peters, are interesting. Born about 1740, kidnapped in 1760, he took the freedom offer in 1776 and ended up in Nova Scotia as a social activist who carried the petition of the destitute ex-slaves to London in 1789. His remarkable eloquence was highly effective.

In England, it became obvious that abolitionist efforts could only succeed if Africa was involved in the solution, as the use of force to restrain the slavers needed local support. Perhaps Britain designed the Freetown experiment to bypass the compromised traditional rulers and create a local, supportive civil society that would use legitimate enterprise to destroy the slave trade at its source. In 1787, the first batch of blacks, accompanied by a number of white prostitutes, was shipped out to initiate the experiment. The project underestimated the damaging potential of the local chiefs who within three years had brought the colony to its knees. Disease also took its toll. It was at this juncture that the Nova Scotian blacks arrived in 1792, to rescue the enterprise with a new temper. They had imbibed the New Light movement, a variety of evangelicalism with Wesleyan spirituality that meshed with charismatic slave religion to produce a corps of powerful indigenous preachers. Among the blacks, preaching was beyond a mere communication technique; preachers were opinion molders and the prayer house served as a political forum, where the ruled freely discussed the rulers and other weighty matters under the guidance of the Holy Spirit. In 1822, a further wave of African-American returnees founded Liberia.

The next phase of abolitionism was connected with a group nicknamed the Clapham Sect: professionals, businessmen, parliamentarians, and politicians who met in St John's Anglican Church, Clapham, South London, under the leadership of Rev. John Venn, to discuss social problems and political solutions. Associated with them are names that became immortalized in West Africa, such as William Wilberforce, Granville Sharpe, and Thomas Clarkson whose son, John, led the Nova Scotians to Freetown. Another of them, Thomas Fowell Buxton, provided a solution in his *African Slave Trade and Its Remedy* (1841) that connected the abolitionist cause to mission. He suggested a solution that was foregrounded in the logic of industrial capitalism: build the self-interest of local chiefs through treaties to encourage them to produce raw materials to feed British industry, establish rational administrative structures and legal systems to provide security and an enabling environment, and use Christian missions as a civilizing agency.

In 1792, a Baptist pastor, William Carey, canvassed his fellow Baptists to obey the Great Commission and mobilize for cross-cultural mission. He called for a voluntary association to sponsor missionaries to places such as India (his special concern) and Africa. Like Buxton, Carey saw the abolitionist cause as wedded to mission, civilization, and commerce. From this period, many missionary bodies sprouted in Britain and Europe, some linked with denominations (like the Anglican Church Missionary Society), and some interdenominational Protestant (like the London Missionary Society). The great age of the Protestant missionary movement was under way. For various reasons, the British societies could not recruit all the personnel they needed at home, so turned to Europe for assistance. Basel, close to the Pietist Lutheran countryside of Baden-Wurttemberg, was prominent in supplying missionaries, because its pious business elite combined trade with evangelism and used their profits for the Lord.

In 1841, Henry Venn, who became the Secretary of the Church Missionary Society, developed a strategy of "three selves" that gave primacy to "native agency" in the enterprise. He advocated the three principles of self-support, self-government, and self-propagation as the recipe for a healthy native church. In America, Venn had a contemporary, Rufus Anderson – born, like him in 1796 – who shared the same missionary goals and strategies, as the American churches stirred in the 1850s. A further vast array of missionary bodies and personnel surged into Africa when the "faith movement," a second wave of evangelical revival, burst out in the 1880s. One thing that differentiated them from the earlier phase was that many individuals, men and women, set out on mission without depending on a funding church or organization. God was expected to sustain them. Then the Roman Catholics, who had pioneered missions in earlier centuries, retooled their structures and joined the affray from the 1840s, when the Sisters of Cluny came to Gorée. Soon the Society for African Missions, the Holy Ghost Fathers, and the White Fathers joined them, working first in the French sphere of influence, and later in anglophone areas.

The role of African Americans in the evangelization of West Africa is a noteworthy aspect of the story. In America, the turn of the century witnessed not only growing numbers but also much confidence among the blacks in forming their own churches. Scholars have argued that by 1830 a new and highly visible Afro-cultural presence had emerged. It rested on the firm foundation of evangelical Christianity. As the only form of organized communal life available to slaves, evangelical institutions came to constitute important loci where black people could develop a sense of belonging and assert a cultural presence in the larger society through the creation of their own moral and social communities. Blacks were mostly Baptists and Methodists, but there were a few Episcopalians and some Presbyterians as these churches split North and South on the slavery question. More importantly, they developed a very strong motivation to evangelize Africa. So, in 1821, a black Carey, Lott Carey, who had bought himself and his two children out of slavery in Charles County, Virginia, and who had been baptized and ordained as a Baptist, set out in the brig *Nautilus* to serve as a missionary in Sierra Leone and Liberia. Black missionaries and white abolitionists stamped early evangelicalism in Africa with an indelible imprint, namely, the quest for a new identity through hot Gospel and responsible citizenship. The African Americans wanted to return home for several reasons: to redeem their motherland through charismatic Christianity; to fulfill the black man's burden; to regain freedom and dignity; to prove their capacity to build a civil society based on the ideals espoused in Europe and America; and to wipe out both the slur and the reality of the slave trade. The contours of these ideals spawned variations till the 1900s. Many associations were formed to promote the colonization project or "back-to-Africa movement," as Marcus Garvey later termed it.

Even before the abolition of slavery in 1838, the West Indies became a recruiting ground for missions to West Africa whose climate made it the proverbial "white man's grave." As white denominations scoured through black colleges such as Oberlin and Tuskegee Institute in the United States, so others looked to Codrington College in Barbados to recruit candidates for the mission fields. Many West Indians went as missionaries to Fernando Po, Nigeria, Cameroon, and the Gold Coast. It was said that the fiery African-American preacher George Liele had so set the region ablaze in the late 1790s, that, in 1806, Jamaican authorities forbade the blacks from holding prayer meetings as these occasions turned increasingly subversive. African-American missionaries served in Ethiopia, Egypt, Mozambique, Rhodesia, Nyasaland, Angola, Congo, and Cape Colony in the 1880s, and groomed the "recaptives" who were rescued in Freetown. Recaptives, such as Samuel Adjai Crowther, set the tone of Christian presence in the early period, characterized by an evangelical temper, strenuous evangelization of the interior, reasoned conversation with Muslims, vernacular translation, maintenance of schools, hospitals and other charitable institutions, and definition of evangelical cultural policy till the Edinburgh Conference in 1910 attempted to plot new dimensions in the face of a new colonial restructuring of Africa.

When Crowther was made bishop of the Niger territory in 1864, the significance went beyond the triumph of black evangelism over the white missionary Christianity of Henry Townsend and others who had opposed his elevation. It was an affirmation of the impact of the alliance of abolitionists and Africans, who at various levels took the Gospel as their own and promoted it among their own people. Yet the imprecise nature of the delimitation of Crowther's episcopacy betrayed the tentative character of the experiment because, by the end of the century, the three black bishops in Haiti, Liberia, and Nigeria were embattled and were replaced by whites at the end of their terms of service. Underneath was the reality that the evangelical spirit was waning under the harsh exigencies of the mission field, its enlargement of scale, and the institutionalization of the enterprise. The evangelization of Africa was still uneven. In Liberia, the various denominations were too locked in competition to prosecute missions into the interior. Among the Episcopalians, for instance, a policy for interior mission had to wait until the elevation of Samuel Ferguson to the bishopric in 1885. The process was even slower in Sierra Leone.

West Africa suffered from inadequate missionary personnel in the face of the enlarged opportunities in Sierra Leone, the Gold Coast, and Nigeria. Islam was steadily advancing in West Africa, partly fueled by a series of *jihad*s across the savannah from Senegambia to northern Nigeria. An early mission to the Susu failed; a second planned by the Methodists hardly took off the ground. An alleged invitation for Christian missionaries to the Futa Jallon did not materialize. European missionaries had no agreed policy toward Islam. Early apologists considered it a false religion but opinion mellowed because Islam was monotheistic, unlike African primal religions. Bosworth Smith's evolutionary theory suggested that Islam might be good for the primitive races, a view taken up by Edward Wilmot Blyden in his severe indictment of the failure of missionary adaptation to African realities, *Christianity, Islam and the Negro Race* (1887). Soon colonial governments were protecting Muslim communities from missionaries. Another concern was the moral effect of the gin trade on West Africa. The easy suggestion was that a religion that avoided liquor was a solution to the gin trade that some considered to be worse than the slave trade in degrading Africans. Few listened to C. H. Robinson's retort in 1896 that in Hausaland, Muslims drank as hard as any pagan and that the slave trade was rife with Qur'anic support. In spite of "Soudan" parties that surged into the Sahelian interior, the obstructive attitude of colonial governments and a failure to design an effective evangelistic strategy hindered missions to the Muslims of West Africa. They have held the numerical supremacy in West Africa to this day.

Colonial Christianity and African Responses, 1885–1914

Certain forces from the home bases of mission combined with the emergent modes of African appropriation to reshape the face of Christianity in the period from 1885 to World War I. The Berlin Conference of 1884–5, which partitioned Africa between the European powers, had an enormous effect on the relationship between white missionaries and Africans. It brought the Gospel and missionary cultural values down to the grass roots, where an attempt was made to domesticate them in the local cultural terrain. Africans responded by weaving Christian strands of their own. Similarly, the Edinburgh Conference of 1910 endeavored to reformulate a new vision of the missionary enterprise, even though it had no enforcement powers. The dominant note of ecumenical consolidation kept the missionary spirit alive in the midst of growing institutionalization, rivalry, the resilience of African cultures, and the rising power of the colonial states. World War I itself reformatted the interior of European culture. As the Anglo-American poet T. S. Eliot described the post-war period, Western civilization was like the moon when it is momentarily covered by a "shadow." The imperial idea lost some of its earlier glow of optimism and thereby created a niche for the reassertion of indigenous creativity.

Partition introduced virulent forms of European nationalism into the continent. The mission churches embellished this spirit with denominational coloring. The Berlin Conference, by requiring the physical presence of the colonizing power rather than mere declarations of areas of influence, opened the bowels of the African interior to missionary occupation too. Self-confidence replaced the initial wary respect for African chiefs, as colonial weaponry was there to back up, if needed, the bearers of the Gospel. The scale of missionary activity was enormously enlarged, making analysis complex. Competition among missionaries became intense: broadly, Catholics squared off against Protestants, but there was competition among the various Catholic Orders, because they often came from different nations. This rivalry determined the pace, direction, and nature of the Christian presence. As the "pacification" of the hinterland provided access to missionaries, the relationship between the two external agents of change became important. The allegation that missionaries colluded with the colonial governments has been modified by the recognition that, like an "odd couple," they often locked horns over cultural policy, educational goals, quality control, and the moral tone of government. Colonial Christianity contained various strands that would challenge the indigenous peoples and provoke responses: the patterns of living imposed in the mission compounds or institutions, the rejection of the large space that some liberals such as Henry Venn had advocated for African initiative, the cultural policy that devalued indigenous realities and embedded racist attitudes, the ecclesiastical structures that ignored the pneumatic resources of the Gospel and sapped the original vigor of evangelical spirituality, the unintended consequences of education, and Bible translations that exposed the underbelly of the enterprise.

Missionaries shared the Enlightenment worldview of the age, with its negative image of Africa. While they used education to create an elite that would carry the Gospel to their people, education served as an instrument of rivalry and a means of evangelization. Missionaries gave much thought to the language of instruction and the range of the curricula. These matters occupied attention during the Edinburgh Conference of 1910. Missionaries disdained the educated "black English men" caricatured in Joyce Cary's novel, *Mister Johnson*, though they had had a large part in creating him. Scholars debate how far colonial mission was a structure of hegemony, both psychological and physical. Others argue that in culture contact, local identities reassert themselves and redeploy externally derived resources in new and complex ways. All admit that nineteenth-century missionary organization was an enterprise run on pietistic principles, emphasizing hierarchy, discipline, and control. Race was a major concern because most whites lived in fear of the African: his dark skin, numbers, and cultures steeped in "heathenism" frightened these outsiders. Control measures were adopted as a survival technique.

Ethiopianism: The Root of African Christianity

From this perspective, the wave of "Ethiopianism" that spread throughout West Africa from 1860 to the turn of the century could serve as an example of African response to colonial Christianity, although it

has been one of the most misconstrued. The reasons include the fact that it was the first organized response that occurred within a few decades of Christianity's insertion into African communities. It bore the imprint of the culture conflict that followed the first massive wave of Western intrusion into African worlds. At that time, missionary structures had just been set up under (or even in advance of) the colonial canopy and were still being consolidated, while many communities in the hinterland had not yet tasted the resources of the Gospel. According to a key figure, the Sierra Leonian medical doctor Africanus Horton (1835–83), Ethiopianism was influenced by the European nationalism of the period that resulted in the partition of Africa, and by the shift in opinion that sought to restrain African initiative under European control. It was a movement with many strands. Its intellectual origins included the impact of Enlightenment ideals, filtered through American revolutionary rhetoric to inspire African Americans who returned to the motherland. The Christianity of the returnees was stamped with the values of anti-slavery and promoted as the cause of the oppressed and the stigmatized. Because in the early contact between missionaries and Africans racial ideology had been so hard-wired into the enterprise, the Ethiopianists called for the freeing of Africans from the religious and political tutelage of Europeans. Their core concerns were a quest for a place of their own, a search for identity and self-respect, and an ambition to nurse Africa back to its old glory. In a conflation of myth and history, that glory was imagined in the cultural achievements of ancient Egypt, Nubia, and Ethiopia. Ethiopia was both a place and an ideological symbol. There is little doubt about the achievements of Egypt in science, architecture, and government, and African contribution to the early formation of Christian doctrine, polity, liturgy, and ethics is incontrovertible.

The translators of the Septuagint Bible around 300 BCE mistakenly translated the Hebrew name *Kush* as *Aithiopia,* a word that the Greeks used for any country south of their known world and that is derived from their word for black face, *aithiops.* The entire region from Egypt to Ethiopia/Abyssinia was known as Ethiopia. This explains how "Ethiopianism" as a movement sought to recreate and attach itself to a golden age of African civilization, the splendor of the kingdoms of Meroe and Aksum that survived the Islamic onslaught of the seventh century and retained the pristine traditions of early Christianity. In European imagination, this was the kingdom of Prester John whose myth had fascinated the Crusaders and served as a beacon for the Portuguese voyages of the fifteenth century. Ethiopia was an enchanted place, whose monarch claimed to be the Lion of Judah, a scion of Queen Sheba and King Solomon, a land said to hold the Ark of the Covenant, yet which also had defeated the Italians at Adwa in March of 1896 – one of the few decisive reverses of European colonialism – to prove that the whites were not invincible. Ethiopia had maintained its independence into modern times, though Nubia had collapsed into the Islamic embrace in the fifteenth century. "Ethiopians" passed into the nineteenth-century imagination as a generic term for blacks, the descendants of Ham and Cush. The Rastafarians of the West Indies equally celebrate this conflation of myth and historical memory because the movement is, as Ethiopianism was, a form of cultural appreciation, a social and historical excavation, a recovery and recontextualization of black traditions of emancipation hidden from the consciousness of black peoples by colonial hegemony.

Beyond myth and ideology, Ethiopianism started from the new confidence gained in the Native Pastorate experiment in Sierra Leone. It expressed the hope that Africans would evangelize Africa, build an autonomous church devoid of denominations, and throw off European cultural domination and control of decision-making in the Church. Psalm 68:31 declared: "Princes shall come out of Egypt; Ethiopia shall soon stretch out its hands to God." Some translations use Nubia and others the Hebrew Cush, but the movement interpreted it as a prophecy of the destiny of the black race. The Native Pastorate experiment flowed from Henry Venn's vision of the euthanasia of missionary control that promoted this counter-imagination, built on confidence in African ability, and created space for them to run their own churches. James Johnson – the charismatic pastor of St Paul's Breadfruit in Lagos – best expressed this view in a letter to M. Taylor on April 19, 1873:

> The desire to have an independent church closely follows the knowledge that we are a distinct race, existing under peculiar circumstances and possessing peculiar characteristics, the desire to preserve this distinction uninjured, the conviction that it would materially contribute to give a purely native character and power to our religious profession, and that the arrangement of foreign churches made to suit their own local circumstances can hardly be expected to suit our own in all their details.

Johnson anticipated the indigenization project of the future. Plans for the Native Pastorate caused a vigorous debate over the availability of educated personnel, funding, and the marginalized role of whites.

Ethiopianism had African-American roots and emigration activists inspired educated West Africans who chafed under white control of decision-making in the churches. Thus, Martin Delany (1812–77) combated the Hamitic theory that postulated a curse from Noah on the black race. It was not Ham who was cursed, he argued, but Canaan, and blacks are not Caananites; and much to the contrary, blacks played prominent roles in both Old Testament events and in the New Testament origins of the Jesus movement. The patriarchs, Abraham and Moses, had married black women. Delany declared, "we are no longer slaves, believing any interpretation that our oppressors may give the word of God, for the purpose of deluding us to the more easy subjugation." Bishop Turner even declared that God is a Negro, and had permitted slavery so that they could bring back the Gospel. Alexander Crummell concurred that the blacks had a manifest destiny to redeem the motherland through Christianity.

Ethiopianism passed from a passive radicalism, where it served as a coping mechanism against ideological and material disadvantage, to an active radicalism that sought to remove the source of white domination. By networking through Sierra Leone, Liberia, the Gold Coast, and Nigeria, Ethiopianists built a formidable following among the rising educated elite. It bonded the stars of West Africa, some of whom I will briefly touch upon.

From Liberia, the West Indian born Edward Wilmot Blyden traveled widely to promote the cause in Africa and America, and helped to inspire the cultural renaissance of late nineteenth-century West Africa.[4] His lecture in Lagos in 1891, entitled *The Return of the Exiles*, encapsulated the heart of the movement. Acknowledging the sacrifices of white missionaries, he argued nonetheless that the destiny of Christianity must lie in the hands of Africans or, as a weekly newspaper in Sierra Leone reported a speech by Mojola Agbebi in 1892, "the sphinx must solve her own riddle. The genius of Africa must unravel its own enigma." Blyden braided cultural, religious, and political nationalism into a prophetic logic of African response to the missionary project. As he put it in a lecture to the American Colonization Society in 1880:

Africa may yet prove to be the spiritual conservatory of the world. Just as in past times, Egypt proved the stronghold of Christianity after Jerusalem fell, and just as the noblest and greatest of the Fathers of the Christian Church came out of Egypt, so it may be, when the civilized nations, in consequence of their wonderful material development, have had their spiritual perceptions darkened and their spiritual susceptibilities blunted through the agency of a capturing and absorbing materialism, it may be, that they may have to resort to Africa to recover some of the simple elements of faith; for the promise of that land is that she shall stretch forth her hands unto God.

Blyden predicted the shift in the center of gravity of Christianity from the North to the South Atlantic and stressed its importance for the future of African Christianity.

In the Gold Coast, J. E. Casely Hayford, a brilliant lawyer and Methodist layman, wrote *Ethiopia Unbound* and initiated a critical literary tradition that rejected the literature of tutelage characteristic of missionary protégés. His compatriot, John Mensah Sarbah, lawyer and educationalist, followed suit. In Nigeria, a Baptist leader, D. B. Vincent, changed his name to Mojola Agbebi. He wore only Yoruba clothes, founded a school with no foreign support, and seceded to found his own Independent Baptists. The Anglican minister E. M. Lijadu, after quarreling with his mission superior (an African as it happened), broke away to found his own Self-Supporting Evangelists Band (1900). He wrote two books in which he sought to articulate Christian theology with indigenous knowledge, arguing that the Yoruba deity Orunmila was a prefiguration of Jesus Christ. The Nigerian educationist Henry Carr asserted that education was a crucial tool for building the African self-image; and with the Ghanaian J. K. Aggrey, he inspired a generation of

teachers. James or "Holy" Johnson, whom I have already mentioned, carried with him when he moved from Sierra Leone to Lagos in 1874 a reputation equally for an unbending evangelical piety and an active commitment to the struggle for ecclesiastical independence for Africans. Yet he insisted on fighting the battle from inside the Anglican Church and would not be persuaded to secede.

The same pragmatism characterized the outlook of the Sierra Leonian Julius Ojo-Cole, who was not averse to borrowing the best of other civilizations to improve Africa as long as it was affirmed that each race of people possessed its genius, and must unite and cooperate to foster a spirit of national consciousness and racial pride. He was a founding member of the West African Students' Union, published the journal *West African Review*, and sought to introduce a new type of education in West Africa. People respond to structures through loyalty, voice (i.e., dissent), or exit. Ethiopianism ran through all the hoops. Its cultural register included the rejection of European baptismal names, the use of African clothes, praying for chiefs instead of the British monarch, and accepting polygamists in the Church. Missionary polity, liturgy, and ethics were all contested. Yet they neither rejected Christianity nor could they fully disavow denominational doctrines and loyalties. Rather they set the missionary message to work by engaging in vibrant evangelism and the advocacy of self-support. This may explain the changing pattern of white responses to Ethiopianism.

The Course of Charisma, 1914–2000

After World War I, West African interest in education increased. It was the era of the "bush school"; the mass growth of Christianity had begun. And alongside this was a new outburst of religious questing outside the boundaries of the mainline churches. African Christianity had experienced localized revivals in the nineteenth century, but their frequency increased greatly in the period 1910–47, and for the first time some revivals spread far beyond their region and country of origin. Prophetic movements, African Instituted Churches (AICs), and charismatic revivals followed upon one another. It must be noted that the prophetic movements that originated under purely indigenous religious leadership differed from those that emerged from individuals who had prior contacts with missionary churches, such as William Wadé Harris and Garrick Braide. Their ministries illustrate the battle for sacred powers that became important around the time of World War I. These prophetic movements and a host of other smaller revivals that occurred in the half-century between 1902 and 1952 can be seen as precursors to the contemporary Pentecostal movement. It removes the strangeness of the charismatic impulse by inserting it into the broad spectrum of African initiatives, appropriations of the missionary Gospel, and relationships with charismatic missionary bodies from the West.

We can use a typology to differentiate five major strands, as detailed below.

(1) *Type 1* is where a diviner or religious leader from the traditional context shifts base by appropriating aspects of Christian teaching and symbolism to create a new synthesis or emergent religious form, in order to respond to the felt needs of his community. In remote Southeastern Igboland, such religious revivals had large political implications, especially when the guardians of the ancestral calabash responded to the new threat of white intruders after 1912. Thus Dede Ekeke Lolo, a priest of the ancestral gods, kept to tradition at the turn of the century among the riverine Akwete community. But his vision was more revelatory than political because he heard whispers of a new covenant, and soon after his prophetic utterances, Christian missionaries came to the community.

(2) With *Type 2*, a prophet emerges from the Christian tradition, emphasizing the ethical and pneumatic components of the Gospel, to intensify the evangelization of the community and its region. Sometimes, he chooses to present himself like an Old Testament prophet with a long beard, staff, and flowing gown, and at the same time to carry a cross. Some go further by employing traditional religious symbols or elements of local culture to communicate the Christian faith; yet at the same time the predominant message is to denounce the indigenous worldview and urge Christian solu-

tions to local existential problems, like sickness and witchcraft. Examples include William Wadé Harris, whose ministry running from Liberia to the Gold Coast started in 1910; Garrick Braide, who operated in the Niger Delta between 1914 and 1918; Joseph Babalola, who left his job as a driver in 1928 in Yorubaland; and Simon Kimbangu, a Baptist whose ministry lasted through one year (1921) in the Congo. Each was arrested by the colonial government and jailed: Harris remained under house arrest until death; Braide died in prison in 1918; Kimbangu's death sentence was commuted to life imprisonment and exile at the intervention of two Baptist missionaries, and he died at Elizabethville in 1951. Babalola was released from prison after a few months when some Welsh Apostolic Church agents intervened on his behalf.

(3) *Type 3* is exemplified in the wave of African indigenous churches that arose all over Africa at different times before and after World War I, and especially during the influenza epidemic of 1918. Known as Aladura ("praying people") in West Africa, Zionists in Southern Africa, and Abaroho ("people of the spirit") in Eastern Africa, some caused revivals, while others did not. The earliest or classical ones emerged from mainline churches by recovering the pneumatic resources of the Bible. Later, new forms appeared that had no linkage with missionary churches. They quickly institutionalized themselves as churches, and many deployed traditional symbols as in Type 2, often to a larger extent. There were variations in just how much of traditional religion there was in the mix: some *messianic* leaders claimed to be one or another person of the Trinity, the *revivalistic* promoted the ideological significance of indigenous religion by privileging its resonance with Christian symbols, while the *vitalistic* tapped occult powers and the *nativistic* came close to being indigenous cults operating with Christian symbols and paraphernalia. The sub-typology is as wide as is their range and importance as lasting contributors to African Christianity. Some worship on Sundays, while others are Sabbatarians. Things are further complicated by the fact that some are political, while others operate as safe

religious havens from the many brutalities of the African experience.

(4) In the case of *Type 4*, a puritan and fundamentalist expression of Christianity breaks out within the boundaries of a mainline denomination challenging its prevailing affirmations and seeking to enlarge the role of the Holy Spirit within its faith and practice. In some cases, the hostile response of the "rulers of the synagogue" forces an exit and the foundation of new congregations, while in others the activists are able to reform their denomination from the inside. Thus some operate as independent churches or ministries, while others remain as movements or sodalities within the main body. The focus of challenge may include doctrine, liturgy, polity, and ethics, or any permutation of these. Many attract enough mass support to become revival movements. In many ways, they resemble Type 2, but they reject the traditional cultural ingredients that are widely found there. Examples include the Ibibio Revival that occurred within the Qua Iboe Church in Eastern Nigeria in the 1920s. Sometimes the revival is catalyzed by contact with Western sources, as in the case of the Faith Tabernacle whose magazines inspired many West Africans in Ghana and Nigeria from 1920. They invited missionaries from the Apostolic Church at Bradford (England) in the 1930s. In Nigeria in 1939 others joined the Assemblies of God (AG), which had been involved with missionary work in Upper Volta and Dahomey since 1928. Other Nigerians invited out the Foursquare Gospel Church in 1954.

(5) Finally, *Type 5* is the contemporary face of Pentecostalism in Africa. This was catalyzed by charismatic movements led by young people from mainline churches, beginning from the late 1960s in some parts of the continent but booming in the 1970s. Some started from the Scripture Union camps in secondary school and others from Christian Union fellowships in the universities. Later, the movements in different countries linked through the activities of the students' organization, FOCUS, and the migrations of students engaged in foreign language programs. By the 1970s, a number of these young people had moved into adult life and founded their own churches off campus. The phenomenon became even more pronounced in the 1980s when these neo-Pentecostal churches linked up with tele-evangelists from the West. The power of media in evangelization and the popularity of prosperity preaching reshaped the religious landscape. Mega-churches appeared and "charismatization" began to affect the mainline churches too. After resisting the youth and women who were so active in the charismatic churches, mainline churches of all hues started following their example. Charismatic insurgence in Ghana, the Republic of Benin, Burkina Faso, the Ivory Coast, and Congo Brazzaville challenged the predominance of either the Vodun cults or Islam, and changed the face of Roman Catholicism. Significantly, the Pentecostal movement has changed its character in every decade, and holiness ethics re-emerged in the late 1990s after the torrent of prosperity Gospel teaching.

The political import is important as intercessors for Africa reappropriated the vision of Ethiopianism and used prayer as political praxis in recovering the lost glory of Africa. Intercession attracted attention by offering a spiritual explanation for the economic collapse and legitimacy crisis of the postcolonial states. Pentecostals have re-engaged the entire region through vigorous evangelistic projects. They have challenged the quality of state-sponsored education by building universities founded on Christian values. By demanding moral standards of political leaders and by raising political awareness among their teeming members, this brand of Christianity has attracted the attention of politicians. Heads of states and senior civil servants now deploy Christian symbols, rhetoric, and active membership as means of consolidating their legitimacy.

Conclusion

There are certainly more Muslims than Christians in West Africa. Several countries are overwhelmingly Muslim: Senegal, Mauritania, Gambia, Mali, Guinea, Burkina Faso, and Niger. Others are more evenly balanced, though with an advantage to Islam, such as Nigeria, Guinea-Bissau, the Ivory Coast, and Chad. Cameroon, Liberia, and Ghana are predominantly Christian, with significant Muslim minorities. Gabon and the other Lusophone states are overwhelmingly Christian. Nigeria is so populous – with about half of West Africa's total population – that it alone contains most of the region's Christians. While the Roman Catholics form the largest single Church, overall, they are outstripped by Protestants, if we include in the latter members of mainline churches, AICs, and Pentecostals (60 percent in Nigeria, 71 percent in Ghana, 81 percent in Liberia, according to a survey conducted in 2008–9 by the Pew Charitable Trusts). Methodists and Baptists are still active in their original fields in Ghana, Liberia, Nigeria, and Sierra Leone. Anglicans are strong in Nigeria, where they have grown to about 17 million members. Presbyterians are strongest in Ghana and Cameroon. Pentecostals now count over 26 percent of the Christian population of Nigeria, Ghana, and Liberia, according to the Pew survey.

The pattern of distribution was partially influenced by colonial policy and partly by new evangelistic thrusts in the independence period. Roman Catholics are strongest in the former French and Portuguese colonies, and they focused on containing the spread of Islam by concentrating on un-Islamized ethnic groups such as the Jola of Casamance in southern Senegal, the Toma, Guerze, and Manon in the Nzerekore district of the forest zone in Guinea, the Bambara, Bobo, Wala, and Dogon of Mali, or the Mossi of Burkina Faso. Policies about Islam shifted in response to geopolitical pressures. But a certain uniform and dogmatic spirituality ensured that African Instituted Churches did much less well in the francophone than in the anglophone sphere. While France secularized education and denied the missionaries a monopoly of this instrument of evangelization, the Portuguese invested little in education and deployed a graded assimilation strategy to create class differences. The British colonies were more open to a plurality of denominations and left much education and charitable provision to missions. Throughout West Africa, Christianity has been challenged by the forces of Islam, indigenous religions, and (in certain times and places) state policies. Though indigenous religions (as an exclusive profession) are now reduced to a dwindling minority, major elements

of them continue to exist alongside or to be incorporated into the practice of the two dominant monotheisms.

Yet Christianity has grown enormously in recent decades because of the cumulative effect of these revivals that have increasingly stamped a charismatic character on its faith and practice throughout West Africa. People have responded to the Christian Gospel from the perspective of a quest for spiritual power to serve their existential needs, a quest grounded within the indigenous worldviews that preceded Christian conversion. At the same time, it helps them negotiate with the demands of modernity and the globalization process that encompasses them. By the 1980s, the Pentecostal movement was beginning to "charismatize" the mainline churches, especially by its use of the new media technology and by exploiting a liberalized air space and privatized radio, television, and print. Advertisements increased public visibility, and charismatic cassettes and videos engaged popular culture. In the late 1990s, after the wave of prosperity preaching, intercessory prayer was used in a more political praxis. Even in francophone West Africa, Christianity has advanced through aggressive evangelization by charismatic movements. In 1995, Pentecostal intercessors challenged the declaration of Vodoun as the state religion of the Republic of Benin and moved into Muslim countries of West Africa.

The political consequences are diverse. The mainline churches are growing, with stronger voices in domestic politics and international conclaves. All the churches have challenged the quality of state-sponsored education by building universities founded on Christian values. By posing morality as a condition for political participation, by creating political awareness among their teeming numbers, West African Christianity has attracted the attention of politicians. Heads of states and civil servants now deploy Christian symbols, rhetoric, and membership as means of consolidating legitimacy.

Notes and References

[1] Dr. Ogbu U. Kalu passed away suddenly on January 7, 2009, in the midst of revising his chapter, having had a successful and productive career as a world-renown professor

of African Church history and global Pentecostalism. The editor extends his gratitude to Dr Derek R. Peterson, from University of Michigan's Department of History, for his helpful comments on Dr Kalu's chapter. The editor is immensely grateful to Professor J. D. Y. Peel, from the School of Oriental and African Studies, University of London, for his close reading of this chapter and helpful suggestions that honor Kalu's work and memory.

[2] See John Thornton, "African Political Ethics and the Slave Trade," in Derek Peterson, ed., *Abolitionism and Imperialism in Britain, Africa, and the Atlantic* (Athens, OH: Ohio University Press, 2010), 38–62.

[3] See John Thornton, *The Kongolese Saint Anthony: Dona Beatriz Vita and the Antonian Movement, 1684–1706* (New York: Cambridge University Press, 1998).

[4] See Philip S. Zachernuk, *Colonial Subjects: An African Intelligentsia and Atlantic Ideas* (Charlottesville, VA: University of Virginia, 2000).

Further Reading

Ayandele, E. A. *The Missionary Impact on Modern Nigeria 1842–1914: A Political and Social Analysis*. London: Longman, 1966.

Fashole-Luke, Edward et al., eds. *Christianity in Independent Africa*. London: Rex Collings, 1978.

Gifford, Paul. *African Christianity: Its Public Role*. London: Hurst, 1998.

Gray, Richard. *Black Christians, White Missionaries*. New Haven, CT: Yale University Press, 1990.

Hastings, Adrian. *The Church in Africa 1450–1950*. Oxford: Clarendon Press, 1994.

Kalu, Ogbu, ed. *African Christianity: An African Story*. Trenton, NJ: Africa World Press, 2007.

Kalu, Ogbu. *African Pentecostalism: An Introduction*. London and New York: Oxford University Press, 2008.

Ojo, Matthews A. *The End-Time Army: Charismatic Movements in Modern Nigeria*. Trenton NJ: Africa World Press, 2006.

Omoyajowo, J. A. *Cherubim and Seraphim: The History of an African Independent Church*. New York: Nok Publishers, 1982.

Peel, J. D. Y. *Religious Encounter and the Making of the Yoruba*. Bloomington, IN: Indiana University Press, 2000.

Ryder, A. F. C. *Benin and the Europeans 1485–1897*. London: Longman, 1969.

Sanneh, Lamin. *Translating the Message: The Missionary Impact on Culture*. Maryknoll, NY: Orbis, 1989.

4

Christianity in Southern Africa
The Aesthetics of Well-Being

Frederick Klaits

Introduction

You may have had the experience of arriving at a party at which you did not know many people, and of feeling awkward at first. After having something to eat or drink, you might begin to feel more comfortable with those around you, and to have a good time with them. As a result of partaking of food and drink in the company of others, you may begin to feel well in yourself in a way you had not before arriving at the party. If you have had such an experience as this, you have access to an important dimension of Christianity in southern Africa, where religious practitioners are commonly attuned to the ways in which substances and materials ingested or brought into contact with their bodies affect their well-being, for better or worse. Imagine, for instance, a party where the food people ate made them angry rather than happy with one another, so angry that they wanted to fight and kill. Many people in southern Africa believe that witchcraft poisons work in a comparable fashion. Such poisons or medicines are said to be introduced secretly by a witch into a victim's food, thereby transmitting the witch's hatred and resentment into the body of the victim. Thus an important element of Christian religious practice in southern Africa involves efforts to reach God and, often, to forestall witchcraft by bringing physical substances to bear upon believers' bodies to beneficial effect. How such substances affect people's well-being is a matter of uncertainty, debate, and polemic for members of the highly diverse range of churches in the region. In many instances, nonetheless, Christian religious practices in southern Africa derive their appeal from believers' awareness of what strengthens, sickens, and heals the body.

The necessity for healing is particularly apparent to many Christians in southern Africa because industrial capitalism, colonialism, and postcolonial rule have often had powerfully destructive impacts on the health of people's bodies. A central aspect of colonial rule in the southern African region, including South Africa and countries extending north to the borders of Tanzania and of the Democratic Republic of the Congo (see map 4.NaN), was the extraction of resources on a massive scale. Such resource extraction was carried out with scant regard for the well-being of the Africans who labored in mines and on farms owned by European settlers, or for those dispossessed of their lands and forced into overcrowded rural reserves, urban slums, or squatter camps. The relationships between Christian movements and the colonial and postcolonial strategies of governance that have been so destructive to people's bodies have been ambiguous. While many Christian leaders have played important roles in movements for democratic liberation, such as the anti-apartheid struggle, Christian missionary work has often legitimated the terms of colonial rule by teaching people to value habits of thinking and acting

Introducing World Christianity, First Edition. Edited by Charles E. Farhadian.
© 2012 Blackwell Publishing Ltd. Published 2012 by Blackwell Publishing Ltd.

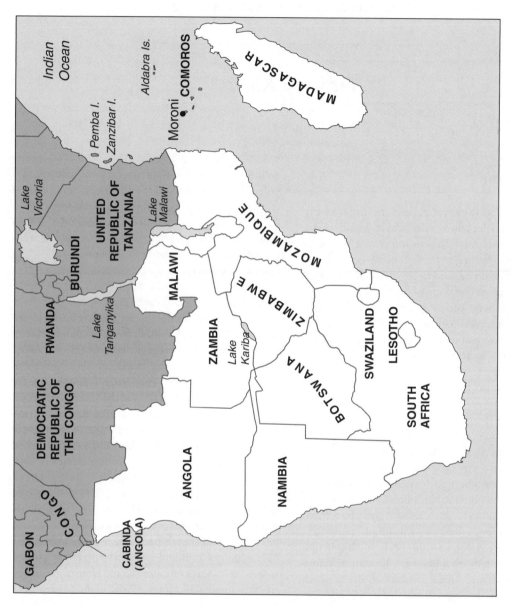

Map 4.1   Southern Africa

deemed "civilized" as opposed to "uncivilized." As elsewhere in the world, a central aspect of missionaries' efforts to preach the word of God has been to carry out a civilizing mission whereby converts would learn to apply a set of dual standards to their behaviors and ways of thinking. In becoming "civilized," converts have been encouraged to regard themselves as saved as opposed to unsaved, educated rather than uneducated, industrious rather than lazy, hygienic as opposed to unclean, and as living healthy lives rather than sickly lives. Contemporary southern African Christians' attitudes toward these normative standards are quite diverse and ambiguous. For many Christians in the region, coming to Jesus in order to find healing spurs reflection on the kind of person one has been and aspires to be, as well as on the histories of communities suffering from extreme inequalities, poverty, and political oppression. In light of the destructive consequences of these forces, believers have aimed to dress themselves and others in well-being and prosperity. The power of the Holy Spirit is often framed in explicitly aesthetic terms, making believers attractive to God and to one another through dress, song, dance, and shared substance.[1]

Mission Encounters

Christianity is a dominant religion in the southern African region. In South Africa itself, there has been a sizable Muslim community since the seventeenth century, when Dutch colonizers employed immigrants from the Moluccan Islands as mercenaries and servants, as well as a large Hindu minority, mainly descendants of Indian laborers brought to work in the sugar fields of Natal during the early twentieth century. In addition, traditional African religious expressions, often combined with Christian elements, remain quite popular. However, Christian expressions have a prominent place in public life in the region. In Botswana, for instance, most paid work stops for the Christmas and Easter holidays, Sunday morning radio is dominated by Christian broadcasts, and Christian prayers open many public meetings convened for secular purposes. On Sunday mornings in the cities, large numbers of men and especially women dress in formal clothing and colorful uniforms as they go to

services, whether in churches that have branches around the globe or in informal structures built in people's backyards. In addition, some of the wealthiest and most influential organizations in the countries of the region are Christian ecumenical societies, charities such as World Vision, and transnational churches. These transnational churches include not only the so-called "mainline" mission churches, such as the Anglican and Roman Catholic Churches, but also Pentecostal Churches founded in southern Africa, such as Zimbabwe Assemblies of God, Africa (also known as Forward in Faith Ministries International, with branches around the world).[2]

Christian movements in the southern African region may be divided into three broad groups:

(1) "Mainline" churches founded by European missionaries, such as Roman Catholic, Dutch Reformed, Anglican, and the United Congregationalist Church of Southern Africa, with branches both in cities and rural areas;

(2) African Independent Churches (AICs), including Zionists, Apostolics, and Nazarites (see below) headed by African leaders, often combining elements of Pentecostal revival movements of the early twentieth century with practices derived from precolonial forms of healing and divination, again meeting both in cities and rural villages; and

(3) Pentecostal revival movements, including churches that have expanded into the region largely from West Africa since the 1980s and stress prayers for prosperity and casting out demons, with branches mainly in urban areas.[3]

In order to account for Christianity's pervasive influence in the region, it is necessary to take a brief look at the history of how Christian missions in the region affected indigenous societies. While the first Christian missionaries in southern Africa were Europeans, African converts engaged in the work of evangelism from an early date. Thus, during the nineteenth century, European missionaries would sometimes find familiarity with Bible stories and hymns among groups of Africans with whom they had had no previous direct contact.

During the early nineteenth century, a period when large-scale missionary work into the interior regions of southern Africa was beginning, many of the indigenous agriculturalist and pastoralist societies were organized as polities headed by rulers responsible for ensuring the fertility of the people and the land. Royalty presided over the initiations of young men and women into age grades. During initiation rituals, young men and women would be instructed to conduct themselves properly as husbands and wives, for instance by engaging in sexual intercourse in ways that did not violate pollution restrictions. For example, it was deemed dangerous for men to have sex with women who were menstruating or nursing, or for them to have sex before engaging in hunting, long-distance travel, and other activities that demanded coolness in their blood.

Apart from such restrictions on sexual activity, the fertility of the land was safeguarded by diviners who engaged in rainmaking rites on behalf of royalty. Diviners appealed to the shades of ancestors in whose hands the well-being of persons and the land were seen ultimately to rest. Divination and mediumship were not necessarily activities limited to local communities and polities. Supplicants to the Mbona regional network of shrines, based in what is now Malawi, venerated a diviner who had opposed and was slain by a tyrannical king during the seventeenth century. Historian Matthew Schoffeleers suggests that the appeal of Christianity in this part of southern Africa might have rested in some measure on the resemblance of Jesus's sacrifice to that of the diviner Mbona.[4] On the other hand, anthropologist Richard Werbner argues that Christians in southern Africa tend to place more emphasis on resurrection than on imitation of Jesus's passion, in keeping with the stress laid on healing and well-being.[5] In general, ensuring the well-being and fertility of persons and the land was a principal aim of divination, initiation rituals, rainmaking rites, and the veneration of ancestors. These practices have shaped in crucial respects the forms Christianity has taken in the region, since many southern African Christians place faith in Jesus and the work of the Holy Spirit as means of sustaining life-giving relationships with spiritual providers.

Over the course of the nineteenth century, the London Missionary Society (LMS), affiliated with Nonconformist Protestant churches in England, sponsored numerous mission stations and travels throughout southern Africa. Mission stations, where converts would learn literacy and artisan skills, served political as well as religious purposes, since they were sites of security for people displaced during the early nineteenth century by a series of wars known as *mfecane* among African groups. Missionaries were also powerful political allies for local rulers aiming to protect their people's lands and livelihoods from European settlers' encroachment. In 1849, Rev. Freeman wrote to the foreign secretary of the LMS in London about the missionaries' role in protecting indigenous Tswana from Afrikaner farmers, who were descendants of Dutch settlers: "there is no doubt that they [the settlers] feel the missionaries are in their way. The missionaries are the protectors of the Natives and the latter cannot be so easily outraged [i.e., exploited] and driven out . . . under the direct observation and remonstrances of the missionary."[6]

Yet many missionaries were frustrated by the slow pace of conversions and by the skepticism local people often showed toward their teachings. Most European missionaries regarded initiation, divination, and the veneration of ancestors as not only inferior to Christian practices but as signs of the Devil's power over inhabitants of what they considered the Dark Continent. Robert Moffat (1795–1883), who spent over 50 years in southern Africa within the London Missionary Society, commented in 1842: "Satan has employed his agency with fatal success in erasing every vestige of religious impression from the minds of the Bechuanas [Batswana], Hottentots [Khoi] and Bushmen [San]; leaving them without a single ray to guide them from the dark and dread futurity."[7] In the view of Moffat and many of his contemporaries, the sexually explicit language and gestures used during initiations were immoral, divination and rainmaking irrational, and the veneration of ancestors a worship of false gods. Convincing converts to begin a new life in Christ was thus regarded as an act of emancipation from traditional beliefs in "fetishes," parallel to emancipation from slavery. Rather than attributing illnesses and misfortunes to the capricious demands of ancestral spirits, converts were encouraged to recognize that it was God and they themselves who truly possessed agency.[8]

Much mission activity was predicated on the belief that Africans and Europeans had equal natural capacities for work and learning, an understanding not widely shared among settlers who dispossessed and enslaved indigenous people. For example, the LMS missionary John Philip (1777–1851) deeply opposed the slavery that was legal in the Dutch and later British Cape Colony until 1834. Missionaries encouraged Christian converts to become literate so that they could read the Bible in translation into local languages. In creating writing systems for indigenous languages for the purposes of Bible translation, European missionaries laid the groundwork for the growth of vernacular literatures, as well as of independent church movements that would draw upon and revise local understandings of holiness and power.[9] Indeed, education was one of the few means of social mobility available to most Africans who were deprived of their land and forced to supply cheap labor for white-owned enterprises.

Together with literacy, missionaries encouraged converts to adopt habits of European domesticity. They insisted that converts abandon polygyny, encouraged local rulers to abolish bridewealth payments, and made efforts to transform daily living spaces, encouraging Christians to live in rectangular houses rather than in outdoor compounds containing round houses. Likewise, the architectural patterns of mission hospitals separated individual patients from their families, in contrast to divination and healing dance practices that would bring others in the community into contact with sufferers.[10] At the same time, a number of missionaries, notably John William Colenso, the Anglican Bishop of Natal from 1863 to 1883, developed sympathetic understandings of African people's beliefs and tried to preserve their ability to sustain autonomous livelihoods. Such efforts prefigured the anti-apartheid and other postcolonial liberation struggles in which many Christian leaders engaged over the course of the twentieth century.

Reaching God: Spirit, Song, and Substance

The antecedents of many of the distinctive Christian movements in southern Africa extend to a set of charismatic revivals that occurred around the turn of the twentieth century. American Pentecostal mission-

aries, inspired by the 1906 Azusa Street Revival in Los Angeles, traveled to South Africa in 1908 to found the Apostolic Faith Mission, preaching a "Foursquare Gospel" of personal salvation through acceptance of Jesus Christ, baptism by the Holy Ghost, divine healing, and the imminence of the Second Coming. These Gospel messages were circulated worldwide through pamphlets and tracts. The enthusiasm and ecstatic nature of the services conducted by the Apostolic Faith Mission and other Pentecostal churches struck many leaders of the previously established mission churches in the region as excessive, and troubling in the impetus they gave to independent church movements headed by African believers.[11] An additional source of revival was the Christian Catholic Apostolic Church in Zion, founded by John Alexander Dowie, a former Congregationalist minister whose experiences with divine healing convinced him to establish a utopian community in Zion City, Illinois, in 1896. As was the case for many Pentecostal converts, those attracted to the Zionist movement in the US were people marginalized by industrialization. Drinking and gambling were banned from Zion City, as were biomedical doctors, since Zionists rejected secular medical practices as having nothing to do with the spirit. In a polemic against missionaries' biomedical practices, Dowie wrote: "The heathen[s] have sense enough to know that the [Bible] in every page teaches divine healing ... Your missionary boards send out your infernal lies, and your medicine chest, and your surgical knives, and tell the Heathen [that] Christ is not the same [as the miraculous healer of Biblical times]."[12] In 1904, Zionist missionaries arrived in South Africa, where the rapid industrialization arising from the 1886 discovery of gold had brought about extremely poor working and living conditions. Congregants were attracted to Zionist and Apostolic Faith Mission churches in Johannesburg by remarkable instances of divine healing of injuries caused by industrial accidents.

These Pentecostal movements spurred an enormous profusion of churches throughout southern Africa that came to differ quite widely in their ritual practices and in their orientations toward God, the Bible, and ancestors. The largest church to arise from the Zionist movement is the Zion Christian Church (ZCC), headquartered in the town of Morija, South Africa, with adherents numbering in the millions, many of whom arrive on pilgrimages to Morija each Easter. Zionist and related Apostolic churches are commonly known as churches of the spirit. Thousands of back-yard churches in the region incorporate the terms "Apostolic" or "Zion" within their names (such as the Holy Sabbath Apostolic Church, or the Faith Gospel Church in Zion). Many churches of the spirit are centered in their bishops' compounds, which are sites of healing and regeneration. In this respect, bishops' compounds recreate the central places of indigenous kings who in pre-colonial times had protected the health and fertility of their subjects. Many Apostolic and Zionist churches adopt practices that recall aspects of the pre-colonial initiation rituals that had strengthened people's bodies, and that many European missionaries had made concerted efforts to end. The uniforms adapted by churches of the spirit from Pentecostal missionaries' frocks and robes provide a case in point. Many Apostolics wear around their waists brightly colored yarn cords, twisted in a manner reminiscent of the human umbilical cord. In initiations practiced by the Tswana ethnic group, the transformation of boys into men took place as cords made of tree bark, woven into kilts, were placed around their waists. Thus, in Apostolic churches, yarn cords are said to strengthen and protect the waist, the central joint of the body.[13] The white robes that members wear signify purity, while the colors of their sashes and shoulder coverings denote the particular churches to which they belong. The beauty of the uniforms, as well as of song and dance, is thought to attract God and the faithful to one another within church spaces. It is common for prophet-diviners in churches of the spirit to sew on to their uniforms signs of moons, stars, and the sun – sources of light that appear to them in dreams, and that signify their abilities to discern causes of affliction while in trance states.

In general, the emphasis within many churches of the spirit is not on transcending the body so as to reach God, but on bringing people's bodies into contact with particular substances, in particular places, and in the company of certain persons, so that they may love one another and thus reach God. Likewise, prophet-diviners defend their clients against occult attacks by fostering an "electrical" atmosphere in church, attracting the empowering force of the Holy Spirit through colorful uniforms and active dance.[14] Thus many

churches of the spirit stress cleansing the interiors and surfaces of members' bodies. Much cultural attention is devoted by Christians and non-Christians alike to the ways in which bathing and cleansing affect people's feelings about one another. In Botswana, a wife shows her love to her husband by preparing his bath for him, while appearing unbathed in public places is apt to bring shame not only on oneself but on others in the household responsible for preparing baths. When a diviner or church prophet attributes an illness to the sorrow or resentment of an elder, traditional remedies stipulate that the elder blow water mixed with certain herbs upon the patient, thereby cleansing the patient's body of dangerous sentiments.[15] While prayer has replaced this practice in many churches, cleansing remains a dominant image in baptism and healing. G. C. Oosthuizen describes how people travel great distances to be baptized in the ocean at Durban. Baptism "washes away the sins," they say, while drinking sea water in order to vomit "cleanses the stomach ... it strengthens one's manhood ... We can have another baby again ... baptism gives one inner well-being."[16] For Zulu Zionists, baptism is an aspect of a broader set of practices by which substances such as water, salt, and ashes cleanse and cool the interior and exterior of the body. The Zulu word *isiwasho*, derived from the English "wash," refers to mixtures of water, ash, salt, and/or burned cow dung that prophets prescribe to patients to drink as emetics when they are ill. *Isiwasho* is said to cleanse the stomach of dirt and sores, and also of witchcraft substances that might have been introduced into a person's food or drink.

Zionists' religious commitments may create tensions with non-Christians. According to anthropologist J. P. Kiernan, Zulu Zionists in Durban tend to suspect their non-Christian neighbors and co-workers of bewitching them.[17] These suspicions spring from Zionists' comparative frugality and prosperity, and from their refusal to engage in beer drinking. Traditionally, beer drinks have been occasions for men to celebrate the completion of labor, and a means of creating feelings of fellowship. Drawing upon missionaries' opposition to beer, members of churches of the spirit argue that beer wastes resources, and that drunkenness prevents men and women from supporting their families. Refusing to drink beer may isolate a man from others in the community and provoke their

Figure 4.1 Women members of an Apostolic church in Botswana dressed in uniforms. Photograph by Richard Werbner. © Richard Werbner. Used by permission of the author.

jealousy of his possessions, a fact that helps to account for the preponderance of women within churches of the spirit.

Rather than being nurtured by beer, Zionists and Apostolics commonly say that they are nurtured by the spoken and sung word of God. In some churches of the spirit, each member preaches in turn, and opens his or her preaching with a personal hymn. These hymns often reflect an experience of conversion or illness, and the sounds of the song are said to remind both individual singers and the congregation as a whole of those experiences. Hearing one's own hymn sung by the congregation is said to give a person the strength to preach, and to drive out jealous or resentful thoughts. When persons are absent or deceased, others may sing their hymns so as to bring them to mind.[18] In other churches of the spirit such as the large-scale Apostolic Church of John Maranke (1912–63), founded in Southern Rhodesia (now Zimbabwe), there are no personal hymns but rather collective chants that may

continue for hours at a time. These chants are expressions of prior spiritual preparation in that they are sung after vigorous confessions of sins. In chanting, these Apostles aim to hear not individual voices but the voice of the group as a whole. Once their chants reach this state, Apostles say, they are singing as saints and as members of the heavenly city.[19]

A different kind of religious experience is elicited by song in the KwaZulu/Natal-based Church of the Nazarites (*ibandla lamaNazaretha*), one of the largest religious communities in South Africa.[20] In singing hymns composed by the Prophet Isaiah Shembe (1867–1935), who founded the church in 1910, Nazarites frame their own experiences of affliction and healing in terms of Shembe's historical struggles to create self-sufficient communities at a time when many Zulu people were being dispossessed of their land by the colonial state, and suffering declines in fertility as a result of sexually transmitted diseases. After receiving a series of visions calling him to preach the word of God, Shembe used contributions from adherents to purchase land where the destitute could farm for themselves. Large numbers of young women, many of whom were fleeing marriages in which their rights had been undermined by colonial legislation, settled at the headquarters of the church, a tract of land known as Ekuphakameni (place of spiritual uplift). At Ekuphakameni, the cosmological power of women is displayed in the prayer mats, gowns, and dance attire that all members must purchase from them in order to be in a state of holiness when entering the temple areas, where the ancestors are said to speak through Shembe and his living descendants to discern and heal afflictions. The well-being of the Nazarite community as a whole rests on the ritual purity of young female virgins and on their arranged marriages as "brides of Christ" to male church members. For their part, married women and mothers gather for prayer over two consecutive days each month to sing hymns to God and Shembe.[21]

While Nazarite hymns situate singers' personal struggles in terms of the experiences of Shembe, hymns sung by apostles of the Zimbabwe-based Friday Masowe church are said to enable members to receive the Holy Spirit "live and direct," in a manner ideally unmediated by any particular person or object.[22] Friday Masowe Apostolics (so named because they take Friday as a holy day) trace the origins of their church to the prophet Johane Masowe (c.1910–73), who after receiving visions during the 1930s preached that he had been sent by God to prepare people to enter the kingdom of Heaven. As did Zionist prophets, Masowe had had contacts with Pentecostal preachers of the Apostolic Faith Mission, whose influence likely shaped his emphasis on enthusiastic reception of the Holy Spirit. Anthropologist Matthew Engelke points out that Masowe's references to a transcendent God in a Heaven separate from the world of humans likely signaled to his hearers a break with traditional understandings of prophets as spirit mediums possessed by royal ancestors.[23] Masowe's emphasis on a transcendent God lent itself to Friday Apostolics' eventual stress on receiving divine power "live and direct" from the voices of angels rather than from the printed words of the Bible. Friday Masowe Apostolics refuse to read or preach from the Bible, rejecting it as a static, even deadening object that can obstruct the immaterial presence of God. Instead, angels of biblical personages

such as John the Baptist are said to possess mediums, whose messages are then shouted to large crowds of Apostles gathered in open-air assemblies. These Apostles' emphasis on receiving divine power without mediation leads them to find ways of conveying God's presence in ways that are as immaterial as possible. For instance, sick people are instructed to carry pebbles from the ground for healing. As mundane objects, pebbles signify nothing in themselves but direct adherents' attention to the immaterial power of God. Likewise, Friday Apostles value spoken and sung words for their ephemeral nature, since they focus attention on the immaterial presence of God.

While Friday Masowe Apostles' preoccupations with the immateriality of God are distinctive, they share with members of other churches of the spirit and with Nazarites a concern with the aesthetic forms by which God's presence is felt and conveyed among persons. As do members of other churches of the spirit, Masowe Apostles grapple with questions of whether and how Christian commitment represents a break from the personal and historical past. For Masowe apostles, as for members of many other Pentecostal churches in the region, Christian commitment often entails an explicit rejection of ancestral spirits, though usually not a refusal to acknowledge their influence. For instance, Masowe ministers may pray to God to drive out from a sick man the spirits of deceased people who had been bewitched by the patient's own ancestor. For Nazarites, on the other hand, Christian commitment expresses the ongoing resonance of a community's historical experience, and the continued salience of measures for ensuring personal security and fertility in the face of colonial and postcolonial depredations.

Christianity's Public Roles

One of the most prominent public roles for churches throughout much of southern Africa is officiating at funerals, where members of multiple churches share tasks of consoling the bereaved and burying the deceased. Most churches operate burial societies that help to defray the costs of family members' funerals in exchange for monthly contributions. Especially in the context of the devastating HIV/AIDS pandemic, burial societies are strong inducements to join churches. Funerals are public occasions that ought to be attended by anyone with a connection to the deceased, his or her relatives, or work or church colleagues. It is important that multiple churches participate in the work of funerals, even if the deceased had been a committed member of one in particular. The participation of pastors from multiple churches ensures that the work of burial and consolation does not fall on one group alone, but rather concerns the widest possible community. At all-night vigils preceding burials in Botswana, church members preach and sing in animated voices to the bereaved kin who lie in a house alongside the coffin, telling them that they must not despair because the Bible shows that the spirit does not die, and that those who believe in Jesus have eternal life. It is important for these words to be spoken forcefully and with conviction, because church members need to show that they have already consoled themselves in order that the bereaved may follow suit. If the bereaved are not consoled, they are liable to remain with jealousy and resentment in their hearts, asking themselves who might have bewitched their loved ones and planning occult vengeance. Funerals bring together members of multiple churches who have diverse and sometimes opposing sets of interests and sentiments. For instance, the question of who has cared most for the deceased during his or her final sickness is liable to give rise to contention and difficult feelings. Thus funerals are often political occasions for assembling persons with a range of backgrounds and intents for the common purposes of consolation and burial.[24]

While funerals are often political events in the sense that they are occasions for negotiating interests and identities on community-level scales, Christian churches have played important roles in state politics as well in southern Africa. Under conditions of widespread poverty across the African continent, joining mission churches and evangelical movements has been a means of gaining access to transnational sources of funding. The comparatively well-financed positions of many large-scale churches have made them some of the most influential political organizations in the region. In many cases, church leaders have used their positions to advocate human rights and to denounce unjust political systems and abuses of power. Such has

been the role of Anglican Archbishop Desmond Tutu, who helped to organize demonstrations against the apartheid South African regime during the 1980s and presided over the national Truth and Reconciliation Commission during the following decade, asking agents of the apartheid state to express remorse for their crimes. Elsewhere, Catholic bishops were some of the few public critics of the autocratic regime of President Hastings Banda in Malawi from the 1970s through the 1990s,[25] and clerics such as Catholic Archbishop Pius Ncube have more recently spoken out, often at great personal risk, against the abuses perpetrated by the regime of President Robert Mugabe of Zimbabwe. Yet the role of churches in bringing about democratic political transitions or broad social transformations in the region has been ambiguous. Paul Gifford takes evangelical movements in Africa to task for failing to preach a liberation theology focused on social injustice (see Escobar's chapter), and for telling parishioners instead that faith in God will provide health and prosperity to themselves as individuals.[26] On the other hand, the efforts of some state officials to ally themselves to Christian movements have compelled lay and clerical participants in evangelical movements to engage in political discussions.

For example, in 1991, President Frederick Chiluba of Zambia declared the country to be a "Christian nation," albeit with full religious freedom for all faiths.[27] After meeting quietly with a few charismatic church leaders, Chiluba made a public declaration that the Bible shows that nations are blessed when they submit to the word of God, and that the nation needed to repent from witchcraft and corruption so as to institute democratic accountability. Zambian church leaders' reactions to this declaration were deeply divided. While Catholic bishops and the ecumenical Christian Council of Zambia supported Chiluba's declaration in principle, Pentecostal leaders who had been struggling for state recognition expressed delight at being brought into the president's inner circle. However, Chiluba's administration during the 1990s was marked by arrests of political opponents, alleged vote-buying, and drug trafficking by politicians. Under these circumstances, the "Christian nation" concept has involved evangelical laywomen and students (members of both Pentecostal and mainline Protestant churches) in discussions of what democracy ought to

Figure 4.2   A burial service in Botswana, conducted by church leaders. Regardless of whether participants at a funeral are church members, most look to Christian pastors to preside over the work of burial. The house-shaped grills over the graves provide shade to the spirits of the deceased. Photograph © Frederick Klaits.

entail. Evangelical women in Zambia have stood for elections and launched political parties, while the Christian nation declaration has prompted university students to discuss whether God calls people to secular reform.

Conclusion

In southern Africa, as elsewhere, Christian movements have provided believers with a sense of God's activity in the world and in their own lives. Distinctive to the region has been the emphasis on God's power to cleanse the body as well as the spirit, and to bring believers' voices to bear on the well-being of their hearers. In embracing Christian teachings, believers throughout southern Africa have been compelled in a variety of ways to come to terms with their personal and collective pasts. For some this has entailed asserting

a sharp break with the veneration of deceased kin, while for others Christian worship involves viewing one's life course in terms of the holy history of a religious community. In contexts of tremendous poverty, frequent debilitating sickness, and fears of the occult, Christian commitments have been crucial to many southern Africans' efforts to ensure a measure of security, enabling them to feel that they are loved by God and by other people.

More specifically, Christianity in southern Africa has played a key role in bringing about transformations in the aesthetics of well-being, and in giving rise to popular discussion and debate about such aesthetics. Aesthetics of well-being involve the appearances and styles of comportment that people feel they should adopt so as to find healing, to become prosperous and respected, and to establish good footings with living and deceased kin. Western mission efforts have often promoted particular aesthetics of well-being: forms of bodily comportment, dress, and architecture signifying "civilization." For their part, adherents of independent Christian movements have aimed to make themselves attractive to God and to one another by drawing on long-standing presumptions about the impact of certain substances on persons' bodies and sentiments. Such aesthetic transformations indicate the penetration of Christianity into many aspects of daily life in the region, and demonstrate as well that Christianity does not necessarily involve celebrating the spirit while belittling the aesthetics of the body.

Notes and References

[1] Richard Werbner, *Holy Hustlers, Schism, and Prophecy: Apostolic Reformation in Botswana* (Berkeley, CA: University of California Press, 2011)

[2] For the global scope of Forward in Faith Ministries International, see the organization's official website: <http://fifmi.org/Home/tabid/7426/Default.aspx>, accessed July 23, 2009. See also David Maxwell, *African Gifts of the Spirit: Pentecostalism & the Rise of a Zimbabwean Transnational Religious Movement* (Oxford: James Currey; Harare: Weaver Press; Athens, OH: Ohio University Press, 2006).

[3] On this more recent wave of Pentecostal movements, see Rijk van Dijk, "Transnational Images of Pentecostal Healing: Comparative Examples from Malawi and Botswana," in Tracy J. Luedke and Harry West, eds, *Borders and Healers: Brokering Therapeutic Resources in Southeast Africa* (Bloomington, IN: Indiana University Press, 2006), 101–24.

[4] Matthew Schoffeleers, "Folk Christology in Africa: The Dialectics of the Nganga Paradigm," *Journal of Religion in Africa* 19 (1989): 157–83.

[5] Richard P. Werbner, "The Suffering Body: Passion and Ritual Allegory in Christian Encounters," *Journal of Southern African Studies* 23 (1997): 311–24.

[6] Quoted Jean and John Comaroff, *Of Revelation and Revolution: Christianity, Colonialism and Consciousness in South Africa, Volume One* (Chicago, IL: University of Chicago Press, 1991), 274.

[7] Quoted in Elizabeth Isichei, *A History of Christianity in Africa: From Antiquity to the Present* (Grand Rapids, MI: W.B. Eerdmans Publishing; Lawrenceville, NJ: Africa World Press, 1995), 121–2.

[8] For a broad discussion of the importance that worldwide Protestant missions place on correctly identifying sources of agency, see Webb Keane, "Sincerity, 'Modernity,' and the Protestants," *Cultural Anthropology* 17 (2002): 65–92.

[9] Lamin Sanneh, *Translating the Message: The Missionary Impact on Culture* (Maryknoll, NY: Orbis Books, 1989).

[10] Stacey Langwick, "Geographies of Medicine: Interrogating the Boundary between 'Traditional' and 'Modern' Medicine in Colonial Tanganyika," in Tracy J. Luedke and Harry West, eds, *Borders and Healers: Brokering Therapeutic Resources in Southeast Africa* (Bloomington, IN: Indiana University Press, 2006), 143–65.

[11] Maxwell, *African Gifts of the Spirit*, 18–21.

[12] Quoted in Jean Comaroff, *Body of Power, Spirit of Resistance: The Culture and History of a South African People* (Chicago, IL: University of Chicago Press, 1985), 182.

[13] Comaroff, *Body of Power*, 226–7.

[14] Richard Werbner, *Holy Hustlers* (DVD, International Centre for Contemporary Cultural Research, University of Manchester, 2009).

[15] Frederick Klaits, *Death in a Church of Life: Moral Passion during Botswana's Time of AIDS* (Berkeley, CA: University of California Press, 2010).

[16] G. C. Oosthuizen, "Baptism in the Context of the African Independent Churches," in G. C. Oosthuizen, S. D. Edwards, W. H. Wessels, and I. Hexham, eds, *Afro-Christian Religion and Healing in Southern Africa* (Lewiston: E. Mellen Press, 1989), 180–2.

[17] J. P. Kiernan, *The Production and Management of Therapeutic Power in Zionist Churches within a Zulu City* (Lewiston, NY: E. Mellen Press, 1990).

[18] Klaits, *Death in a Church of Life*.

[19] Bennetta Jules-Rosette, *African Apostles: Ritual and Conversion in the Church of John Maranke* (Ithaca, NY: Cornell University Press, 1975).

[20] Carol Ann Muller, *Rituals of Fertility and the Sacrifice of Desire: Nazarite Women's Performance in South Africa* (Chicago, IL: University of Chicago Press, 1999).

[21] See *In Pictures: South African Pilgrims,* a series of photographs of a Nazarite pilgrimage posted on January 21, 2008, on the BBC News website. Available at: <http://news.bbc.co.uk/2/hi/in_pictures/7196477.stm>; accessed July 29, 2009.

[22] Matthew Engelke, *A Problem of Presence: Beyond Scripture in an African Context* (Berkeley, CA: University of California Press, 2007).

[23] Engelke, *Problem of Presence*, 95–6.

[24] Klaits, *Death in a Church of Life*.

[25] Schoffeleers, *In Search of Truth and Justice: Confrontation between Church and State in Malawi 1960–1994* (Blantyre, Malawi: Christian Literature Association of Malawi, 1999).

[26] Paul Gifford, *African Christianity: Its Public Role* (Bloomington, IN: Indiana University Press, 1998).

[27] Isabel Apawo Phiri, "President Frederick Chiluba and Zambia: Evangelicals and Democracy in a 'Christian Nation,'"

in Terence O. Ranger, ed., *Evangelical Christianity and Democracy in Africa* (Oxford: Oxford University Press, 2008), 95–129.

Further Reading

Bornstein, Erica. *The Spirit of Development: Protestant NGOs, Morality, and Economics in Zimbabwe.* New York: Routledge, 2003.

Comaroff, Jean. *Body of Power, Spirit of Resistance: The Culture and History of a South African People.* Chicago, IL: University of Chicago Press, 1985.

Comaroff, Jean and John L. *Of Revelation and Revolution: Christianity, Colonialism, and Consciousness in South Africa. Volume One.* Chicago, IL: University of Chicago Press, 1991.

Comaroff, John L. and Jean. *Of Revelation and Revolution: Christianity, Colonialism, and Consciousness in South Africa. Volume Two.* Chicago, IL: University of Chicago Press, 1997.

Engelke, Matthew. *A Problem of Presence: Beyond Scripture in an African Context.* Berkeley, CA: University of California Press, 2007.

International Centre for Contemporary Cultural Research. *Encountering Eloyi* and *Holy Hustlers.* DVDs. Dir. Richard Werbner. Films distributed by International Centre for Contemporary Cultural Research, University of Manchester, 2008, 2009.

Isichei, Elizabeth. *A History of Christianity in Africa: From Antiquity to the Present.* Grand Rapids, MI: W.B. Eerdmans Publishing, 1995.

Klaits, Frederick. *Death in a Church of Life: Moral Passion during Botswana's Time of AIDS.* Berkeley, CA: University of California Press, 2010.

Maxwell, David. *African Gifts of the Spirit: Pentecostalism & the Rise of a Zimbabwean Transnational Religious Movement.* Athens, OH: Ohio University Press, 2006.

Muller, Carol Ann. *Rituals of Fertility and the Sacrifice of Desire: Nazarite Women's Performance in South Africa.* Chicago, IL: University of Chicago Press, 1999.

Ranger, Terence O., ed. *Evangelical Christianity and Democracy in Africa.* Oxford: Oxford University Press, 2008.

Sundkler, Bengt G.M. *Bantu Prophets in South Africa.* London: Published for the International African Institute by Oxford University Press, 1961 (first edition, 1948).

Time Life. *Zulu Zion.* VHS. Dir. Mischa Scorer. Time Life Video, distributed by Ambrose Video. *The Long Search,* vol. 10, 1977.

Part II

Europe

5

Christianity in Western Europe
Mission Fields, Old and New?

Simon Coleman

Historical Introduction

Christianity did not start in Western Europe, but the region played a key role in its development in the centuries immediately after the birth of Christ. Following the conversion of the Emperor Constantine in the fourth century CE, Christianity was transformed from being a persecuted sect into the state religion of the Roman Empire, with Rome itself becoming the primary political and religious center of Western Christianity. Missionaries spread the new faith into sometimes initially hostile pagan lands throughout Europe. Scandinavia proved the hardest region to convert, and yet it became fully Christianized after around 1000 CE.

Three features of the early centuries of the Western Church are worth mentioning here. First, the emergence of monastic Orders, which developed powerful economic and political, as well as religious, networks across Western Europe and beyond, were to become intellectual powerhouses during the Christian Middle Ages. Indeed, with the decline of classical Roman culture, monasteries became sites for education, with boys handed over to their care at the age of six or seven, and frequently becoming monks in adult life. Second, we need to consider the link between Christianity and conquest. The Holy Land itself was disputed territory, claimed by both Christians and Muslims, and the cutting off of access to the Christian shrines in

the eleventh century gave an apparently religious justification to a violent response. Prompted by the papacy, Crusades were led against Muslims not only in the Holy Land but also in parts of Europe. Thus St James (martyred 44 CE), whose relics were said to be located in the Spanish pilgrimage site of Santiago de Compostela, became known as *Santiago Matamoros* ("Saint James the Moor-slayer"), honored and depicted as both soldier and pilgrim. Third, we need to be aware of the deep-felt disputes within Christianity itself. In the eleventh century, after much theological wrangling, the so-called "Great Schism" (1054) would occur between "Western" (Latin) and "Eastern" Churches over such issues as liturgy, the role of the priest, and above all the extent of the power of the papacy in Rome.

Significant as these elements of early Christianity proved to be in the West, they were eclipsed by another set of events in the sixteenth century: those that culminated in the Protestant Reformation. The Reformation itself was a long drawn-out process rather than a single occurrence, and took numerous local forms in European contexts. At its root, however, was a single idea that was as much destructive as it was creative, since it involved an attack on what were perceived to be the moral corruption and liturgical compromises of the Roman Church. Martin Luther, the German theologian (1483–1546) who is often seen as the instigator of the Reformation, emphasized the

Introducing World Christianity, First Edition. Edited by Charles E. Farhadian.
© 2012 Blackwell Publishing Ltd. Published 2012 by Blackwell Publishing Ltd.

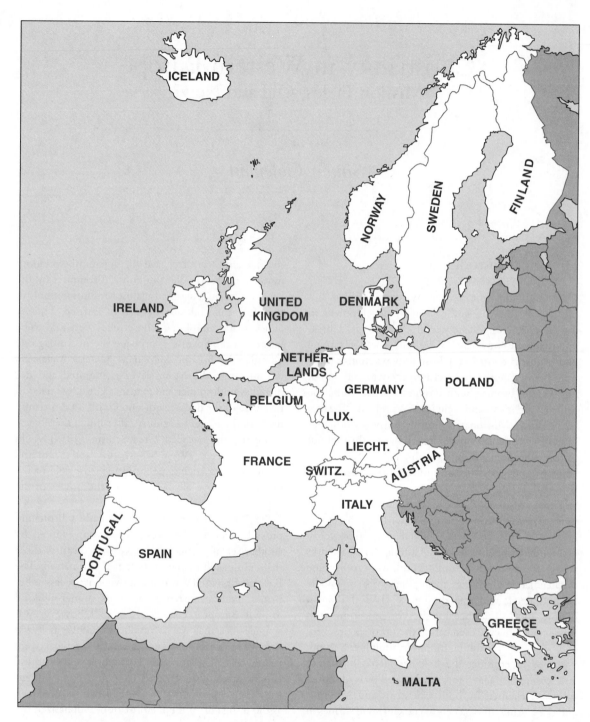

Map 5.1 Western Europe

power of the Bible and the faith of ordinary believers over the assumed authority of entrenched Church hierarchies. Subsequently, the French reformer John Calvin (1509–64) made Geneva a center of a new, morally and culturally rigid – "reformed" – way of life. The Reformation would remain more of a Northern than a Southern European phenomenon. At times, it would become deeply entangled in monarchical politics. In England, for instance, the Tudor King Henry the Eighth's struggles with Rome led him to establish the English – "Anglican" – Church in opposition to the authority of Rome. The years after his death witnessed often bloody struggles over the supremacy of Catholicism or Protestantism in England, before Elizabeth I settled the argument in favor of the reformed Church.

Thus were laid the basic theological and ecclesiastical configurations of Western Christianity in Europe, even as they would be transformed and challenged further in coming centuries. In turn, they would be exported beyond Europe, as missionaries – often sponsored by monastic Orders – would spread versions of the Catholic or Protestant faith alongside the exploration and exploitation of "newly discovered" continents, such as North and South America, and Africa. The earliest forms of such expansion took place in the fifteenth and sixteenth centuries, though they gained renewed power as industrializing nations of the eighteenth and especially nineteenth centuries required resources and markets around the globe. Western European Christianity has never been an isolated phenomenon.

Bodies of Christ: Models of the Church

The early history of the Western Church reveals a series of tensions that have recurred in later centuries, even up to the present: the authority of Church leaders versus that of political rulers; official, clerical religion versus the lived faith of ordinary people; Christianity as a site of social and cultural resistance versus its role as an agent of political and religious (and sometimes military) domination. The sociologist Steve Bruce characterizes the nature of formal religion in pre-Reformation Europe as involving a small number of

highly trained officials, acting on behalf of the state, and conducting services in Latin that excluded the active participation of lay people.[1] At the same time, pilgrimage shrines offered more popular remedies for problems, as people appealed to saints for healing, or sprinkled holy water over houses, fields, and even livestock. As Bruce puts it, "What one sees in pre-Reformation religious life is a sophisticated complex organization of formal religion laid over a mass of popular superstition."[2]

Given this background, the Reformation in Western Christianity represented more than just a protest against corruption. It was a remodelling of the very idea of a Christian Church, of the "Body of Christ," even as it evolved alongside a more general breakdown of older, feudal, social and economic hierarchies. "Reformed" services used simpler hymns, as laity (ideally) took a more prominent and committed role in the life of the Church, and as a more personal, individual relationship to God was assumed to be cultivated in each person. The translation of the Bible into local languages combined with slowly increasing literacy and the development of the printing press in shifting the understanding and deployment of religious language away from purely clerical control. In due course, and along with the development of "sectarian," schismatic groups such as the Quakers, the principles of such religion could be said to be challenging not only old hierarchies, but also the assumptions behind older, "magical" ways of thinking.

The contrasts can be overdrawn, but in very broad terms we see two basic models of the Church emerging out of such disputes and developments. As Philpot and Shah note,[3] a Roman Catholic form emphasizes an ecclesiology – an ideal of Church order – that stresses visible unity centered upon a single, hierarchical institution. Since the Middle Ages, this model has conceived of Europe itself as a Christian civilization, brought together through, and accountable to, the Church. In this view, the Church may cooperate with but must also be skeptical of the power of the sovereign state and its rulers. In general, Protestant Churches (which after all have lacked a "Pope") have been less keen to promote the idea of such pan-European unity, not least as the Reformation encouraged the embrace of national and linguistic particularities, with national churches being formed in such countries as Sweden and Denmark (both Lutheran), England (Anglican), and Scotland (Reformed).

Fascinatingly, such past differences retain resonances in much more recent European history. After World War II, and fearing the spread of both renewed fascism and secular communism, the Roman Catholic Church took an important role in working with Christian Democratic movements to promote forms of cultural, economic, and political integration that would be realized in the foundation of the European Economic Community (EEC), now the European Union (EU).[4] Arsène Heitz, who in the 1950s designed the European flag of 12 yellow stars on a blue blackground, is said to have been inspired by the reference in the Book of Revelation to "a woman clothed with the sun . . . and a crown of twelve stars on her head."[5] The link between politics and Christianity was also expressed in the success of individual parties in the post-war years. In France, Italy, and West Germany newly founded Catholic or inter-confessional Christian Democratic Parties won high levels of support.[6]

Secularization: From Cathedrals to Cults?

Bruce's characterization of the early Church in Europe is a preface to his wider project of tracing the transformation of Christianity in the Western world, from the time when Luther instituted the Reformation to the present day. The subtitle of Bruce's book – *From Cathedrals to Cults* – says much about the basic thesis of his book. Mention of these two very different kinds of religious organization is intended to make us think about shifts in the locations of religious activity over the centuries since the Middle Ages. The cathedral – massive, confident, dominating its surroundings in spatial and economic, as well as religious, terms – represents a form of Christianity that is at the center of the life of a city, with its temporal rhythms known to all, whether they attend its services or not. The idea for the cult, on the other hand, comes from a very different and much more fragmented set of religious, cultural, and social conditions, as mainstream Christianity is challenged by a multitude of other (often smaller) faiths and religious groupings, but also by the very idea of choice, that the (modern) individual is offered an array

of often obscure religious options that can be dipped into, and experimented with. But there is also a larger thesis contained in the depiction of the movement from cathedral to cult, and it is one that has emerged powerfully from the work of many scholars who have studied Western Christianity: that of secularization. To understand what this term means, and why it should have particularly preoccupied those who have studied religion in the West, we need to go back again into history before returning to the present.

We have seen that one way of understanding the Reformation and the wider upheavals accompanying it is to see such transformations as leading to the popularizing, even the democratizing, of religion, and ultimately (after decades or, in some cases, centuries) providing the catalyst for an efflorescence of religious denominations, each dependent on the idea of developing strong and personal religious commitments, ranging from Methodists and Quakers to Pentecostals, and so on. But from another point of view, the Reformation and its aftermath ironically contributed to the decline of religious activity in many parts of the West, especially the Northern European strongholds of the Protestant churches. Why should this be?

Briefly put, we might say that the very emphasis on the need for personal engagement, for choice in religious affiliation, for seeing religion as a matter of inner conviction and not just external ritual, provided the potential for religious fervor among some, but also indifference among others. At the same time, as the great German sociologist Max Weber pointed out, the new Calvinist way of thinking about the world resonated with the emergence of a new capitalist order, driven not by tradition, sentiment, or age-old human bonds, but rather by the impulse to give all spheres of life maximum productivity. While such values could be given a religious meaning, in the notion of a "calling" to save others or prosper through hard work and dedication, they could easily be translated into a more secular striving after material success alone.

Faced with the challenges to taken-for-granted faith provided by science, the gradual emergence of a multiplicity of religious organizations, and by the break-up of the stable communities in which the Church could be taken for granted as a part of everyday life, mainstream Christianity has faced particular challenges in the West. One study indicates that the number of people who "never" or "practically never" attend church has gone up in many Western European countries over the past 20 years.[7] In Finland in 1981, for instance, the proportion of people who generally avoided church was 15 percent, whereas by 2000 it was 28 percent; for Spain the shift was from 26 to 33 percent, and for the Netherlands it was from 41 to 48 percent. The capacity of the Church to influence individual behavior also seems to have reduced. Thus the birth rate throughout much of Western Europe has been falling considerably in recent years, indicating the use of artificial birth control, despite the teachings of the Roman Catholic Church. Attitudes toward divorce, abortion, and gay marriage have also become less strict. A fascinating indication of the unease felt by some Europeans regarding the expression of religious faith in the public sphere was contained in the recent British prime minister Tony Blair's attitude toward his deeply felt religious convictions. While it was generally known in the UK that Blair was a practicing Christian, he was careful to avoid any mixing of his personal beliefs and his public persona – in marked contrast, for instance, to his American counterpart, George W. Bush. Only after Blair left office did he convert to Roman Catholicism and begin to talk openly about the connections between religion and politics, while setting up a faith foundation in London.

Despite the widespread signs of secularization, we should clearly not assume that living in the modern world automatically encourages indifference to religion. Thus debate rages over whether the apparently secularizing tendencies of Western churches represents the future of all religion in the modern world, or rather a reflection of exceptional conditions in Europe, where the power of the Church has often promoted equal and opposite reactions (as in the anti-clericalism of revolutionary France), or where its ubiquity as a state institution has prompted a mixture of indifference and tolerance (as in the UK or the Scandinavian countries). In general, Catholic countries have retained churchgoing habits for longer than those of the Protestant North, with Ireland as well as Poland the most "practicing" countries of Europe.[8] We must also keep in mind the role of the churches in marking the life cycles of people who would not otherwise consider themselves to be religious: for instance, it has long been a feature of supposedly "secular" Scandinavian countries that rates of participation in baptism have been relatively high, carried out by the majority of the population.

Arguments about the significance of these trends must rest on the very measures one uses to identify the presence or absence of the secular. Jose Casanova[9] has recently explored some of the nuances of the debate by noting that, in recent decades, Western European societies seem to have undergone rapid, drastic, and seemingly irreversible processes of secularization – a kind of "post-Christianity" – in the sense that an increasing majority of the population has ceased regular participation in "traditional" religious practices. But along with Casanova we might ask how we are to assess the importance of participation in the Church alongside the much more diffuse holding of beliefs. In Casanova's view, if we focus on the persistence of inner convictions – however unorthodox or inchoate they may be – we might talk of the "unchurching" rather than of the secularization of Western Europe. Grace Davie has indeed characterized such an attitude as "believing without belonging," given that large numbers of Europeans, even in the most apparently secular countries, still identify themselves as "Christian."[10] Yet what is most striking is how little we actually know about what such identification means. Examining the results of responses to census data collected in the UK in 2001, Abby Day has recently pointed to the apparent anomaly of 72 percent of respondents describing themselves as "Christian," and yet many not seeing themselves as religious as such.[11] A similar point is made by Danièle Hervieu-Léger, when she characterizes the European situation as "belonging without believing," in other words expressing a general sense of closeness to Christian heritage while feeling uneasy about its religious content.[12]

Whether we see "belief" or "belonging" as primary in our assessment of attachment to Christianity, we need to acknowledge the role of Christianity in orientating people both ideologically *and* socially; in terms of religious identity but also, potentially, in relation to national or ethnic identity. Nor can we associate Christianity with church attendance alone, or purely with the explicit articulation of religious dogma, just as we need to be clear when we talk of secularization whether we are talking about a lack of influence in the public sphere (e.g., over political and social policy), or a more profound loss of faith at the level of individual experience. We might also consider the problems over interpreting the actions of Churches as promoting "secularization" or doing the exact opposite. Some more conservative commentators might regard the Second Vatican Council (1962–5), the famous set of reforms carried out by the Roman Catholic Church, as a form of internal compromise of faith, as it democratized forms of worship and promoted use of local languages rather than Latin (just as Protestant Reformers had done centuries earlier). Similarly, some might argue that the growth in the number of women priests in Reformed churches in recent decades is a concession to secular values. But one might equally well argue that these are signs and causes of revival in the Church, and ways of reaching out into the lives and needs of many Christians.

Forms of religious practice are far more complex and multifaceted than any single measure can reveal, and we see how the distinctions between cultural and religious identity might be very difficult to untangle in a continent that has seen itself as predominantly "Christian" over the last millennium. Davie also encourages us not to see churches as autonomous social phenomena: they are after all social groupings as well as locations of the sacred, and as voluntary (albeit sometimes state-sponsored) organizations they must hold their own along with other leisure-time activities. In these terms, apparently "secularizing" religious institutions are actually doing relatively well compared with, for instance, political parties and trade unions in many parts of the West. For the British context, at least, Davie intriguingly points to the disproportionate numbers of the religiously active that can be found in the unpaid but highly trained voluntary sector – advice workers, prison visitors, charity workers, bereavement counsellors, and so on.[13]

In a curious sense, Davie's depiction of religion – and especially Christianity – in the modern world has a parallel with that described by Bruce for pre-Reformation Europe. Davie refers to the frequently vicarious nature of modern religion for the mass of people, suggesting that many people who do not themselves see the need to take part in religious services or to observe strict moral codes are nevertheless happy that such activities are carried out by somebody else.[14] At first glance, this perspective echoes that of the Catholic

laity in the early Middle Ages, who were unable to participate in complex ceremonials but very aware of their existence. And yet we are in fact seeing two rather different forms of vicariousness, reflecting wider social and cultural transformations: one a product of social hierarchy, where exclusion is produced by rigid social norms and exclusive forms of religious expertise; the other a result of the opposite process, a democratization of faith, a removal of the sense of obligation from Christian identity, and a reduction in liturgical competence not through barriers but through relative – if usually benign – indifference. In the latter, democratized version of religious practice, active participation in Christianity becomes one "lifestyle" choice among many possible ones.

Beyond the Secular?: Transformations of Christianity in the West

If people are going to Church less than they were before, and if it is perfectly acceptable to say that one is an atheist or an agnostic in most places in Western Europe, what might be the future of Christianity in this part of the world? In the following, I shall explore some of the ways in which Christianity in Western Europe might be revived, or more probably transformed, in ways that might not always have been predictable just a few decades ago. While Christianity will undoubtedly retain its place within church-like organizations, such churches in the future might look rather different to the old state-churches of post-Reformation Europe; and there might be other locations for engagement in Christian faith and culture that bypass or complement attachment to parishes and congregations. Let us therefore explore some of these possibilities.

Christianity as heritage?

Whether or not Christianity is becoming less of an active faith in people's lives in Western Europe, there is no doubt that Christianity has been one of the mainsprings of European culture and civilization, though not the only significant world faith on the continent, given the presence of Islam and Judaism, and in more recent years Buddhism and Hinduism. The cathedrals may have been challenged by new religious movements, in Bruce's terms, but great religious buildings and other sites of Christian heritage such as monasteries, older churches, and shrines are all a valued part of the historical and aesthetic landscape of Europe, at a time when tourism has become one of the major growth industries in the world.

Some scholars have explored the notion of religious heritage and linked it to the idea that Christianity might act as a store of national "memory" in many European contexts. For Davie, for instance, active members of the mainstream churches – many of them older women – might be serving as guardians of an admittedly increasingly precarious knowledge of Bible stories, liturgies, and ecclesiastical histories.[15] The French scholar Danièle Hervieu-Léger has even written a book called *Religion as a Chain of Memory*, where she speaks of the important but again possibly dwindling function of religious tradition in generating social links and historical lineages. Such tradition itself may be shifting in significance, as it moves under contemporary conditions from being a "sacred trust" into becoming a "an ethico-cultural heritage,"[16] in other words, a fund of memory and symbolic resources at the disposal of, and subject to, the choices of individuals. We see here a movement of tradition and truth from the institution to the believer.

Yet heritage and tradition can be revived in other ways, also well suited to the current emphasis on leisure, travel, and the consumption of heritage sites in Western Europe. Hervieu-Léger notes, for instance, "top-down" attempts to revive consciousness of an historical chain of belief in the form of initiatives taken by the Roman Catholic Church in launching pilgrimages of young people to places of special significance in the European Christian past, such as Rome, Santiago de Compostela (in Spain), and Czestochowa (in Poland). Thus, for her, there might in such efforts be an "emotional remembrance and historico-cultural reconstruction of the failing memory of the continuity of belief."[17]

Certainly, pilgrimage has been carried out by Christians throughout Europe ever since the early centuries of the religion. Its popularity has continued, with some interruptions, throughout the centuries, and shows signs of growing in the present, despite the supposed secularization of the churches. The Protestant Reformers in the sixteenth century might have regarded it as a corrupted and corrupting influence on believers, but later centuries have seen the revival and rebuilding of many shrines, some of which, such as Compostela (in Spain), Lourdes (in France), and Rome, attract many thousands if not millions of visitors each year. A feature of some of the important shrines has been their willingness to embrace a more ecumenical attitude, bringing Roman Catholic and other Christians together, at least for short periods, as is evident at the important English sites of Walsingham and Glastonbury.

At the same time, pilgrimage again reveals the complexities of attempting to define any single activity as solely or definitely "Christian," or even "religious." One of the significant attractions of pilgrimage sites is less their liturgy and more their identity as pleasant places for tourists to visit. The precise motivation of the journey – religious, secular, or a mixture of the two – may be unclear to the tourist/pilgrim. Thus Nancy Frey writes of contemporary journeys across ancient pilgrimage tracks to Compostela as an activity carried out by a huge variety of people, with exceedingly varied intentions and ways of traveling. Some go by car; others on bicycle or on foot. It is clear that, for many, the journey provides an opportunity to slow down the hectic pace of normal life, to re-engage with one's own body as well as with others, and even with nature. Such practices may of course be given Christian interpretations – as sacrifice, fellowship, worship – but they might be of equal value to an avowedly secular tourist searching for a more "authentic" or active holiday than simply lying on a beach.[18] Even the massive pilgrimages sponsored by the Pope, which have for instance seen hundreds of thousands of young people gathered together in Spain, might be seen either as revivals of piety among the newer generations, or as celebrations of youth culture with Christian pilgrimage providing a convenient opportunity for enjoyment.

Away from the State?

Pilgrimage can add a powerful dimension to Christian experience, taking it away from everyday forms of worship, combining it with the excitements of travel and with resonant – sometimes seemingly miraculous – traditions of healing or prophetic vision. It is not the

SIMON COLEMAN
72

only way to breathe life into the Church, however. We have seen that, in the past, some Christian Churches have gained power and influence in Western Europe through their close association with, and support of, the state, such as the Anglican Church in the UK or the Scandinavian Churches (which have acted as important administrative arms of the state). Such associations with power can become a liability, as the Church comes to be seen as a part of the establishment, with little moral leverage in relation to secular authority. Thus, in France, anti-clericalism led to the separation of Church from state in 1905. Nowadays, a number of the established Churches in Western Europe have begun to question their own status as national bodies that have lost a sense of spiritual purpose in attempting to appeal to, and encompass, the population as a whole. One obvious contrast here is with the United States, where arguably the lack of any single, official faith has encouraged the vitality of all denominations as they compete for members.

This point is made by Zsolt Enyedi in a piece attempting to track the current situation concerning Church–state relations in Europe, and interestingly one of Enyedi's conclusions is that "while in the USA churches and politicians have begun to embrace the idea of closer co-operation between church and state, in Europe, the principle of separation finds growing support among religious sectors."[19] A non-established Church has more of a chance to engage actively within civil society, to protest against state policies, indeed to encourage the very spirit of voluntarism that Davie refers to in her examination of the role of activism in a number of areas of modern life. In 2000, the Swedish Lutheran/state Church even took the step of separating from the state: the Church hopes that what it loses in state taxes it will gain in support from a committed membership. Such a move was reflected upon in the following way by a Swedish Lutheran priest in two interviews, conducted just at the time of separation:

We're a heavy organization, not very efficient, suffering from a lack of confidence, with tired and confused priests. There's no future for such a Church. But the Church doesn't exist for itself. It has the purpose of giving the gospel to the people. We had that debate back in the 1950s, and then they said, "This isn't a missionary church" – and I regret that deeply.[20]

We see here in summary a plea for the notion of a Church – whether allied to the state or not – that is also an energetic "mission," reaching out to its potential flock rather than being weighted down by its "heavy" bureaucracy.

Conversion and Charisma?

If the increasing power of voluntarism within state churches is one possible indication of the future, it is notable that some of the most vital and dynamic churches in Western Europe (and elsewhere) are those that require not birth into the Church, but an active decision to enter into the faith, often through a "born-again" experience. Protestant forms of worship in Northern and Western Europe have been revived by varieties of Pentecostalism and charismatic worship, ranging from the smaller "house churches" of the 1980s to the emergence of mega-churches (broadly defined as congregations with more than 2,000 regular attendants) in more recent years.

One of the most striking examples of this tendency in Europe is provided by the Word of Life ministry, located in Sweden, but expressing a faith that is self-consciously global, opposed to the staidness of more traditional churches, and preaching a message of Christianity as leading to material prosperity rather than to pious sacrifice. Despite its foundation in supposedly one of the most secular countries in Europe, the Word of Life has developed possibly the largest Bible School in Europe, explicitly oriented toward the attraction of Christians from all parts of the world, as well as a congregation with some 2,000 members.

Charismatic styles of worship have also helped to rekindle Catholic movements in Europe, involving international movements such as the Focolare and the Emmanuel Community. Both share the dynamic outreach and emphasis on youthful dynamism that is characteristic of Protestant evangelicalism, combined with the unabashed use of modern communications media to spread their message. In all of these movements we see how Western Europe cannot be viewed as an isolated region: it hosts global movements of renewal that link its Christians with those of other denominations and even faiths. Energetic church

Figure 5.1 Jesus House Ministry in Brent Cross, Northwest London, a church run by the predominantly Nigerian Redeemed Christian Church of God. Photograph © Simon Coleman.

organizations such as the newer Pentecostal/charismatic ministries are able to locate themselves on a map of perceived revival that includes countries of the global South, such as Ghana or Brazil, as well as the United States.

A New Mission Field?

Ironically, the very "secularism" of Western Europe has made it a new mission field for Christian and other religious groups, especially since the wealth and colonial history of the region have made it a target for migrant groups since World War II. A fascinating by-product of the emergence of Islam as a prominent faith within Europe has been a renewed discussion about whether the state has the right to control the religious lives of its citizens. Thus discussions about whether a "secular" government can ban the use of the *burqa* (traditional Islamic dress for women) outside the home raise profound questions concerning the

boundaries between assumed "national culture" and religious adherence, as well as between private and public expressions of that adherence.

Meanwhile, the significance of immigrant Christian congregations can hardly be underestimated, given their high levels of participation and activity compared with older, established churches. On a typical Sunday, perhaps half of all churchgoers in London are African or Afro-Caribbean. In a similar vein, Afe Adogame and Cordula Weissköppel argue that: "The implosion of new African immigrants in diasporic contexts is significant in that it also forms the bedrock for an extensive reordering of European and American religious life."[21] In this perspective, religious proselytization may not only be a by-product of migration, but also a central motivation for migrants, many of whom are also training to be effective professionals in their own or adopted country. An organization such as the Redeemed Christian Church of God, founded in Nigeria in 1952, attracts some 30,000 people to its "Festival of Life," held every six months in London, and many of those attending are

Figure 5.2   A women's conference in London run by the Redeemed Christian Church of God, on April 4, 2009. Photograph by Katrin Maier. Used by permission of the author.

young students or professionals, aiming to make an impact on economic as well as religious life in Europe as well as Africa.

Thus today, more than ever, it is impossible to study "African" Christian Churches as purely geographically or culturally "African," or "European" Churches as reflecting the same cultural heritage – or memory – that they might have done 50 years ago. Churches, along with other contemporary institutions, are both products and producers of globalized religious cultures. A "Southernized" Christianity is returning to the places from which it departed, as postcolonial Christianity turns Western Europe into a location of prime missionary opportunity.[22]

Concluding Remarks

The German philosopher and social theorist Jürgen Habermas has remarked that "Christianity, and noth-

ing else, is the ultimate foundation of liberty, conscience, human rights, and democracy, the benchmarks of Western civilization. To this day, we have no other options [than Christianity]. We continue to nourish ourselves from this source. Everything else is postmodern chatter."[23] Habermas's confidence indicates the potential influence of Christianity far beyond talk of churches and theology, into the roots of European and Western notions of what it means to be a human being, or how to run the ideal state. At the same time, in tracing the history and current position of Christianity in Europe, we also see the dangers of assuming that we can grasp the significance of religion along any single dimension of activity – theological, cultural, social, or economic. Nor can we think of Christianity as an isolated religion or culture. Today in Western Europe it exists alongside, but is also influenced by, many other faiths, in what has become a deeply multicultural and multireligious context, and to some extent always has been. Perhaps, ultimately, the cathedral is not isolated from the cult; nor the cult from the cathedral.

Notes and References

[1] Steve Bruce, *Religion in the Modern World: From Cathedrals to Cults* (Oxford: Oxford University Press, 1996), 2.

[2] Bruce, *Religion in the Modern World*, 3.

[3] Daniel Philpott and Timothy Samuel Shah, "Faith, Freedom, and Federation: The Role of Religious Ideas and Institutions in European Political Convergence," in Timothy A. Byrnes and Peter J. Katzenstein, eds, *Religion in an Expanding Europe* (Cambridge: Cambridge University Press, 2006), 36, 62.

[4] Peter Katzenstein, "Multiple Modernities as Limits to Secular Europeanization?," in Timothy A. Byrnes and Peter J. Katzenstein, eds, *Religion in an Expanding Europe*. (Cambridge: Cambridge University Press, 2006), 32.

[5] Quoted in Katzenstein, "Multiple Modernities," 32.

[6] See Hugh McLeod, *Religion and the People of Western Europe 1789–1989* (Oxford: Oxford University Press, 1997), 132.

[7] A 2000 study by the Swedish-based World Values Survey, quoted in "Religion Takes a Back Seat in Western Europe," by Noelle Knox, *USA Today*, available online at <http://www.usatoday.com/news/world/2005-08-10-europe-religion-cover_x.htm>.

[8] See Grace Davie, *Religion in Modern Europe: A Memory Mutates* (Oxford: Oxford University Press, 2000), 47.

[9] José Casanova, "Religion, European Secular Identities, and European Integration," in Byrnes and Katzenstein, *Religion in an Expanding Europe*, 65.

[10] Grace Davie, *Religion in Britain Since 1945: Believing Without Belonging* (Oxford: Blackwell, 1994).

[11] See, for instance, Abby Day, "Believing in Belonging" *Network* 97 (summer 2007): 33. British Sociological Association.

[12] Danièle Hervieu-Léger, *Religion as a Chain of Memory* (Cambridge: Polity, 2000).

[13] See Davie, *Religion in Britain Since 1945*, 55 and 67–8. Davie also notes that more women than men attend European churches, and that this difference holds across a variety of theological types and across all age groups. In the West, churchgoing attracts disproportionate numbers of relatively well-educated and professional classes; in Central Europe, says Davie, this pattern is largely reversed.

[14] Davie, *Religion in Britain Since 1945*, 49.

[15] Davie, *Religion in Modern Europe*, 177–80.

[16] Hervieu-Léger, *Religion as a Chain of Memory*, 168.

[17] Ibid., 175.

[18] Nancy Louise Frey, *Pilgrim Stories: On and Off the Road to Santiago* (Berkeley, CA: University of California Press, 1998).

[19] Zsolt Enyedi, "Conclusion: Emerging Issues in the Study of Church–State Relations," in John T. S. Madeley and Zsolt Enyedi, eds, *Church and State in Contemporary Europe: The Chimera of Neutrality* (London: Frank Cass, 2003), 219.

[20] The interviews by William J. Tighe, entitled "Swedish Dissent Life as an Orthodox Churchman in the Church of Sweden," were undertaken with Dag Sandahl. They are available online at: <http://www.touchstonemag.com/archives/article.php?id=13-06-035-i>.

[21] Afe Adogame and Cordula Weissköppel, "Introduction," in Afe Adogame and Cordula Weissköppel, eds, *Religion in the Context of African Migration*. (Bayreuth: Bayreuth African Studies Series, no. 75, 2005), 5, 122.

[22] Arguably, the expansion of the EU might also bring religious revival to Western Europe, with influence from the more active and dynamic churches in Eastern Europe, such as those of Poland.

[23] Quoted in Phillip Jenkins, "Europe's Christian Comeback," *Foreign Policy*, June 2007, online at: <http://www.foreignpolicy.com/story/cms.php?story_id=3881>.

Further Reading

Adogame, Afe and Weissköppel, Cordula. "Introduction," in Afe Adogame and Cordula Weissköppel, eds, *Religion in the Context of African Migration*. Bayreuth: Bayreuth African Studies Series, no. 75, 2005, 1–15.

Bruce, Steve. *Religion in the Modern World: From Cathedrals to Cults*. Oxford: Oxford University Press, 1996.

Casanova, José. "Religion, European Secular Identities, and European Integration," in Timoth Byrnes and Peter Katzenstein, eds, *Religion in an Expanding Europe*. Cambridge: Cambridge University Press, 2006, 65–92.

Davie, Grace. *Religion in Modern Europe: A Memory Mutates*. Oxford: Oxford University Press, 2000.

Day, Abby. "Believing in Belonging" *Network* 97 (summer 2007): 33. British Sociological Association.

Enyedi, Zsolt. "Conclusion: Emerging Issues in the Study of Church–State Relations," in John Madeley and Zsolt Enyedi, eds, *Church and State in Contemporary Europe: The Chimera of Neutrality*. London: Frank Cass, 2003, 218–32.

Frey, Nancy Louise. *Pilgrim Stories: On and Off the Road to Santiago*, Berkeley, CA: University of California Press, 1998.

Katzenstein, Peter. "Multiple Modernities as Limits to Secular Europeanization?," in Timothy Byrnes and Peter Katzenstein,eds, *Religion in an Expanding Europe*. Cambridge: Cambridge University Press, 2006, 1–33.

McLeod, Hugh. *Religion and the People of Western Europe 1789–1989*. Oxford: Oxford University Press, 1997.

Philpott, Daniel and Shah, Timothy Samuel. "Faith, Freedom, and Federation: The Role of Religious Ideas and Institutions in European Political Convergence," in Timothy Byrnes and Peter Katzenstein,eds, *Religion in an Expanding Europe*. Cambridge: Cambridge University Press, 2006, 34–64.

6

Christianity in Eastern Europe
A Story of Pain, Glory, Persecution, and Freedom

Peter Kuzmic

East and West: Definitions and Boundaries

Europe is a complex and not easily definable continent. Geographically it is the Western peninsula, a part of the much larger land mass stretching between the Atlantic and Pacific Oceans (Euroasia). When it is conventionally defined as the continent running "from the Atlantic to the Urals," Russia, east of the Ural Mountains, is actually assigned to the continent of Asia. The present definition of Europe is based upon particular cultural, religious, economic, and political factors and developments that gradually led to the well-known equation of Europe with Christendom. A contemporary of Martin Luther, the geographer Wachelus, published in 1537 a woodcut map of Europe as "The Queen Virgin" that was to illustrate the unity and integrity of "Christian Europe" as conceived by medieval Catholic ideology related to the concept of the "Holy Roman Empire." Wachelus's map shows Spain as the head of the virgin, Italy as its right arm, and Denmark the left; Germany, France, and Switzerland are the breast; Poland, Hungary, "Illyricum," Albania, Greece, Lithuania, Romania, Bulgaria, and others are all identified on the (continental) virgin's illustrious gown.[1]

For the purposes of this chapter, the pertinent question is: what is "Eastern Europe?" There is no standard definition because Europe's political and geographic boundaries do not always match and have been subject to frequent fluctuation and multiple overlaps. The dilemmas and ambiguities of boundaries between the European East and West can be illustrated at the very point of the arrival of the Christian message. Following the Jerusalem Council in c.48 CE, St Paul, the Apostle to the Nations, and his missionary team crossed over from Asia to Europe with the Gospel of Jesus Christ, in response to an unusual vision of the "Macedonian call" (Acts 16: 9ff). Thus began the early Church's evangelization of the continent of Europe and the long process of the universalization of Christianity. At this point, however, it might be appropriate to ask whether this mission began in Western or Eastern Europe? Greek Macedonia is geographically and culturally considered to be part of "Southern/Eastern Europe" and yet, as the working definition of this chapter will show, modern Greece, though Eastern Orthodox by religion, is by the very reconfiguration of European geopolitical realities considered a Western country.

The division of Europe into "Western" and "Eastern" is traceable back to the division between the Western and Eastern parts of the Roman Empire. Following the Middle Ages, the Ottoman line of division was imposed with the Turkish Muslim advance on Europe and its centuries-long subjugation of the Balkans. The East–West division is thus marked by several important and fluctuating boundary lines on the map of the diverse continent that is historically marked by numerous ethnic frontiers and cultural

Introducing World Christianity, First Edition. Edited by Charles E. Farhadian.
© 2012 Blackwell Publishing Ltd. Published 2012 by Blackwell Publishing Ltd.

Map 6.1 Eastern Europe

divides, along with traditional and modern political divisions.

Historically speaking, the most durable division of the continent is the thousand-years long religious "fault-line" separating Western Catholic (Latin-based, after sixteenth-century, including Protestant) Christianity, and Eastern Orthodox (Greek-based and later Slavonic) Christianity. Geographically, this line begins in the very north with the border between Finland and Russia and then moving south separating the Baltic states (Estonia, Latvia, and Lithuania) from its recent ruler Russia, proceeding to draw the religious line of distinction along the border between Poland and its eastern neighbors Belorussia and Ukraine. It continues south separating Hungary and, somewhat less precisely, Transylvania from its larger modern home state of Romania, dividing Catholic Croatia from Orthodox Serbia within the former Yugoslav federation, to touch the Adriatic coast south of the religiously more complex Bosnia and Albania, assigning Monte Negro and (former Yugoslav Republic) Macedonia to the larger Slavic Orthodox world. To the east of the continent there is no real or religiously definable boundary, but simply, geographically, the Ural Mountains and the Caspian Sea.

The term "Eastern Europe," as it is generally used today, is actually a political concept based on the realities of the post-World War II division of the continent. Although there are considerable shared ethnic (Slavic nations) and religious (Orthodox-dominated lands) commonalities, the concept in no way indicates geographic or cultural unity. For our purposes here, "Eastern Europe" denotes primarily that geographical area from the Elba River to the Ural Mountains that was until recently named "Eastern Bloc," and that stood for the political entity consisting of the communist countries in Central, East Central, and Southeast Europe. This bloc of countries was until 1990 represented by its powerful political patron, the Soviet Union (USSR), and included Bulgaria; (former) Czechoslovakia; (former) German Democratic Republic (GDR); Hungary; Poland; Romania; and, to some extent, Albania and (former) Yugoslavia. Under Soviet control and direction, they constituted a new entity in world politics as expressed by their economic and military unifying bodies (Comecon, Warsaw Pact). During the dangerous Cold War era of the twentieth century, this communist-dominated "Eastern Europe"

was considered the arch-enemy of the free Western world and its brutally imposed "Iron Curtain" division of Europe was powerfully symbolized by its physical expression in the Berlin Wall.

The countries of formerly communist-dominated Eastern Europe represent diverse cultural landscapes, which often have very little or nothing in common. It includes the homeland of the Reformation – Germany's eastern part, which enjoyed Soviet-controlled "independent" existence as the German Democratic Republic (GDR) from 1949 to 1990, as well as Catholic-dominated Poland and Czechoslovakia (now Czech Republic and Slovakia), while Hungary, Slovenia, and Croatia were and continue to be regularly counted as "East" European, even though as lands of "Mitteleuropa" they despise that designation for cultural and religious reasons, considering themselves to be more Western than Eastern. Several of these also took pride in their history of the Habsburg tradition. Finally, there are the Balkan states of Albania, the ethnically related youngest and most vulnerable independent nation of Kosova (2008), Monte Negro (2005), Serbia, Romania, and Bulgaria – the latter four largely Orthodox in religion, and all with shared experience of centuries of Ottoman Turkish rule.

Consequently, Eastern Europe's history and religious topography are characterized by an unusual variety conditioned by the intersections of competing historical forces and their attendant civilizations, cultures, and faiths. The limited length of this chapter necessitates a broad sweep in our panoramic overview, as we contextually define "Eastern Europe" using the modern political concept developed in the aftermath of World War II and problematized by the events of the "Great Transformation" (1989).[2] Older Christian confessional divisions of Europe, the role of Islam, and their implications for and impact upon "new Europe" – a continent presently undergoing comprehensive and intensive integrative processes prior to full membership in the European Union – will be explored.

Introducing and Assessing Eastern Christianity

With the collapse of communist totalitarian regimes and the opening of Eastern Europe and the former

Soviet Union, Orthodox churches of the East, especially the Russian Orthodox Church, once again became major players in the religious theater of world communions. And yet they are still the least well known of the three major branches of world Christianity (i.e., Roman Catholic, Eastern Orthodox, Protestant). While not completely neglecting the better-known Catholic Church and various expressions of Protestant Christianity in Eastern Europe, this introduction will (especially for the benefit of Western readers) pay more attention to the disproportionately neglected Eastern Orthodoxy. Due to the broader focus of this chapter, I will forego any pretensions of being comprehensive in historical treatment, doctrinal expositions, and contextual particularities. It is a picture painted with rather broad strokes, pointing out only those developments and features that help us understand less familiar and yet crucial ecclesial characteristics, cultural habits, and socio-political dimensions of Orthodox churches of Eastern Europe today.[3]

Eastern Orthodoxy is the generally accepted designation referring to the majority of the self-governing (autocephalous) national Orthodox churches that are theologically defined as Chalcedonian (Council of Chalcedon, 451) so as to distinguish them from the (non-Chalcedonian) Oriental Orthodox churches (Coptic, Syrian, Armenian, Ethiopian, and other less numerous bodies). All Orthodox churches in Eastern Europe are Chalcedonian in their creed and confess fidelity to the seven ecumenical councils beginning with Nicea (325) as their norm. They became Eastern as a result of a long and complex process of estrangement from Rome-based Western Christianity. The Eastern Orthodox, in a similar way and yet in competition with the Roman Catholic Church, claim a direct and unbroken continuity with the faith and authority of the apostles and appeal to the tradition of the "undivided church," which preceded the final break ("Great Schism") between Rome and Constantinople ("New Rome") in 1054.

The theological and cultural divide was reinforced when in 1204 Western crusaders went on the rampage to slaughter, rape, and mutilate the inhabitants, and then destroy and pillage the beautiful and wealthy city of Constantinople,[4] the center of Byzantium. The atrocities committed against Eastern Christians deepened the distrust, increased the enmity, and widened the chasm between the Western and Eastern Christendom. These painful historic memories have become germane again in the discussions about the present erosion of confidence between Orthodoxy and Catholicism, as well as in the context of current debates about increased animosity and perceived threats to Christian civilization due to the growth of Islam in Europe. I agree with one of the most learned and ecumenically open Orthodox bishops that "the crusades brought a result that was just the opposite of what they intended. These wars created for centuries a fear and a suspicion between Christians and Muslims. In the end, they mutilated and mortally wounded not Islam, but one of the most vital and flourishing cultures, the Christian Byzantine."[5] Attempts at reconciliation and reunion between Rome and Byzantium (prompted by renewed threats of Islamic expansionism) at the Councils of Lyons (1274) and Florence (1439) failed because of the opposition by the Russian Orthodox and Greek monastic communities. Relations between the "First Rome" and "Second Rome" (Constantinople, the seat of the Ecumenical Patriarch) have been considerably improved since 1965 when mutual excommunications of 1054 were solemnly lifted during a remarkable meeting of the Ecumenical Patriarch Athenagoras (otherwise known as a reconciler of churches) and Pope Paul VI. Relations with the theologically and culturally even more estranged Protestant Christianity have improved in the twentieth century through their common membership and intensive cooperation in the ecumenical bodies, particularly in the World Council of Churches (WCC), which most of the national Orthodox churches joined in the 1960s, and the Conference of European Churches (CEC), which the Protestants and Orthodox jointly established in 1959.

The Orthodox Church is one and many at the same time, as it is a family of churches that share the same ancient faith, being in communion with each other while remaining independent in their administration in the context of their own nations. The majority of the countries of Eastern Europe are religiously shaped and dominated by Eastern Orthodox Christianity. The Slavic nations were first evangelized in the ninth century by Byzantine missionaries Cyril and Methodius (and their disciples) who are, in both bridge-building and competitive ways, venerated and claimed by both the Orthodox and Catholic churches.[6] The most numerous attendants of the Eastern churches today are those of the Russian Orthodox Church (76 million). Following are approximate statistics of nominally declared Orthodox in other nations: Ukraine (28 million), Romania (19 million), Serbia (7 million), Bulgaria (6 million) and Greece (9 million). The Georgian Orthodox Church (2.5 million) is the oldest in the territory of the former Soviet Union (Georgia is now an independent nation in conflict with Russia) and was founded in the fifth century through missionary work by St Nina, a slave woman who is counted as "equal to the apostles" in the Orthodox register of saints, a noteworthy curiosum for a Church adamantly opposed to the ordination of women. It is not as well known that the Orthodox tradition represents strong religious minorities (recognized as autonomous churches) in dominantly Roman Catholic lands of Eastern Europe in former Czechoslovakia and Poland (850,000 Orthodox), in mainly Lutheran Finland, and in Albania. One should add that Orthodox churches in the Ukraine and Bulgaria are sadly divided, and that Macedonian and fledgling Monte Negro Orthodox churches are (due to Serbian opposition) not recognized by other autocephalous Orthodox churches. Divisions and lack of recognition have ramifications on political and other levels since:

> Church autocephaly has usually been valued both as an authentication of Christian culture/national identity and as an assurance of the exclusion of foreign clerical or even political influence. It is something more as well, namely, a definition of the arena in which church–state issues will be resolved and of the status and prerogatives to be enjoyed by the ecclesiastical organization in this relationship.[7]

In the Ukraine, Belorussia, and Romania there are large numbers of Christians who worship like the Orthodox but recognize the authority of the Roman Pope. They are properly named Eastern-rite Catholics, but are frequently also called "Greek Catholics" or (in a somewhat derogatory way) "Uniates."[8] Their clergy marry and they were able to retain Eastern Orthodox liturgy, spirituality, ecclesiastical customs, and rites when they re-entered into full communion with the Roman Catholic Church. These hybrid churches are a result of religious compromises, created under political pressure from the Rome-favoring local rulers in "fault-line" areas of shifting borders. Over the centuries, however, these Eastern-rite Catholic Churches acquired a distinctive cultural and ecclesial character and a genuine identity. In regions under Soviet control they were forced by Stalin to join the more easily subdued Russian Orthodox Church. In terms of relations between East and West, they have remained an open wound and a serious bone of contention, a cause of constant tensions and periodic conflicts. These conflicts have intensified following recent political changes, especially as Eastern-rite Catholics (Uniates) regained their religious freedom and came once again under the jurisdiction of papal authority. Violent clashes ensued, especially in western Ukraine, over the (re)claiming of properties and places of worship. Although the Vatican ideally sees these churches as ecumenical bridge-builders, pointing to the desired full reunion of the Catholics and Orthodox,[9] the Orthodox interpret their very existence and territorial corollaries as an explicit Roman negation of their own (Orthodox) ecclesial character and as an instrument of Western proselytism.

Safeguarding Spirituality

The majestic city of Constantinople, the historical center of Eastern Orthodoxy, was named after its founder, Roman Emperor Constantine the Great (285–337). He is considered a saint in the Eastern Church, not only for making Christianity the privileged religion of empire and convening the first Ecumenical Council in Nicea (though he was not even baptized at the time), but also for laying the foundations to Christian Byzantium. In order to break with the republican and pagan traditions of Rome, he moved the capital to the new city, and so from the fourth to the eighth centuries the Roman Empire, now centered in Constantinople, intentionally developed into a "Christian Empire." This process was made easier by the dissolution of the West into numerous barbarian kingdoms, while the East remained strong and united under the powerful Byzantine emperor who reigned over a large empire, legally Christian and theologically viewed as an earthly expression of the heavenly reign of Christ. The emperor was viewed as the head of both the Church and state, or at least in control over the head of the Church. This strengthened the link between the two and shaped the background for what modern Orthodoxy came to understand as the desirable "symphony" between the temporal (state) and spiritual (Church) rulers. There were, viewed from a modern perspective, numerous abuses by emperors claiming absolute power over both realms who frequently took advantage of the Church's spiritual authority to support and extend their political and earthly ambitions. Some of the emperors, however, sincerely sought (as both "priest and king") to make their earthly empire a replica of the kingdom of Heaven and allowed the Church to share the state's judicial authority. This led to some beneficial results in the area of public welfare and in the provision of imperial funds to support ecclesial causes, such as the construction of magnificent church buildings, among which, as the most outstanding example, the world-famous Hagia Sophia Cathedral still stands (though transformed into a mosque after the fall of Constantinople to Turkey in 1453).

The Byzantine theocratic totalitarianism, frequently referred to in a derogatory sense as "caesaropapism," was curbed in the ninth century when the rights and lines of authority of the emperor, and those of the patriarch as head of the Church, were more clearly delineated, thus reducing the power of the emperors to impose their absolute will on the Byzantine Church. It took considerable time and obvious abuses of power, with consequential damages for both the Church and the state, before the lesson was learned that an earthly empire cannot be transformed into a "Christian society" and that God's Kingdom will only be fully realized in the eschatological future. Today's search for a modern equivalent of a "symphony" between secular and spiritual authorities, in Orthodox dominated Russia, Serbia, and to lesser extent in other postcommunist nations, should also be politically and theologically questioned, as it is based on antidemocratic ethno-religious homogenization of their nations and leads to marginalization, as well as occasional legally induced discrimination of religious minorities, including well-established Protestant churches.

In the Byzantine imperially patronized Church, which became additionally stained by growing moral laxity through the centuries, we must notice three significant developments that served as protective redemptive responses to these and other spiritually disparaging forces. First was the search to safeguard the heart of the Gospel through monasticism. In the previously persecuted Church, it had been the martyrs, as the community of the committed followers of Christ, who clearly marked the line of radical separation between the pagan state and the Church. In the imperially privileged Church there was no need for martyrs, and the committed Christians who became monks now replaced them as "white martyrs" who through ascetic lives of self-denial died daily to the vain glory and luxury offered by the earthly powers. In addition to spiritual disciplines, some early monastic communes also developed work disciplines that made them prosperous economic cooperatives. The spiritual and social influence of the monks (the Byzantine Church's "democratic front") was important in balancing and moderating the power of both emperor and bishop by pointing to the primacy of the transcendent and by acting as reminders of the eschatological dimensions of divine reign. Monks play a similar role within the contemporary Orthodox world, with spiritual and theological influence beyond measure. The largest and most influential monastic center in the Orthodox world today is Mount Athos in Greece, with about 20 semi-independent monasteries, including Russian, Serbian, and Bulgarian communities.

The second response to the secularizing threat of an increasingly shallow and officially favored Christian religion was a move to preserve the purity of Orthodoxy by protecting its very heart, namely the sacred liturgy. Georges Florovsky (1893–1997), a universally recognized spokesman for Orthodoxy and a formative theological figure in guiding its participation in the wider ecumenical search for Christian unity, summarized the nature of their faith most aptly: "Christianity is a liturgical religion and the Church is first of all a worshiping community."[10] The roots of this commitment go back to the times when ancient sanctuaries were filled with superficially baptized masses and the spiritual center of the liturgy had to be safeguarded by its withdrawal behind an iconostasis (a wall covered with icons), where the laity were (and still are) forbidden to enter. The consequences of spiritually motivated withdrawal from the world into monastic communities, with the safeguarding withdrawal of the heart of liturgy into a sanctuary separating its most sacred functions from the less spiritual laity, can be questioned at several levels. This dual move within a superficially "Christian empire" did, however, help preserve Orthodoxy through the centuries of persecution under both the onslaught of Islam and the antagonistic communist attempts to destroy religion. As a third structural safeguard at the level of Church leadership came the early rule mandating that a bishop had to be chosen from a monastic community.

Later centuries were not kind to Christianity in many lands of Eastern Europe when their nations and churches faced major political, military, and religious threats to their very survival. It was the spirituality and the learning of the monastic communities that preserved the sense of nationhood, language, and culture under the Islamic Ottoman-Turkish imposition for nearly half a millennium. They also, in an uncompromised way, kept alive certain endangered national and spiritual values under communism, to which we now turn.

Religion under Pressure: Communism's Treatment of Christianity

Dogmatic Marxism and historic Christianity have by and large consistently viewed each other as irreconcilable enemies because of fundamental differences in their worldviews, though one could also argue that they are actually relatives – relatives historically and philosophically at odds with each other. Oswald Spengler, for example, claimed that "Christianity is the grandmother of Bolshevism," while Nicolas Berdyaev argued that communism and Christianity were rival religions, and William Temple explained the similarity of Christian and Marxist social ideas by pronouncing the latter a Christian heresy.[11] One thing is sure: "Generally speaking, Marxists hate all gods, including the Christian God-man Jesus Christ."[12]

It is a well-known fact that wherever Marxist communists came to power, their long-term goal was not only a classless but also a non-religious society. Consistent with their politics, derived from the philosophy

of dialectical materialism and joined with revolutionary practice, they viewed Christian faith as superstitious, obscurantist, obsolete, pre-scientific, and thus a totally irrelevant way of thinking and living. Christian institutions were treated as reactionary remnants of the old social order and a hindrance to the progress of the new society and full human liberation of their citizens. Since the Communist Party and its members had a monopoly on both power (which they abused) and truth (which they distorted), they developed comprehensive strategies and powerful instruments for the gradual elimination of all religion. This included restrictive legislation, comprehensive programs of systemic atheization of younger generations through educational institutions and fully controlled media, manipulation of selection of Church leadership, and effective monitoring of their activities. In contrast, for example, to the government-sponsored educational agencies and youth organizations pursuing a comprehensive campaign of indoctrination of children and youth in "scientific atheism," Christian organizations for youth and children were forbidden, Sunday schools outlawed, and youth under the age of 18 years old forbidden to attend church services. As late as the 1980s, the Soviet government proudly claimed that one of the successes of its educational system was evident in the fact that around 90 percent of young people aged 16 to 19 adhered to atheism as their worldview.

Within communist-dominated nations specialized legislation regulated and restricted the status and practice of religious communities. The USSR first introduced "A Law on Religious Associations" in 1929, after Stalin consolidated power. The law contained some 60 Articles that stated what religious organizations could or could not do and what the rights and duties of believers were. During the Stalinist period of intense persecution, especially up to World War II, limiting Articles were vigorously applied and almost regularly over-enforced through common abuse of political power by ambitious regional and local administrators and police. The Law on Religious Associations became a model for similar legislation that was introduced in the late 1940s in other Eastern bloc and socialist countries. More instruments for the control and oppression of Christian communities were introduced, such as central government offices, administrative apparatuses at all levels of governance, and

Figure 6.1   Evangelical Pentecostal Church "Radosne Vijesti" (a former synagogue), next to the Theological Seminary in Osijek, Croatia. Photograph by Maja Sequin, used by permission of the author.

specialized police and judicial departments. Cooperative leaders of registered Christian bodies were given some incentives and government-controlled unions were imposed on smaller Christian denominations. The best known among these was the All-Union Council of Evangelical Christians and Baptists (AUCECB) in the former Soviet Union, composed of Evangelicals, Baptists, Pentecostals, and Mennonites. Their unregistered counterparts were treated as enemies of the state, exposed to harsh treatment and periodic physical persecution. Waves of comprehensive and vigorous national anti-religious campaigns, such as during the Kruschev era in the early 1960s, did not succeed in eliminating religious life but contributed rather paradoxically to a resurgence of spirituality and the growth of all religious communities.

It must be pointed out, however, that practical policies differed from country to country and, in different periods of time, even within the same nation, depending on what was considered to be politically expedient during various historical periods and in diverse regions. Generalizations are problematic, for Eastern Europe has never been totally monolithic regarding the treatment of religion, due to the complexity of the national, cultural, and religious history of different nations, and at times depending on international relationships and considerations.[13] It is legitimate, however, to conclude that at best Christian faith was reluctantly tolerated, with its adherents socially marginalized and discriminated against as "second-class citizens," while, at worst, practicing believers were brutally persecuted, church buildings closed or destroyed, and their institutionalized religion outlawed. In Albania, for example, all visible expressions of religion were, by the force of the law, totally eradicated, with that small neo-Stalinist country at that time (following 1967) priding itself as being the "first atheistic state in the world."

Modes of Survival: Between Resistance, Resignation, and Accommodation

What lessons can be drawn from the precarious existence of the Church under pressure? Christians who live under repressive political (or religious, as in case of countries with Islamic governments) systems that are antagonistic to their faith face serious trials and severe temptations. Valuable lessons have been learned in observing and comparing how Christians in their vulnerable existence responded to the challenges of a totalitarian society. I shall briefly outline the experience of the churches under communism through three different kinds of responses, fully aware that there were occasional overlaps and circumstantial inconsistencies in all of them. These observations are partially based on my first-hand experience and study of the social behavior of minority Protestant communities, their encounter with the challenges of the Marxist rule in general, and communist treatment of Christian churches and believers in particular.[14]

The first impulse of many Christian communities who suddenly found themselves surrounded by an aggressive enemy and ruled over by an atheistic system was to *react by fighting back*, taking a posture of *active opposition* to the government and its policies. The simple reasoning was that the new system was ungodly and evil, inspired by the devil, and so should neither be obeyed nor tolerated, but rather actively opposed in the name of Christ. At times it was simply the fight for Church property and resistance to revolutionary overthrow of the established order. There are obvious dangers in this posture of unrelieved hostility in any context of social change. In Eastern Europe, such opposition was recurrently based on an oversimplified political and correspondingly spiritual division of the world, with the accompanying character of an eschatological struggle between the children of light and the children of darkness. "During the times of the 'Cold War' when the political antagonism between the Western and Eastern bloc countries came to a very critical and dangerous climax, there was in fashion much over-generalized and simplistic speaking of the 'Christian West' and 'atheistic East' and mutual denunciation in almost mythological terms."[15] History

records that in most countries the first years of the communist takeover were marked by bitter and at times *violent confrontations*. In some cases the state resorted to the most brutal repressive measures, producing countless Christian martyrs, and causing enormous devastation of Church property and institutions. Christians who were trapped into the assumption that their major task was to fight communism (modern-day Crusader mentality) handicapped themselves by becoming incapable of practicing forgiveness and being a living witness to the communists.

The second, materially and physically less costly, reaction was to *withdraw from the social scene*, literally to "flee the world." This *posture of resignation* in order to avoid confrontation and compromise took place either by internal or external emigration. Both are caused by fear of engaging with the new system that was conceived as evil, powerful, and bent on the total destruction of those who dared to oppose it. Most of the communist countries practiced a "closed borders" foreign policy and thereby refused to allow their citizens to immigrate to other lands. Yet history records periods in which the governments granted passports and encouraged "undesirable elements" to leave their homelands on grounds of ethnic or religious differences. The best-known cases were the Jewish and, among Christians, large numbers of Pentecostal emigrants from the Soviet Union in the late 1980s.[16] Those who opted for the easier *internal withdrawal* by isolating themselves from the surrounding secular society, though spiritually motivated like the monastic communities, were by and large lost for any effective social impact. They very often developed a ghetto mentality, with a passive if not reactionary lifestyle, and were conspicuous by a high degree of legalism and insulation that made them incapable of a positive "salt and light" influence on their society. They often developed their own pietistic subculture with its own pattern of behavior, language, dress code, and even hymnology. By the neo-Protestant groups (Baptists, Pentecostals, Adventists, and Mennonites), such internal withdrawal was very often doctrinally undergirded by apocalyptic, escapist eschatologies that, in their general outlook on life, seemed to validate certain aspects of Marxist criticism of religion as offering only a "pie in the sky." Extreme examples of such isolated groups of conservative Christians, both Orthodox and

Protestant, have at times been highlighted in Soviet and allied anti-Christian propaganda to prove the socially and mentally harmful effects of Christian faith. This internal withdrawal universally tends to lead to a loss of relevance, denies the mission of the Church, and undermines the Christian impact on culture, for it deals with outdated issues, answers questions that are no longer asked, and has very little to say to its contemporaries and their society.

The third model of responding to the new ideological environment was to *conform or compromise*, to tailor the message and the method to the new situation, thereby *accommodating to the prevailing ideology*. Some Christian leaders were denigrated by others for yielding ground theologically and otherwise establishing rapport with the new rulers and gaining some concessions, if not privileges, in the areas of limited religious freedom, social status, international travel, and so on. Charges of opportunism and selfish careerism by the suffering believers and religious dissidents were not uncommon. In all Christian churches, but especially within the neo-Protestant camp, different degrees of accommodation and resistance often led to splits between those denominations that registered with the government and agreed to observe the restrictions of the letter of the law and those that rejected the legal regulations and operated in a clandestine way and thereby became known as "underground churches."

The compromising approach may at times appear to have been naive and motives questionable, though in many cases it also provided evidence of the diplomatic skills of Church leaders who were able to negotiate settlements that led to temporarily beneficial (to critics: morally and theologically dubious) modus vivendi between Church and state. The obedient attitude to the government by some apparently sincere leaders was additionally justified by their patriotism (as it is frequently done today in China) and by appeals to the apostolic admonition to "submit to the governing authorities, for there is no authority except that which God has established" (Romans 13:1).

A brief concluding theological observation about the most important lesson from and for the Christians under pressure: the Church of Jesus Christ is a pilgrim community – *communio viatorum* – "in the world" but not "of the world," still on the journey to the eternal city and, therefore, never comfortably at home in any society. As Jan Milic Lochman, a Czech theologian, reminded us at that time, "any attempt to relate the gospel too closely to an ideology is dangerous for its integrity and its identity."[17] An uncritical identification with the world inevitably leads to critical loss of both identity and spiritual authority and thereby discredits the preserving and transformative mission of the Church in the world.

From Painful Transition to Hopeful Future

Challenges for the post-communist era Christians and their churches in Eastern Europe are many. With the rather sudden collapse of totalitarian regimes, as dramatically illustrated in November 1989 by the tearing down of the most powerful symbol of a divided Europe – the Berlin Wall – a new spirit of hope filled the widened horizons of unexpected freedom. Many Christians all across Eastern Europe interpreted those events as *The Gospel's Triumph Over Communism,* to borrow the title of Michael Bourdeaux's book,[18] describing them as the providential work of the Lord of history who has seen their suffering and longing for freedom, answered their prayers, and provided them with a special *kairos* period to call their nations back to God and to the spiritual foundations for a free and truly "new society."

The general euphoria of East Europeans with a newly found freedom in the early 1990s, however, has been quickly replaced by the sober encounter with many grim realities that appeared to threaten the prospects of free, peaceful, and prosperous societies. Lack of developed political culture and other obstacles to the consolidation of democratic institutions are key reasons why some nations of Eastern Europe are still going through the very difficult political transitions away from one-party totalitarian regimes toward stable multi-party parliamentary democracies. Transition continues to be equally painful economically as several nations have moved too rapidly and in ethically dubious ways away from the centrally planned "command" economies toward desired viable free-market economies. Large-scale corruption in the process of privatization of formerly state-owned factories and land has created new injustices, causing massive unemployment and social disparities as a result of chaotic "wild capitalism." Social unrest, disillusion- ment of the impoverished masses, and the general mentality of dependence has created environments conducive to new authoritarian rulers, as well as to manipulations by populist politicians hungry for power and personal enrichment. Unfortunately, by and large, East European churches failed to provide effective and credible ethical correctives to these dubious processes. Developing a spirituality for trans- formative social engagement remains one of the priority tasks of the churches if they are to be credible and effective instruments of the Kingdom of God among the broken kingdoms of the post-communist world.

One of the major problems for the national churches is the temptation to return to a quasi-Constantinian model of Church–state relationship. After prolonged periods of external persecution, societal marginaliza- tion, and internal weaknesses, the Church is again favored by (frequently former communist!) rulers and bestowed privileges of public treatment incompatible with modern democratic societies. For example, in 2007, the government of Serbia passed a law that does not recognize Baptist, Pentecostal, and Adventist re- ligious communities as churches and refuses to give them legal status. Laws in Russia, Belarus, and several other countries have in recent years adopted similar restrictive legislations. Although the intensive process of replacement of a singular communist ideology by nationalistic ideologies did lead to partially valid redis- coveries of ethno-religious identities, the discernible shifts "from totalitarianism to tribalism" (issuing in inter-ethnic conflicts and wars) and "from rights to roots" threatened democratic processes and dimin- ished the liberties and human rights of vulnerable minorities. In such contexts, some national Orthodox churches seemed to still operate with the outdated view of canonical authority over a territory, which caused many tensions, for example, in Russia where both Catholics and Protestants were accused of proselytism and illegitimate encroachment on areas supposedly under their control. A competent scholar of religion in Eastern Europe has identified and described this phenomenon as follows:

Ecclesiastical nationalism consists in several distinct as- pects of church activity: in the church's preservation and development of the cultural heritage, in the church's use of a special language for liturgy and instruction, in the advancement of specific territorial claims on putative ethnic grounds, and in the cultivation of the social idea itself, that is, the idea that a given people, united by faith and culture, constitutes a nation.[19]

Since the fall of communism, both Orthodox churches (in the republics of former Soviet Union and Yugoslavia) and Catholic churches (in Poland, Hungary, Slovakia, and Croatia) have in varying de- grees reasserted their claims of monopoly on the religious life of their nations. In these countries, be- longing to the national Church has become less a question of doctrinal persuasion or moral conviction, and more an issue of national identity, patriotism, and ethno-religious folklore.

Protestant churches are small minorities in most of these nations and are in general looked upon with suspicion as adherents of that radical movement that in the past has divided Christendom, and as a modern- ized, Western faith, and thus a foreign intrusion that in the present, in its various fragmented forms, threatens the national and religious identity and unity of the people.[20] Democratically and ecumenically illiterate clergy, with intolerant militant fanatics among them and in their flocks, are fiercely opposed to evangelizing evangelicals and their Western partners, for they view them as disruptive sectarians involved in dangerous proselytizing and unpatriotic activities. Most tradi- tional Protestant churches are in decline, while Baptist, Pentecostal, and charismatic churches are attracting young people and flourishing in countries like the Ukraine and Romania.

Now that the "Iron Curtain" is down, most East European nations, for reasons of security and economic prosperity, aspire to membership in NATO and the European Union (EU). Although the enlargement of these transnational entities and Europe's integrating processes cause tensions with Russia and its neighbors, further unification of the continent is inevitable. In addition to political and economic reasons, it is obvious that the common Christian history and culture make it unacceptable for the continent to be divided permanently between the more advanced

Figure 6.2 St Andrew's Orthodox Church sits atop historic "Andrew's Descent" cobblestone street where local artisans and craftsmen sell their wares in Kyiv, Ukraine. Photograph by Cara Denney, used by permission of the author.

Western part, marked by democracy, economic prosperity, and general vitality, and the Eastern part, as less democratic, prosperous, and stable. Such a division is unsustainable and would do damage to both. The new and united Europe and its churches need each other to rediscover the full meaning and respect for life and personhood, provide for protection of human rights of minorities, work for social justice, practice solidarity, and bear witness to a future that transcends the vision of a common economic and political space. Europe also needs, as frequently reminded by the late Pope John Paul II, an intensive re-evangelization and rediscovery of the Gospel based on spiritual values.

Over the last 20 years, European churches' otherwise frustrated search for ways of finding greater unity and cooperation across the age-long and deeply entrenched confessional divisions has made some significant advances. The Conference of European Churches (CEC), to which almost all Orthodox, Protestant, Anglican, and independent churches belong, and the Council of European Bishops' Conferences (CCEE), composed of all National Catholic Bishops Conferences, have organized three significant European Ecumenical Assemblies: in Basel (1989), Graz (1997), and – the first one in an East European country – Sibiu, in Romania (2007). And in 2001, after a prolonged and careful pan-European study period, they also jointly adopted a finely balanced document, *Charta Oecumenica: Guidelines for the Growing Cooperation among Churches in Europe*, in whose preamble we read: "Europe – from the Atlantic to the Urals, from the North Cape to the Mediterranean – is today more pluralist in culture than ever before. With the Gospel, we want to stand up for the dignity of the human person created in God's image and, as churches together, contribute towards reconciling peoples and cultures."

A search for a more hopeful future for Christian witness in a more unified and secularized Europe continues, with the full realization that it requires a renewed definition of the mission of the Christian churches. This has been programmatically expressed by the document *Churches in the Process of European Integration,* issued by CEC in 2001:

> The substantial role of Christian Churches in society – in debate about values in society, politics, culture, and science, in their pastoral and diaconal roles and their ethical contribution – needs to be recognized. Christian churches are not only part of European history, but also a vital and integral part of the functioning social infrastructure. In spite of the fact that there is not an ecclesial unity, the voice of the Christian churches needs to be taken into consideration. The variety of church and religious traditions in Europe is to be understood not as an obstacle but as an enrichment, which could be of use in the creation of a common European structure. It is completely unsatisfactory to pursue exclusively the pattern of market values to create a common Europe. Accompanying ethical and spiritual dimensions are essential for the success of the project. . . . There is a role for the churches and religious communities as guardians, independent of state power, of many European traditions as well as guardians of the specifically ethical dimension of this process. This role is substantial and truly irreplaceable.[21]

Notes and References

[1] See Peter Kuzmic, "Europe," in James M. Phillipsand Robert T. Coote, eds, *Toward the 21ˢᵗ Century in Christian Mission* (Grand Rapids, MI: Eerdmans, 1993), 148–63.

[2] "Great Transformation" in this context applies to the dramatic change related to the collapse of communism as most vividly and symbolically expressed in the November 9, 1989, tearing down of the Berlin Wall and subsequent dismantling of single-party regimes and socialist federations under their control.

[3] The most helpful general resource work on Orthodoxy written by insiders is: Ken Parry, David J. Melling, Dimitri Brady, Sidney H. Griffith and John F. Healey, eds, *The Blackwell Dictionary of Eastern Christianity* (Oxford: Blackwell, 1999).

[4] See Jonathan Phillips, *The Fourth Crusade and the Sack of Constantinople* (New York: Penguin Group, 2005).

[5] Anastasios Yannoulatos, "Culture and Gospel: Some Observations from the Orthodox Traditions and Experience," *International Review of Mission* 74/294 (1985): 195.

[6] Peter Kuzmic, "Slavorum Apostoli, The Enduring Legacy of Cyril and Methodius," in Tim Perry, ed., *The Legacy of John Paul II* (Downers Grove: IVP Academic, 2007), 267–89.

[7] Pedro Ramet, "Autocephaly and National Identity in Church–State Relations in Eastern Christianity: An Introduction," in Pedro Ramet, ed., *Eastern Christianity and Politics in the Twentieth Century* (Durham, NC: Duke University Press, 1988), 19.

[8] "Uniates" and "uniatism" are widely used pejorative terms to label the thorny ecumenical and political problem of the status and relationships of the Eastern Christians who are under Roman Catholic jurisdiction.

[9] See R. G. Robertson, *The Eastern Christian Churches*, 3rd edn (Rome: Pont. Institutum Studiorum Orientalium, 1990); and "Decree on Eastern Catholic Churches," *Orientalium Ecclesiarum*. Vatican II, November 21, 1964.

[10] Georges Florovsky, *Christianity and Culture* (Belmont: Nordland, 1974), 132.

[11] Cf. David Lyon, *Karl Marx: A Christian Appreciation of His Life and Thought* (Tring: Lion Publishing, 1979), 11–12.

[12] Peter Kuzmic, "How Marxists See Jesus," in Robin Keeley, ed., *Handbook of Christian Belief* (Tring: Lion Publishing, 1982), 108.

[13] One of the most reliably balanced studies of the topic is presented by Trevor Beeson, *Discretion and Valour* (London: Collins, 1974).

[14] See Peter Kuzmic, "Evangelical Witness in Eastern Europe," in Waldron Scott, ed., *Serving Our Generation*: Evangelical Strategies for the Eighties (Colorado Springs, CO: WEF, 1980), 77–86; and "Pentecostals Respond to Marxism," in Murray A. Dempster, Byron D. Klaus, and Douglas Petersen, eds, *Called and Empowered: Global Mission in Pentecostal Perspective* (Peabody, MA: Hendrickson Publishers, 1991), 143–64.

[15] Peter Kuzmic, "Christian–Marxist Dialogue: An Evangelical Perspective," in Vinay Samuel and Albrecht Hauser, eds, *Proclaiming Christ in Christ's Way: Studies in Integral Evangelism* (Oxford: Regnum Books, 1989), 161.

[16] Kent R. Hill, *The Puzzle of the Soviet Church: An Inside Look at Christianity and Glasnost* (Portland: Multnomah, 1989), 292–3.

[17] Jan Milic Lochman, *Encountering Marx: Bonds and Barriers Between Christians and Marxists* (Philadelphia, PA: Fortress Press, 1977).

[18] Michael Bourdeaux, *The Gospel's Triumph over Communism* (Minneapolis, MN: Bethany House Publishers, 1991).

[19] Ramet, "Autocephaly and National Identity in Church–State Relations in Eastern Christianity: An Introduction," 10.

[20] See the excellent symposium John Witte, Jr., and Paul Mojzes, eds, "Pluralism, Proselytism, and Nationalism in Eastern Europe," special issue, *Journal of Ecumenical Studies* 36/1–2 (winter–spring, 1999): 1–286.

[21] Peter Pavlovic, "Churches in the Process of European Integration, " Conference of European Churches – Church and Society Commission. Available at: <http://www.cec-kek.org/English/IntegrationprocE-print.htm >; accessed May 15, 2009.

Further Reading

Bourdeaux, Michael. *The Gospel's Triumph over Communism*. Minneapolis, MN: Bethany House Publishers, 1991.

Ellis, Jane. *The Russian Orthodox Church: Triumphalism and Defensiveness*. Basingstoke: Macmillan, 1996.

Mejendorff, John. *The Orthodox Church: Its Past and Its Role in the World Today*, 3rd edn. Crestwood: St Vladimir's Seminary Press, 1981.

Mojzes, Paul. *Religious Liberty in Eastern Europe and the USSR: Before and After the Great Transformation*. East European Monographs 337. New York: Columbia University Press, 1992.

Nielson, Niels Christian, ed. *Christianity after Communism: Social, Political, and Cultural Struggle in Russia*. Boulder, CO: Westview Press, 1994.

Ramet, Sabrina P., ed. *Eastern Christianity and Politics in the Twentieth Century*. Durham, NC: Duke University Press, 1988.

Ramet, Sabrina P., ed. *Protestantism and Politics in Eastern Europe and Russia*. Durham, NC: Duke University Press, 1992.

Ramet, Sabrina P. *Nihil obstat: Religion, Politics, and Social Change in East-Central Europe and Russia*. Durham, NC: Duke University Press, 1998.

Sawatsky, Walter W., and Penner, Peter F., eds. *Mission in the Former Soviet Union*. Schwarzenfeld: Neufeld Verlag, 2005.

Walters, Philip. *World Christianity: Eastern Europe*. Monrovia: MARC, 1988.

Weigel, George. *The Final Revolution: The Resistance Church and the Collapse of Communism*. Oxford: Oxford University Press, 1992.

Part III

Asia

7

Christianity in South Asia
Negotiating Religious Pluralism

Arun Jones

Historical Introduction

To understand Christianity in South Asia today, we
need to remember that the Christian faith has come to
this part of the world in a number of waves, each of
them different, each of them giving birth to strong and
vibrant Asian Christian communities, most of which
endure to the present time. Given the differences
between the Christian traditions that have come to
South Asia, what is quite amazing is that within each of
the countries in this region the majority of Christians
generally share a sense that they are all members of one
Church. This basic theological conviction is nourished
and strengthened by a fundamental sociological fact:
Christianity in South Asia is a minority religion.

Let us turn to the different forms of Christian faith
that have found a home in South Asia. The oldest came
from the Middle East or West Asia, early in the history
of Christianity.[1] There are numerous strong oral traditions in South India that St Thomas, one of the 12
disciples of Jesus, himself brought the Gospel to India.
While this tradition is disputed by scholars, a number
of different and independent written sources from the
early Church support this claim. Archaeological evidence has also bolstered the argument for Thomas's
founding of the Church in South Asia. A second
tradition, not as well attested and not known in India
itself, is that the Apostle Bartholomew founded the
Christian community in South India. Whatever one

may make of the various arguments for and against the
apostolic founding of the Indian Church, there is a
general scholarly consensus that by the middle of the
third century Christianity had been planted at least in
South India, and was starting to sprout and grow as an
Asian religious community. This Christian community saw itself as connected to the Church in Syria and
Persia, and so was deeply influenced by Syrian liturgy
and theology. In the fifth and eighth centuries the
South Indian Church was greatly strengthened by
groups of Christians coming from Mesopotamia, perhaps fleeing persecution in the Persian Empire.

In the fifth century, due to a major theological
controversy, large portions of the church in Asia were
deemed to be heretical and were called "Nestorians"
by the church in the Roman Empire.[2] The so-called
Nestorians referred to themselves as The Church of the
East or the East Syrian Church. This church was highly
missionary, for example planting churches in Sri Lanka
that were noted by the Alexandrian merchant Cosmos
Indiclopeustes in the year 525. From Mesopotamia it
was the Church of the East (or Nestorians) that
continued to support the church in South India by
providing bishops and occasionally priests for its ongoing sacramental and ecclesial life until the eighteenth
century.

The second group of Christians to come to
South Asia was the Roman Catholics.[3] While there
had been occasional contacts between European

Introducing World Christianity, First Edition. Edited by Charles E. Farhadian.
© 2012 Blackwell Publishing Ltd. Published 2012 by Blackwell Publishing Ltd.

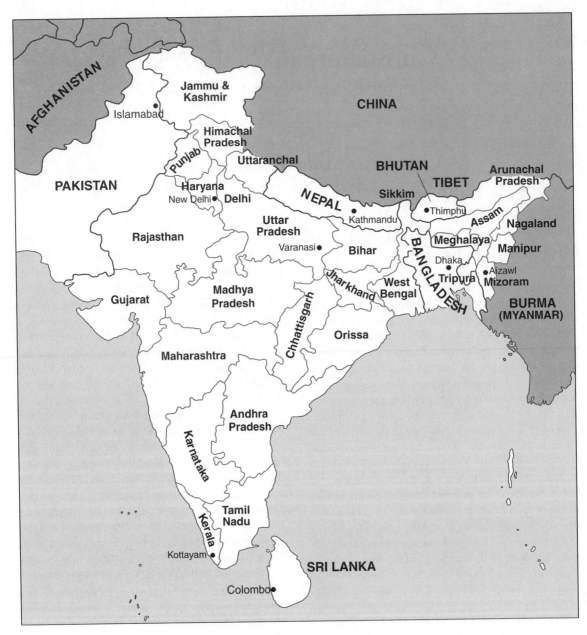

Map 7.1 South Asia

and Indian Christians through the centuries, the character of Indian Christianity was not really affected by Catholicism until the arrival of the Portuguese as a trading and colonizing force in South Asia, beginning in 1498. The Portuguese were unable to conquer or colonize large tracts of land in Asia, and as a result they had to be content to establish small trading enclaves that functioned as European outposts in Asia. In India they took over the port of Goa, making it the base of Roman Catholic work in all of Asia (with the exception of the Philippines). From here, the Church sent missionaries to all parts of India and the rest of Asia through the centuries. The success of the Catholics in South Asia, however, was confined mostly to the southern part of India until the nineteenth century. Franciscan and Jesuit missionaries began the task of evangelization in the sixteenth century, in what are today Sri Lanka and Bangladesh, although with few results in terms of an Asian church until the nineteenth century.

The final wave of Christianity to come to South Asia was that of Protestantism. The first bearers of this tradition were the Dutch, who established their rule in a number of places in Asia, including the Indian subcontinent, during the seventeenth century. The greatest influence of Dutch Protestantism in South Asia is to be found in Sri Lanka, which the Dutch captured from the Sri Lankans and the Portuguese in 1658 and ruled until 1802. Early in the eighteenth century, two German Lutheran missionaries, Bartholomäus Ziegenbalg and Heinrich Plütschau, introduced Protestantism to the eastern coast of South India in the Danish-ruled territory of Tranquebar, sowing the seeds for Protestantism on the subcontinent. The nineteenth century, when Britain became the paramount imperial power in South Asia, was also when Protestantism secured a permanent place in the South Asian landscape. Due to the work of Asians, Europeans, and North Americans, Protestants established Christian communities that today are still developing and maturing into a form of Asian Christianity.

Christianity in the Context of South Asian Religious Pluralism

The long history of Christianity in South Asia is important on at least two counts. First of all, it demonstrates that Christianity has very deep and ancient roots in Asia. So, when thinking of South Asia, for example, it is important to remember that there were Christians in India and Sri Lanka before there were Muslims in Pakistan and Bangladesh, or Sikhs in North India. Christianity is an Asian religion. The second importance of this history is that the different waves of Christianity have exhibited different attitudes toward the dominant religion and culture, especially Hinduism. The Syrian form of Christianity, by and large, has developed the attitude of accommodation to the local culture. Christians of Syrian background in South India function quite harmoniously within the structures of Hindu caste society: they "form part of the total segmentary caste structure and are ranked to each other and to the Hindu castes."[4] Syrian Christians also wear the same dress and observe many of the same social customs as their Hindu and Muslim neighbors.[5] The Roman Catholic tradition generally displays ambivalence toward the predominant religion and culture. On the one hand, there are strands of Catholicism that have sought a radical accommodation of Christianity to the local religion. Thus one of the most famous Catholic missionaries of the seventeenth century, Roberto de Nobili (1577–1656), settled in Madurai where he became "thoroughly Brahminized," studying Hindu religious texts in Sanskrit and Tamil, "scrupulously abstaining from all pollution from defiled or tainted things (e.g., flesh), subsisting only on one simple meal, and wearing the 'sacred thread' of the 'twice-born' (dvija) along with the ochre robe of a sannyasi."[6] On the other hand, some strands of Catholic thought and practice have rejected Asian religions and the accompanying social traditions as unchristian. The priests and missionaries that settled Goa in the sixteenth century banished all Hindus from the state if they did not convert, banned the performance of Hindu religious rituals and festivals, and prohibited Hindu priests from exercising any religious activities in the colony.[7] Finally, Protestantism generally established itself as a religion of protest against other Asian religious traditions; it has tended to provide the most radical alternative to local social and religious traditions. The famous early Baptist missionary William Carey (1761–1834) and his colleagues, for example, believed that Hinduism was a "satanic" religion, "not merely devoid of salvific value but an idolatrous system which was an affront to God's sovereign rule of his world."[8] Of course there are numerous exceptions to be found to this general characterization of the various Christian traditions; nevertheless, it does show that Christians and Christian traditions in South Asia exhibit substantial variety in their self-understanding with respect to their neighbors of differing faith traditions.

A few general comments need to be made about Christianity in South Asia. First of all, as noted above, Christianity is a minority religion, albeit not the only one, in the region. Hinduism is by far the largest religious tradition in India (75 percent of the population) and Nepal (77 percent), with Islam the dominant religion in Bangladesh (86 percent) and Pakistan (96 percent), and Buddhism the religion of the majority of the population in Bhutan (74 percent) and Sri Lanka (68 percent).[9] Second, while Christians are to be found throughout all of South Asia, there are areas with higher concentrations of Christians. In India, Christians make up a small percentage of the population – estimates range all the way from 2.3 percent to 6.2 percent.[10] However, Christians are to be found in larger numbers relative to the whole population in the states of Andaman and Nicobar Islands (77,000 or 22 percent), Goa (360,000 or 27 percent), Kerala (6 million or 19 percent), and the northeastern states of Manipur (740,000 or 34 percent), Meghalaya (1.6 million or 70 percent), Mizoram (773,000 or 87 percent), and Nagaland (1.8 million or 90 percent).[11] In Pakistan, Christians constitute somewhere between 1.6 percent and 2.5 percent of the population, and the majority are from the state of Punjab.[12] Christians in Bangladesh (between 0.3 percent and 0.7 percent of the population) come mostly from low-caste Hindu groups and from so-called tribal people such as the Garo, Santal, Khasi, and Kurulel.[13] The Christians of Sri Lanka (between 7 percent and 9.4 percent of the population), four fifths of whom are Roman Catholic, are to be found mostly on the western coast of the island, and make up 30 percent of the population of the city of Colombo.[14] Third, even though the introduction of both Roman Catholic and Protestant Christianity is linked to European imperialism, Christianity is not first and foremost a political force in South Asia. Rather, it needs to be understood primarily as a religious movement and

force. That being said, the fourth point to be made is that there is no neat division between the religious and the secular in South Asian life. People's religious background directs not only where they worship, but also what kind of occupation they have, with whom they associate socially, whom they marry, and for whom they vote. In other words, in South Asia one's economic, political, and social life is deeply influenced by one's religious affiliation; religion is a matter of identity. This is why social conflict in South Asia sometimes manifests itself as religious conflict.

There are many ways to describe the Christian presence in South Asia, but perhaps the most helpful one is to see Christianity as an alternative religious tradition to the dominant religions in the area, Hinduism and Islam. In other words, to varying degrees, Christians distinguish themselves from the majority religion in the area where they live. In this matter, they are just like the other religious minority communities in South Asia. As mentioned above, exactly how Christians distinguish themselves varies greatly across the subcontinent. Let us look at three characteristic ways in which Christian communities relate to the dominant religions of South Asia. In order to illustrate these three ways, we shall consider three very different groups of Christians in India.

Christianity in Harmony with the Dominant Religion

In a recent autobiographical essay, the Roman Catholic theologian Michael Amaladoss remembers his childhood as one of easy relationships with his Hindu friends in the Indian state of Tamil Nadu. "I grew up in a village of about 1,000 families, only three of which were Christian," he writes. "My friends and playmates were Hindus. It was a natural, human relationship, not hindered by ignorance or prejudice. My Christian identity was recognized and respected, as I respected their different identities."[15] For many of us Christians who have grown up in South Asia, this brief description of a boy's friendly and respectful interaction with Hindus accurately captures the nature of our earliest and most formative interactions with our neighbors of the dominant religious tradition in our area.

While the Western media tends to focus on friction between Christians and Hindus or Muslims – and such friction certainly exists – the majority of Christians live peaceably in the South Asian context. Christians of any number of traditions have become part and parcel of the religious landscape of South Asia, and live as productive members of their society.

Perhaps the Indian Christian community that has most blended into the religious landscape is the Syrian Orthodox branch of Christianity (this branch having many smaller branches of its own), with its roots in the state of Kerala, South India. As mentioned above, Syrian Christians (or Syrians for short) have lived in Kerala since at least the third century, and as a result have become well integrated into the larger Hindu society. In fact, sociologically speaking they function as one of the privileged groups with high status in Kerala. They gained this position in society due to their skills and services as warriors, merchants, and revenue officers to the kings in the area. They have maintained this position by a strict adherence to Hindu codes of pollution and purity in their social interactions. In other words, they avoided association with persons of low status, who were seen as religiously polluted, and associated rather with persons of high status. So, for example, Syrian Christians will generally not contemplate marrying low-status Pulaya Christian converts of Kerala, and, until the 1960s, Pulaya Christians would not even be fed inside the home of a Syrian Christian. Today, however, Pulaya and Syrian Christians of similar economic backgrounds attend each others' weddings and sit at table and eat together.[16]

The integration of Syrian Christians into the Hindu society of Kerala is further evidenced by their religious observances. For many centuries they performed life-cycle rituals that were almost identical to the rituals of high-caste Hindus. In this way, Syrian Christians ensured their status within the sacred and moral order of Hinduism. They acted as patrons and sponsors at Hindu festivals and shrines; their churches were often located right next to local temples, and they even shared processional regalia with their Hindu neighbors.[17] Thus Syrian Christians share many religious and social customs with their Hindu neighbors. Syrians also served as "pollution neutralizers."[18] This means that objects that had been defiled for Hindu rituals could be purified for them through the mediation of Syrian Christians. So, for example, the touch of a Syrian Christian could purify provisions bought for use at a Hindu temple. In addition, Syrian Christians and Muslims, who each comprise very roughly one quarter of Kerala's population, have borrowed traditions from one another. So it is not surprising that just as with aspects of Hinduism, Islamic ideas and traditions have been interwoven with Christian ones in this area.[19]

However, it would be wrong to think of Syrian Christianity as simply an extension of Hindu or Muslim religion. To begin with, Syrian worship is thoroughly Christian, even though like other Christian worship around the world it picks up influences and expressions from the surrounding cultures and religions. This is made easier by the fact that the liturgy is in Syriac, and so well suited to the Asian context. Syrian Christians baptize their children and partake of the Eucharist just like other Christians. Their understanding of death is specifically Christian: old people wait for death in anticipation of meeting Christ and their loved ones who have died before them.[20] Similarly, the liturgical calendar is based upon the Jewish and early Christian calendar. Syrians celebrate Advent, Christmas, Lent, and Easter with great ardor and deep devotion, and with uniquely Christian rituals, beliefs, and understandings. Unlike high-status Hindus who are vegetarian, Syrian Christians eat fish, pork, and beef; these foods are considered polluting in the Hindu worldview.[21] Syrian Christians generally marry within their own group, thus preserving their Christian identity. Nowadays, with the permission of the parents, a young adult may marry a Christian from some other group, as long as the mate comes from a commensurate economic background. The wedding service takes place in the church, with the Pauline symbolism of marriage found in Ephesians being of central importance.[22]

One of the best illustrations of how Syrian Christians both adapt to local Hindu culture and keep their distinctive Christian identity is seen in the way that Syrians in Kottayam, a small city in Kerala, have their houses built.[23] A Syrian will hire a Hindu master builder to construct the house; however, the master builder uses the same customs and rules in building this house as he would for a Hindu client. He follows the rules of construction found in the Hindu Scriptures

Figure 7.1 A Syrian Orthodox Church in Kerala. Photograph by Arun Jones, reproduced with permission of the author.

called the *Thaccu Shastra*. The Christian house therefore looks just like a Hindu one of a family of similar status. The master builder uses astrological signs and other omens to calculate where the house should be situated, and when it should be built. The site of the land needs to be carefully determined; three, five, or six-cornered plots of land are considered inauspicious. Land in which certain materials like bones or ash are found is considered polluted and therefore not suitable for building. A house cannot be built facing a church, because the church gives off *shakti* or supernatural power. Only certain trees are to be planted on certain sides of the house. The builder carefully chooses the months for construction; April–May is associated with disease, for example, while May–June is associated with jewels and money. Sundays and Tuesdays are inauspicious days for building.

There are a number of rituals that accompany the house construction, so as to ensure good fortune. Among them are prayers to the Hindu god Ganapathy when the foundation stone is laid. Fried rice, beaten rice, molasses, plantains, fruit, money, and flowers are offered to the god, and the master builder conducts his own worship or *puja*. The Syrian Christian clients do not partake in these Hindu rituals; however, they provide the food and other offerings necessary for the worship. They also accept as a matter of fact the auspicious nature of powerful sacred materials – gold, silver, copper, bronze, and iron, sugar crystals, grapes, and pounded and puffed rice. Once the five sacred metals are buried in the ground, the foundation is laid and the Syrian priest is called to say prayers at the construction site. During the process of construction, the master builder will continue to read omens and pray to spirits to guide and protect him and the workers. Again, while the Christian clients do not participate in these rituals and prayers, they insist on them being performed by the master builder so as to ward off any bad luck, and they purchase any materials needed for the builder's religious activities.

When the house is built, the master builder, carpenters, and workers are given a feast by the owner of the house, and then their contract is completed and they are sent on their way. The Christians then make the house ready for habitation by exorcising the Hindu influence. The Syrian priest and deacon are called for a purification ritual. Prayers for peace and grace are said for the living and the dead of the household. The priest and deacon visit every room of the house with a censer, holy water, and strips of palm leaf, marking each door with the sign of the cross. After this Christian ritual, the house is ready to be occupied by its owners.

The construction of a house is just one way in which Syrian Christians harmoniously both join in but also mark themselves off from the surrounding Hindu culture. All in all, Syrian Christians are able to hold on to their particular identity because they are looked upon as a distinct group within the Hindu social system. Their incorporation into the system allows them both to interact with their neighbors of differing religions as members of a high-status group, but it also insulates them from pressure to conform to the dictates of the Hindu or Muslim religion. They are respected as important but distinct members of Kerala society.

Christianity in Tension with the Dominant Religion

While Syrian, Goan, and other Christians live amicably with their Hindu and Muslim neighbors, there are substantial numbers of Christians who experience more friction with communities of other faiths, even though these Christians live much like their religiously different neighbors and share much in common with them. Chief among such groups of Christians are those from an outcaste background, who call themselves *dalit*, a word meaning "oppressed." Estimates of the proportion of Christians from outcaste backgrounds vary significantly, but *dalits* comprise a majority of the Christians in India and Pakistan.[24] The caste system is a highly complicated and intricate ordering of Indian society, and indeed sociologists and anthropologists do not agree on what exactly constitutes the Indian caste system and how powerful a force it is in shaping and forming society.[25] Caste continues to exist, if in attenuated form, in Pakistan, Bangladesh, Nepal, and parts of Sri Lanka; however, it is not the mode of social organization of the peoples in Northeast India or the tribal peoples of Bangladesh. What can be said generally is that the caste system orders the thousands of Hindu communities of India into a hierarchy that has strong religious, social, and economic components.

Communities that are higher in the hierarchy tend to live a religiously purer (i.e., less polluted), socially more prestigious, and economically more advantageous life in comparison to groups lower in the hierarchy. This characterization has numerous and interesting exceptions both on the individual and group level; but especially from the perspective of the outcaste or *dalit*, this is how the system functions. Outcaste or *dalit* communities are composed of the religiously most polluted, socially most despised, and economically poorest people in society.

In order to get a glimpse into the kind of religious tensions with which the majority of Christians in South Asia live, let us move from a small city in the South Indian state of Kerala to a small village in the North Indian state of Uttar Pradesh, from the upper echelons of Indian society to its bottom-most rung, from Syrian Christians who trace their ancestry to the first century to Roman Catholics who trace their Christian origins to the 1950s and 1960s.[26] The Christians of the pseudonymous village of Shantinagar near the city of Varanasi (or Benares) converted to Roman Catholic Christianity from the Chamar caste, an outcaste or "Untouchable" community that traditionally lived by tanning – which involved dealing with carcasses of dead animals, a highly polluting substance. Not only the touch but even the proximity of Chamars was considered polluting to high-caste Hindus. In addition to tanning, the Chamars have worked as landless indentured laborers in the fields of the richer and higher-caste landowners from the Bhumihar caste, and also performed as musicians in bands that play at weddings and other functions. To this day, the Chamars work in fields at harvest in order to obtain foodstuff for the coming year.

These particular Chamar Christians in eastern Uttar Pradesh were introduced to Roman Catholicism by European Capuchin missionaries in the late 1940s. Despite resistance from the local Bhumihars, who feared that Christianity would disrupt their relationship to the Chamars, the missionaries were able to buy a piece of property and establish a mission that had a school, a dispensary, and a church. Slowly, Chamars started to convert to Christianity. At that time they worked the fields of the Bhumihar families to whom they were indentured, living at a subsistence level on a diet of rice and lentils. Sometimes Chamars would extract undigested pieces of grain from cow dung in order to obtain a little extra food for themselves. Since wheat was an extremely valuable commodity at the time, the Chamars were paid for a day's labor not with wheat but with a kilogram of feed reserved for cattle and other livestock. In addition, Bhumihar families would demand that young boys and girls from Chamar families work as household servants.

The men of the Chamar caste also worked as tanners. When livestock died they removed the carcasses, skinned them, and used the meat for food. In payment, the owners of the livestock received sandals made from the hide of the dead animals. Chamar women also had hereditary work in society. They served as midwives, caring for pregnant women and cutting the umbilical cord of newborns. They also looked after the mother for 12 days after birth, making sure that the fire in the delivery room was constantly burning. Their service included "disposing of the feces of the mother by hand after she had defecated into a clay pot."[27] After years of such service, a Chamar midwife would reek of human feces.[28] At the birth of a male child, a midwife received the payment of a sari; at the birth of a female, she was given a kilogram of coarse grain.

Because their work was considered highly polluting, the Chamars were quite literally outcaste. They had to live on the outskirts of villages, and were not allowed access to the wells and hand pumps that upper-caste Hindus used for drawing water. When talking to their social superiors, the outcastes had to squat on the ground, signifying their inferior status. They were not allowed access to temples, let alone Brahmin priests. As a result, the Chamars had their own religious leaders, very often someone like the headman of their caste, who would officiate at their weddings and other religious functions. Chamars are also known to be extremely superstitious and gullible, leaving them open to manipulation by other members of society.[29]

Given their status (or lack of it) in society, some Chamars decided to become Christian in order to leave behind the terrible stigma of their outcaste position.[30] Generally, however, their efforts at social mobility have been largely futile. The reason for this is that they cannot find work other than that which is relegated to them by society. Once in a while, through education provided by Christian mission schools,

Chamars are able to break through the economic and intellectual barriers of their group and find clerical or other professional work. Despite this apparent success, they and their family members live with the social stigma of their outcaste background. They also face strong resistance and at times outright violence when they try to move up the hierarchical ladder of their society. Thus Christians from outcaste backgrounds often face a double oppression: that which comes from being an outcaste and that which comes from being a Christian trying to move away from one's outcaste background.

One can see that for Chamars and other outcastes in India and Pakistan, to become a Christian (or Buddhist or Muslim) is to make a statement of defiance to one's Hindu society; one purposely lives in tension with the dominant religion.[31] However, *dalit* Christians are still very much a part of the larger society in which they are located: their economic, political, social, and even religious activities are carried out in constant contact and conversation with other castes and groups around them. A good example is the religious life of the Chamar Christians of Shantinagar. The type of worship that is most favored by these Catholics is a charismatic service, which is a Catholic adaptation of Pentecostalism.[32] This Pentecostal or charismatic Christianity involves ecstatic forms of religious practice, typified by speaking in tongues (glossolalia), strong emotional outbursts in worship, seeing and interpreting visions, long hours of prayer and contemplation, and healing through prayer from physical ailments and diseases.

A Catholic charismatic prayer and healing service is in certain ways exclusively Christian. There is an intense focus on Jesus, on Mary the Mother of Jesus, on the Host (the bread used during communion or Eucharist), and other such uniquely Christian figures and elements. Charismatic Christianity is itself identified with the United States, at least for Roman Catholics, because it was brought to India by priests who had been exposed to it while studying in America.[33] Through charismatic renewal, prayer, and healing services, Catholics around the Varanasi area desire to strengthen and deepen their Christian identity. They also want to proclaim God's word to Hindus who have not yet heard God's message given to the Christians.

The following description of charismatic Catholic worship is taken from observations made in the North Indian city of Varanasi (or Benares). In October of 1995, a number of Catholic charismatic clergy and laity, both women and men, met at a Christian *ashram* near Varanasi to prepare themselves for a three-day charismatic prayer service. An *ashram* is a religious retreat center, quite common in the Hindu world. The planning retreat began with Mass (a worship service with communion), and then the members broke into small groups where they prayed, confessed their sins, and shared personal experiences. While most of those gathered were holding their discussions in small groups, the leaders of the diocesan charismatic team got together in order to plan for the upcoming prayer service. Praying "in tongues" and interpreting visions they had received, they set the daily schedule for the service. The planning retreat ended a few hours before the charismatic prayer service itself began. By this time, Hindus who were devoted to Jesus had begun to arrive at the *ashram* on their way to the Catholic cathedral, where the prayer service was to be held. They were going there after having heard from neighbors and friends that healings occurred during the service. These Hindus are called *Khrist Panthis*, which literally means "Christ followers" or "followers of Christ." They are deeply devoted to Jesus, and carry with them pictures or paintings of him. What distinguishes them from Catholics is that they refuse to convert to Christianity, and since in Hinduism it is perfectly legitimate to devote oneself to following a particular god (one's *ishtadevta*), they find a home for devotion and worship of Jesus within Hindu religious structures. The presence of *Khrist Panthis* reveals yet another facet of Christianity in South Asia – it is sometimes difficult to clearly demarcate Christians from followers of other religious traditions. If we define a Christian as anyone who says she or he follows Jesus, then the *Khrist Panthis* would be numbered among Christians. However, because *Khrist Panthis* are not baptized members of a Christian church, most Indian Christians would not count them among the body of believers.

In the chapel of the Christian *ashram*, as *Khrist Panthis* arrived, they sat down next to Catholics in order to look reverently upon the Host that was placed on the altar. Catholics believe that the Host – the bread used for Communion – becomes the actual body and

Figure 7.2 A Khrist Panthi worshiping Jesus. Photograph by Mathew Schmalz, reproduced with permission of the author.

blood of Christ while retaining the physical attributes of bread. The Christians and *Khristh Panthis* in the *ashram* did not have identical understandings of the Host and reasons for gazing upon it; however, they both did believe that it is holy and contains divine power. Soon the charismatic Christians and the *Khristh Panthis* were praying in tongues. Their voices grew louder and louder, and then slowly subsided. The charismatics became silently contemplative. The quiet of meditation was broken by a catechist (a Catholic teacher of doctrine who is not a priest) who started singing a song that he had composed. Such singing is also typical of charismatic services. Soon the Christians and the Hindu followers of Christ made their way to the cathedral in Varanasi, where the actual charismatic prayer service was held. The service consisted of praying in tongues, long sermons, veneration of the Host, singing of religious songs, and a closing Mass at which Communion was shared.

One of the deep paradoxes of the large three-day charismatic prayer service is that while it was meant to strengthen and demarcate Christian identity in a Hindu culture, the great majority of people attending the service were themselves Hindus. They had come to experience one of the most powerful aspects of the service, its healing aspect. And the source of the healing was said to be the Host, since Christ himself is believed to be present in it.[34] Therefore, Hindus attending the service venerated the Host as fervently as did the Christians; there were many stories told of how simply viewing the bread brought about healing in various people. Thus an exclusively Christian symbol, the Host of Communion, became the means for a religiously inclusive worship and prayer service. Yet the power of healing was not restricted to the Host. There were certain charismatic Christians in the city known to be healers, and these Christian charismatics would be visited by Hindus and Muslims seeking healing for themselves or family members. The charismatic Christian healers would pray over those who were brought to them, and would perform exorcisms of evil spirits believed to be causing physical, mental, and emotional illness; yet Muslims or Hindus felt no compunction to convert to Christianity. If the sick or possessed person was healed, the clients did not care to which religious tradition the healer belonged, only that the healer's particular prayers and god were efficacious.

The conflict between adaptation and resistance to the surrounding Hindu culture is perhaps best illustrated in the Communion service during the final Mass of the three-day charismatic prayer service. In Roman Catholic belief, only baptized Catholics are supposed to receive the Host at Communion. Hindus attending the charismatic prayer service, however, also wanted to receive and eat the Host, because for them it is laden with effective supernatural power. So, as people came to receive the Host during communion, nuns strategically positioned in the cathedral interrogated them. The nuns "asked whether communicants were Christian, whether they had received baptism, or whether they had attended Mass before."[35] Those who did not give the correct answers were prevented from receiving the Host.

The charismatic prayer and healing service is just one way in which Chamar Christians live in tension with the Hindu society from which they have emerged, a tension caused by their being pulled into a society from which they are trying to move away. The tension continues in political, economic, educational, and social arenas. On the one hand, living as Christians and therefore as outsiders in the predominantly Hindu culture, Catholic Chamars are defying their prescribed role in society. On the other hand, these Christians are still absorbed into the ebb and flow of life of the society in which they live, and they must participate peacefully in this ebb and flow to a significant extent in order to survive.

Christianity in Contradistinction to the Dominant Religion

The states of Meghalaya, Mizoram, and Nagaland are unique in India because a majority of their populations is composed of Christians. In fact, in Mizoram and Nagaland, over 80 percent of the population professes Christianity. However, it is not only the religion of these states that is unique. The original inhabitants of these northeastern states are culturally and ethnically very different from the vast majority of the population of South Asia. The majority of the indigenous people are of "mongoloid racial stock. They are believed to have migrated from north and east of their present homeland. . . . [T]he Mon-Khmer group in the present day Meghalaya is the other dominant race."[36] Unlike the Sanskrit-based languages of the majority of South Asians, the language of the indigenous peoples of the three states is Sino-Tibetan or Tibeto-Mongolian. In addition, their social organization is quite unlike the hierarchical caste system that pervades much of South Asia; it is much more communal and egalitarian. Finally, the pre-Christian religion of the people of Northeast India is not dependent in any way on Hinduism or the Hindu worldview. Rather, the traditional religions of this area pay close attention to spirits and to the forces of nature. In the Indian Constitution, such people are called "tribals," although this is a term that at least some of the people themselves resent because it has been used pejoratively. What the Indian Constitution knows as tribal people are not only to be found in Northeast India, however; they are scattered throughout South Asia, and significant concentrations of tribal people have traditionally resided in the states of Bihar, Orissa, and Madhya Pradesh, as well as in the country of Bangladesh, where the majority of Christians are from these groups.

Many of the Christians of Northeast India have developed their religion so that it stands in fundamental distinction to the Hinduism of the majority population of the nation. In this case, Christianity both preserves and accentuates the ethnic and cultural differentiation of the minority population in a nation-state. This preservation is carried out in the face of pressure, which is sometimes intense, on the nation's minority population to give up its cultural, social, and sometimes political independence and be assimilated into the majority. The case of the Protestant Christians in Mizoram is a good example.[37]

The state of Mizoram is in the northeast corner of India, in a hilly part of the country sandwiched between Myanmar to the east and Bangladesh to the west, and is home to the Mizo people. Mizoram and several other northeast states became politically linked to the Indian subcontinent in 1826 due to the economic, political, and military maneuverings of the British East India Company. The British had great difficulty controlling and subduing the peoples of the area, who militarily resisted foreign incursion on to their ancestral lands.[38] After 70 years of military expeditions, the British Empire was finally able to establish a permanent military presence in Mizoram in the mid-1890s. An uneasy truce resulted in what the British termed indirect rule, whereby the "traditional village chiefs continued to administer their villages on behalf of the new colonial rulers."[39]

Attempts at Christian mission, first Protestant and then Roman Catholic, followed on the heels of the British annexation of the area. The Baptist and Calvinistic Methodist missions began work in Mizoram in 1894; however, there were no baptisms for five years. This is not surprising, given the political situation where Europeans were occupying Mizo lands. The first two baptisms came in 1899, and that only because a Christian from the neighboring Khasi people was working with European missionaries. A few others converted to Christianity due to visions received by a local seer in southern Mizoram.[40] Slowly a small but vigorous Mizo Protestant church formed in the first decade of the twentieth century, with the Presbyterians in the north and Baptists in the south. "These early Christians were mostly among the lower class of the society, and they were mocked, despised, and sometimes persecuted by their fellow villagers and even by the chiefs."[41] We can see, then, that from the first, Christianity in Mizoram was developed in contradistinction to the local culture and religion.[42]

A number of revivals beginning in 1906 brought more and more adherents to the Protestant churches. Beginning around 1920, Mizo Protestant Christianity slowly began to be identified with Mizo culture and identity. Indigenous elements such as traditional drumming, singing, and dancing started to make their way into Mizo worship and church life. For example, around 1920, new hymn tunes started to appear in Mizo worship services. These tunes were neither strictly traditional Mizo nor traditional Western, but an adaptation of indigenous singing to the strictures of Christian hymnody introduced by missionaries. They were composed by Mizo poets and singers, who in

turn were inspired by the local people's singing. Also during the 1920s the traditional Mizo drums, which were used for religious festivals and dancing, slowly appeared in Mizo Christian worship. Dance had been introduced into Christian revivals even earlier by the Mizo, who in the first revivals of 1906 were stamping their feet on the floor in motions highly reminiscent of Khasi dancing. So today any visitor to a Mizo Protestant worship service will notice a pair of drums being used, will hear unique hymns set to what is now known as "the traditional Mizo-Christian-tune," and may very well find some inspired worshipers dancing in front of the altar-pulpit.[43] By 1950, 80 percent of the population of Mizoram was Christian, and Christianity was being identified as the religion of the Mizo people.[44] Since the 1970s, there has been a conscious and concerted effort by Mizo Christian leadership to indigenize Church life: that is, to bring Church and traditional culture into harmony with each other.

While the Church was becoming increasingly Mizo over the first half of the twentieth century, the Mizo were differentiating themselves more and more from the Sanskritic Indian majority of the British Empire, into whose orbit they were being ineluctably drawn. When India and Pakistan attained their independence from the British on August 15, 1947, the Indian flag was not hoisted in Mizoram. No act could speak more loudly of Mizo resentment against the claims of the Indian nation-state on their traditional lands. Soon a movement for an independent Mizo nation emerged, and gained great strength in the 1960s. Over the next 20 years the Indian government and the Mizo independence movement waged a bitter and cruel war for supremacy. A Peace Accord was finally signed in 1986, with Church leaders acting as key mediators between the warring factions.

The relationship between Christianity and Mizo nationalism is complicated.[45] What we can say is that as the Mizo people found themselves living in a context first of the British Empire and then of the Indian national state, they integrated their traditional culture with their new religion, Christianity, to form a new Mizo national identity. Traditionally, the Mizo people had lacked any political unity, since each village governed itself. The incursion of a modern empire and nation-state unified the Mizo in a number of ways, and

Christianity was one of the means of unification. So it is not surprising that in the 1940s, leaders in the Church often became the spokespersons of their people, and the Church bodies became deliberative assemblies for political matters. However, as politics took on a life of its own, Church leaders became wary of their institution becoming simply a vehicle for political action. So as the full-fledged armed resistance to the Indian nation-state developed in the 1960s, the relationship between Church and political movement was one of ambivalence. On the one hand, the Church sympathized with some of the aims of the resisters, and the resistance movement identified itself as a movement to preserve Christianity in the face of Hindu fundamentalism. On the other hand, the Mizoram Presbyterian Church was the first Mizo body to raise objections and criticisms to the violence being perpetrated by both Mizo nationalists and the Indian army.[46] Soon the Baptist Church issued messages condemning violence. A further development was that the churches came together ecumenically and initiated several moves to bring peace between the warring factions, and in fact the churches were the key mediators in forging a ceasefire in 1986. Still, the churches could not have performed this function had they not been seen by both sides as representatives of the Mizo people as a whole.

Today, although Mizoram is a state of India, the Mizo people see themselves as distinct from the majority of Indians who have completely different ethnic, cultural, and religious roots. A key component in this distinction is the Christian religion, which the Mizo have appropriated as their own religion. Christianity among the Mizo, Naga, Khasi, and other peoples of Northeast India is a religion that has helped the peoples define themselves against the majority peoples of their countries.

Conclusion

The three different Christian communities that we have looked at in our exploration of Christianity in South Asia illustrate three different modes in which Christians live out their faith in their religious context. Notice that we have defined "context" in a variety of ways. For the Syrian Christians, the context was the

state of Kerala; for the Chamar Christians, the context was their local Hindu community; and for the Mizos, the context was the nation-state of India. The three communities we have looked at certainly do not characterize the only ways that South Asian Christians live among their neighbors of differing faith traditions. Rather, they illustrate typical modes of living out a Christian identity in the midst of religious pluralism, in societies and nations where Christianity is a minority religion.

One may ask what difference Christian communities make in the midst of communities of many other faiths. Generally speaking, there are two important contributions that Christianity makes in South Asia. The first is that it provides a religious alternative to the various dominant religions in this area of the world. Christianity provides an alternative worldview, ethos, belief structure, and community to that of the majority of the population in any particular context. How different this alternative is varies considerably, as we have seen, in various parts of South Asia. Yet there is no question that Christianity provides a somewhat unique religious vision and experience in the mix of South Asian religions. This alternative is important for those who for whatever reason find the dominant religion unsatisfactory. People become Christian and remain within the Christian fold because this particular faith addresses the existential questions or life problems in ways that are compelling to them. Over the last few centuries, Christianity as an alternative religion has been especially important to those who have felt oppressed within the religious system of the majority. Thus Christians from outcaste or *dalit* backgrounds throughout the Indian subcontinent have found the Christian message of God's love and concern for all humanity, and the Christian concept of religious community as a fellowship of sisters and brothers equally beloved by their Lord Jesus, particularly liberating. The same is true for peoples of Northeast India, as they have struggled to maintain their identity and way of life in the midst of an enormous nation-state that has a radically different worldview and ethos from their own. How well any Christian community actually realizes its ideals is of course open to debate. Yet the ideals themselves remain appealing and compelling to those who are oppressed.

One of the attractive features of Christianity as an alternative religion is that it does not require people to give up their cultural identity when they become Christian. South Asian Christians generally speak the same language, dress the same way, and are free to eat the same food as their neighbors from different religious backgrounds. In fact, as the case of the Mizo demonstrates, Christianity can help people maintain and even strengthen their cultural identity, by channeling it into Christian forms that can withstand the pressures of the modern world. Thus for many South Asians, Christianity is an alternative religious vision and social reality that provides different perspectives and possibilities from the dominant religion, without demanding a loss of Asian or ethnic identity.

The second way in which Christianity makes a difference in South Asia is that it provides a vital link to the wider world. Along with Islam and Buddhism, Christianity is a highly international religion. South Asian Christianity has provided valuable access to international resources, not simply for Christians but more importantly, perhaps, for the countries' populations in general. Thus Western education, which has come to be highly prized in South Asia, has been introduced, developed, and strengthened by Christians in their respective countries. The same can be said about certain modern ideas and ideals, such as those of human equality across social boundaries, of the dignity of each individual, and of the equality of women and men. Christians in South Asia also have at times provided access to helpful technologies and material developments, for example, in agriculture.

Let me close with four general observations that emerge from our survey. The first is that Christians in South Asia have developed their own identity in a religiously pluralistic context. They provide an alternative religious vision and experience to the dominant religions in this part of the world. The second observation is that South Asian Christians have developed a number of different ways to live out that identity in their respective contexts. How Christianity actually interacts with other religious traditions in South Asia varies greatly over the region. The third observation is that Christians in South Asia have always maintained ties and relationships with Christians from other countries such as Syria, Persia, England, and the United States of America. Since the 1960s strong ties have developed between Christians in South Asia and in other parts of Asia. The fourth observation is that no matter how different are the ways of being Christian in South Asia, and no matter how valuable the links with Christians in other parts of the world, all Christian communities in this region have been deeply influenced and shaped by the religious and cultural milieu in which they have found themselves. In other words, South Asian Christianity is profoundly South Asian: Christians have learned to fashion and live out their faith through constant interaction with their neighbors of different faiths and religions.

Notes and References

[1] For early Christianity in South Asia, see A. M. Mundadan, *History of Christianity in India, Volume 1: From the Beginning Up To the Middle of the Sixteenth Century* (Bangalore: Church History Association of India, 1984); Ian Gillman and Hans-Joachim Klimkeit, *Christians in Asia Before 1500* (Ann Arbor, MI: University of Michigan Press, 1999), 154–202; and Samuel Hugh Moffett, *A History of Christianity in Asia, Vol. 1: Beginnings to 1500* (New York: HarperCollins, 1992), 24–44, 265–71.

[2] For Nestorian Christianity, see Moffett, 168–84; and Gillman and Klimkeit, 13–19.

[3] For Roman Catholic beginnings in South Asia, see Mundadan, 240–521; *New Catholic Encyclopedia*, 2nd edn. (Detroit, MI: Thomson Gale, 2003), s.v. "Bangladesh: The Catholic Church In," "Bhutan: The Catholic Church In," "India: Christianity In," "Nepal: The Catholic Church In," "Pakistan: The Catholic Church In," "Sri Lanka: The Catholic Church In."

[4] C. J. Fuller, quoted in Susan Visvanathan, *The Christians of Kerala: History, Belief and Ritual among the Yakoba* (New Delhi: Oxford University Press, 1993), 2.

[5] S. G. Pothen, *The Syrian Christians of Kerala* (Bombay: Asia Publishing House, 1963), 55, 91.

[6] Robert Eric Frykenberg, *Christianity in India: From the Beginnings to the Present* (Oxford: Oxford University Press, 2008), 139.

[7] Rowena Robinson, *Christians of India* (New Delhi: Sage Publications, 2003), 44.

[8] Brian Stanley, *The History of the Baptist Missionary Society, 1792–1992* (Edinburgh: T&T Clark, 1992), 43.

[9] David B. Barrett, George T. Kurian and Todd M. Johnson, *World Christian Encyclopedia, Vol. 1*, 2nd edn. (Oxford: Oxford University Press, 2001), 98, 117, 360, 527, 570, 695.

[10] The 2.3 percent figure is from the 2001 census of India, which is compiled by the government of India, available online at:<http://censusindia.gov.in/Census_Data_2001/India_at_glance/religion.aspx>; the 6.2 percent figure is from Barrett et al., 360.

[11] Figures are from: <http://censusindia.gov.in/Census_Data_2001/India_at_glance/religion.aspx>, 2001census of India.

[12] The figure of 1.6 percent is from: <www.statpak.gov.pk/depts/pco/statistics/other_tables/pop_by_religion.pdf>, the 1998 census of Pakistan, while the 2.5 percent is from Barrett et al., 570.

[13] The figure of 0.3 percent is from <http://www.bbs.gov.bd/dataindex/datasheet.xls>, the 2004 Bangladesh, and the 0.7 percent figure from Barrett et al., 98. For the background of Bangladeshi Christians, see Barrett et al., 99.

[14] See: <http://www.statistics.gov.lk/PopHouSat/PDF/Population/p9p9%20Religion.pdf> for 2001 government statistics, and Barrett et al., 696. According to Barrrett et al., 117, 527, Bhutan's population comprises 0.5 percent Christians, and Nepal's 2.4 percent.

[15] Michael Amaladoss, "My Pilgrimage in Mission," *International Bulletin of Missionary Research* 31/1 (Jan. 2007): 21.

[16] Robinson, *Christians of India*, 41, 78, 81.

[17] Ibid., 41.

[18] Ibid., 106.

[19] Susan Bayly, *Saints, Goddesses and Kings: Muslims and Christians in South Indian Society, 1700–1900* (Cambridge: Cambridge University Press, 1989), 263–5.

[20] Visvanathan, *The Christians of Kerala*, 133.

[21] Robinson, *Christians of India*, 105.

[22] Visvanathan, *The Christians of Kerala*, 106–8.

[23] Ibid., 6–8.

[24] Dr Sathianathan Clarke of Wesley Theological Seminary, a well-known scholar of Dalit Christianity, estimates that of the 25 million Christians in India, Syrian Christians number about 5 million (20 percent), Christians in the Northeast about 3.5 million (15 percent), plains tribal and Nadar Christians between 1 and 2 million (5 percent), which means that Dalit Christians comprise roughly 60 percent of the total Indian Christian body (private correspondence with the author on December 16, 2009). The website <www.dalitchristians.com/Html/survey.htm> estimates that Dalits make up 80 percent of Indian Christians.

[25] For a useful discussion of the overall framework in which to study South Asian Christianity, see Rowena Robinson, *Conversion, Continuity and Change: Lived Christianity in Southern Goa* (New Delhi: Sage Publications, 1998), 9–31; and Rowena Robinson, *Christians of India*, 11–25.

[26] Material for this section is taken from Mathew Schmalz, *A Space for Redemption: Catholic Tactics in Hindu North India* (PhD Dissertation, Chicago, IL: University of Chicago, 1998).

[27] Schmalz, *A Space for Redemption*, 135.

[28] Ibid., 36.

[29] Ibid., 136–8.

[30] Ibid., 30–1.

[31] Ibid., 10–11.

[32] Ibid., 21 ff.

[33] Ibid., 28.

[34] Ibid., 30.

[35] Ibid., 31.

[36] Lalsangkima Pachuau, *Ethnic Identity and Christianity* (Frankfurt: Peter Lang, 2002), 45.

[37] Material for this section is taken from Pachuau, *Ethnic Identity*, 130ff.

[38] Pachuau, *Ethnic Identity*, 68.

[39] Ibid., 71.

[40] Ibid., 74–5.

[41] Ibid., 76.

[42] Ibid., 119–20.

[43] Ibid., 131.

[44] Ibid., 78.

[45] For an extended discussion, see Pachuau, *Ethnic Identity*, 145–71.

[46] Pachuau, *Ethnic Identity*, 163.

Further Reading

Brown, Judith M. and Robert Eric Frykenberg, ed. *Christians, Cultural Interactions, and India's Religious Traditions*. Grand Rapids: Eerdmans, 2002.

Fernando, Leonard and G. Gispert-Sauch. *Christianity in India: Two Thousand Years of Faith*. New Delhi: Penguin Books India, 2004.

Frykenberg, Robert Eric. *Christianity in India: From the Beginnings to the Present*. Oxford: Oxford University Press, 2008.

Mundadan, A. M. *History of Christianity in India, Volume 1: From the Beginning up to the Middle of the Sixteenth Century*. Bangalore: Church History Association of India, 1984.

Pachuau, Lalsangkima. *Ethnic Identity and Christianity*. Frankfurt am Main: Peter Lang, 2002.

Robinson, Rowena. *Christians of India*. New Delhi: Sage Publications, 2003.

Schmalz, Mathew. "A Space for Redemption: Catholic Tactics in Hindu North India," PhD diss., Chicago, IL: University of Chicago, 1998.

Visvanathan, Susan. *The Christians of Kerala: History, Belief and Ritual among the Yakoba*. New Delhi: Oxford University Press, 1993.

Webster, John C. B. *The Dalit Christians: A History*. New Delhi: ISPCK, 2000.

8

Christianity in Southeast Asia
Similarity and Difference in a Culturally Diverse Region

Barbara Watson Andaya

Introduction

Consisting of 11 nations divided between "mainland" (Myanmar, Thailand, Cambodia, Laos, Vietnam) and "island" (Philippines, Malaysia, Singapore, Brunei, Indonesia, Timor Leste), Southeast Asia has a combined population of around 586 million. As followers of the last world religion to reach Southeast Asia, Christians number approximately 21 percent. Roman Catholicism is overwhelmingly dominant in the Philippines and Timor Leste, but elsewhere all Christians are national minorities and are concentrated in areas that were historically less influenced by Buddhism or Islam.

Overviews of Southeast Asian Christianity are rare, and academic studies tend to concentrate on specific countries, ethnic groups, or denominations. This tendency can be attributed to the difficulty of generalizing about the Christian experience. Not only was missionizing initiated by six different colonizers (Portugal, Spain, France, the Netherlands, Britain, the United States), but the two broad streams of Catholicism and Protestantism incorporate numerous interpretations and practices. The variety of regional Christianity also reflects Southeast Asia's cultural diversity and the different historical contexts in which Christianization occurred. In some areas mission work began as early as 400 years ago, while in others it only gathered pace in the late nineteenth century or as recently as the 1960s.

Despite these disparities we can still identify themes that highlight similarities and contrasts among Southeast Asia's Christian communities and that find a counterpart in many societies discussed in this volume.

Historical Background

Christianity came to Southeast Asia because of the expansion of European maritime trade in the late fifteenth century. The religious and commercial rivalry of the foremost Catholic powers, Spain and Portugal, led to the Treaty of Tordesillas (1494), which divided the world into two spiritual jurisdictions. In return for a commitment to missionize, the Portuguese Crown was allotted all newly encountered realms East of a line drawn through the Atlantic; the Western half was given to Spain. In the late sixteenth century the Spanish successfully challenged Portugal's claim to the Philippine archipelago, and with the imposition of colonial rule Christianity spread over all lowland areas except the Muslim South. The Portuguese committed fewer resources to their Southeast Asian domain and the Catholic heritage today is most evident in Timor Leste and Eastern Indonesia. The Dutch East India Company (VOC), which arrived in the early seventeenth century, was primarily interested in trade, but the company's Protestant ministers did undertake evangelization among Catholic and animist groups, especially in Eastern Indonesia.

Introducing World Christianity, First Edition. Edited by Charles E. Farhadian.
© 2012 Blackwell Publishing Ltd. Published 2012 by Blackwell Publishing Ltd.

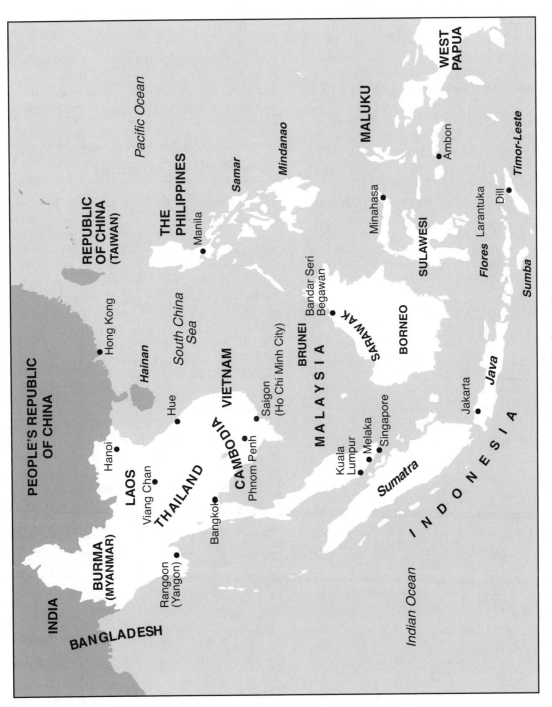

Map 8.1 Southeast Asia

Missionary efforts in mainland Southeast Asia were generally half-hearted, since commercial attractions were considerably less than in the island world and Buddhist societies showed little interest in adopting Christianity. Because Vietnam lay within the orbit of China, where Catholicism had been relatively successful, there were hopes that missions here would yield better results. From the early seventeenth century several Catholic Orders and subsequently the French-sponsored Society for Foreign Missions began work in Tonkin (North Vietnam) and its Southern rival, Co-chinchina. Despite the proscription of the ancestor veneration so central to Confucian philosophy, Christianity continued to attract followers and a local priest-hood helped maintain small congregations even when missionaries were expelled or went into hiding. A concerted Vietnamese campaign against those who refused to renounce the "perverse religion" of Christianity provided the justification for the French invasion of 1858.

During the nineteenth and early twentieth centuries, European colonization of all Southeast Asia (except Siam, known as Thailand from 1939) was rationalized by the argument that local populations were being "civilized." Protestant churches and missionary societies devoted serious attention to evangelism, while new Catholic Orders joined those already well established in the field. For the first time Protestant women arrived in Southeast Asia as missionaries, while Orders of nuns, previously confined to the Philippines, began to work as teachers and nurses in other areas of Southeast Asia. The privileging of Christians in the colonial system led to a noticeable increase in conversions, especially among animist groups and migrant Asians. As nationalist movements developed, however, questions were raised about the depth of Christian commitment to independence because of perceived ties to colonial administrators.

The outbreak of the Pacific War in 1941 marks a watershed in the history of Southeast Asian Christianity, since most Western clergy were imprisoned during the Japanese Occupation. Over the last 60 years there has been a steady process of "indigenization," and Church administration in all countries is now under local control. The nature of missionizing across Southeast Asia helps explain variations in the size of Christian populations, but also raises questions about the moti-

vations that have drawn people to Christianity and their relationship with the state and other belief systems. Because many areas are still perceived as fertile areas for evangelization, Southeast Asia is an intriguing arena in which to study the process of localization as ordinary Christians seek to reconcile the demands of their own environment with a world religion that is itself being reshaped by globalized communication on an unprecedented scale.

Encountering Christianity

An appreciation of the ways in which becoming "Christian" has varied over time and in different contexts is central to any analysis of Christianity in contemporary Southeast Asia. We need to understand how beliefs change and why individuals and communities assume new Christian identities because so often the ideas missionaries introduced were not merely alien, but at odds with local values. During the first encounters, when missionaries ordered the destruction of statues, objects, and buildings associated with beliefs in ancestral deities and powerful spirits, potential converts often expressed fear of supernatural retaliation. In this context any calamitous event – epidemic, drought, crop failure – could easily be attributed to non-human forces angry at an unwelcome intrusion. In the seventeenth century rivalries between Christian denominations imposed another layer of contention when VOC ministers in Eastern Indonesia reviled Catholic priests as the devil's agents, denounced veneration of holy images as idolatry, and pressed Catholics to convert to Protestantism.

Repeated complaints from early missionaries, both Catholic and Protestant, that new converts were essentially "baptized heathens" whose lifestyles remained largely unchanged remind us that Christianity's stipulations were often difficult to accept, especially in relation to marriage and the family. Missionary stress on monogamy and virginity conflicted with social norms in cultures where men customarily displayed wealth and status by supporting numerous women, or where pre-nuptial sex was accepted as part of village life. The exhortation that Christians should "turn the other cheek" was equally bewildering in communities where internecine raiding was motivated by the cultural demand for vengeance, or where the taking of heads was necessary to prove manhood, to end a period of mourning, or ensure community fertility. Vietnamese rulers, outraged that converts would no longer bow before ancestral altars, believed that priests had "mesmerized" their people, and even in the 1960s Akha villages in Northern Thailand were expelling Christians who refused to join in community rituals.

On the other hand, Christianity had its attractions, sometimes reflecting simple pragmatism. Pressured to affirm their religious affiliation, many people in what is now Indonesia have chosen Christianity rather than Islam because they can then continue to keep pigs and eat pork. At a deeper level, acceptance has been facilitated when there are perceived parallels with local traditions. In nineteenth-century Myanmar legends of a lost "Golden Book" that would one day be returned contributed to Karen reception of American Baptists and their Bible, while myths about a magical text containing "songs of teaching" helped Timorese make connections to Dutch missionaries and their "holy writ." In a similar vein, the most favored Catholic saints were those whose lives invoked elements of familiarity. San Roque was popular in the Philippines because he protected the sick, but statues depicting a dog as his constant companion struck an empathetic

Figure 8.1 Our Lady of Antipolo was brought to the Philippines from Mexico in 1626. From Monina A. Mercado, *Antipolo: A Shrine to Our Lady*. Craftnotes/ Aletheia Foundation: Manila, 1980. Plate 47. Photograph by Monina A. Mercado, reproduced with permission of the author.

chord in cultures where hunting was intrinsic to male roles. In all Catholic areas we can see the universal appeal of the Virgin Mary. Her representation as a dark-skinned Filipina or wearing a Vietnamese *ao dai* symbolizes the central role she occupies in Catholic life, and points to Southeast Asia's rich potential as a field for Marian studies.

Healing

Over the centuries, in Southeast Asia as elsewhere, potential converts have been drawn to Christianity by its reputation as a religion of healing. When missionaries first arrived in the sixteenth and seventeenth centuries they found that stories of Christ's miracles and their own knowledge of medicinal remedies melded easily with indigenous notions that linked healing with ritual expertise. Women in particular saw the Virgin Mary as a human mother who would have a special interest in maternal and infant welfare; crosses, rosaries, and holy images were regarded as protective amulets; the sacraments, most notably baptism, were viewed as a potent defense against illness, especially for infants. Missionaries exploited these beliefs by deliberately making the baptismal ceremony as solemn as possible and by using holy water freely, especially when administering to the sick. Even when Christian sacraments did not bring about recovery, faith in the efficacy of holy water remained, and the outbreak of any epidemic typically saw a marked rise in the number of baptisms of adults as well as children.

Nevertheless, because the rituals of baptism and confirmation were interpreted as symbolic alliances with Europeans, the Christianity/healing association was not without problems. In nineteenth-century Vietnam there were even rumors that missionaries cast spells over their patients by administering potions containing the crushed eyeballs of dying converts. At a more prosaic level, it has been difficult to discourage the notion that an individual can "bargain" with God or the saints for recovery from illness, while for many Southeast Asians spirit propitiation has retained its attraction as an alternative source of supernatural assistance when Western medicines are unavailable or ineffective. Although medical missionaries and their dispensaries were relatively successful in drawing potential converts into a church environment, especially the poor and disadvantaged, doubts were also raised about whether gratitude for medical treatment led to long-term Christian commitment. In Buddhist Siam, where all missionaries were termed "mo" or doctor, it became all too clear that a growth in patients treated by mission hospitals (890 in 1908 and 4,999 in 1936) did not translate into an increased number of converts.[1]

For their part, despite periodic anti-clericalism among politicians at home, colonial regimes were generally willing to provide subsidies to Church-supported health care, realizing its value in reaching remote areas beyond European administrations. In subsequent years, governments of Southeast Asian countries where Christianity is a minority religion have also agreed to admit medical missionaries, although the claim that hospitals become centers for proselytizing has heightened sensitivities. In some cases government suspicion has resulted in extreme measures. Following the 1962 military coup in Myanmar, for example, all foreign missionaries were expelled and all medical institutions nationalized. In contemporary Indonesia, where Christian hospitals enjoy a reputation for providing superior medical services, many Muslims believe that poor patients are deliberately targeted for conversion. These suspicions have been fueled because of a marked rise in revivalist assembles where reports of miraculous healing have given Christianity an unprecedented visibility. Although leaders of mainstream churches are concerned about unsupported claims of divine intervention, these gatherings serve to remind us of the entrenched belief that Christianity and its agents offer those sick in body and spirit a unique access to supernatural power.

Education

If the promise of physical as well as spiritual healing has been central to the appeal of Christianity and its localization in Southeast Asia, so too have the opportunities for gaining practical skills through education. Missionaries have always accorded school attendance a high priority because the classroom is considered the most effective environment in which to redirect a community's attitudes and behavior. By the seventeenth century, Catholic Orders, especially the Jesuits, had developed highly efficient teaching methods for use in non-European cultures, such as training a cohort

of senior students (*decuriones*) who could assist in the classroom. The results of this religious pedagogy were most evident in the Philippines because children in Christian settlements came under strict friar surveillance. Meanwhile, the solidification of the Spanish regime underscored the benefits of a Catholic education, since literacy and knowledge of Spanish were essential for appointment to the low-level administrative offices available to Indios. The possibility of entry into the service of the Catholic Church was also enticing. Although the regular Orders refused to accept even well-born Indios, a very small number (including *mestizos*, less than 50 during the first 200 years of Spanish rule) gained higher education at mission-run seminaries and were ordained as parish priests. The *beaterios*, or houses for pious women, also received Filipino women and helped provide basic education for many Filipino girls.

In Eastern Indonesia, where the VOC displaced Portuguese and Spanish interests in the seventeenth century, considerable effort was expended in persuading local leaders to accept Protestantism and thereby affirm their alliance with the Dutch. This involved a twofold conversion, not merely of "heathens" but of individuals who had been baptized as Catholics by Portuguese or Spanish priests. Malay, long established as a lingua franca in the Western archipelago, was selected as the medium for religious instruction, although it was still unfamiliar to many communities in the East. A succession of ministers produced translations of prayers, catechisms, and biblical selections, while Malay-speaking Ambonese Christians were assigned as teachers. These men were often the only religious authority in their community because there were so few Dutch ministers. Charged with monitoring church attendance and preparing congregations for baptism and Holy Communion, their influence in Eastern Indonesia's scattered island settlements was considerable. Indeed, it was schoolteachers, angered by salary reductions and rumours of changes in Church and school organization, who provided the major support for an anti-Dutch movement in Ambon in 1817.

During the nineteenth century the imposition of colonial regimes reinforced the value of a Western education, then available only in religious institutions. The influence missionary teachers could exercise is

Figure 8.2 Cathedral, Vigan, the Philippines. Because of frequent earthquakes the Spanish built churches low to the ground with separate belltowers. Photograph: Barbara Watson Andaya, reproduced by permission of the author.

remarkably demonstrated in a newly discovered autobiographical Malay text, *Hikayat Hikamat* (*The Story of Hikamat*), composed around 1861. Hikamat's memoirs include not merely descriptions of boyish escapades but of the theological discussions with his headmaster and the spiritual visions that eventually led to his acceptance of Christianity. The attraction of mission schooling was also evident in Java, where converts to Christianity had typically been from lower socio-economic groups. By the early twentieth century, however, a new generation of middle-class Javanese was also severing links with tradition by accepting the vision of modernity that Christianity offered. Such examples served to reinforce the colonial view that missionary education was a valuable means of spreading "civilization." Accordingly, although the United States attempted to separate Church and state following its colonization of the Philippines in 1898, Protestant initiatives were encouraged in an effort to

break the Catholic hold over education. Some Filipinos, largely middle-level bureaucrats, servants, lawyers, and small entrepreneurs, elected to convert to Protestantism and a few families became nationally prominent. Fidel Ramos, thus far the only Protestant president of the Philippines (1992–8), came from such a background.

It should nevertheless be emphasized that colonialism by no means opened the door to unrestricted mission education, since governments remained concerned that evangelism in areas where Christians were a minority would cause social unrest. The decision to restrict missionary activities to specific districts thought to be amenable to Christianization fostered stereotypes of certain ethnic groups as "more loyal," and colonial armies and police forces included a disproportionate number of Christians. Christian soldiers from Ambon and Minahasa were thus a majority in the colonial army of the Netherlands Indies, and during

World War I, three of the 16 companies in the Burma Rifles were composed of Christian Karens.

The association between ethnic identity and certain ways of "being Christian" was strengthened because missionary organizations were frequently assigned to separate areas in order to avoid conflict. The long-term effects of such policies are especially obvious in Indonesia. Dutch missionaries arrived in Minahasa (Northern Sulawesi) in 1821, and by the end of the nineteenth century the population was more than 90 percent Christian. Today, other Indonesians still regard Minahasans as Westernized, well-educated, and commercially astute. Another example of the mesh between education, ethnic identity, and a particular church is provided by the Toba Batak of North Sumatra, where representatives of the German-based Rhenish Missionary Society (RMG) began working in the 1880s. By developing congregations based on existing clan structures, by appointing rajas as church leaders, and by retaining the Toba language for liturgy, the RMG helped in the formation of a Toba Batak identity that placed a high value on education as a path to *hamajuan* or progress. A different basis for local identity is found in the district of Larantuka (Eastern Flores), where the Nagi trace their Portuguese heritage and their Catholicism back to the seventeenth century, and maintain a particular veneration for Bunda (Mother) Maria, Larantuka's Queen.

Figure 8.3 Good Friday procession in Larantuka, Flores, Indonesia. The lay brotherhood, the Confreria of the Holy Rosary, escorts the image of Bunda (Mother) Maria. Photograph: Barbara Watson Andaya, reproduced by permission of the author.

The perceived advantages of obtaining a Christian education can also be seen among migrant Asians, especially the overseas Chinese. In Thailand, where missionaries had little success in attracting Thai Buddhists, Bangkok's Maitri Chit Church (1837) was the first Chinese church in Asia and Chinese assistants became a mainstay in the mission posts. In the 1920s, missionaries in the Netherlands Indies began to develop strategies to attract Chinese to Christianity, especially outside Java. Though Christian schools slowly began to attract more Chinese pupils, family pressure to remain "Chinese" was strong and conversion did not necessarily result from a Dutch-style education. However, membership in the Chinese-dominated Gereja Kristen Indonesia increased dramatically after the 1965 army coup as Chinese sought to avoid accusations of communist sympathies, and today around 70 percent of Indonesian Chinese are Christian. From a Christian perspective the most painless absorption of Chinese has been in the Philippines. In the seventeenth century the decision to convert may have been purely pragmatic, since non-Christian Chinese were periodically subject to expulsion edicts and baptism, necessary for marriage to a Christian Filipina, could also open access to land acquisition. Yet a substantial number of those ordained as parish priests were Chinese *mestizos*, and in 1987 the Pope canonized the first Filipino saint, the part-Chinese Lorenzo Ruiz (*c*.1600–37).

The association of specific groups with Christianity became more pronounced through the twentieth century as colonial administrations extended their control over remote highlands and islands regions. Regarded as inferior by the more dominant ethnic and religious groups, these areas had often been targets for exploitation and slave raiding, or regarded as "primitive." Whether working among hill tribes in Northeast Thailand, mountain peoples in the Philippines, or the highlanders of Western New Guinea, missionaries became bearers of "civilization" and its symbols of modernity – soap, needles, beads, and steel axes. "Becoming Christian" was associated with the adoption of a very different lifestyle, as choices of marriage partners were aligned with missionary preferences, bride-price and polygamy abandoned, housing became more "hygienic," semi-clothed bodies were covered, and work patterns changed to follow the calendar of Church services, prayer meetings, and feast days.

In some cases, it has been argued, these lifestyle changes so challenged existing cosmologies and social relationships that a vacuum was left in which the new religion could be accommodated. The eradication of head-hunting so central to the culture of upland societies like the Ilongot of the Philippines deprived men of a traditional means of acquiring status, while forcing fundamental reconfigurations about the affirmation of community fertility. Christian rituals, the acquisition of a Western-style education and the ability to access prestige through gaining leadership roles in Church life have become an important means by which tribal minorities seek to claim they that are both equal to and different from more dominant religious and ethnic groups. The use of minority languages in translations and Christian teachings affirm a local relevance, while the sense of belonging to a world religion imbues marginalized communities with a new confidence. The Iban of the Malaysian state of Sarawak, with access to mission education, provide one example of an ethnic group that has been well placed to record their own histories and oral legends, and thus to reinforce their identity within the nation-state.

Yet the acceptance of education has not always proceeded smoothly. In the early years the loss of family labor was seen as akin to *corvée*, and gifts such as rice or punishment in the form of fines were often necessary to persuade parents to send their children to the Christian school. Of necessity, missionaries often relied on teachers from ethnic groups where Christianity was well established, but this could arouse resentment. On the Indonesian island of Sumba, for instance, there was considerable resistance to Christianity because Dutch missionaries used teachers from neighboring Savu and only slowly became aware of the long-standing enmity between the two societies. In some cases the very relevance of a religious education may be questioned. Despite the very high value placed on biblical knowledge, a younger generation of Dani in West New Guinea is concerned that mission-sponsored schools are insufficiently oriented toward the practical and vocational skills needed to advance in the modern world. A more serious issue concerns the restrictions that governments may impose. Although there are still over 400 mission schools in Malaysia, where Islam is the state religion, their character has changed since independence. The curriculum is now under the surveillance of the Ministry of Education that also appoints or approves staff; even display of Christian symbols like the cross has come under fire. Nonetheless, these schools have still retained a reputation for quality education and their graduates include prominent men and women from all races.

In regional terms the most far-reaching effect of Christian-based education became apparent in the new opportunities provided for women. Even in the sixteenth century, the great missionary Francis Xavier held special classes for women and girls because he realized that the family environment would be critical in any effort to inculcate Christian teachings. In later years the arrival of missionary wives and female religious Orders meant the opening of more schools for girls. Initially the focus was on housekeeping skills intended to produce Christian wives and mothers, but the emphasis soon shifted to vocational training that would equip girls to become teachers, nurses, and midwives. In many Southeast Asian societies women had played a prominent role in indigenous ritual, and even as these roles disappeared Christianity opened up new spaces for female agency. In the Philippines, for example, the number of primary schools for girls steadily increased, and by 1860 Orders of nuns had established several institutions dedicated to female education. In 1973, the Ateneo de Manila University began to admit female students, and can count two presidents, Cory Aquino and Gloria Macapagal-Arroyo, among its graduates. Nuns have also taken a leading role in political and social life, like Sister Mary John Manazan, the founder and President of GABRIELA, an umbrella organization for women's activist groups. In other countries Christian women may be less prominent, but there can be no doubt that their support has been crucial. Although the Catholic Church does not ordain women, congregations are heavily female and women are the backbone of lay organizations. Female leadership is more obvious in Protestant churches, where pastors are quite commonly women, and on several theological campuses in Indonesia female students well outnumber males.

Christianity and the State

Christianity has had an ambiguous relationship with independent nations in Southeast Asia because of its association with colonialism and Western influence, and because of shifting political environments. In Timor Leste, the newest Southeast Asia state, the Catholic Church was once regarded as an arm of the Portuguese colonial government, but membership rose dramatically after the Indonesian invasion in 1975. Under the leadership of Bishop Carlos Belo, the Church emerged as the focus of Timorese resistance, benefiting from the Vatican's endorsement of inculturation and the sense of identity fostered by using Tetum rather than Indonesian as the liturgical language. Because 97 percent of Timor Leste's population is Catholic, the Church continues to exercise considerable influence in the formulation of government policies and in shaping public opinion.

The recent history of Timor Leste clearly illustrates that successful opposition to unpopular governments is dependent on the support of ordinary people and on the degree to which Christianity has established its patriotic credentials. Nowhere is this better exemplified than in the Philippines, where Filipinos have long understood that "being Christian" does not entail unquestioning support of the Church or the government. Anti-Spanish rebellions frequently invoked Christian symbols and the *Pasyon,* the vernacular version of Christ's life, inspired peasant movements by comparing Filipino sufferings to those of the persecuted Christ. Devout Filipinos were also ready to challenge the regular Orders, which steadily refused to ordain native priests and condemned advocates of clerical equality as enemies of both the Church and Spain. Indeed, it was the Spanish execution of three priests as insurrectionists that eventually led to the anticolonial Revolution of 1896. Revolutionary *illustrados* (enlightened men) like the national hero José Rizal were products of an elite Catholic education but were bitterly opposed to the stranglehold of the "friarocracy" (*frialocracia*) and its alliance with the Spanish administration. In more recent times clerics have continued to see themselves as the nation's conscience. President Ferdinand Marcos (1965–86) initially enjoyed Church approval because of his opposition to communism, but his declaration of martial law in 1972 aroused much

criticism from priests and nuns influenced by liberation theology. Led by Cardinal Jaime Sin, the Church played a central role in the "people's movement" that toppled the Marcos regime, and continues to exercise enormous influence over Philippine politics and family life. Clause XV of the 1987 Constitution, for example, specifically forbids both divorce and abortion.

The great issue confronting the Philippine government today concerns the future of the Muslims in the South, who number around 5 percent of the total population and are concentrated on the large and fertile island of Mindanao. By the late 1960s, a policy of assisted migration from the Christian North to Mindanao meant that Muslims were becoming an impoverished minority in their own homeland. Christian arrogation of Muslim land and growing economic disparities exacerbated calls for secession from Islamic leaders. During the past 40 years continuing violence between Muslim forces and government armies has displaced more than a million people and left more than 120,000 dead. An Autonomous Region of Muslim Mindanao was created in 1989, but leaders of the Muslim separatist movement still envisage themselves as defenders of Philippine Muslim territory and traditions against Christian chauvinism. Indeed, a 1997 study indicated that the Christian image of Muslims is invariably more negative than the reverse, and Christians are often unenthusiastic about interreligious dialogue. While both Christians and Muslims agree that land disputes have been a basic cause of hostility, Christians believe the minority Muslims are trying to control Mindanao, while Muslims feel the government has consistently failed to treat them fairly. In 2008, violence erupted once more after the collapse of protracted peace negotiations, with tensions worsening because of the re-emergence of Christian vigilantes.

A contrasting situation is found in countries where Christianity is a minority faith because the relationship with the state involves issues of patriotism and personal loyalty. In colonial Vietnam, for instance, the Catholic Church had been a vehement opponent of communism. This position was substantially modified when Ho Chi Minh declared independence in 1945, and Vietnamese priests made a deliberate effort to demonstrate support for the fledging republic. The Catholic minority, however, still feared retribution for its historical links with the French. In the ensuing years

Church opposition to Ho Chi Minh intensified, and the division of the country in 1954 pitted the communist North against the more Catholic South. Church land in Northern Vietnam was confiscated and Southern churches became a target for communist hostility when the country was re-unified in 1975. From 1986 government attitudes became more liberal with the policy of *doi moi* ("renovation"), and in 1999 religious rights were guaranteed as long as the state was not threatened.

This modus vivendi remains fragile because a revitalized Church has now become more open in pressing the government on matters like the return of land. Another concern relates to the presence of Protestant missionaries, who have been permitted to initiate aid programs in the highlands. Hanoi's suspicion that Christian communities have become centers for subversion has led to harassment as well as reported cases of violence. A comparable situation holds in Laos, where government distrust has been reinforced by evangelism among the Hmong hill tribes, many of whom were used by the French and Americans against the communist armies. Although some training colleges remain under the control of Vietnamese Catholics, a number of churches have been closed and no foreign missionaries are permitted.

In these state–Church interactions, the globalization of all religious faiths has injected new tensions into communal disputes that might once been contained at the local level. The roots of ethnic violence are commonly economic, but the articulation of differences in religious terms often leads to accusations of persecution and appeals for assistance to a worldwide audience. Myanmar, where Christians comprise only 4 percent of the population, is a case in point. The military junta has imposed tight restrictions on Church activities, claiming that they act as a conduit for Western influence and encourage opposition among Christianized ethnic minorities. The foremost example is the Karen, whose embattled campaign to acquire their own homeland has continued since 1948. Although only around 40 percent of the 4.5 million Karen are Christian, the fact that baptism and church meetings can precede a military operation make it easy to portray their resistance as a Christian rather than an ethnic struggle. This impression is intensified because international supporters publicize the Karen cause

through Church networks, websites, and sponsorship of lecture tours like that by General Bo Mya (1928–2007), former president of the Karen National Union and a devout member of the Seventh-day Adventist Church.

The interaction between Christian minorities, the state, and international Christian connections is particularly evident in those countries where Islam is a majority religion. Islam is the state religion in Malaysia and Brunei, and since virtually all Malays are Muslim, Christian congregations are overwhelmingly comprised of Chinese, Indian, and Eurasian, with the addition in Borneo of non-Malay indigenous groups. The extension of the Malay/Muslim and non-Malay/ non-Muslim divide to include even linguistic issues is well illustrated in ongoing debates as to whether "Allah" can be used in Malay publications referring to the Christian God. The shadow of the 1969 ethnic riots still hangs over the country, and Church leaders are fully aware of the potential for conflict when opposition is couched in religious terms. Despite heated Internet exchanges, public debate on government policies toward Christianity has therefore been relatively restrained.

Friction resulting from the ethnicity/religious overlap is especially pronounced in Indonesia, where the relationship between Christianity and the state has been a controversial issue from the nation's very birth. Christianized ethnic minorities feared discrimination under a postcolonial government dominated by Javanese Muslims, and their support of Dutch proposals for federalism was widely viewed as betrayal of the national cause. Against this background Indonesian leaders made several concessions to allay Christian anxieties, and the 1945 Constitution omitted the stipulation that the president be a Muslim and replaced "Allah" by the more generic "Tuhan" (Lord). When the Suharto regime was in power (1965–98) religious involvement in politics was proscribed, but over the last decade suspicion of world Christianity has become more pronounced, since many Muslims seriously believe an international conspiracy aims at Christianizing Indonesia. In the early 1990s, Muslim–Christian violence erupted in Maluku, Central Sulawesi, and Eastern Java, areas previously known for their relative tolerance. In just two years of fighting in Maluku, for instance, over 5,000 people were killed and a majority of the estimated 350,000 displaced persons in Indonesia are victims of religious conflict.

Although clashes have declined since 2001, the periodic disturbances that still erupt as an escalation of some minor incident are a disturbing indication of underlying animosities. Muslims remain angry at the proliferation of churches, a trend exacerbated in recent years because certain streams of Christianity like the Pentecostals have a tendency to subdivide. A number of churches have apparently been built without reaching a mandatory congregation of 90 or obtaining the neighborhood approval now required by law. The international media has tended to focus on Muslims, but in Sulawesi and Maluku armed Christian militias have also been responsible for initiating and escalating violence. The most serious conflict is occurring in the resource-rich and Christianity-majority province of Western New Guinea, where a growing number of Muslims enjoy political and economic advantages denied to local Papuans. During the violence in Maluku, militant Christians invoked the hymn *Onward, Christian Soldiers* (*Maju, Laskar Kristus*) as their battle cry, and the Papuan Liberation Movement (Operasi Papua Merdeka) has done the same. Sung defiantly during anti-government parades or demonstrations, the hymn becomes a medium for expressing Papuan frustration at the perceived Indonesian colonization and a statement of Christianity's engagement with the public sphere.

"Old" and "New" Christianity

Although one might have expected that Christian churches in Southeast Asia would make vigorous efforts to speak with one voice, the ecumenical movement remains rather weak despite some cooperation in matters such as Bible translation. In Indonesia, where "Katolik" and "Kristen" (i.e., Protestant) are still categorized as two separate religions, a long-standing rivalry, and the frequent conflation of denomination and ethnic identity, has militated against inter-faith initiatives. Regionally, Church organizations do bring many Catholic and Protestant leaders together at the national level, but the impression of a Christian patchwork has been accentuated because a number of congregations follow their own path. In the Philippines, for

example, around 5 percent of Filipinos are members of the Aglipayan Church, which broke with Catholicism in 1902. Asia's largest independent church, the Iglesia ni Cristo, was established in 1914 and now has branches in over 80 countries. It has taken an active role in Philippine politics, sometimes opposing candidates favored by the powerful Catholic Church.

As elsewhere in Asia, however, the religious landscape in the Philippines has changed noticeably because of the rise of charismatic Christianity and Pentecostalism. Originating in the United States in the early twentieth century and emphasizing direct personal experience with God, these new churches have proliferated worldwide, with the Assemblies of God being the largest. In the Philippines militant evangelism by Filipinos, Westerners, and other Asians has been encouraged by the belief that many Catholics are simply "nominal." Although mainstream Protestant churches appear to have maintained numbers, they have also lost members to the independent evangelical and Pentecostal churches that now account for approximately 15 percent of the Christian population. It is thus significant that the charismatic renewal movement known as El Shaddai, with its strong working-class base, has been retained within Catholicism.

While still a minority among Protestants, Asia's Pentecostal churches share much in common. Largely urban based, they draw people of different backgrounds together in a common experience that reasserts biblical authority, emphasizes Christianity as a religion of physical and spiritual healing, and affirms belief in extraordinary signs as evidence of God's presence. With charismatic preachers exhorting individuals to be "born again" and an emotional atmosphere heightened by music, vibrant praise, and "high-tech" performances, Pentecostalism is extremely appealing to those seeking assurances in an uncertain world. Its pervasiveness is evident across the region, especially in the large cities where well-funded and well-marketed mega-churches attract a high percentage of middle-class professionals and young people. In Indonesia, Pentecostal congregations developed as early as the 1920s, but they grew rapidly in the 1980s in response to increasing modernization, a more obvious Islamic pietism, and perhaps in reaction to the austere Calvinist Protestantism bequeathed by the Dutch. By 1998, the Pentecostals were said to be the fastest growing of all Indonesia's churches, with estimates of members as high as 10 million. The expansion is even more striking in Singapore, where Pentecostalism has been expanding since the 1980s. The City Harvest Church, for example, draws congregations estimated at around 24,000 people, and well over half of its members are below the age of 25 years. Pentecostal leaders see lay involvement as critical to the goal of missionizing in the region, and to Singapore's future as the "Antioch of Asia."

What is particularly striking about Asian Pentecostalism is a global reach that extends far beyond specific cultures. In 30 years the Bible study group begun by Filipino activist Eddie Villanueva has mushroomed from 15 students to the huge Jesus Is Lord Church, which now has more than 3 million members spread across 36 countries. Mel Tari, the Timorese whose account of the 1965 "Timor Revival" has been translated into 19 languages, is the founder of World Mission International and is in universal demand as a speaker. Southeast Asians also flock to hear visiting preachers reputed to have healing powers, like the charismatic Filipino-Canadian priest, Fernando Suarez, or the American television evangelist Benny Hinn.

At the same time, the belief that even ordinary people can be granted special powers or singled out to receive the Holy Spirit, as well as the emphasis on healing and spiritual rebirth, also resonates with traditional religions. It is not surprising, therefore, to find that the Pentecostal movement has found a fertile ground in local revival movements that stress prophecy, speaking in tongues, miracles, and delivery from satanic powers. One of the most interesting Pentecostal developments has taken place among the Chin peoples of northwest Myanmar, where American Baptists began to work in 1899 but where no foreign missionaries have been permitted since 1966. From the late 1970s, a Pentecostal renewal took hold among the Chin, with thousands of people entering newly established Assemblies of God churches through village crusades, claims of miraculous cures, deliverance from evil spirits, trance worship, and prophecies of Christ's imminent return. By 1997 the activities of independent preachers had reached such extremes that Church leaders felt compelled to bring the prophetic movement into line with biblical teachings by differentiating "false" from "true" prophecies. Despite government opposition, the Pentecostal movement has survived and today there are more than 700 churches in the Chin Hills alone.

Inculturation

The accusation from Myanmar's military government that Chin Christianity is pro-Western directs our attention to another cross-regional theme: the extent to which Christianity has been detached from its European and American origins to become truly localized. To a considerable degree this localization process depends on the leadership of local men and women who can take their place on the national stage and serve as respected representatives in world assemblies. This has not been a rapid development. From the sixteenth century, Church authorities exhorted missionaries in Southeast Asia to support clerical education, but 200 years later the figures were disappointing. By 1871, for example, only 181 of 792 Philippines parishes were under *mestizo* or Filipino control, and the first Filipino cardinal was only appointed in 1960. Theological colleges and seminaries established by Protestants may have produced greater numbers of ordained preachers, but the internment of most expatriate clergy during the Japanese Occupation revealed the inadequacy of pre-war efforts.

The remarkable advances since that time mean that in contemporary Southeast Asia well-educated and internationally experienced leaders have assumed key roles in virtually all denominations. Their very theological sophistication, however, raises a question that in many ways echoes earlier concerns of Western missionaries; is there a danger that local control will dilute or misrepresent Christian teachings? The history of Christianity in Southeast Asia provides innumerable examples of the tensions that could occur when it was felt that doctrinal boundaries had been exceeded. Despite his success in attracting followers, the teachings of the "Apostle of Java," Kiai Sadrach (c.1835–1924), were regarded by most Dutch ministers as heretical because they presented Christian teachings as a form of Javanese esoteric wisdom. In a similar vein, modern Roman Catholic leaders in the Philippines dismiss independent communities like the Apostolic Catholic Church, founded in 1992, as cults.

Although debates about the limits to "localization" continue, it is generally accepted that some compromise is necessary if Southeast Asian Christians are to become active agents in religious praxis rather than passive recipients of imported teachings. In Northern Sulawesi, for example, educated Minahasans have led a move to synchronize Christianity and traditions associated with pre-colonial culture. Church services have developed a new form of baptism based on early missionary accounts of rituals in which people purified themselves by going to a mountain stream where water was poured over their bodies, while requesting assistance from ancestors and powerful spirits. By replacing the names of ancient deities with that of the Christian God, ministers have successfully combined baptism with a pre-Minahasa form of ritual cleansing, and have thus asserted a specifically "Minahasa" identity. Similar developments can be seen in Catholicism, where the Second Vatican Council (1962–5) inaugurated a new chapter by allowing Mass to be said in the vernacular. Church music and hymns had previously been based on Western compositions, but in recent years choirs and musicians have tried to incorporate instruments and musical traditions that speak to the local environment. Formerly the Catholic Church in Sumatra did not allow the playing of traditional drums and gongs because their rhythmic beating was associated with trance-inspired dancing and spirit possession. Though still selective in choosing melodies, the Church now actively encourages the use of traditional instruments and the composition of *lagu inkulturasi* (inculturation hymns) that are suitable for incorporation as "church music."

It is likely, however, that the most powerful localizing forces are operating outside church walls, as ordinary people integrate ancient beliefs into their own practice of Christianity. Across the region, sacred grottos, springs, and mountains, home to powerful

Figure 8.4   Tomb of a Toba Batak Christian, Sumatra, Indonesia. Courtesy of Sara E. Orel.

spirits or revered ancestors, have been injected with Christian potency through association with miracle-working images and prophetic achievement. While thousands of devotees visit old Marian shrines such as Antipolo in the Philippines or La Vang in Vietnam, there is also a proliferation of newer sanctuaries like Sendang Sono, the so-called Lourdes of Java. Although Catholicism is usually regarded as more amenable to this type of syncretism, ancient practices have also resurfaced in Protestant communities. Around 50 years ago, Toba Batak ceremonies honoring the dead appeared to have vanished, but from the 1960s remittances from wealthy migrants financed the impressive monuments to lineage founders that now dot the Toba landscape. A reminder of the veneration long accorded mountain spirits, Mount Banahaw in the Philippines and Sarawak's impressive Mount Murud are both major pilgrimage sites, in the one case for Catholics and in the other for the Sidang Injil Borneo (Borneo Evangelical Church), Malaysia's largest Protestant denomination. Gathering force in the twenty-first century, this ongoing domestication of Christianity mirrors the selective adaptation and adoption that has always characterized Southeast Asian responses to global influences.

Christianity has been part of Southeast Asia's history for over 500 years. Offering a new explanation for human existence, bringing ideas that were often quite alien to indigenous cultures, but sometimes curiously familiar, it has become deeply embedded in notions of self and community among millions of people. Diversity has always been a Southeast Asian hallmark, but even the difficulty of regional generalization can be beneficial to cross-cultural and comparative discussion. As participants in the meteorical rise of the non-Western "Third Church," Southeast Asia's Christians are themselves helping to reshape global understandings of " orthodoxy" and of Christianity as a truly world religion.

Notes and References

[1] Alex G. Smith, *Siamese Gold: A History of Church Growth in Thailand: An Interpretative Analysis 1816–1982* (Bangkok: Kanok Bannasan, 1981), 165.

Further Reading

Anderson, Allan and Edmond Tang, eds. *Asian and Pentecostal: The Charismatic Face of Christianity in Asia*. Baguio City: Regnum Studies in Mission, 2005.

Aritonang, Jan Sihar and Karel Steenbrink, eds. *A History of Christianity in Indonesia*. Leiden: Brill, 2008.

Forest, Alain. *Les Missionnaires Français au Tonkin et au Siam XVIIe–XIIIe Siècles: Analyse comparée d'un relatif succès et d'un total échec*. Paris: L'Harmattan, 1998.

Hunt, Robert, Lee Kam Hing and John Roxborough, eds. *Christianity in Malaysia: A Denominational History*. Petaling Jaya, Malaysia: Pelanduk Publications, 1992.

Lao Christian Service. *Life after Liberation: The Church in the Lao People's Democratic Republic*. Phai Sali, Nakhon Sawan, Thailand: Lao Christian Service, 1987.

Ngaihte, Tuan Khaw Kham, *Christianity in Myanmar and its Progress*. Yangon: Tedim Baptist Church, nd.

Phan Phát Huồn, *The History of the Catholic Church in Vietnam*. Long Beach, CA: Cu Thế Tùng Thu, 2000.

Ponchaud, François. *La Cathédral de la rizière; 450 ans d'histoire de l'Eglise au Cambodge*. Paris: Fayard, 1990.

Ramsay, Jacob. *Martyrs and Mandarins*. Stanford, CA: Stanford University Press, 2007.

Smith, Alex. G. *Siamese Gold: A History of Church Growth in Thailand: An Interpretative Analysis 1816–1982*. Bangkok: Kanok Bannasan, 1981.

Steenbrink, Karel. Catholics in Indonesia; A Documented History 1808–1942. Vol. I: A Modest Recovery 1808–1903; Vol. II: The Spectacular Growth of a Self-Confident minority, 1903–1942. Leiden: KITLV Press, 2007.

Wiegele, Katherine L. *Investing in Miracles: El Shaddai and the Transformation of Popular Catholicism in the Philippines*. Honolulu: University of Hawai'i Press, 2004.

9

Christianity in East Asia
Evangelicalism and the March First Independence Movement in Korea

Timothy S. Lee

Introduction

In East Asia, as elsewhere, Christianity's fortunes have ebbed or flowed depending on how it interacted with political interests of the societies to which it was introduced. East Asia is defined here as the region encompassing China, Korea, Japan, Taiwan, and Mongolia. Christianity arrived in East Asia as early as 635. Since then, for the most part, the faith has failed to coalesce with political interests of Chinese and Japanese, the largest societies in the region. Nor has it made much headway in Mongolia, the smallest society in terms of population.[1] The exception has been Korea – chiefly South Korea, where nearly 30 percent of the population identified themselves as Christian at the end of the twentieth century.[2] Among Korean Christians, evangelical Protestants have predominated, both in numbers and influence. This is the case partly because evangelicalism has successfully coalesced with political interests of the Korean people. One event in which such coalescence occurred was the 1919 March First Movement, a pivotal event in the rise of Korean nationalism, which occurred when Korea was under the colonial rule of Japan. Examining this coalescence will be the main object of this chapter. Before doing so, however, we will briefly examine the history of Christianity in China and Japan, focusing on Christianity's interaction with the political interests of these societies.

China

Earliest traces of Christianity in China goes back as far as 635 when Nestorian missionaries arrived in Chang'an, the capital of the Tang dynasty. But the religion did not take hold till the early seventeenth century, with the arrival in Beijing of Jesuit missionary Matteo Ricci. Ricci and other Jesuits adopted an accommodationist policy, which allowed Chinese converts to retain customs such as ancestral rites. They won over many Chinese, including influential persons in the literati class. In 1644, the Ming was toppled by Manchu, who established the Qing dynasty (1644–1911). Under the Qing, the Catholic Church continued to thrive, until the Jesuits conflicted with missionaries from other Orders, who accused them of condoning idolatry in the name of accommodation. The ensuing "rites controversy" proved costly, as the Vatican and the Chinese imperial court took opposite sides. Eventually, in 1715, the Vatican unequivocally condemned ancestral rites; and in 1724, the Chinese emperor outlawed Christianity.[3] A series of persecutions against the Christians ensued. In 1700, around 300,000 Chinese were Catholic; by 1800, the number had shrunk to half of that figure.[4]

In the nineteenth century, Christian missionaries once again arrived in China, this time led by Protestants. The first Protestant missionary to arrive was Robert Morrison of Scotland, who arrived in Guangzhou in 1807. Morrison and other missionaries

Introducing World Christianity, First Edition. Edited by Charles E. Farhadian.
© 2012 Blackwell Publishing Ltd. Published 2012 by Blackwell Publishing Ltd.

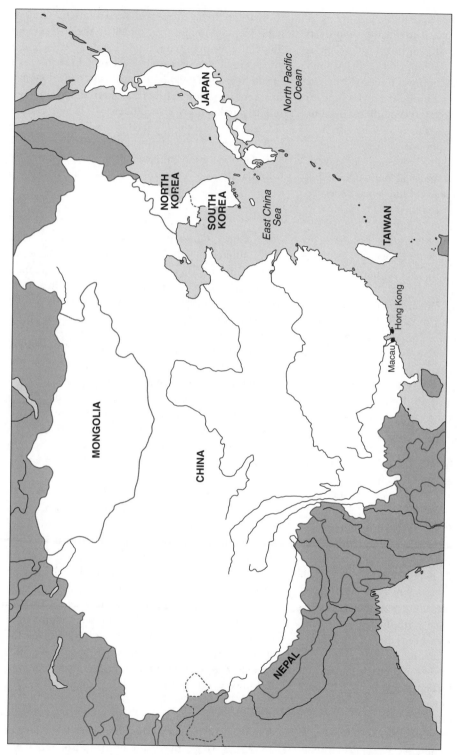

Map 9.1 East Asia

who followed him struggled in evangelizing, owing to the laws against Christianity. The situation improved only when China lost to Britain in the two Opium Wars, the first between 1839 and 1842, the second between 1856 and 1860. China was forced to open its ports to Britain and other European powers, and to allow trade in opium and other commodities. Eventually China was also compelled to allow Christian missionaries within its borders. Soon missionaries poured in from Europe, Australia, and North America. Converts were made and churches built all over China, but Christianity's gain was tainted because it was associated with nations that had imposed their will on China.

Such association proved costly to Christianity. In 1900, during the Boxer Uprising, for example, Christians were specifically targeted by Chinese nativists. Christians perished by the thousands, including hundreds of missionaries. In the 1920s, Christian churches suffered during anti-imperialist demonstrations. In the 1930s, when China was engaged in war against Japan, the Church redeemed itself somewhat by succoring helpless Chinese victims. At that time Christianity won many admirers, but not enough to decouple its association with Western imperialism. When Japan was defeated in 1945, the civil war between the nationalists and the communists intensified. In 1949, the communists emerged victorious, with the nationalists evacuating to Taiwan.

The new communist regime disapproved of Christians. Christianity was denounced as an opiate, and the missionaries as imperialists. The remaining missionaries were evacuated and Church properties nationalized. Christian leaders were forced to undergo re-education. In 1958, denominational distinctions were prohibited among the Protestants: all Chinese Protestants now came under the oversight of the Three-Self Patriotic Movement, a government-controlled body.[5] The Catholics met a similar fate. Priests who refused to yield and toe the party line were imprisoned. Many recalcitrant Christians practiced their faith underground. During the Cultural Revolution (1966–76), Chinese Christians suffered even more. It looked as if Christianity would be totally stamped out in China.

Christianity obtained a new lease on life in China in 1979, when China and the United States normalized their relations. In the 1980s, the Chinese government eased its control over the churches, allowing Christians to worship freely in a registered church, without harassment, so long as they abided by the government guidelines. With the communist ideology in decline, a great many Chinese eagerly seized on Christianity as a means to ground their lives. At the turn of the twenty-first century, churches, both registered and unregistered, rapidly grew in numbers. It is notoriously difficult to gauge the number of Christians, Catholic and Protestant, in China. But at the turn of the twenty-first century, a good estimate is held to be around 65 to 70 million.[6]

Japan

As in China, Christianity has failed to coalesce with political interests of Japan. Japanese became aware of Christianity in 1549 when the Jesuit missionary Francis Xavier arrived to disseminate the faith. After some false starts, Xavier and other missionaries successfully established thriving Catholic communities in Japan. In achieving their success, the missionaries were aided by feudal divisions that existed in the land. Many of the feudal lords, *daimyos*, seeking profits and firearms, desired trade relations with Portugal, which monopolized the West's early trade with Japan. To promote such trade, and knowing that the missionaries wielded influence among the Portuguese, many of the *daimyos* allowed them to engage in missions in their realms.[7] In some cases, *daimyos* underwent genuine conversion, with their subjects following suit.

By 1614, Christians numbered around 300,000, about 1.5 percent of the entire population of Japan. By then, however, Japan had become unified under the shogun Tokugawa Ieyasu, and in that year the shogun outlawed Christianity. He did so partly out of the suspicion that Portugal had political designs on Japan – and that Christians might play a role in effecting such a design. Under the reign of Ieyasu's son, Tokugawa Iemitsu, Christians were subjected to fierce persecution. Japanese converts were given the choice of apostasy or execution. A great many submitted. Many chose martyrdom rather than to submit. And many others pretended to submit before the authorities, but practiced their faith in secret, giving rise to the tradition of the Hidden Christians (*Kakure Kirishitan*) of Japan. In the Shimabara Rebellion of 1637 and 1638, the last Christian stronghold was crushed. In 1639, Japan officially declared itself off limits to Westerners; missionaries who still ventured into the country risked execution.

Japan kept itself isolated from the West and Christianity for nearly 220 years. It finally opened again to the West in 1854 – and then only because it had been compelled to do so in the previous year by the gunboat diplomacy of the United States. In 1858 Japan signed an amity and commerce treaty with the United States, in terms that were disadvantageous to Japan, such as conceding extraterritoriality. Similar treaties followed with other Western nations. Along with merchants and diplomats, Christian clergy also arrived, with Catholic and Protestant clergymen first arriving in 1859, ostensibly to serve Western residents in Japan.

Initially Japanese authorities maintained their hostility toward Christianity. But in their quest to hurriedly modernize their country and to be accepted as an equal by Western powers, Japan became more tolerant toward Christianity. In 1873, the edict proscribing Japanese from converting to Christianity was repealed. By 1890 Japan had become sufficiently modernized, especially militarily. It defeated China and Russia in 1895 and 1905, respectively. In 1905 Japan forced itself upon Korea as a protectorate, forcibly annexing it in 1910.

In the 1890s Japanese nationalism reached new heights. The emperor emerged as a deity (kami). Anything that stood in the way of the emperor cult was fiercely resented. Christianity, which had already been identified with Western imperialism, was severely castigated when some Japanese Christians refused to submit to the emperor cult. After 1890, missionary efforts made little progress in Japan. Things worsened in the new century. In the 1930s, as it waged war in China and colonized Korea, Japan sought to tighten its reign over religious institutions, enacting a law that required all organizations – religious or not – to begin their activities with Shinto rites, throwing many a Christian community into agonizing turmoil. In June 1941, under government coercion, most Protestant denominations in Japan joined together to form the United Church (Kyōdan). After the Japanese bombing of Pearl Harbor in December of 1941, Protestant missionaries were rounded up and sent to the United States, in exchange for Japanese civilians. And during World War II, the churches suffered severely.

After the war, the emperor cult was dismantled, the missionaries returned, and Japanese churches regrouped. Evangelistic efforts went well for the first 10 years, and then they fizzled out, not having regained the momentum since. In the 60 years thereafter, the number of Christians in Japan have remained at about 1 percent of the general population.

Christianity in Korea

Koreans first learned of Christianity early in the seventeenth century, through Jesuit-published Chinese Catholic literature that their envoys brought back from Beijing. Although most Korean literati deemed the literature mere curiosities, some took them seriously. In 1784, one of them, Yi Sŭnghun, underwent baptism in Beijing and returned home, where he baptized others, thereby laying the foundation of the Korean Catholic Church – a full decade before any Catholic priest arrived in Korea. Thus the Catholic Church in Korea was started by the natives themselves – not missionaries – a rarity in the history of Christian mission.

Planted in a proud Confucian society where ancestral rites permeated – at a time when the Vatican had prohibited the accommodationist policy – the nascent Catholic community stood little chance of flourishing. Indeed its first century was punctuated by a series of persecutions – provoked partly because the Catholics refused to observe ancestral rituals, which they regarded as idolatrous. The more noteworthy of these persecutions occurred in 1801, 1839, 1846, and especially 1866–73. In 1886, when Korea and France signed a diplomatic treaty, the Catholics finally attained religious freedom. By then, 10 thousand or so Catholics had been executed; in 1984 when Pope John Paul II visited Korea, he canonized 103 of them, including 10 French missionaries.

Protestants sought to evangelize Korea in earnest in the last quarter of the nineteenth century. As early as the late 1870s, Korean converts of the Scottish missionary John Ross, stationed in Manchuria, evangelized in Northern Korea. In 1884 Horace N. Allen arrived as the first resident missionary of Korea, hailing from the United States, representing the Northern Presbyterian Church. Allen was followed in 1885 by

Figure 9.1 Women's Bible study group in Chemulp'o (Incheon). Date unknown. Courtesy of University of Southern California, on behalf of the Reverend Corwin & Nellie Taylor Collection of the USC Korean Heritage Library.

Horace G. Underwood (Northern Presbyterian Church) and Henry G. Appenzeller (Methodist Episcopal Church).

In the late nineteenth century, a corrupt officialdom and rapacious imperial forces, especially from Japan, wreaked havoc in Korea. With the government seeking aspects of Western culture for its own survival, the missionaries were tolerated. From 1885 to 1910, Korean reformers favored the Protestants as they built not only churches but also hospitals, schools, and orphanages. The Protestants also engaged in Bible studies and door-to-door evangelism; in 1907, an evangelistic revival erupted in Pyŏngyang that swept through all the Protestant communities, imparting an indelibly evangelical character to the Church.

The Orthodox Church arrived in Korea in 1899, via Russia. Initially the priests ministered only to the Russians affiliated with the legation in Seoul, but they soon evangelized among the natives. The Church

encountered major setbacks owing to Russia's defeat in the Russo–Japanese War (1904–5), the Russian Revolution (1917), and the Japanese occupation of Korea. But it managed to survive, albeit with only a few thousand adherents at the end of the twentieth century.

Japan colonized Korea from 1910 to 1945. The colonial government exploited the land and attempted to extirpate the national identity of the Korean people. In this period, the churches fared badly. The Catholic Church, with French missionaries at its helm, sought to comply with the colonial policy – to the extent of excommunicating the renowned Catholic nationalist An Chung'gŭn for assassinating a leading Japanese colonialist. Near the end of World War II, Western priests were expelled from Korea. Their expulsion ironically enabled native priests to move up in the Church hierarchy.

For the Protestant churches, the colonial period was a turning point, enabling them to coalesce with

Korean nationalism. The Protestant missionaries sought to maintain a neutral stance throughout the period, but they could not prevent Korean converts from actively participating in the nationalist cause. As will be seen, their participation was especially conspicuous in the 1919 March First Independence Movement. The movement did not result in Korean independence but nevertheless galvanized Korean nationalism. In 1935, when Japan imposed a Shinto ritual on the churches, the Catholics and Methodists complied, accepting it as a civic ceremony. But the Presbyterians regarded it as idolatrous and closed all their schools rather than comply. The colonial government eventually coerced all the Presbyterian bodies to accept the ritual. Many Protestants resisted it till the end, however, with some 50 of them losing their lives over it and thousands suffering imprisonment. After liberation, the churches' participation in the Shinto ritual became a divisive issue among Korean Protestants.

Between the liberation in 1945 and the end of the Korean War in 1953, both Catholics and Protestants suffered under communism, which had emerged in Korea in the 1920s. When the war ended, most Christians in the North had fled to the South. At the end of the twentieth century, the North had no more than 15,000 Christians and three churches. In the South it was a different story. The Catholic Church became a full archdiocese in 1962 and, thanks in part to the Second Vatican Council, actively engaged in societal issues. Its Myŏngdong Cathedral and Cardinal Kim Suhwan emerged as icons of the South Korean democracy movement. For much of the period the Protestants were divided. Liberals such as Moon Ik Hwan vigorously opposed dictatorships and were supported by theologians such as Suh Nam Dong, who helped to develop liberation-oriented *Minjung* theology. But the vast majority of the Protestants were evangelicals who sympathized with the government's anti-communist policy. Led by the likes of Han Kyung Chik, they eschewed political activism and concentrated on evangelism. Thanks to their efforts, churches grew phenomenally in the latter half of the twentieth century. In 1950, Christians approximated 600,000, about 3 percent of the Korean population. By 1997 they numbered about 13 million, almost 30 percent of the South Korean population, with the Protestants outnumbering the Catholic by three to one.

Thus Korean Protestantism's growth took off only in the second half of the twentieth century. But such a take-off could not have occurred had the faith not become indigenized in Korean history by the midpoint of the century. And such indigenization could not have occurred had evangelicalism not contributed profoundly to Koreans' political interests: that is, to Korean nationalism, as was revealed during the 1919 March First Independence Movement.

Protestantism and Korean Nationalism

In September, 1884, American physician Horace N. Allen arrived in Korea as the first Protestant missionary to reside there. With his arrival, there occurred an exception to the general trend of conflict between Protestantism and East Asian societies. Changed political circumstances had predisposed rulers of Chosŏn (1392–1910), the last Korean dynasty, to be more receptive to foreign influences. Already a few years before Allen's arrival, Chosŏn had abandoned its xenophobic policy, realizing it could no longer ward off foreign encroachment by sealing up the borders. Indeed, by 1876, Chosŏn had been compelled by Japan's gunboat diplomacy to sign its first modern diplomatic treaty with that nation – much the same way that Japan did with the United States in 1854, under duress and with guarantees of extraterritoriality to the other party. Shortly, similar treaties followed suit with the United States (1882) and other Western nations. Clearly by the 1880s Chosŏn leaders had caught on to the international realpolitik in which their country was enmeshed. They had also resigned themselves to the view that assimilating at least some aspects of Western culture – namely, sciences and technology – was essential for their nation's survival. This resignation, in turn, led the Korean court to tolerate the arrival of the missionaries.

In addition to benefiting from changes in international politics, the Protestant missionary enterprise profited from struggles in Korean domestic politics. It benefited especially from a failed *coup d'état* of December, 1884, in which a group of the nation's progressives attempted to force a reform on the government by murdering their conservative rivals. In the midst of this coup, Min Yongik, a nephew of the

Figure 9.2   Prayer meeting in Pyongyang. Date unknown. Courtesy of University of Southern California, on behalf of the Reverend Corwin & Nellie Taylor Collection of the USC Korean Heritage Library.

queen and a powerful figure in the conservative camp, was gravely wounded, and could not be healed by court doctors. To the good fortune of the Protestants, however, he was nursed back to health by Allen. Subsequently, through the aid of Min and the queen, Allen was able to convince King Kojong (1852–1907) to start a Western hospital in the country. Thereafter, it was only a small step for him to arrange for the arrival of other missionaries.

Partly owing to these missionaries, the Korean Protestant Church experienced one of its most explosive growth periods between 1890 and 1907. In 1896, for example, the total number of Protestants was 4,356; by 1900 the number reached 20,918, nearly a fivefold increase. By 1907, when a nationwide revival swept through the churches, the figure increased to 106,287 – a growth that multiplied the original number by 24 – in a space of 11 years. And in 1909–10, 20,000 more were added to this number as a result of the nationwide "One-Million-Souls-for-Christ" movement.[8]

Two factors figured into this rise of Church membership, aside from the missionary efforts: Korea's deteriorating political circumstances and Koreans' perception that the Protestant Church sympathized with their misfortunes. Between 1890 and 1910, Korea's political fortunes declined precipitously. The cause lay in internal and external conditions. Among the numerous internal conditions were a government beset by baneful factional struggles, corrupt officialdom, and overtaxed peasants. Among the external factors, the most important was the imperialistic struggle to dominate Korea that developed among China, Russia, and Japan. These two conditions, in the end, combined to engender in Korea a series of upheavals and disasters that devastated the people. These included the Tonghak peasant rebellion of 1894; the Sino–Japanese War of 1894–5 and the Russo–Japanese War of 1904–5 (both won by Japan); the imposition of a Japanese protectorate over Korea in 1905; and finally the Japanese annexation of Korea in 1910, which formally ended Korea's existence as an independent country.

As one disaster after another befell Korea, the already distorted society became even more contorted, distressing and disorienting the people. Most of the traditional worldview and structures were now irreparably damaged. Disillusioned people strove beyond traditional options to search for salvation. Once such option was the Protestant Church, which promised a new life to whoever would convert. In China and Japan, such a promise might have sounded sanctimonious. In Korea, however, none of the imperialistic powers that plagued the natives were Protestant, affording the missionaries' promise prima facie appeal.

Missionaries and Korean Nationalism

For the most part, Koreans sought the Church for apolitical reasons – to seek personal salvation, to cope with distress caused by societal turmoil – and were of the lower class. But Protestantism was also making inroads into the ranks of politically minded *yangban*, the dominant class. Like commoners, *yangban* also started to join the Church in the 1880s when the country was still under Korean sovereignty. Most early *yangban* Christians were from the disaffected portion of their class. Many of them, such as Kil Sŏnju, were attracted to the faith primarily for religious reasons.[9] For a significant portion of them, however, politics played a role in their adoption and support of the religion. Such was the case with two of the first *yangban* to be converted to Protestantism: Sŏ Chae-pil (Philip Jaisohn) and Yun Ch'iho, influential progressives linked with the failed *coup d'état* of 1884. Yun, Sŏ, and other *yangban* like them, believed that Protestantism could help to reform their people and nation. Thus they encouraged their countrymen to embrace the religion. Moreover, after the Russo–Japanese war of 1904–5, many Korean officials who used to disapprove of the religion also endorsed it.[10]

In part influenced by such endorsements, many Korean nationalists turned to Protestantism to find ways to ameliorate their nation's woes. Faced with politically motivated seekers, the missionaries became concerned lest the Church turn into a hotbed of independence movement. So they began to emphasize

to the Koreans, especially to the converts, their long-standing policy of disallowing political activities within the Church.[11] By doing so, the missionaries believed they were taking a non-partisan stance.[12] In reality, such a stance was extremely difficult – if not impossible – to achieve in Korea at the time. Indeed except in the minds of certain Koreans whom later generations stigmatized as collaborators, between Japanese colonialism and Korean nationalism, there was hardly middle ground. One had to choose a side. And the refusal to take a side – which was what the missionaries did with their declaration of political neutrality – was tantamount to accepting the status quo: Japanese rule.

Moreover, while espousing political neutrality, missionaries did more than just disallow political activities from taking place in the Church. They actively discouraged their flock from cultivating nationalistic sentiments. Thus, in 1906, when 12 students from P'yŏngyang Academy participated in a rally against Japan's imposing a protectorate over Korea, they were promptly suspended.[13] During the great revival of 1907, the converts were urged to repent of their hatred for the Japanese. It so happened that 1907 was also the year Japan abolished the Korean army, prompting former Korean soldiers to lead guerrilla uprisings all over the country. Many in the Church were tempted to join the guerrillas, only to be dissuaded from doing so by the missionaries.[14] Similarly, in 1910, the missionaries used the opportunity afforded them by the Million Movement to discourage the Koreans from participating in protests against the Japanese annexation of their country.[15] That was not all. From 1910, when Japanese rule over Korea began in earnest, the missionaries made it clear they were willing not only to accept the status quo but also to regard the Japanese as a partner in their self-appointed task to enlighten Koreans. Thus, in 1918, a *Korea Mission Field* editorial stated the following, as it welcomed the arrival of the second governor-general of Korea, Hasegawa Yoshimichi:

We are pleased thus to honor our Governor General; firstly because the Bible commands us to honor the Powers that be;... Thirdly, because the Governor General and the missionaries are both interested in the Koreans to improve their condition. Though methods employed are different they need not conflict, but, on the other hand, should be mutually helpful and complementary.[16]

The missionaries had good reasons to discourage Korean nationalism. After 1905, to safeguard and continue their evangelistic work in Korea, they needed to obtain Japanese toleration. And Japanese authorities were ever wary of the Church's potential for political subversion, as evidenced by the Conspiracy Case of 1911, in which the colonial government arrested a hundred or so Korean Protestant leaders on the trumped-up charge of having plotted to assassinate Governor-General Terauchi Masatake, torturing many of them.[17] It was clear to the missionaries that unless the colonial authorities could be assured that the Church was "apolitical" their prime mission of preaching the Gospel would be jeopardized.

But having led the Church to accept the status quo – the Japanese rule – the missionaries could not help but disappoint Korean nationalists within the Church, and alienate those outside it. Inevitably, many Koreans left the Church – at least the Church as institutionally conceived. By the same token, fewer and fewer Koreans were attracted to the Church. Thus the missionaries' "apolitical" stance, and the consequent depoliticization of the Church, was an important reason that the Church's growth stagnated between 1910 and 1919.[18] Such stagnation was documented by Alfred W. Wasson in his 1934 study, *Church Growth in Korea*, where he titled the section covering the period between 1911 and 1919 as "Nine Lean Years."[19]

It is not a historian's task to speculate what might have happened in the past had certain events transpired differently. But it is hard to resist speculating about what might have happened to Korean Protestantism had it maintained its "apolitical" stance throughout the Japanese occupation. Were that the case, the Korean Church might have taken the path taken by the Protestant Churches of Japan and China. In other words, it might have never become positively associated with Korean national interests and would have become no more successful in Korea than it did in China or Japan.

Protestantism in Korea, as it turned out, did not follow that path. Unlike its Japanese and Chinese counterparts, the Church was to share in and contribute to Korean collective interests. This happened despite the missionaries' effort to depoliticize the Church. This was possible because though the missionaries succeeded in depoliticizing the Church qua an institution, they failed to depoliticize it qua Korean men and women. That this was the case was attested by the 1919 March First Independence Movement.

Evangelicalism and the 1919 March First Independence Movement

The March First Movement marked a turning point in modern Korean history.[20] It was a movement in which Koreans of varied backgrounds congregated en masse to defy their colonizers and demonstrate to the world their fervent desire for independence. In the end the movement failed to achieve its objective of Korean independence, but it did succeed in galvanizing and uniting Koreans. And as Michael E. Robinson states, "the memory of this uprising plays a significant role in the narrative of modern Korea and the evolution of Korean nationalism."[21]

The March First Movement is pregnant with diverse meanings and interpretations. Even so, consensus has emerged – at least among historians in South Korea and the United States – on the major factors that went into the making of the movement. One was Koreans' persistent desire for independence, a desire fueled by their historical memory and imagination as one nation whose history stretched back to 2333 BCE, when the mythical Tan'gun purportedly founded the earliest Korean kingdom, Old Chosŏn.[22] The overtly repressive nature of Japan's first 10-year rule in Korea constituted a second factor. During this period the government-general employed ethnic discrimination, systemic terror, and torture as instruments of its policy – prompting historian Frank P. Baldwin to observe in 1969, "The political, social and educational disqualification imposed on Koreans from 1910 to 1918 resemble the plight of the American negro living a precarious, subservient existence in America."[23]

Koreans' desire for independence and Japan's cruel repression were deep-seated and fundamental to the March First Movement. The more immediate factor was the Fourteen-Point speech made by President Woodrow Wilson of the United States. First delivered in January of 1918, nine months after he had persuaded Americans to join the Allies in world war, Wilson's speech seemed to promise the right of self-determination to colonized people everywhere.[24] Later, this ideal would turn hollow, as it was not applied to the colonies held by Allies, such as Japan. But when the speech was first aired, Korean nationalists embraced it as a clarion call to action. The first Koreans to act on it were those outside Korea, who were freer and had greater access to the news than their counterparts in Korea. They were soon joined by their supporters in Korea, led by 33 signers of a Declaration of Korean Dependence, all of them religious leaders, adherents of Buddhism, Ch'ŏndokyo (Heavenly Way, an indigenous religion of Korea), and Protestantism.

On March 1, 1919, Protestantism's most potent encounter with Korean nationalism took place. On that day, in Seoul's Pagoda Park, thousands of Koreans – men and women, young and old – had been gathering since the morning for a rally. Many of them had come from the countryside for the funeral of King Kojong, who had died in January of that year. Then at two o'clock in the afternoon, a young Protestant man mounted the platform in the middle of the park and stirred the crowd by reading the Declaration of Independence. As soon as he was finished, the crowd burst into deliriously resounding cheers: "*Taehan Tongnip Manse!*" ("Long Live Korean Independence!"). Shortly after, Koreans elsewhere in the city and in the country at large staged similar demonstrations. Within days, the movement for independence erupted in virtually every corner of the country, in nearly all segments of the Korean society, with upwards of 2 million people directly participating in more than 1,500 gatherings, occurring in all but seven of Korea's 281 country administrations.[25]

The March First Independence Movement was meant to be non-violent. It started out that way, but in the end it failed to remain so. The leaders intended to appeal to the conscience of the Japanese colonizers and, more importantly, to the Wilson-led victors at the Paris Peace Conference, by using peaceful demonstrations.[26] Instead of affecting the Japanese conscience, the demonstrations only galled the gendarmes, who, assisted by Japanese residents in Korea, indiscriminately

beat and shot at the demonstrators. In the face of such reaction, the peaceful demonstration soon turned into riots. Riots continued sporadically through the summer. The situation came under full control only with the arrival of additional troops. By that time a great many casualties had been suffered by the Koreans: 7,645 killed and 15,961 injured – with 715 houses, 47 churches, and 2 schools destroyed and burned.[27]

Soon after the independence movement broke and it became clear that it was not a random but a carefully planned phenomenon, many Japanese – given their low opinion of Koreans – denounced the missionaries, suspecting them to be behind it. Such a denunciation, for example, was published on March 12 by *Chosen Shimbun*, a Japanese daily in Korea:

> The stirring up of the mind of the Koreans is the sin of the American missionaries. This uprising is their work. . . . They take the statement of Wilson about the self-determination of nations and hide behind their religion and stir up the people. However, the missionaries have tried to apply the free customs of other nations to these Korean people who are not fully civilized. From the part that even girl students in Christian schools have taken it is very evident that this uprising has come from the missionaries.[28]

Despite this newspaper's contention, the truth was that the demonstrations surprised the missionaries no less than the Japanese. Accused of having abetted and aided the Koreans, the missionaries vigorously denied the accusation and protested their political neutrality. Eventually, in mid-March, influenced by protestations and pressure from the American consulate, the government-general publicly exonerated the missionaries.

In hindsight, given the missionaries' indifference toward Korean nationalists' aspirations, it is understandable that they were not apprised of the activities. And if by keeping the missionaries in the dark the planners intended to minimize any hindrance to achieving their goal, subsequent developments proved them to have been prudent. For when the demonstrations erupted, many a missionary's immediate reaction was to dissuade their Korean converts from joining them. One particularly poignant example of such dissuasion is described in the journal of Methodist missionary Mattie Wilcox Noble, who wrote the following in her March 1 entry:

Today has been a great day for Korea. How long their joy will last, who can say? At two P.M. all the schools, from grammar grades or middle schools up went on strike against Japan's governing Korea, and all started out on the streets in parade, hands thrown in air, caps swung, and Hurrahs ("Ten Thousand Years of Korea") shouted. People of the streets dropped in line with them; and such joyful shouting all over the city. I could see from our window one long procession filing past the corner around the palace wall. The Government School for Girls also paraded, and when a company of boys came past Ewa Haktang [a Methodist school for girls], they rushed into the compound and called to the girls to come on. The girls rushed out to go but Miss Walter in her kimono ran down to bolt the big gate and head off the girls. Mr. Tayler and Mr. Appenzeller went over to her assistance and they succeeded in keeping the Ewa girls from going. They cried, and some of the boys grew almost wild, but had to go on and leave them.[29]

On the one hand, missionaries like Tayler and Appenzeller genuinely feared for the safety of Korean Protestants, even if much of that fear emanated from paternalism. On the other hand, the missionaries were alarmed lest by their converts' taking part in the demonstrations their own apolitical stance would be jeopardized. But despite their efforts the missionaries could not stem the tide of nationalistic fervor that swept through their schools and churches. Nor could they prevent the Japanese violence that was perpetrated on the demonstrators.

Seeing Koreans, especially their co-religionists, brutalized, the missionaries could not remain aloof. They took a stand, insisting on "no neutrality for brutality" – a slogan born of moral indignation. They became actively involved in caring for the injured, and they urged the colonial authorities to desist from using brutal tactics against the demonstrators.[30] Failing to make much impact by a direct appeal, they drew on the resources of their overseas contacts. They documented clear cases of Japanese atrocities and reported them to mission boards and influential friends in Europe and America, using unofficial channels. Such documents comprising 1,000 pages or so were compiled by the Commission on Relations with the Orient of the Federal Council of the Churches of Christ in America. In July of 1919, a select portion of them were published as a pamphlet under the title, *The Korean Situation: Authentic Accounts of Recent Events by Eye Witnesses.*

Among the numerous accounts cited in the pamphlets are the following:

On March 4th, about 12:30 noon, loud cheering was again participated in by the Koreans. With this cheer the Japanese fire brigade was let loose among the crowds with clubs; some carried pickax handles; others their long lance fir-hooks, some iron bars, others hardwood and pine clubs, some with short-handled club hooks. They rushed into the crowds, clubbing them over the heads, hooking them here and there with their lance-hooks, until in a short time many had been seriously wounded, and with blood streaming down their faces were dragged to the police station by the fire brigade.[31]

At Maungsan: During the first part of the March after the people at this place had shouted for independence, fifty-six people were asked by the gendarmes to come to the gendarme station, which they did. When they were all inside the gendarmerie compound the gates were closed, gendarmes climbed up on the wall and shot all the people down. Then they went in among them and bayoneted all who still lived. Of the fifty-six, fifty-three were killed and three were able later to crawl out of the heap of dead. Whether they lived or not is not known. A Christian woman in whom we have confidence made her way to foreign friends after several days' travel and made the above statement. Undoubtedly it is true.[32]

Accounts such as these proved to be a public relations nightmare for the Japanese government: they provoked international outcries and provided ammunition to senatorial critics of Japan in the United States.[33] Consequently, the government was compelled not only to renounce using brutal tactics against the demonstrators, but also to overhaul its colonial policy in Korea. As part of this overhaul, in September of 1919, heavy-handed Governor-General Hasegawa was recalled, replaced by more diplomatic but just as imperious Saito Makoto.

By the time Saito arrived in Korea, the uprising had been contained. Also by this time a clear link had been made between Protestantism and Korean nationalism, owing to the contributions made to the uprising by the Protestants, Korean and missionary. The March First Movement was a pan-Korean phenomenon to which no single group could lay an exclusive claim. But once the movement got under way, the contributions rendered by Korean Protestants – roles played and sufferings borne – stood out. Protestants, for example, were most numerous among the top tier of the leaders, the 33 signers of the Declaration of Independence: 16 as opposed to 2 Buddhists and 15 Ch'ŏndokyoists.[34] For the movement to have spread so quickly and cohesively, communication and organization were key. Here, the Church's national network and local leadership played crucial roles. Moreover, according to a report issued by the Japanese military police near the end of 1919, 19,525 persons were arrested in connection with the demonstrations. Of these, 3,371 were Protestants – more than 17 percent of the arrested – an impressive figure considering that, by 1919, Protestants comprised only about 1 percent of the total population.[35]

One of the few missionaries, perhaps the only one, who had any inkling of the uprising before it erupted was Frank W. Scofield. He was a Canadian medical missionary and was asked to take pictures of the planned rallies. As the movement proceeded, he became a vigorous advocate of Korean rights, speaking out against Japanese brutality, for example, at a conference of Far East missionaries in Tokyo in September of 1919. But his most potent and enduring contribution consisted of the numerous pictures he took of various aspects of the movement. These pictures, especially those of the massacres at Suwŏn and Cheamni, helped to galvanize international pressure against Japan. In 1920, Scofield left Korea but returned in 1945 when the country was liberated. His contributions were appreciated by Koreans, who affectionately referred to him as the "thirty-fourth" signer of the Declaration of Independence. In 1960, he was decorated with an Order for Cultural Merits by the South Korean government. Upon his death on February 20, 1970, his body was interred in the *Tongnip Yugongja* section of the Korean National Cemetery, reserved for those who had rendered distinguished services for the independence of Korea.[36]

The missionaries' moral stand in the face of colonial brutality proved crucial for Protestantism. Their treatment of the injured and their publicizing of the Korean plight went a long way toward redeeming them – and their religion – in the eyes of many Koreans. This was borne out by Wasson, who, after noting an upturn in Church membership in the wake of the uprising, states, "the charges against the missionaries [that they instigated the uprising], instead of discrediting them in the minds of the people, put them in greater favor. They were looked upon as comrades in spirit even though they remained neutral in political action."[37] Unwittingly the missionaries had contributed to the Korean nationalist cause. After March of 1919, no Korean could accuse the missionaries of being self-serving without provoking a loud cry of dissent from their more discerning countrymen. By bonding with Korean nationalism, evangelicalism also gained something much more enduring – its right as a legitimate religion of Korea. For by virtue of its participation in Koreans' struggles for freedom and power, evangelicalism had acquired a nationalistic credential no Korean could gainsay. Thus evangelicalism had become indigenized in Korean history.

Conclusion

Indigenized in Korean history, evangelicalism grew rapidly in (South) Korea, becoming the faith of every fifth South Korean.[38] In the last decade of the twentieth century, evangelicalism wielded more influence in South Korean economy, politics, and civil society than any other religion in the country.[39] Moreover, given its global worldview and pan-ethnic disposition, evangelicalism has served as a check against nativistic impulses in Korean society, impulses that may degenerate into ultra-nationalism if left condoned.[40] This is not to say evangelicalism did not bring challenges to Korean society. Evangelicals' aggressive missional activities, for example, sometimes conflicted with traditional religions of Korea, such as Buddhism.[41] Holding respect toward other religions while remaining true to their calling remains a challenge to Korean evangelicals. Protestantism is also represented in Korea by a liberal wing that is much smaller than evangelicalism but just as essential. In the 1970s and 1980s, it was this wing of the Church that led South Korea's democratic movement, along with the Roman Catholic Church.[42]

Compared to Korea, Christianity's impact on Japan and China is less dramatic. Nonetheless it is significant. In Japan, Christianity's influence has been disproportionate to the number of its adherents. This is apparent in the educational sector, where Christian institutions from kindergartens to graduate schools number close to 2,000.[43] In realms of politics, social services, and artistic endeavors, as well, Christians have been amply represented. Christianity's impact on China is just as significant, if not more so. Despite its unhappy association with Western imperialism, Christianity has genuinely contributed to China's modernization, especially in areas such as medicine and education.[44] It has also influenced key leaders of modern China: for example, Sun Yat-Sen, often called the father of the Chinese republic.[45] Christian contribution is also linked to the horrific event known as the Nanjing Massacre of December of 1937, when a handful of missionaries helped to shield 2–300,000 hapless Chinese from the murderous rampage of the Japanese imperial army.[46] In the twenty-first century, Christian churches are gaining in appeal as more and more Chinese search for meaning amid a nation that is increasing becoming capitalistic. The appeal is especially strong for unregistered churches, a great many of which are found in rural areas, and are imbued with nationalism and millenarianism.[47]

Notes and References

[1] Hugh P. Kemp, *Steppe by Step: Mongolia's Christians: From Ancient Roots to Vibrant Young Church* (London: Monarch Books, 200); on the Taiwanese story, see Hollington K. Tong, *Christianity in Taiwan: A History* (Taipei: China Post, 1961).

[2] Robert E. Buswell and Timothy S. Lee, eds *Christianity in Korea* (Honolulu: University of Hawaii Press, 2006), 330.

[3] George Minamiki, *The Chinese Rites Controversy* (Chicago, IL: University of Loyola Press, 1985), 67; Jason Kindopp and Carol Lee Hamrin, eds, *God and Caesar in China: Policy Implications of Church–State Tensions* (Washington, DC: Brookings Institution Press, 2004), 86.

[4] Moffett, *Christianity in Asia, Vol. II: 1500–1900* (Maryknoll, NY: Orbis, 2005), 130.

[5] The Three-Self Patriotic Movement arose among certain Chinese Protestants in the 1950s with the backing of the state. It has emphasized Chinese ownership of the Church. The three "selves" refer to self-governance, self-support, and self-propagation. Yihua Xu, "'Patriot' Protestants: The Making of an Official Church," in Kindopp and Hamrin, eds, *God and Caesar*, 107.

[6] Philip Jenkins, "Notes from the Global Church: Who's Counting China?," *Christian Century* (August 10, 2010), 45.

[7] C. R. Boxer, *The Christian Century in Japan, 1549–1650* (Berkeley, CA: University of California Press, 1951), 91.

[8] Timothy S. Lee, *Born Again: Evangelicalism in Korea* (Honolulu: University of Hawaii, 2010).

[9] On Kil Sŏnju's motive for embracing evangelical Protestantism, see Kil Chingyŏng, *Yŏnggye Kil Sŏnju* (Seoul: Chongo Sŏjŏk, 1980).

[10] C. E. Sharpe, "Motive for Seeking Christ," *KMF* 2 (August 1906): 182–3; and C. A. Clark, "Not Unpromising Now," *KMF* 2 (August 1906): 198–9.

[11] IKCHS, *History of Korean Church*, vol. 1, 303.

[12] Cf. "A strict neutrality has been maintained and a determination to keep hands out of politics is a well known fact to all who are acquainted with the missionary plans and policy of the Christian Church" editorial, *KMF* 3 (October 1907): 153–6.

[13] W. M. Baird, "Pyeng Yang Academy," *KMF* 2 (October 1906): 221–4.

[14] Ibid.: 221–4.

[15] William Blair, "Report of an Address to the Presbyterian Mission on the Million Movement," *KMF* (November 1911): 310–11.

[16] "Editorial Notes," *KMF* 14 (January 1918): 1–3.

[17] *A History of Korean Church*, vol. 1. (Seoul: Institute for Korean Church History, 1989), 308.

[18] "Some Changes in the Korean Church," *KMF* 10 (March 1914): 69.

[19] New York: International Missionary Council, 1934.

[20] For detailed treatment of this event, see Frank Baldwin, Jr, "The March First Movement: Korean Challenge and Japanese Response" (PhD diss., Columbia: Columbia University, 1969).

[21] Michael E. Robinson, *Korea's Twentieth-Century Odyssey: A Short History* (Honolulu: University of Hawaii Press, 2007), 47.

[22] The *classicus locus* of the Tan'gun myth is in the thirteenth-century work by Iryŏn: see his *Samguk Yusa: Legends and History of the Three Kingdoms of Korea*, trans. Tae-hung Ha and Grafton Mintz (Seoul: Yonsei University, 1972).

[23] Baldwin, "March First Movement," 12.

[24] On the influence of the Versailles Peace Conference on the March First Movement, see Baldwin, "March First Movement," 14–51.

[25] Ki-baik Lee, *A New History of Korea* (Cambridge, MA: Harvard University Press, 1984), 344. There is some dispute over the number of Korean participants in the uprising. Robinson cites the conservative figure of 1 million – *Korea's Twentieth-Century Odyssey*, 48. Baldwin cautiously endorses the figure of 2 million.

[26] Baldwin, "March First Movement," 53.

[27] Lee, *New History of Korea,* 344; Baldwin, "March First Movement," 232–5.

[28] Quoted in Cynn, Hugh Heung-Woo, *Rebirth of Korea: The Reawakening of the People, Its Causes, and the Outlook* (New York: Abingdon, 1920), 64.

[29] *The Journals of Mattie Wilcox Noble, 1892–1934* (Seoul: Han'guk kidokkyo yŏksa yŏnguso (Institute of Korean Church History Study), 1993), 275.

[30] Baldwin, "Missionaries and the March First Movement," 197.

[31] Federal Council of the Churches of Christ of America (FCCCA), comp., *The Korean Situation: Authentic Accounts of Recent Events by Eye Witnesses* (New York: FCCCA, 1919), 30–1.

[32] FCCCA, *The Korean Situation,* 33.

[33] Baldwin, "March First Movement," 185.

[34] Kim Sung-t'ae, "*Chonggyoin-ŭi 3.1 Undong Ch'amyŏ-wa Kidokkyo-ŭi Yŏkhwal*" (Religionists' Participation in the March First Movement and the Role of Christianity), in *Journal of the Institute of Korean Church History Studies* 25 (April 1989): 17–24.

[35] Kim, "*Chonggyoin-ŭi 3.1 Undong Ch'amyŏ,*" 39.

[36] "The '*Such'ŏn kyohoe panghwa-haksal sakŏn*' (The Arson-Massacre Incident at the Such'on Church), *Kŭrisch'an sinmun* (Christian Press) (February 27, 1965); and "*Sŭkop'ldŭ paksa*" (Dr Scofield) in the same newspaper (April 18, 1970).

[37] Alfred W. Wasson, *Church Growth in Korea,* (Concord, NH: International Missionary Council, 1934), 103. On the upturn in Church membership, Wasson states, "Since 1910 the curve representing the total number of Southern Methodist members and probationers had been steadily going downward; in 1920 the curve turned sharply upward again, and within five years there was a net gain of 102 percent. In each of the other churches in Korea also the year 1920 marks the beginning of a period of growth. ... This period of rapid growth was ushered in by the Independence Movement" (98).

[38] See Donald Baker, "Sibling Rivalry in Twentieth-Century Korea: Comparative Growth Rates of Catholic and Protestant Communities," in Buswell and Lee, eds, *Christianity in Korea,* 283–308.

[39] Timothy S. Lee, "Beleaguered Success: Korean Evangelicalism in the Last Decade of the Twentieth Century," in Buswell and Lee, eds, *Christianity in Korea,* 330–50.

[40] Timothy S. Lee, "What Should Christians Do about a Shaman-Progenitor?: Evangelicals and Ethnic Nationalism in South Korea," *Church History* 78/1 (March 2009): 66–98.

[41] Ibid.

[42] Paul Yunsik Chang, "Carrying the Torch in the Darkest Hours: The Sociopolitical Origins of Minjung Protestant Movement," in Buswell and Lee, eds, *Christianity in Korea,* 195–220.

[43] Scott W. Sunquist, ed., *A Dictionary of Asian Christianity* (Grand Rapids, MI: Eerdmans, 2001), s.v. "Japan," 412.

[44] Daniel H. Bays, ed., *Christianity in China: From the Eighteenth Century to the Present* (Stanford, CA: Stanford University Press, 1996).

[45] Sunquist, ed., *A Dictionary of Asian Christianity,* s.v., Sun Yat Sen.

[46] Iris Chang, *The Rape of Nanking: The Forgotten Holocaust of World War II* (New York: Basic Books, 1997); Hua-ling Hu, *American Goddess at the Rape of Nanking: The Courage of Minnie Vautrin* (Carbondale, IL: Southern Illinois University Press, 2000).

[47] Lian Xi, *Redeemed by Fire: The Rise of Popular Christianity in Modern China* (New Haven, CT: Yale University Press, 2010).

Further Reading

Bays, Daniel H., ed. *Christianity in China: From the Eighteenth Century to the Present.* Stanford, CA: Stanford University Press, 1996.

Buswell, Robert E., Jr., and Timothy S. Lee, eds., *Christianity in Korea.* Honolulu: University of Hawai'i Press, 2006.

Choi, Hyaeweol. *Gender and Mission Encounters in Korea: New Women, Old Ways.* Berkeley, CA: University of California, 2009.

Chong, Kelly H. *Deliverance and Submission: Evangelical Women and the Negotiation of Patriarchy in South Korea.* Cambridge, MA: Harvard University Asia Center, 2008.

Grayson, James Huntley. *Korea: A Religious History,* rev. edn. London: RoutledgeCurzon, 2002.

Hunter, Alan and Kim-Kwong Chan, *Protestantism in Contemporary China.* Cambridge: Cambridge University Press, 1993.

Lee, Timothy S. *Born Again: Evangelicalism in Korea.* Honolulu: University of Hawaii Press, 2010.

Moffett, Samuel H. *A History of Christianity in Asia, Vol. II: 1500–1990.* Maryknoll, NY: 2005.

Mullins, Mark R. *Christianity Made in Japan: A Study of Indigenous Movements.* Honolulu: University of Hawai'i Press, 1998.

Reid, David. *New Wine: The Cultural Shaping of Japanese Christianity.* Berkeley, CA: Asian Humanities Press, 1991.

Thomas, Winburn. *Protestant Beginnings in Japan.* Rutland, VT: Charles E. Tuttle, 1959.

Yip, Kap-che. *Religion, Nationalism and Chinese Students: The Anti-Christian Movement of 1922–1927.* Bellingham, WA: Washington University Press, 1980.

Part IV

Americas

10

Christianity in North America
Changes and Challenges in a Land of Promise

Kevin J. Christiano

Introduction: "Supremely Pluralist in Religion"

All that is recognizably Christian in North America initially came to the continent, and then suffused through its historical passages and its social patterns, with the movements of migrating people. In their exchanges with European cultures, the resettled people of North America became net importers (and often imposers) of religion for themselves and for the native population. Later, North Americans produced and promoted, revised and renewed, varieties of Christianity for transmission through religious missions around the world.

This is not to say, however, that everything about Christianity throughout the history of North America has been clear and consistent – far from it. The Christian experience in North America has been marked repeatedly by controversy and conflict when emphases in society swing from pious purity to the purely practical. In the case of the United States, the social critic Max Lerner has noted how "history reveals a striking mixture of theocracy and secularism, of dogma with indifferentism." As a result, the American religious record, writes Lerner, "is at once deeply individualist, anti-authoritarian, salvation-minded yet secular and rationalist in its life-goals. . ."[1]

Tinged with an inclination toward such instrumental concerns as economic development and nation-building rather than grand theory or philosophy, the culture of the United States is additionally the product of what historian William G. McLoughlin terms a "dynamic, sectarian form of pietistic-perfectionism."[2] His description is something of a mouthful, but what it means is that Americans were disinclined to perpetuate "remnants of the European civilization" in their new nation. Instead, their particular version of Christianity ignited "in America from the outset . . . a continual spirit of reformation, a constant search for a more perfect union between God and man."[3] The collective striving of Americans for an improved moral order led to a society that is characterized to this day by a relentless spiritual restlessness, so that perfection is pursued always anew, not by means of a static regulation of society but by active resort to the moral freedom that God provides, through the government and its laws, to individuals.

For this reason, the religious history of the continent has exhibited one bold continuity: a tendency, proceeding over several centuries, to greater and greater levels of freedom in matters of conscience. The logical consequence of this freedom has been the creation, through both choice and happenstance, of a religious environment that, with time, has grown ever more *diverse* and *pluralistic*. At first, the legitimation of religious pluralism in North America enabled a huge range of beliefs and actions to take concrete shape – as single congregations or entire bodies of churches –

Introducing World Christianity, First Edition. Edited by Charles E. Farhadian.
© 2012 Blackwell Publishing Ltd. Published 2012 by Blackwell Publishing Ltd.

Map 10.1 North America

and to flourish in the new nations. Wrote David S. Schaff back in 1912, "it might seem as if it had been ordained that every known type of the Christian faith should be brought together here."[4] At the same time, religious impulses conceived and guided an expanding array of inter- and para-denominational organizations.

Yet, among individuals, the elevation of freedom of conscience as a prime value encouraged types of religion that could be tailored to personal tastes, that could thrive outside of institutional settings, and that could be maintained faithfully even in total privacy. For example, by the late 1970s, 81 percent of Americans in a Gallup survey agreed with the assertion that "an individual should arrive at his or her own religious beliefs independent of any church or synagogue." Moreover, almost the same proportion of respondents (78 percent) endorsed the statement that "a person can be a good Christian or Jew without attending" such an institution.[5]

A second consequence of the multiplication of spiritual stances in North America is the development of *tolerance* as the modus vivendi (the method of everyday living) of relations between and among religious groups. The very principle of freedom that permits one to embrace one's own beliefs necessarily supports the right of others with differing perspectives to do the same without interference.[6] This end is accomplished peacefully by shunting potential points of interreligious conflict into the personal realm, because "the more extensive the range of denominational inclusion within the American system the more the denominationally specific components of religious belief, practice and organization must be 'privatized.'"[7]

The New World: Christianity Comes to a Continent

One of the most salient attributes of North American history is how much of the European settlement of the continent proceeded from religious interests and imperatives. As an esteemed church historian wrote 100 years ago, "in the discovery and colonization of the continent, the planting of the Christian religion was an avowed and prominent purpose." To offer just one example: "In the minds of the Spanish sovereigns and the emperor, religion was a paramount concern in the occupation of the new world."[8] To demonstrate this, one only need cite Queen Isabella herself: "Our chief intention" in dispatching explorers to the West, she said, "was to attract the peoples of these regions and to obtain their conversion to our holy religion."[9]

Between the time of the first European exploration of the New World and that of the American Revolution, approximately 1.2 million Spanish and Portuguese and about 750,000 British settlers came to the western hemisphere. Smaller numbers of French and Dutch subjects followed as well. Against their will, nearly 3.9 million African slaves also made the Atlantic crossing in those centuries, and about one third of this total were taken to colonies that were under the control of Great Britain.

Most histories of North America credit the Spanish with founding in 1565 the first permanent settlement on the continent (but not without killing some French Huguenots on the site in Florida). More notable still is the lengthy chain of mission stations that Spanish clergy established up the Pacific coast and throughout what is now the American Southwest. For their part, the French concentrated on exploring from their base at Québec, founded in 1608, the continent's vast network of lakes and rivers, from the upper Midwest all the way down the valley of the Mississippi to the Gulf of Mexico. En route, Jesuit priests among them sometimes made converts, yet the trappers and traders of New France seldom tarried long enough to do other than cement lucrative relationships with native communities. The British in turn were as dedicated to occupying the land as the Spanish were to exploiting it and the French to paddling and portaging smoothly through it. Hence their colonies hugged the Atlantic coastline and were heavily dependent for their survival upon religious inspiration, military backing, and oceangoing commerce from the mother country.

Sacred Liberty: The Colonial Religious Experience

To make a long story somewhat shorter, Spanish control in the Southeast and along the shores of the Gulf eventually gave way to British domination, while a brief but decisive confrontation with British troops in

1759 on a cliffside plain overlooking the St Lawrence River ended forever any French hopes of turning a North American foothold into a continental empire.[10] Just a few years in the future, however, lay the revolution against England's colonial rule that would produce the United States. This uprising, too, possessed a religious dimension that was supplied and nourished by the Christian churches of the colonies. More particularly, the religious enthusiasm of the eighteenth-century revivals set the stage for "religious and political ideas with powerful social significance and ideological urgency. . . a radical, even democratic, social and political ideology."[11]

In a century when public sources of information were few, and newspapers in particular were scarce, the churches became centers of communication and their services acted as gatherings of the local community.[12] In that context, sermons from the pulpits of especially the dissenting churches ("protestants from Protestantism itself "[13]) did much to fan the flames of ire among liberty-loving colonists – to the point that they discoursed more on political philosophy than on theology. When the Bible was called into play, it was to assist the patriots' side. England's King George III was equated with the Pharaoh from the Hebrew Scriptures who held captive the people of Israel; the aggrieved colonists were compared to the ancient Israelites.[14] The effect was to invite churchgoers to view themselves as actors in a world-historical struggle between good and evil, the sacred and the worldly, and ultimately to mobilize them to take up arms against their oppressor.

A New Nation: Republican Ideas and Christian Ideals

The Christian churches of the new American nation immediately began jockeying to claim credit for having animated the spirit of the successful revolution. The Baptists boasted that republican government owed its values to their church polity, "which was founded upon free assent, sovereignty of each congregation, and dependence of ministers upon the people." Presbyterians drew a parallel between their own form of governance, which they deemed to have been ordained by God, and the government of

the republic, which must therefore, they reasoned, enjoy similar divine favor.[15] Not to be outdone, the Episcopalians (recently shorn of their English connections) contended that both their church and the new civil sphere featured "a unified executive power, limitations on the judicial process, guaranteed safeguards of individual rights through hearings and judgment by one's peers, and a bicameral legislature of sorts."[16] Even Roman Catholicism, not the most democratic of denominations, pointed to the Swiss cantons and the Italian city-states as examples of free republics that operated under its principles of order.[17] Why not the United States?

In at least eight of the 13 original colonies, religion was established by the state or funded out of tax revenue.[18] However, with the adoption of the First Amendment to the Constitution in 1791, the United States became the first nation with a Christian majority formally to separate church and state, a move that has been described as possibly "the most dramatic widespread change in governance since the era of Constantine 1,400 years earlier."[19] Although many critics of the move warned fearfully of the likely consequences of the withdrawal of state support for religion, in the new United States formal faith did not deteriorate but blossomed.

Canada: Loyalty in the Lord's Dominion

As we have already seen, Christian religion was integral to the founding of the United States. In contrast, few of the original settlers of Canada arrived on its shores as refugees from religious persecution.[20] Nor was Canada's formation, called Confederation, accomplished directly through invoking the Christian beliefs of the majority of its inhabitants.

More mundane factors held sway in the decision to consolidate the British possessions north of the border into a new political entity in 1867. For one, the United States in 1865 had concluded a horrible civil war, and had embarked upon a path of sectional reconciliation. Leaders in Canada were fearful that a powerful neighbor, again united, could endanger the sovereignty of their fragmented territory.[21] To knit together a scattered people and to attain greater solidarity from east to west across their fledgling nation, Canadian business and political elites planned grand projects of canal and railroad construction. For such transcontinental ambitions to be realized they required new laws and governmental institutions, which came in the guise of Confederation. Canada's founding act thus had more to do with rights of way than with the Rights of Man.[22]

Rallying to repel territorial threats, Canada's political architects, the Fathers of Confederation, had no time to remake their society according to a list of central philosophical or religious precepts – even were one available and accepted – and no warrant to do so either. Instead their handiwork is marked by accommodations to, and compromises with, conditions that they found in place.[23] These conditions included a vast physical landscape covered with only a small population; the deep and enduring division of that population into aboriginal, French-speaking, and English-speaking camps; the stubborn strength of local and regional identities as opposed to a truly national sentiment; and the unrelenting pull of the wider continental culture.

All of these contingencies bred for Canadians a regular habit of negotiation and compromise rather than a commandment of conformity to a single ideal. This habit in turn blunted some of the potential for absolutism in thought and the acute conflict in behavior that it can trigger. "The necessity of continuous compromise in the interests of religion, regionalism, and race," wrote the Canadian economic historian Harold A. Innis, "explains the paucity of political thinking and the importance of pretence in mediocrity to political leaders."[24] The contemporary literary critic Noah Richler has implied much the same thing about his country, though in more intimate terms: "We are a nation founded on uncertainty and doubt – and querulous and wonderfully modern as a consequence."[25]

Many who participated in or supported the process of Canada's creation were descended from persons who specifically rejected the revolution to their south (or, in the case of Québec, who pre-dated the one in the original mother country),[26] and who remained loyal to the idea of state-sponsored religion. Harold Innis stated this fact tersely when he remarked, "a counter-revolutionary tradition implies an emphasis on ecclesiasticism."[27] Seymour Martin Lipset put the identical matter in comparative terms when he

asserted, "The United States has been a sectarian country. Canada has been a church country."[28] The aftermath of the two nations having followed diverging paths in religious organization is visible today in the

Table 10.1 The 10 largest religious affiliations – United States (2008)

Denomination	Proportion of the adult population in percent
Roman Catholic Church	23.9
(Unaffiliated or "don't know")	(16.9) (but 1.6 "atheist")
Southern Baptist Convention	6.7
"Protestants" (unspecified)	5.2
United Methodist Church	5.1
Evangelical Lutheran Church in America	2.0
National Baptist Convention	1.8
Jewish	1.7
Church of Jesus Christ of Latter-day Saints (Mormons)	1.6
Church of Christ	1.5
Total	66.4

Source: The Pew Forum on Religion and Public Life, *U.S. Religious Landscape Survey. Religious Beliefs and Practices: Diverse and Politically Relevant* (Washington, DC: The Pew Research Center, 2008)

Table 10.2 The 10 largest religious affiliations – Canada (2001)

Denomination	Proportion of the population in percent
Roman Catholic Church	43.2 (83.2 in Québec)
("No religion")	(16.2) (37.4 in Yukon; 35.1 in B.C.)
United Church of Canada	9.6
Anglican Church of Canada	6.9
"Christians" (unspecified)	2.6
Baptists	2.5
Lutherans	2.0
Muslims	2.0
"Protestants" (unspecified)	1.9
Presbyterians	1.4
Total	88.3

Source: Census Operations Division, Statistics Canada, *Religions in Canada* (Ottawa: Minister of Industry, 2003)

PA-023350

Figure 10.1 A community of Trappist monks poses next to their original rustic monastery building in the Canadian wilderness around Mistassini, Québec. Today, these monks perform religious works at the same time that they support themselves making chocolate candy (*Source*: Jules-Ernest Livernois/Library and Archives Canada/PA-023350).

relative concentration of Canadian Christians in a handful of large nationwide denominations, but also with the dispersion of their American brethren throughout a much more extensive and varied collection of bodies (for an indication, compare tables 10.1 and 10.2).

In 1791, the act that established two Canadian provinces (Upper Canada, where today one finds Ontario, and Lower Canada, or Québec) also allocated the proceeds from one seventh of all public ("Crown") lands to pay for the Protestant clergy. The law intended that "Protestant" mean the Church of England, but ministers of other Christian denominations later challenged this interpretation and sought portions of state funds for themselves. Partly to quell the rising conflict, the bulk of these monies was shifted in 1854 to a public fund that would underwrite the expenses of schools.[29]

It would seem that Christians in nineteenth-century Canada had advanced far toward their goal of forging a godly nation when they took part of a verse from the Psalms as the country's official motto: *A mari usque ad mare*, Latin for "From sea unto sea."[30] However, their dream eventually foundered on the sharp seams of their nation's own internal cleavages. Because these differences persisted against a backdrop of religious establishment (formal at first, then informal),[31] the rampant type of pluralism that caused Christianity to grow and expand in the United States held the churches in check in Canada.

From an American perspective, denominational variety could be a good thing. For Canadians, however, rivalry among the churches was taken as a sign of the fragility and thus the vulnerability of institutional religion. Instead of competing against one another, head-to-head, to gain material resources, to open new fields of endeavor, and to add further members, Canadian Christians learned early the virtues of cooperation and church comity. "Christianizing an immense territory shortly to be populated by millions of people of foreign birth, ideals and traditions," predicted Canadian churchman S. D. Chown, "could not be accomplished with reasonable speed by competing Churches duplicating their resources upon a single task."[32]

The cooperative ethic sometimes entailed, for the sake of efficiency, a clear demarcation of tasks and terrain. In Alberta, for example, Presbyterians limited themselves to work among people "contiguous to the lines of the Canadian Pacific Railroad" (CPR), while the Methodists served those along the tracks of the Canadian National (CN) Railway.[33] At other times, it surpassed simple sharing and stimulated actual mergers of church bodies. Between 1874 and 1884, six groups of Canadian Methodists became one; four Presbyterian groups combined in 1875; and by 1893, all of the dioceses of the Church of England in Canada were unified under a sole structure.[34]

All of this activity was a mere prelude, though, to the sweeping action in 1925 that created the United Church of Canada out of a union of the Methodist, Congregationalist, and most Presbyterian churches.[35] "Such a thorough breaching of historic denominational lines," it has been said, "had never taken place within the old Christendom."[36] The resulting combination, in the words of the same commentator, "is as Canadian as ice hockey."[37]

The Lord's Song in a Foreign Land: Migration and Immigration in North American History

Even as the people of North America were enjoying the benefits of new political arrangements, their social worlds were again tossed into a maelstrom of change, this time by a mass migration to the continent that was without historical precedent. Between 1790 and 1860, the population of the United States increased from 3.9 million to 31.5 million, and it more than doubled from there to 1890.[38] What is more, indices of church growth such as numbers of adherents and clergy outstripped this rapid rate of expansion. For example, from 1,200 American parishes in 1850, the Roman Catholic Church entered the twentieth century with around 12,000.[39]

Much (though certainly not all) of this trend was contributed by a wave of immigration, primarily from the nations of Europe, which began in the 1830s and 1840s and continued through to the end of World War I.[40] By the first years of the twentieth century, more than 1 million immigrants per year were making the passage to America and to a new life. This demographic upheaval did more than simply jam ports of entry and feed the voracious appetite for labor that the enterprises of a burgeoning continent had incurred. Its composition also challenged the once dominant Protestant Christian heritage of the United States. "From the colonial period to the late nineteenth century," notes historian Patrick Allitt, "most Americans regarded the English-speaking part of the New World to be an essentially Protestant place."[41] That all began to change at the onset of the twentieth century, with the insertion into the culture for the first time of substantial numbers of Catholics and Jews, and their concentration in the densely settled cities of the continent.

Not long after the mass immigration of people from Europe, African Americans commenced an enormous internal migration of their own. By 1930, more than 1.2 million blacks from rural hamlets in the South had migrated to the industrial cities of the North, leaving behind the legal segregation of Jim Crow and entering for the first time a truly heterogeneous urban environment. "More than any other single social phenomenon," the Southern novelist Richard Marius has written, "religion has marked the South."[42] So it is no surprise that black migrants from the South brought religion northward with them. There they constructed a distinctive African-American religious culture that melded elements of Southern folk life with new interpretations of gospel and jazz music.[43]

This domestic migration, to be sure, acted to introduce some characteristic elements of Southern religion to life in the North. Religion in the South featured events as different as the Mardi Gras of the Gulf states and the mass revival meeting of a thousand rural churches: it was, reflects historian Donald G. Mathews, "a broad and mischievous diversity." Yet, he ruminates, "the nation would not be what it is without the South, and the South would not be what it is without African Americans." Indeed, Mathews ventures the assessment that "Absent race, and North Carolina becomes Iowa."[44]

Much of the national drama about race, of course, traces back to conflict over "the peculiar institution" of slavery.[45] Southern Christians were especially notable for their estrangement from their Northern brethren over the morality of holding other humans as property, a division that began well before the Civil War (1861–5). Throughout the nineteenth century, in fact, Hebrew and Christian scriptures alike were contorted and twisted from end to end in a theological and ideological tug-of-war, invoked both to justify and to attack the practice of slave-holding.[46]

Protestants, Catholics, and Jews: Conflict and Comity among Christians and Others

For the greatest stretch of its history, the United States was an overwhelmingly Protestant nation. Indeed, of the approximately 4.5 million free white colonists at the time of the American Revolution, just 30,000 (about seven tenths of 1 percent) were Catholics and perhaps 3,000 (one tenth that proportion) were Jews.[47] Roman Catholics showed up in great numbers in the United States only in the 1840s, when economic crisis in Ireland and political strife in Germany prompted them to leave their homes to establish themselves in the American republic. Before the end of the nineteenth century, enormous numbers of Catholics came as well from places in Southern Europe (such as Italy) and Eastern Europe (such as Poland).

The response to this new presence, on the whole, was not positive. Catholic immigrants, aside from simply being "foreign," often looked foreign and spoke in foreign tongues. And their religion, though Christian in belief, was a mixture of severe practices and sensory spectacles that were far removed from anything that the Protestant majority would acknowledge. Prejudice against Catholics spread widely in the nineteenth and early twentieth centuries. Although much of this anti-Catholic sentiment was not put to rest until the victory of Senator John F. Kennedy in the presidential election of 1960, the middle years of the century were a kind of prologue to the religious *rapprochement* that awaited Americans in later decades.

Few historical events can match the involvement of the United States in World War II (1941–5) for either the speed or the span of its effects on how average Americans would live through the second half of the twentieth century. More particularly, among the first victims of the nationwide mobilization for battle abroad were the overt religious prejudice and discrimination that in the recent past had prevailed at home. As an ideological matter, they mirrored too closely for comfort the most repugnant aspects of the racial theories of the Axis powers.[48] As a practical matter, they carried too high a price to be borne into the fight, for they represented an insult to the unity and solidarity that loyal citizens, regardless of background, were expected to exhibit in the face of an immediate and demonstrably lethal enemy.[49]

Millions of young Americans served in uniform during World War II, and their experiences caused them to regard each of "the three fighting faiths of democracy" as equally legitimate mechanisms for enacting one's identity as an American. Whereas religion was beforehand a basis for division and exclusion, it now functioned for many as a foundation for consolidation and commonality of purpose. The symbol that perhaps best communicated the union of American faiths in the sacrifices of World War II stemmed from a real episode: the torpedoing and sinking in 1943 of a crowded troop carrier, the SS *Dorchester* (a former merchant vessel), in the North Atlantic, and the heroism of her four on-board chaplains (two Protestant ministers, a Catholic priest, and a Jewish rabbi). Each of the four clergymen voluntarily relinquished his life preserver to a beleaguered soldier or sailor; they then perished together while praying as the crippled ship slipped below the ocean's surface. It was, in the words of a later memorial, a timeless instance of "Interfaith in Action."[50]

Conformity in the Mainstream, Combusion at the Margins

With the Japanese surrender in 1945, the military triumph over Nazism and fascism in Europe and the defeat of imperial aggression in Asia left the United States briefly without a visible enemy on the world stage. However, that place in geopolitics soon came to be occupied by America's erstwhile ally, the Soviet Union. Yet, as powerful as the regime of the Soviet commissars may have seemed in the post-war world, it was perceived to suffer at least one great vulnerability: "Marxist atheism was the Achilles' heel of Soviet communism, which was portrayed as a fanatical pseudo-religion that only a superior spiritual force could resist."[51]

To many, that force of resistance in the so-called Cold War was the combined Judeo-Christian piety of the American faithful: Protestant, Catholic, and Jewish – and maybe others.[52] "It makes no difference," preached a celebrated Catholic homilist, Monsignor Fulton J. Sheen, "if one be a Jew, a Protestant, or a Catholic, a Hottentot, a Mohammedan, Hindu, German or Japanese."[53] In this opinion, a national leader such as Dwight D. Eisenhower was no less a believer than a churchman such as Billy Graham; each could insist, in the words of the general-turned-president in 1955, "Without God, there could be no American form of government, nor an American way of life."[54]

Yet, every bit as much *because of* the plurality of religion in the United States as *in spite of* it, President Eisenhower was hard put to flesh out his patriotic form of faith with much official doctrine beyond a vision of the fatherhood of God and the brotherhood of humanity. Quipped William Lee Miller about the chief executive's beliefs: "President Eisenhower, like many Americans, is a very fervent believer in a very vague religion."[55] Speaking sociologically, Ike's predicament was unavoidable: what Parsons clumsily called "the main common normative structure" had "to include wider ranges of pluralistic diversity," and so, to achieve the desired consensus, it "has come to be placed on a level of higher and higher generalization."[56]

Beneath feelings of material comfort and spiritual coziness, however, lurked a sense of unease in the culture. Americans evidently believed in their country and their God, but many nevertheless privately doubted the ability of either to deliver them to a more meaningful existence. Popular piety had penetrated family ritual and civic expression, and was not neglected either in the television schedule or on the bestseller lists.[57]

Thus were the seeds sown for a new type of religious consciousness in North America, one that did not flourish fully until a decade or more later in the movement called "Beat." True, the Beats were not enamored with "organized" religion, but to imply that their outlook was fashionably negative was far off the mark too. In contrast, as Stephen Prothero has argued, their "*flight from* the churches and synagogues of the suburbs to city streets inhabited by whores and junkies, hobos and jazzmen, never ceased to be a *search for* something to believe in, something to go by." Later Prothero identifies the constant motion of the Beats as a drive to sanctify the grimiest byways of their world: "They aimed not to arrive but to travel and, in the process, to transform into sacred space every back alley through which they ambled and every tenement in which they lived."[58] One of the leading figures in Beat circles, the prose poet Jack Kerouac, told an interviewer that the "Lost Generation" of F. Scott Fitzgerald and Ernest Hemingway "from what I can tell from the books, was based on an ironic romantic negation"; he contended that the Beats, on the other hand, were "sweating for affirmation."[59]

The cultural conformity that overtook organized religion in the 1950s easily spilled into the succeeding decade. In terms of conviction, pollster Louis Harris established by 1965 that fully 97 percent of American adults professed a belief in God. With respect to conduct, his counterpart George Gallup discovered in the same period that 44 percent of Americans claimed to attend religious services on a weekly basis. Yet of the nearly unanimous theists whom Harris encountered in the national population, a mere quarter or so (27 percent) would describe themselves as "deeply religious."[60]

Americans All vs Multicultural Canadians: The New Religious Pluralism in North America

In 1965, the Congress of the United States passed legislation that finally repealed the national-origin quotas on immigration that it had instituted back in 1924 in a naked attempt to curtail the flow into the country of non-Protestant migrants from Southern and Eastern Europe.[61] The main effect of this belated change, however, was not to re-establish an earlier mix of newcomers from old places, but to open the gates more widely to an entirely different tide of people:

Figure 10.2 Richard M. Nixon, who served as president of the United States from 1969 to 1974, joins the famed Christian evangelist Billy Graham on stage at the Rev. Graham's massive 1970 East Tennessee Crusade in Knoxville. (*Source*: Oliver F. Atkins for the White House Photo Office/Richard Nixon Library, U. S. National Archives and Records Administration/NLNP-WHPO-MPF-C3587[04]).

those from Latin America, the Caribbean, Southern and Eastern Asia, and elsewhere. By the 1990s, there were two immigrants from Asia and about four from the Americas for every immigrant to the United States from Europe. In the 30 years of movement that followed the lifting of the quotas, the majority of the immigrants to land in the United States were born in one of only seven countries: China (and Taiwan), the Dominican Republic, India, Korea, Mexico, the Philippines, or Vietnam.[62]

Not only did this new wave of immigration bring with it a diversity of races, ethnicities, and languages, but it also introduced into American society, or augmented existing examples of, religions from outside the middle-class mainstream of Anglo-European Christianity. "This migration," notes David Wills, "is refashioning Christianity... away from its European past and toward its global future."[63] In the United States and Canada, stained-glass windows once shone their colors from whitewashed sanctuaries camped confidently on downtown squares. Now they were joined by novel types of religious institutions: storefront churches, basement prayer and healing fellowships, non-denominational worship venues, shrines and other pilgrimage destinations, Islamic mosques, Buddhist and Hindu temples, and Sikh *gurdwaras* – not to mention meditation centers under a number of different auspices.

A similar dynamic is at work to the north in Canada, which has erected an even more hospitable environment for the maintenance of religious diversity. From its very beginnings a country committed to (or captive of) its essential plurality, Canada came by the 1960s to enshrine in federal law *bilingualism*, the equality of its two principal languages (English and French), and in 1971 it instituted an official policy of *multiculturalism*. Canada's Constitution, patriated from Great Britain in 1982, included a landmark Charter of Rights and Freedoms that protects "freedom of conscience and religion" (Section 2), as well as provisions banning religious discrimination (Section 15) and instructing that the document itself be interpreted in a manner in keeping with the nation's multicultural reality (Section 27).[64]

But Canadian legislation dealing with cultural diversity is not simply defensive: the federal government in Canada, through several granting agencies, provides financial subsidies to organizations that help immigrants actively to retain and develop their cultures in North America.[65] Finally, the Multiculturalism Act of 1988 identifies Canada as a polity "dedicated to the promotion and incorporation of cultural diversity, linguistic diversity, and somewhat less explicitly, religious pluralism." One concomitant of these changes in Canada was an explosion of official evidence of that pluralism. In fact, between 1971 and 1981, its census (which, unlike the census of the United States, collects data on the religious preferences of individuals) could be read to indicate increases of at least fourfold in the numbers of Muslims, Hindus, and Sikhs.[66]

The Religious Future: Fissures in Faith?

As many commentators have already observed, Christianity in North America is facing social facts and societal trends prefiguring a future that likely will not be diminished so much as it will be different from the patterns of the past.[67] Signs of the magnitude of this difference are repeated in the millions of North Americans who, over the course of a single lifetime, switch from one religious affiliation to another, who "pick, mix, and choose" from the sacred practices of numerous cultures, or who abandon religion altogether out of boredom, frustration, or competing commitments.[68]

The penultimate point in this progression is the oft-heard confession these days that one is "spiritual, but not religious." What can be inferred from such an identification is that one feels some impulse toward understanding and experiencing the sacred, but at the same time one believes that organizations or communities either do not assist, or positively obstruct, this aspiration. A possible endpoint, however, is an exit from religion entirely. Two sociologists, Michael Hout and Claude S. Fischer, have calculated that the proportion of American adults with no religious preference doubled during the 1990s, from 7 to 14 percent, while those who remember being raised with no affiliation tripled, from 2 to 6 percent.[69] (Among Canadians, the rate of those without a religion is slightly higher, at approximately 16 percent.) Although these fractions are relatively small, they give every reason to expect growth among the unchurched in the future.

Sure to be witnessed during the coming years is the further attenuation of denominational affiliations. More and more markedly, religious loyalties will cease primarily to be the passively accepted consequences of family ties, group traditions, or other cultural inheritances. Instead, they will emerge with greater frequency as the product of personal choices.[70]

In this "reinvented" locus for faith, the focus of believers will bypass doctrine, not out of disbelief but from uninterest.[71] Instead, participants in religion will center their concern on the local congregation, and these churches, sociologist Donald E. Miller predicts, will accord themselves to a specific prototype:

> The fastest-growing churches in America are independent congregations that typically share the following characteristics: they were started after the mid-1960s; the majority of congregational members were born after 1945; seminary training of clergy is optional; worship is contemporary; lay leadership is highly valued; the churches have extensive small-group ministries; clergy and congregants dress informally; tolerance of different personal styles is prized; pastors are understated, humble, and self-revealing; bodily, rather than merely cognitive, participation in worship is the norm; the gifts of the Holy Spirit are affirmed; and Bible-centered teaching predominates over topical sermonizing.[72]

Although this new organizational model is congregationally based, it ironically privileges the personal search for a trustworthy source of cultural authority to which autonomous persons may surrender themselves. Theirs is "a task of personal and cultural reconstruction"; according to Miller, "The goal is for members to have a relationship with Jesus, not to pledge allegiance to a particular catechism or doctrinal statement."[73]

From his strategic vantage monitoring cultural innovation in southern California, at the "hither edge" of the North American continent, the sociologist Wade Clark Roof advises that "it should come as no real surprise that multi-layered meaning systems are commonplace," because today's believers have embarked on voyages of "faith exploration" that resemble pastiche, "combining elements from such diverse sources as Eastern meditation, Native American spirituality, psychotherapy, ecology, feminism, Jungian psychology, as well as more traditional Judeo-Christian beliefs." Despite the fact that this habit of improvisation signals, in its "liberation from ascriptive bonds," a thinning of venerable religious heritages, Roof argues that it also clears the way for "new forms of belonging and community organized around people's deeper expressive concerns."[74]

Conclusion: Christianity and Christians in the Thick

Is the contemporary trade-off that is implied by Roof's thinking unique, or does it suggest any parallels with the past? Is it a development in religion throughout North America that ought to be welcomed? Welcome or not, is it probably inevitable? If inevitable, does it threaten to be irreversible? The answers to all of these doubts are not yet determined. The future of Christianity in North America may, in the end, be as open as the many courses of change that its practitioners and their institutions have traversed in five centuries of exertion and expression on the continent.

As important as will be future forms of religious organization and practice, in North America and elsewhere around the world, the impact of Christianity – in whatever forms it may take over the remainder of the twenty-first century – doubtlessly will be evident and earnest. Christians as a group historically have sown their share of discord and destruction in the midst of their very own societies. Yet it is worth remembering, too, that they continue to be the largest single providers of education and healthcare in the world.[75] In many places, at home and abroad, theirs are the sometimes lonely and imperiled voices insisting on the recognition of human rights and the extension of political freedoms, and standing against poverty, slavery, and allied indignities, while arguing also for a sustainable environment. These are crucial conflicts, and North American Christians can be found in the thick of each of them, where they will be for decades to come.

Notes and References

[1] Max Lerner, "Christian Culture and American Democracy," *The American Quarterly* 6 (1954): 129–30.

[2] William G. McLoughlin, "Pietism and the American Character," *The American Quarterly* 17 (1965): 164.

[3] Ibid., 165.

[4] David S. Schaff, "The Movement and Mission of American Christianity," *American Journal of Theology* 16 (1912): 57.

[5] Wade Clark Roof and William McKinney, "Denominational America and the New Religious Pluralism," *Annals of the American Academy of Political and Social Science* 480 (1985): 25.

[6] Talcott Parsons, "Religion in a Modern Pluralistic Society," *Review of Religious Research* 7 (1966): 127–8.

[7] Ibid., 134.

[8] Schaff, "The Movement and Mission of American Christianity," 52 and 53. See also 56.

[9] Quoted in Martin E. Marty, *The Christian World: A Global History* (New York: Random House, 2007), 139.

[10] Schaff, "The Movement and Mission of American Christianity," 55.

[11] Harry S. Stout, "Religion, Communications, and the Ideological Origins of the American Revolution," *The William and Mary Quarterly* (Third Series) 34 (1977): 521.

[12] C. H. Van Tyne, "Influence of the Clergy, and of Religious and Sectarian Forces, on the American Revolution," *American Historical Review* 19 (1913): 54–5. See also Stout, "Religion, Communications, and the Ideological Origins of the American Revolution," 526–30.

[13] Van Tyne, "Influence of the Clergy, and of Religious and Sectarian Forces, on the American Revolution," 64.

[14] Ibid., 58.

[15] William Gribbin, "Republican Religion and the American Churches in the Early National Period," *The Historian* 35 (1972): 66 and 67.

[16] Ibid., 67–8.

[17] Ibid., 69–71.

[18] Martin E. Marty, "The Land and the City in American Religious Conflict," *Review of Religious Research* 18 (1977): 227; Marty, *The Christian World*, 168–70; and David W. Wills, *Christianity in the United States: A Historical Survey and Interpretation* (Notre Dame, IN: University of Notre Dame Press, 2005), 11–17.

[19] Hugh McLeod, "Introduction," in Hugh McLeod, ed., *World Christianities, c. 1914– c. 2000* (Cambridge: Cambridge University Press, 2006), 8. The quotation is from Marty, *The Christian World*, 171.

[20] John Webster Grant, *The Canadian Experience of Church Union* (Richmond, VA: John Knox Press, 1967), 7.

[21] John Webster Grant, "Canadian Confederation and the Protestant Churches," *Church History* 38 (1969): 329.

[22] For a discussion, see Kevin J. Christiano, "Church and State in Institutional Flux: Canada and the United States," in David Lyon and Marguerite Van Die, eds., *Rethinking Church, State, and Modernity: Canada Between Europe and America* (Toronto: University of Toronto Press, 2000), 71–3.

[23] See Andrew E. Kim, "The Absence of Pan-Canadian Civil Religion: Plurality, Duality, and Conflict in Symbols of Canadian Culture," *Sociology of Religion* 54 (1993): 257–75; and Seymour Martin Lipset, "Historical Traditions and National Characteristics: A Comparative Analysis of Canada and the United States," *Canadian Journal of Sociology* 11 (1986): 121–2 and 142–3.

[24] Harold A. Innis, "Political Economy in the Modern State," *Proceedings of the American Philosophical Society* 87 (1944): 337.

[25] Quoted in Olga Stein, "Literally Across Canada: Interview with Noah Richler," *Books in Canada: The Canadian Review of Books*, December 2006: 10.

[26] This historical fact is the foundation for Seymour Martin Lipset's numerous analyses of differences between the United States and Canada. See, e.g., Lipset, "Historical Traditions and National Characteristics," 114–15 and 117–19; and Lipset, *Continental Divide: The Values and Institutions of the United States and Canada* (New York: Routledge, 1990).

[27] Harold A. Innis, "The Church in Canada" [1947], reprinted in Harold A. Innis, *Essays in Canadian Economic History*, ed. Mary Q. Innis (Toronto: University of Toronto Press, 1956), 385.

[28] Seymour Martin Lipset, "Culture and Economic Behavior: A Commentary," *Journal of Labor Economics* 11 (1993): S333. See also Lipset, "Historical Traditions and National Characteristics," 119 and 124–8.

[29] The disposition of the "clergy reserves" is one of the pivotal episodes in the religious development of Canada. For background, see Grant, *The Canadian Experience of Church Union*, 15–17; and Henry H. Walsh, "A Survey of Canadian Church History," *The Americas: A Quarterly Review of Inter-American Cultural History* 14 (1958): 369–73.

[30] "He shall have dominion also from sea to sea, and from the river unto the ends of the earth" (Psalm 72:8; KJV).

[31] Kim, "The Absence of a Pan-Canadian Civil Religion," 266–8; and Lipset, "Historical Traditions and National Characteristics," 125–6.

[32] S. D. [Samuel Dwight] Chown, *The Story of Church Union in Canada* (Toronto: The Ryerson Press, 1930), 12. See also Grant, *The Canadian Experience of Church Union*, 26–7.

[33] Chown, *The Story of Church Union in Canada*, 53–4.

[34] Grant, "Canadian Confederation and the Protestant Churches," 332.

[35] See C. E. [Claris Edwin] Silcox, *Church Union in Canada: Its Causes and Consequences* (New York: Institute of Social and Religious Research, 1933).

[36] Grant, *The Canadian Experience of Church Union*, 5.

[37] Ibid., 64. (Compare 37.)

[38] Mark A. Noll, "Nineteenth-Century Religion in World Context," *OAH* [Organization of American Historians] *Magazine of History*, July 2007: 51; and Kevin J. Christiano, *Religious Diversity and Social Change: American Cities, 1890–1906* (Cambridge: Cambridge University Press, 1987), 20.

[39] Noll, "Nineteenth-Century Religion in World Context," 52; and Christiano, *Religious Diversity and Social Change*, 20.

[40] Wills, *Christianity in the United States*, 22–5.

[41] Patrick Allitt, *Religion in America Since 1945: A History* (New York: Columbia University Press, 2003), 6. Compare Parsons, "Religion in a Modern Pluralistic Society," 128: "At least for the first century of its independent existence, American society ... was basically a *Protestant* society" (emphasis in the original). See also Wills, *Christianity in the United States, 2–3.*

[42] Richard Marius, "Musings on the Mysteries of the American South," *Daedalus* 113 (1984): 154.

[43] Colleen McDannell, "Christianity in the United States During the Inter-War Years," in McLeod, ed., *World Christianities, c. 1914–c. 2000*, 244–7.

[44] Donald G. Mathews, "Forum: Southern Religion," *Religion and American Culture* 8 (1998): 148 and 154.

[45] Marius, "Musings on the Mysteries of the American South," 143–4.

[46] See J. Albert Harrill, "The Use of the New Testament in the American Slave Controversy: A Case History in the Hermeneutical Tension Between Biblical Criticism and Christian Moral Debate," *Religion and American Culture* 10 (2000): 149–86.

[47] Marty, *The Christian World*, 169.

[48] Mark Silk, "Notes on the Judeo-Christian Tradition in America," *The American Quarterly* 36 (1984): 66–9.

[49] Philip Gleason, "Americans All: World War II and the Shaping of American Identity," *Review of Politics* 43 (1981): 500–1; see also 515–16.

[50] Deborah Dash Moore, "Jewish GIs and the Creation of the Judeo-Christian Tradition," *Religion and American Culture* 8 (1998): 37; and Edward S. Shapiro, "World War II and American Jewish Identity," *Modern Judaism* 10 (1990): 74.

[51] Dianne Kirby, "The Cold War, the Hegemony of the United States and the Golden Age of Christian Democracy," in McLeod, ed., *World Christianities, c. 1914–c. 2000*, 285.

[52] Robert S. Ellwood, *1950: Crossroads of American Religious Life* (Louisville, KY: Westminster John Knox Press, 2000), 11 and 104; Michelle Mart, "The 'Christianization' of Israel and Jews in 1950s America," *Religion and American Culture* 14 (2004): 109, 111, and 113; and Silk, "Notes on the Judeo-Christian Tradition in America," 69–70 and 76.

[53] Quoted in Martin E. Marty, *Under God, Indivisible: 1941–1960* (Chicago, IL: University of Chicago Press, 1996), 93.

[54] Dwight D. Eisenhower, "Remarks Recorded for the 'Back-to-God' Program of the American Legion (February 20, 1955)," as quoted in "Belief in God Is Vital to Americanism, Eisenhower Asserts in Filmed Talk Here," *The New York Times,* February 21, 1955: 24; and in "Words and Works," *Time* (US edition), March 7, 1955: 58.

[55] Quoted in Marty, *Under God, Indivisible*, 303. See also 295–6.

[56] Parsons, "Religion in a Modern Pluralistic Society," 138.

[57] On the religious communications triumvirate of the Rev. Dr Norman Vincent Peale [Protestant], Monsignor (later Bishop) Fulton J. Sheen [Roman Catholic], and Rabbi Joshua Loth Liebman [Jewish], see Robert S. Ellwood, *The Fifties Spiritual Marketplace: American Religion in a Decade of Conflict* (New Brunswick, NJ: Rutgers University Press, 1997), 11–13, 60–1, and 83–4; Ellwood, *1950: Crossroads of American Religious Life*, 7–8, 65, 72, 111–14, and 135–7; McLoughlin, "Pietism and the American Character," 178–9; and Marty, *Under God, Indivisible*, 89–97 and 314–29.

[58] Stephen Prothero, "On the Holy Road: The Beat Movement as a Spiritual Protest," *Harvard Theological Review* 84 (1991): 210 and 211 (the emphases appear in the original). As Allen Ginsberg wrote in "Footnote to *Howl*" [1955]:.

Everything is holy! everybody's holy! everywhere is holy!/everyday is in eternity! Everyman's an angel!

Reprinted in Ann Charters, ed., *The Portable Beat Reader* (New York: Penguin Books, 1992), 71.

[59] "On the Road Back: How the Beat Generation Got That Way, According to Its Seer" [1958], reprinted in Kevin J. Hayes, ed., *Conversations with Jack Kerouac* (Jackson, MS: University Press of Mississippi, 2005), 7.

[60] "THEOLOGY: Toward a Hidden God," *Time* (US edition), April 8, 1966: 82–7.

[61] Parsons, "Religion in a Modern Pluralistic Society," 130–1; and Wills, *Christianity in the United States*, 47–51, 66, and 76–9.

[62] Wills, *Christianity in the United States*, 77; and Wade Clark Roof, "Religious Borderlands: Challenges for Future Study," *Journal for the Scientific Study of Religion* 37 (1998): 2.

[63] Wills, *Christianity in the United States*, 77.

[64] Lori G. Beaman, "A Cross-National Comparison of Approaches to Religious Diversity: Canada, France, and the United States," in Lori G. Beaman and Peter Beyer,

eds, *Religion and Diversity in Canada* (Leiden, The Netherlands: Brill Academic Publishers, 2008), 206–11.

[65] George M. Fredrickson, "America's Diversity in Comparative Perspective," *Journal of American History* 85 (1998): 866 and 868.

[66] Peter Beyer,"From Far and Wide: Canadian Religious and Cultural Diversity in Global-Local Context," in Beaman and Beyer, eds, *Religion and Diversity in Canada*, 10 and 16–17.

[67] Hugh McLeod,"The Crisis of Christianity in the West: Entering a Post-Christian Era?," in McLeod, ed., *World Christianities, c. 1914–c. 2000*, 329; and Wade Clark Roof, "Toward the Year 2000: Reconstructions of Religious Space," *Annals of the American Academy of Political and Social Science* 527 (1993): 164.

[68] Sean McCloud, "Bibliographical Essay: Religion and Modern American Culture," *Choice: Current Reviews for Academic Libraries* 44 (2007): 1439–51.

[69] Michael Hout and Claude S. Fischer, "Why More Americans Have No Religious Preference: Politics and Generations," *American Sociological Review* 67 (2002): 165–90.

[70] Phillip E. Hammond, *Religion and Personal Autonomy: The Third Disestablishment in America* (Columbia, SC: University of South Carolina Press, 1992); and Roof, "Toward the Year 2000," esp. 164–9.

[71] Donald E. Miller, "Postdenominational Christianity in the Twenty-First Century," *Annals of the American Academy of Political and Social Science* 558 (1998): 199 and 203.

[72] Ibid., 198. See also Miller, *Reinventing American Protestantism: Christianity in the New Millennium* (Berkeley, CA: University of California Press, 1997); and Gerardo Martí, *Hollywood Faith: Holiness, Prosperity, and Ambition in a Los Angeles Church* (New Brunswick, NJ: Rutgers University Press, 2008).

[73] Miller, "Postdenominational Christianity in the Twenty-First Century," 200 and 203.

[74] Roof, "Toward the Year 2000," 165 and 167.

[75] Rupert Shortt,"Resurgent Rome: There Are Now Almost as Many Catholics as Citizens of China – Why?," *TLS: Times* [London] *Literary Supplement*, April 10, 2009: 22.

Further Reading

Ahlstrom, Sydney E.,with David D. Hall. *A Religious History of the American People* [1972], 2nd edn.New Haven, CT: Yale University Press, 2004.

Balmer, Randall H. *Mine Eyes Have Seen the Glory: A Journey into the Evangelical Subculture in America* [1989], 4th edn. New York: Oxford University Press, 2006.

Butler, Jon. *Awash in a Sea of Faith: Christianizing the American People.* Cambridge, MA: Harvard University Press, 1990.

Canada. Statistics Canada. Census Operations Division. *Religions in Canada.* Ottawa: Minister of Industry, 2003.

Gaustad, Edwin S.,and Philip L. Barlow, with Richard W. Dishno. *The New Historical Atlas of Religion in America* [1962], 3rd edn. New York: Oxford University Press, 2001.

Gillis, Chester. *Roman Catholicism in America.* New York: Columbia University Press, 1999.

Handy, Robert T. *A History of the Churches in the United States and Canada.* Oxford, England: Clarendon Press, 1976.

Herberg, Will. *Protestant, Catholic, Jew: An Essay in American Religious Sociology* [1955]. Chicago, IL: University of Chicago Press, 1983.

Hutchison, William R. *Religious Pluralism in America: The Contentious History of a Founding Ideal.* New Haven, CT: Yale University Press, 2003.

Lipset, Seymour Martin. *Continental Divide: The Values and Institutions of the United States and Canada.* New York: Routledge, 1990.

Marsden, George M. *Fundamentalism and American Culture: The Shaping of Twentieth-Century Evangelicalism, 1870–1925* [1980], 2nd edn. New York: Oxford University Press, 2006.

Marty, Martin E. *The New Shape of American Religion.* New York: Harper Brothers, 1959.

Marty, Martin E. *Pilgrims in Their Own Land: Five Hundred Years of Religion in America.* Boston, MA: Little, Brown, 1984.

Moore, R. Laurence. *Religious Outsiders and the Making of Americans.* New York: Oxford University Press, 1985.

Pew Forum on Religion and Public Life, *U.S. Religious Landscape Survey. Religious Beliefs and Practices: Diverse and Politically Relevant.* Washington, DC: The Pew Research Center, 2008.

Silk, Mark. *Spiritual Politics: Religion and America Since World War II.* New York: Simon and Schuster, 1988.

Wuthnow, Robert. *The Restructuring of American Religion: Society and Faith Since World War II.* Princeton, NJ: Princeton University Press, 1988.

11

Central America and the Caribbean
Christianity on the Periphery

Virginia Garrard-Burnett

The Colonial Period in Central America

Christianity came to Central America, as it did to all of Spanish America, with the Spanish Conquest. Because Spanish claims to the New World were based on Pope Alexander VI's 1493 declaration of *Inter Caetera* (also known as the *Patronato*), which divided new lands between the "Catholic Kings" of Spain and Portugal, and because Spanish ideas of citizenship formed by the 700-year long Reconquest were framed around religious identity, Cross and Crown were closely linked in the colonial enterprise. In Central America, the expansion of the Catholic Church closely followed patterns of conquest and colonization of the region.

By the mid-sixteenth century, the institutional Church was firmly in place throughout most of Central America. Ecclesiastical divisions roughly paralleled the secular *audiencias* established in the 1560s: the Diocese of Guatemala included present-day Chiapas, Honduras, El Salvador, and Guatemala. The southern jurisdiction was based in Panama and included present-day Costa Rica and Nicaragua. Although it was territorially large, the population in southern Central America, Spaniards, *castas*, and indigenous combined, was much smaller than in the north. As a result, the institutional Church in the south left a much smaller colonial footprint than did the Church in the north, despite the sustained efforts of the missionary Orders

such as the Franciscans, the Dominicans, the Jesuits, the Capuchins, and the Augustinians, who started work in the region early in the sixteenth century and retained a presence there throughout the colonial period.

Clergy came with the Conquest and set up institutions (monasteries) in Guatemala and Nicaragua almost immediately. Dioceses of Honduras and Chiapas received bishops slightly later, but Central America did not get an archbishop until 1745.[1] Although the Church and Crown in Central America, as in the rest of Spanish America, were closely linked, sectors of the Central American Church also served as agents of royal policy of humanitarianism toward the indigenous population, which often pitted the Church against the secular authorities and planters.

Above all, Central America was home to one of the Catholic Church's most important experiments in human rights, led by one of Latin America's most noted early clergy, Fray Bartolomé Las Casas (1484–1566).[2] Las Casas originally came to the New World as a conquistador in 1502, but, horrified by Spanish treatment of the Indians during the Conquest of Hispaniola, he retreated to Spain, where he eventually wrote the highly influential *A Short Account of the Conquest of the Indies* (1542), and took the vows of a Dominican friar. Las Casas returned to the New World to become a spokesman for indigenous protection from Spanish abuse, a role he undertook so tirelessly

Introducing World Christianity, First Edition. Edited by Charles E. Farhadian.
© 2012 Blackwell Publishing Ltd. Published 2012 by Blackwell Publishing Ltd.

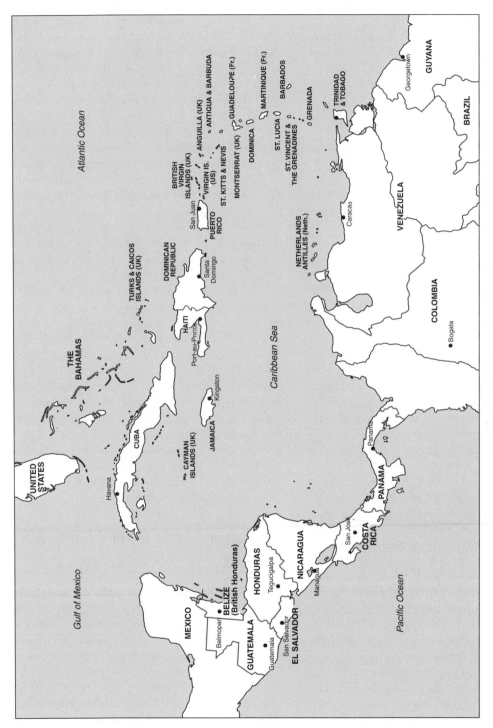

Map 11.1 Central America and the Caribbean

that the Crown eventually granted him the title of "Protector of the Indians."

In Guatemala, Las Casas became a vocal spokesman against Indian maltreatment, appealing to Alvarado and other Spanish authorities on their behalf. The following year, Las Casas, with the support of Bishop Marroquín, convinced Spanish authorities to allow him an experiment in conversion through "peaceful persuasion" rather than force.

Inadvertently, the friar's efforts brought the region – now known as "Verapaz" ("True Peace") – and its people under sufficient control for effective Spanish subjugation, although some years after Las Casas's departure the population rose up in revolt and killed many Spaniards. Las Casas returned to Spain and persuaded the Crown to promulgate the New Laws in 1542 to put an end to the abusive *encomienda* system. Las Casas returned to Central America as the Bishop of Chiapa(s) (under which jurisdiction Verapaz fell) in 1544. Even after Las Casas's death in 1566, the Dominicans retained a strong presence in Guatemala.[3]

Both secular and regular clergy came to Central America, and competition among them, as in other parts of Spanish America, could be intense. Franciscans and Dominicans, in particular, competed with one another for authority over the indigenous population in Guatemala, as evinced by the relatively large number of friars who established a presence early on in this important regional colonial center. By 1600, there were 22 Franciscan, 14 Dominican, and 6 Mercedarian *conventos* in Guatemala, located primarily in the Santiago de los Caballeros (now Antigua), Guatemala.

The Jesuits came to Central America in 1582, where they played a significant role in education and agricultural production, but they were neither as numerous nor as prominent in Central America as they were elsewhere during the Spanish colonial period. Even so, the Jesuits' enthusiasm and aggressive efforts in Central America earned them the enmity of some of the clergy in other Orders, who resented their wealth and influence. Nevertheless, despite vows of poverty, even some of the mendicant and secular clergy accumulated considerable wealth and power in colonial Central America; this was especially true in Guatemala and in Nicaragua, where the ecclesiastical base of the province was, around Grenada.[4]

Over time the Catholic Church came to maintain a local presence unparalleled by any other colonial institution; in major population centers, monasteries employed and were supported by large numbers of the indigenous residents, while even in remote areas, each *pueblo* was responsible for maintaining both clergy and small chapels. The liturgical calendar came to mark the course of the year, and the cycle of fiestas to mark both the feasts of the Church and identity of each locality through the celebration of its patronal festival. In most towns, sodalities (*cofradías*), consisting of prominent local men and community elders, were formed by the Church to help the communities maintain support of the clergy and manage the community's coffers.[5] Eventually these very *cofradías* assumed much of the ecclesiastical responsibility for their communities as well, becoming mediators between the locality and colonial (later national) authorities.[6]

The colonial Catholic Church performed social and economic functions that extended far beyond its spiritual authority. It served a banking function, loaning money and administering trusts; it managed real estate, the Church itself gradually becoming the largest single landowner in all of Latin America by the end of the eighteenth century. It also provided an education for multiple generations of colonial elites. The Church, as a uniquely ubiquitous colonial institution, maintained social order and hierarchies through socio-religious institutions such as convents for young women from good families, as well as the ecclesiastical courts that monitored and punished social deviancies such as witchcraft and sexual misbehavior.[7]

Church and State in the Nineteenth Century

Given the Church's pervasive influence in colonial society, it is not surprising that when independence came to Central America, first from Spain in 1821 and then from Mexico in 1823, the Catholic Church found itself in the vortex of controversy. Clergymen, believing Mexico's Iturbide represented their interests, led the charge for independence from Spain in all of Central America except Guatemala. Three years later, when Central America separated from Mexico and formed the Central American Union – a political entity that proved to be not only ineffectual, but also hostile to Church interests – the new government nonetheless declared Catholicism to be "the only religion of the Federation."[8]

Impeding the cause of state formation in the early years of Central American nationhood was the conflict between two political parties, the Liberals and the Conservatives, whose conflicting visions for national development were neatly mirrored in their attitudes toward the Church. The Liberals were modernists, seeking to create modern nations by way of a theoretical belief in democracy and a genuine affection free trade, alongside rapid "progress" measured by roads and investment. The Conservatives preferred a more gradual approach to nationhood and economic development, the Spanish colonial model providing the template for patriarchal social, economic, and political development.

For both, the Catholic Church was a potent symbol and power broker. To the Liberals, the Church represented the worst of the region's colonial heritage; worse still, it was the only early "national" institution that could compete with the emerging state for the hearts and minds of the populace. To the Conservatives, the Church symbolized the very best of the colonial legacy, providing a moral and political bulwark against the "calumnies" of Liberalism.

In light of this, it is not surprising that the fate of the institutional Catholic Church rose and fell with political fortune. During the brief years of the unified Central American republic (1823–39), Liberal governments systematically attacked the Church, dramatically reducing its secular power by secularizing and selling off Church property, legalizing Protestant immigration, and giving to the secular state authority formerly claimed by the Church, such as the secularization of public records and cemeteries to Central America. This embodied a Positivist agenda of "order and progress" that included a series of strong anti-clerical laws and gestures designed to strip the Church of what little remained of its secular influence. Across the region, liberal anti-clerical, indeed anti-Catholic, legislation such as the reintroduction of laws permitting freedom of worship, the limitation of Church ownership of property, and the banning of religious education combined with serious restrictions on the number of clergy and on new clerical vocations permitted in most countries to become the order of the day.

In 1884, the Vatican signed a new concordat with Guatemala in which that state gave up its claims to national patronage, but the Church made the more significant and highly realistic concession of renouncing its claims to a position of privilege in Guatemalan society.[9] By the first decades of the twentieth century, the institutional Catholic Church in much of Central America was greatly weakened and remained so throughout the first half of the twentieth century. As John Lloyd Mecham noted of this period, "The Catholic Church in two republics, Guatemala and El Salvador, undoubtedly suffered more vicissitudes in its fortunes than in any other Latin-American countries, with the possible exception of Mexico."[10]

The Church in Central America in the Early Twentieth Century

As Liberal anti-clerical measures put increasing pressure on the institutional Roman Catholic Church, it slowly began to recede from the social landscape of Latin America. Yet, while the Church as an institution began to vanish from the distant countryside in the late nineteenth and early twentieth centuries, Catholicism as a lived religion did not. To the contrary, a type of popular Catholicism, as practiced and interpreted by an enthusiastic local laity, quickly emerged to supplement and eventually replace orthodox Catholicism. The manifestations of popular religion were not merely reactions to the reduced presence of the Church, but instead represented local adaptations of vital elements of the faith, with or without the benefit of clergy.

In some areas, this unlicensed "folk Catholicism" typically grafted elements of local spirituality, legend, and shamanism on to orthodox Catholic dogma, resulting in a fusion of indigenous and Catholic beliefs that were specific and resonant to a given locality and community. Elsewhere, traditional beliefs that centuries of Christian contact had never fully snuffed out again achieved a more public forum. Much later, in the 1940s, the Catholic Church sent missionaries to Latin America to weed out syncretic practices and reintroduce Catholic orthodoxy into communities where "folk Catholicism" remained the dominant system of belief. As late as 1958, clergy from the Maryknoll

Figure 11.1 Cathedral Of Santo Domingo. *Source*: Agguizar (http://commons.wikimedia.org/wiki/File:San_Crist%C3%
B3bal_de_Las_Casas_02.jpg)

Order in El Salvador reflected on this tension, noting that in a country where the ratio of priests to Catholics was 1:7,600, rural Catholicism was "not Christian but pagan" and that "Catholicism was practiced only occasionally."[11]

The Church at large had begun much earlier to address the threat to its spiritual hegemony in a papal encyclical issued by Pope Leo XIII, popularly known as the "working man's Pope," whose pivotal 1891 encyclical, *Rerum Novarum*, advanced the position that social morality and the principles of justice and charity should regulate the relationship between capital and labor.[12] Although this encyclical resulted in important new currents in Catholic social thought and praxis, most notably the Catholic Action movement, *Rerum Novarum* nonetheless had a much greater effect in Europe than in Latin America, at least in the first half of the twentieth century.

Rerum Novarum's limited influence changed dramatically, however, in the post- World War II period, as new kinds of ideologies – mostly political – began to inflame the passions that had once been kindled by active Catholic religiosity in the region. In particular, the Cuban Revolution (1959) served notice to the Church that it would consider no land to be inexorably Catholic, not even in Latin America. Many of these hostile forces were those associated with the "modern" world: communism, secularism, urbanization, and other demographic changes that pulled people away from traditional lifestyles and worldviews. In addition, by the early 1960s, Protestantism also presented an ever greater challenge to Catholic spiritual hegemony.

With this in mind, in October of 1962, Pope John XXIII convened the Second Vatican Council. The object of the Second Vatican Council was to "open the Church," that is, to reclaim Catholicism's moral and temporal authority by reasserting its relevance in the modern world. Between 1962 and 1965, the Council issued 16 major documents that set the course for the most dramatic change in universal Catholicism to take place since the Counter-Reformation. The most important of these changes included the following: a dramatically increased role for the laity; an emphasis on Bible reading and reflection over formulaic ritual; increased accessibility to the sacraments through liturgical revision and abandonment of the Latin Mass for modern vernacular languages; a conciliatory attitude

to ecumenism, including a definition of Protestants as "separated brethren"; and a renewed emphasis of the Church's role in the problems of the secular world.[13]

Liberation Theology in Central America

It is this last element that caught the interest and enthusiasm of many clergy in Latin America, who believed that the Second Vatican Council signaled a new commitment in the Church's obligation to the poor. In 1968, the bishops of Latin America convened the Second General Conference (CELAM) in Medellín, Colombia, where they called for a specific application of the Second Vatican Council decisions to the region. In particular, the convening bishops articulated the Church's "preferential option for the poor" and called for "concientización" (consciousness-raising) through Bible reading and discussion in small groups known as Christian Base Communities (CEBs), to help the poor take control of their lives in the secular world. This rearticulated action-based faith became known as liberation theology. Liberation theology had a galvanizing effect throughout Latin America, but most of all in Central America, bringing thousands of the faithful to informed understanding of their beliefs and to social action for the very first time.

Nicaragua

Liberation theology took root in Central America earlier and deeper than in virtually any other place in Latin America, except perhaps Brazil, often guided by clergy associated with the Maryknoll and the Jesuit Orders. The terrible inequities of wealth, the poverty of its people, and the deep religiosity of people who had for many decades been largely responsible for their own spiritual welfare, coinciding as it did with the emergence of new guerrilla movements fighting for the overthrow of autocratic governments, provided fertile ground for the liberationist message. Nowhere was this more true than in Nicaragua. There, priests of the Jesuit Order established CEBs in rural areas and poor urban slums early on; it was the 1977 publication of Jesuit Ernesto Cardenal's accounts of Gospel exegesis in a small island community, *The Gospel in Solentiname*, which helped popularize the basic teachings of liberation theology across Latin America, Europe, and the United States.[14] By the mid-1970s, especially after the devastating 1972 earthquake brought the mendacity and cruelty of Nicaragua's leader, Anastasio Somoza Debayle, to the fore, membership in CEBs soared, alongside opposition to the regime. By the end of the decade, the participation of radical Catholics in the armed movement contributed significantly to the success of the Frente Sandinista Liberación Nacional (Sandinistas) in the overthrow of the dictatorship in July of 1979, and Catholic clergy formed a key sector of the original Sandinista directorate.

In 1983, Pope John Paul II, a conservative Pope whose experience as a Catholic in communist Poland made him wary of Church associations with revolutionary popular movements, paid a visit to Sandinista Nicaragua. He chastened the radical clergy for their over-investment in what he considered to be a dangerously socialist regime, while later on the same visit, Sandinista cadres attempted to drown out the Pope's homily with political slogans during the celebration of Mass in the Plaza of the Revolution. By the mid-1980s, the Nicaraguan Church had become seriously divided between pro-Sandinista Catholics (the "popular Church") and an institutional Church led by Archbishop (later Cardinal) Miguel Obando y Bravo, who increasingly opposed the regime. In 1989, the Sandinistas relinquished power after losing in presidential elections where the winning candidate, Violeta Chamorro, credited her victory in large part to the support of Cardinal Obando y Bravo and the conservative sector of the Catholic Church.[15]

El Salvador and Guatemala

In neighboring El Salvador, by contrast, the institutional Church took a somewhat different role. As in Nicaragua, "lower" clergy – parish priests and religious who worked among the poor – in El Salvador took an active role in establishing CEBs in poor rural areas. Over time, liberationist Catholics began to ally themselves with popular movements that sought a fundamental reorientation of politics and society that would redistribute wealth, land, and power from the military government and the so-called "Fourteen Families" who controlled more than 80 percent of the nation's

wealth in the mid-1970s. Although Salvadoran Catholics were generally reluctant to take up arms and join one of several armed guerrilla movements that coalesced in 1980 into a single organization, the Frente Farabundo Martí Liberación Nacional (FMLN), radical Catholics eventually played key roles in the movement, particularly in running social programs in the ravaged cities and in the "liberated territory" that the FMLN claimed in Chalatenango and Morazán provinces during most of the 1980s.

El Salvador's history between 1979 and the end of hostilities in 1992 is unusually bloody. Between approximately 1979 and 1982, in particular, the government's counterinsurgency campaigns and its approval of paramilitary activities, especially the use of "death squads," resulted in a chaotic and violent social milieu that killed more than 70,000 by the war's end. The Church itself was hardly immune from this violence, as activist lay Catholics and clergy were especially targeted. One of the most prominent victims of the entire civil war was San Salvador's archbishop, Oscar Arnulfo Romero. Romero, a political moderate who had become a vocal opponent of organized violence, was assassinated while saying Mass on March 24, 1980, the victim of a right-wing death squad.

Although Romero's death shocked the world and made him a martyr across Latin America, his murder was not the last of its kind. At the end of the same year, in December of 1980, four American churchwomen associated with the Maryknoll Order were raped and killed by members of the Salvadoran security forces. Then, in 1989, clergy deaths formed grim parentheses around a decade of violence, when officers from the Salvadoran military ordered the assassination of six Jesuit priests associated with the University of Central America (UCA), who were killed as a warning from the Salvadoran authorities to all who might wish to be "intellectual authors of insurgency." In Guatemala, too, during the same period of time, Catholic activists and clergy paid a heavy price for their efforts toward bringing social justice to the poor. According to one of the Guatemalan Truth Commission reports, outside of labor rights activists and trade unionists, lay Catholic and clergy suffered the highest number of victims of any category of people during that nation's armed struggle, which lasted from 1961 until 1996 and killed nearly 200,000 people.[16]

Protestantism

Against this backdrop of Catholic activism and persecution, an alternative religious form was rapidly emerging on the Central American spiritual landscape: evangelical Protestantism. Although the number of Protestants in Central America was very small until the 1960s (in no place did Protestants number more than 5 percent of the total population), Protestantism has a long history in the region, much of it tied negatively to the expansion of the political and economic hegemony of Protestant nations, specifically Great Britain and the United States. Protestantism came to Central America alongside forces that have been traditionally hostile to the totality of the Hispanic experience. It is perhaps not insignificant that British pirates from the "Spanish Main" – which included the Atlantic coast of Central America – were tried as heretics rather than as criminals when taken before the Spanish colonial Inquisition in the seventeenth century.[17]

Largely because of the political rivalry that underscored religious difference, Protestantism remained outlawed (either by practice or actual decree) in Central America through the eighteenth century. This status changed with independence, however. As the Catholic Church suffered under Liberal rule, Protestantism benefited from Liberals' dreams of "modernity." The 1824 Constitution of the United Provinces of Central America included a freedom of religion clause in its new Constitution, which legalized Protestant practices in Latin America for the first time in order to facilitate the immigration of "desirable" foreigners from Europe who might be willing to invest their lives and capital in the emerging republics. However, throughout the middle part of the nineteenth century – roughly from 1840 to 1860 or 1870 – while under the rule of the pro-Catholic Conservative government, Protestantism was once again outlawed.

It was during this period, nevertheless, that Protestant *colporteurs* began to work illicitly within Central America, selling or giving away Scripture and covertly trying to evangelize. In the middle years of the nineteenth century, international organizations such as the Society for the Propagation of the Gospel in Foreign Parts and the British and Foreign Bible Society – an organization founded in 1804 to spread the Gospel in the many vernacular languages of the vast British Empire – also began to actively support *colporteurs* in Central America, using British outposts in British Honduras and Jamaica as bases for operations. Although many Bible Societies were officially non-sectarian and they often offered the Scripture "without note or comment,"[18] the very nature of their work – the distribution of Bibles – reflected the fundamental tenet of Protestant belief of *sola scriptura*, that God's truth is revealed solely in Holy Writ, in contrast to Catholicism's emphasis on God's revelation through Scripture and tradition through the Church. Within Latin America, this sharp theological divide underscored the fact that the Bible Societies' *colporteurs* were widely understood to be advance agents of imperialism.

It was not until the return of Liberal, Positivist (modernization-oriented) governments to most of Latin America in the last decades of the nineteenth century that Protestant missionary work began in earnest in the region. The second half of the nineteenth century was an era of enormous expansion in US political and economic influence in Central America and the Caribbean, and the work of Protestant missionaries went hand in glove with the spread of US hegemony.

During this period, North American "mainline" (Reformational) denominations came to the region bearing a message of salvation that was deeply imbedded in the cultural norms and behaviors of Victorian society and, to some extent, wrapped in the flag of political imperialism. At the end of the nineteenth century and the beginning of the twentieth, missionaries of mainline denominations such as Presbyterians, Methodists, Quakers, and Baptists, many of whom equated Protestant religion with social and economic development, produced an extensive network of mission-run institutions such as schools, clinics, hospitals, and literacy programs throughout the region. Missionaries and Liberal Latin American governments alike foresaw a close and symbiotic relationship between a mission education and the governments' modernizing projects.

Despite the long and diligent efforts of missionaries, however, Protestantism did not take root in any significant way among the local populations in Latin America until the second half of the twentieth century. This is not to say that missionary work went unnoticed during this early period. To the contrary, mission-run hospitals and clinics were among the first to bring then-modern medicine to much of Central America, even in Costa Rica, where Liberal reforms did not take the same anti-Catholic rigor as elsewhere in the region. Even more significantly, mission schools educated a generation of future statesmen and leaders, including, but by no means limited to, Guatemala's great Liberal historian, Lorenzo Montúfar, and its most famous revolutionary, Jacobo Arbenz (who was baptized and educated in Protestant schools). Yet despite the missions' influence in building institutions, they largely failed in their primary goal, which was to evangelize and convert the people of Central America. Although missionaries consoled themselves by turning to the parable of the sower of seeds that would someday be "ripe for the harvest," by the late 1950s not a single Central American nation had a Protestant minority that was larger than 5 percent of the native population.[19]

By the late 1940s and 1950s the pioneering missionaries, with their zeal and confidence, had begun to pass away, replaced by a new generation of workers who, at least at some level, had begun to seriously question the methodologies and motives of their predecessors, especially the unchallenged equation that early missionaries had made between Protestant mission work and "modernity."

Younger missionaries found the paternalistic language and Victorian worldview of old-school mission work to be outdated and insufficient to withstand a series of contemporary challenges. These included, among other things, rising nationalism, increased political activism (especially from the left), and emerging anti-imperialism within the host countries. The wholesale expulsion of Christian missionaries from China in the wake of the Maoist Revolution in the late 1940s served as a wake-up call for foreign missionaries working in all parts of the world. Mao's ability to shut down virtually overnight what had once been the largest mission field in the world offered clear warning that the missions needed to devise new methods and strategies to cope with the rising tide of Marxist and nationalistic revolutions.

Mainline denominations such as the Presbyterians, Methodists, and Baptists found one solution in the nationalization of their work, creating new administrative structures in-country so that churches could be accountable to a local *iglesia nacional* ("national Church") instead of to a US-based board of foreign missions. Although it had been a long-time goal to let the churches "go native," as the phrase went – that is, to turn the leadership of the "national Church" over to local administrators and pastors – few denominations were prepared for the transitions and most had still failed to nurture local leadership. The reality of this meant that the "national Church" of each area generally retained close ties to the parent denomination, and many, even in the early twenty-first century, still depend on the US denomination for at least some of their funding, training, and personnel.

Given these constrained achievements, the real growth of Protestantism within Central America in recent decades has not, generally, come from the historic mainline denominations. The 1960s are a pivotal era in the Protestant story in Latin America. In the wake of the 1959 Cuban Revolution, a new type of missionary from North America began to operate in Latin America, promoting Protestantism as a "spiritual alternative to communism." In Central America, much of this effort was channeled through the organization Latin American Mission (LAM). In 1962, LAM launched a major evangelization campaign in Guatemala. The timing of the event coincided with the emergence of the nation's first guerrilla movement, thus making LAM's claims to offer a "spiritual alternative to communism" both immediate and timely; it soon also placed them in direct competition against Catholic liberation theology.[20]

It is worth noting that this saturation marketing came at a time when the Catholic Church was suffering from a severe shortage of clergy and the institutional Church itself was in turmoil due to the many changes wrought by the Second Vatican Council. Given what was for the new missions such a favorable convergence of factors, the efforts of such interdenominational agencies quickly bore fruit, and Central Americans' innate distrust of evangelical religion began to break down. By the middle of the decade, locally run Protestant churches began to sprout in urban slums and rural villages of Central America for the first time, especially in Guatemala, where rapid urbanization, a Green Revolution, and the exigencies of the armed conflict and a repressive state pushed ordinary people into seeking new solutions.

The links between socio-political conditions and religious change were especially clear in Guatemala, which today, with more than one third of the population self-identified as *evangélico*, is not only one of the most "Protestant" countries in Central America, but in all of Latin America. Prior to the 1960s, less than 5 percent of Guatemalans were Protestants. Protestantism, and particularly Pentecostalism, did not truly register on the scene until a horrific earthquake killed tens of thousands of Guatemalans on February 4, 1976; in the aftermath of the disaster, Protestant aid agencies flooded the country with assistance, and conversions boomed. Yet the conversions largely continued, particularly during the darkest years of the nation's war, a period now known as *la violencia*, when government troops, under orders from a commander-in-chief who was himself a newly converted Pentecostal, General Efrain Rios Montt, ordered the massacres that killed many tens of thousands of Maya victims, including many activist Catholics, and also nearly defeated the guerrilla movement. Although the role that Ríos Montt's religion played in this drama is still subject to debate, there is no question that people flocked to Protestant churches in search of physical and spiritual survival.[21]

One thing that is significant about the development of the new Protestant churches in Central America during the 1960s and into the 1970s was not their size or number – indeed, during this early period, Protestant conversion was still something of a novelty, and congregations were typically small enough to meet in a house or storefront – but that for the first time, Protestant churches were being established, pastored, and attended exclusively by local converts, without the controlling paternalism of missionaries. As such churches began to branch out, Protestantism, Pentecostalism in particular (an expression of Christianity that emphasizes the miraculous power of the Holy Spirit as described in the Book of Acts), in Latin America began to assume a more Latin face.

In Guatemala, Nicaragua, and El Salvador, a boom in Pentecostal conversions took place during the late 1970s and 1980s, coinciding with those nations' decade of civil war and crisis. This is not to suggest that Pentecostalism was a new phenomenon, as missionaries had moved into the region in the early part of the twentieth century; for instance, a renegade CAM missionary, Frederick Mebius, introduced Pentecostalism to rural El Salvador as early as 1915, where, in violation of CAM rules against "holiness" practices, he conducted "ecstatic and boisterous" services on the side of Santa Ana volcano.[22] However, the movement did not take off anywhere in the region until the 1960s and 1970s, when religious, social, and political conditions all contributed to its rapid and precipitous expansion.

Elsewhere, a variety of studies examine how Protestantism and Pentecostalism in particular affect community relations. Historically, the affect of conversion on community and family life has tended to be divisive in the extreme. There is little dispute that the "traditional community" as an integrated social system did once define the countryside of much of Central America, but the ongoing challenges of civil wars, natural disasters, and migration mean that in many areas these "places of being" no longer exist. For some observers, religious conversion is one of the key culprits in this decline; that is, when people exit the system of *costumbre* that tends to be constructed around Catholic rituals and beliefs, they also abandon the historical patterns of living in that community.[23] They may be systematically excluded from community life, but even more importantly, they exclude themselves. As David Martin has noted, for Protestants and Pentecostals in particular, "[the church] is its very own fiesta."[24]

One of the reasons why Latin Americans elect this new identity as Protestants is because the old identities that once designated one's place in life gave way over the course of the twentieth century. In countries like Guatemala and El Salvador, which experienced civil violence and large-scale out-migration, or like Honduras and Nicaragua, which endured catastrophic natural disasters like Hurricanes Mitch and Stan, the key social and sacred places, including those found in parish and community, may no longer be present. In such contexts, Protestant churches can provide a new locus of meaning and identity: the new community is one of *hermanos* ("brothers") and *hermanas* ("sisters"), which is both geographically smaller and metaphysically larger than the community of old.

The desire to recreate community and meaning may account in part for why a place like El Salvador has experienced such an expansive growth in Protestant conversion, not, like Guatemala, during the war, but after it. El Salvador today is more than one-quarter Protestant, a sector that is growing rapidly, perhaps attributable to the immense social disruptions that continue to plague Salvadoran society – the inequities that existed prior to the war, combined with massive out-migration and family disruptions, horrific crime, and transnational gang activity. Alongside all this, churches can and do provide safe havens for protecting and reorganizing lives.[25] Hondurans, too, are converting to Protestantism in record numbers, accounting for perhaps as much as 35 percent of that nation's population. Given Pentecostalism's tendency to thrive within environments of intense suffering and loss, it is not surprising that much of this growth has taken place since the catastrophic disruptions of Hurricane Mitch in 1998.[26]

An Exceptional Case: Christianity in Contemporary Cuba

Christianity before Castro

Cuba represents an anomalous case in Christianity within Latin America, not only because of its half-century of communist rule, but also because of the unique historical status of the Catholic Church and the prevalence of African beliefs, most notably Santería, on the island. The Cuban Roman Catholic Church is among the oldest in the Americas. Catholicism arrived with Christopher Columbus's "discovery" of the island on his first voyage in 1492. In 1518, Leo X established the Diocese of all Cuba, which included also the Spanish possessions of Louisiana and Florida. Pope Adrian VI in 1519 established a see in Havana, and in Baracoa in Santiago de Cuba; in 1522 the smaller bishopric was transferred to the city of Santiago de Cuba, where it remains to the present day.[27]

Despite this long history, however, the Catholic Church did not have a strong social and religious presence on the island, outside of the major cities. The Church is closely associated both in fact and in the popular imagination with the Spanish colonial interests; in the words of John Lloyd Mecham, "the Catholic Church of Spanish Cuba was really a Spanish

institution."[28] As with the nearby colony of Puerto Rico, about which one nineteenth-century bishop explained, "[Catholicism] . . . sustains empires with a firm hand and constant support, inspires in the citizenry the true love of the fatherland," Spanish monarchs and Church leaders in Cuba used Catholicism to enforce political loyalty and compliance with the colonial regime throughout the nineteenth century.[29] This strong Spanish association, along with the failure of plantation owners to actively introduce Christianity to their slaves (beyond baptism) and the deftness with which Afro-Cubans were able to retain their former beliefs, meant that by the time Cuba won its independence from Spain in 1898, the Cuban Church was among the least influential in the hemisphere. As historian Louis Pérez has described it, "the colonial church had been ineffective, if not indifferent to Cuban spiritual and material needs."[30]

Catholicism's weak hold in Cuba and Americans' notion that the new republic could serve as a Petri dish for conversion and "uplift" made the island a particular target for Protestant missionary efforts in the years following the Spanish–American War. Between the end of the war in July of 1989 and the termination of the American military occupation of Cuba in 1902, no fewer than 20 different Protestant denominations, including Northern and Southern Baptists, Methodists, Presbyterians, Episcopalians, Disciples of Christ, Quakers, Congregationalists, and "Pentecostals" (an anachronistic term for a group probably considered to be followers of "Holiness" traditions), sent missionaries to the newly liberated Cuba. Within the decade, at least 12 more Protestant denominations had begun work on the island. Although these missionaries did not directly collude with the American government in Cuba (or, for that matter, elsewhere in the region), they did envision their goals – of redemption, salvation, and improvement – to be quite similar. In the words of Pérez, "National policy fused indistinguishably from evangelical purpose and distinctions were blurred early; no need for conspiracy or even need for formal collaboration, rather a construction of ideological constructs and shared cultural norms that yielded common purpose toward shared norms."[31] By the middle of the twentieth century, Cuba had a relatively large and vigorous Protestant population compared to other countries in Latin America, but the triumph of the revolution in 1959 put an immediate end to this expansion.

Christianity in Cuba under Castro

Nevertheless, in modern Cuba, Christianity – both Catholicism and Protestantism, particularly Pentecostalism – (along with Santería) has grown rapidly over the past 10 to 20 years, although precise numbers are difficult to obtain, since many Cuban Christians prefer to not identify themselves as such in official tallies, for reasons we will discuss below. In 1980, approximately 43 percent of Cubans self-identified as Christians, of whom nearly 40 percent were Catholic and slightly more than 3 percent were Protestant.[32] While the number of Cuban Catholics has expanded somewhat since that time (experiencing a notable jump in the wake of Pope John Paul II's 1998 visit), the number of Cuban Protestants has increased fairly dramatically. One reason for this expansion is that since the turn of this century, there has been an expanded space for religion in official discourse, which has resulted in increased numbers of people attending Catholic and also Protestant churches in Cuba over the past decade, both as a response to the crisis of the Special Period (1989 to the late 1990s) and because of increased access to religious services that were not available to them before.

This political opening for churches came after years of suppression and repression by the Castro regime, which has generally viewed religion through a classically Marxist lens, as a tool of repression and an instiller of false consciousness. The historical peculiarities of Cuban Catholicism also contributed to its suppression by the regime, given its strong Spanish and colonial references and its association with the *ancien régime* of Fulgencio Batista (who had been overthrown by the Castro Revolution). Generally speaking, Cubans have historically viewed the institutional Catholic Church as urban, white, upper class, and anti-revolutionary. As a trope, white elite *habeneros* are Catholic, but poor people of color outside of the capital are followers of Santería or other religious expressions of the African diaspora, if they are religious at all. This means that the Castro regime's systematic repression of the Church for nearly four decades caused relatively little social

outrage, especially after white elites, Catholic clergy, clergy, and Catholic adherents fled from the island. In the meantime, the Cuban Church largely missed out on liberation theology due to its isolation, its conservatism, and because the revolution had already laid claim to the language of liberation.[33]

The Catholic Church

Despite all these negative factors, the Catholic Church remains the largest single institution in Cuba that is not under the direct control of the government, and as such it offers, at least potentially, a unique venue for resistance or reform. As such, the government has tried to control the Church through two methods: (1) repression and (2) cooption or accommodation, both of which the government enforces cyclically.

While the regime actively repressed religion for many years, it moved into a cycle of accommodation in the 1990s and into the first years of this century. There is evidence that the cycle is moving back into repression, especially if the government perceives that the growing number of professing Christians represents a discursive threat to the regime at a particularly vulnerable moment in its history.

It was the era of the 1990s that witnessed the greatest period of rapprochement between the state and the Church, beginning in the Special Period (roughly, the decade of the 1990s) – the time of grave economic and political isolation that Cuba faced with the loss of its great patron, the Soviet Union. The Special Period began with the fall of the Berlin Wall in 1989, and the Cuban government – seeking to solidify its political base among a potentially volatile population – reached out to the Christian Church almost immediately. One of the most monumental of these changes came about in 1991, when the Cuban Communist Party changed its by-laws to allow practicing Christians to join the party. Up until that time, no one who openly professed Christian faith could belong to the Communist Party, which had excluded them from eligibility to hold government positions, professional jobs, or from traveling outside of the country.[34] Before 1991, restrictions on Christian membership in the party took a serious toll on religious participation in churches, although religious expression increased in popular religious practices (such as Santería) that the government had never actively suppressed.[35] Like Christianity, Santería has expanded dramatically in Cuba over the past four decades, gaining many adherents who are not part of its black, Afrocentric traditional base, suggesting that the religious market is very much at work in Cuba even if the capitalist free market is not.[36] The de facto "decriminalization" of Christianity provided an immediate boom for institutional Christianity, especially in the Protestant sector, which has established more than 700 new official churches (this figure does not include house churches) affiliated with 54 different Protestant denominations since 1992; by contrast, the Catholic Church has some 650 official parishes on the island.[37]

A second major change took place in 1992, when the language of the Cuban Constitution was amended to make Cuba no longer an "atheist" state (hostile to religion), but a "secular" country, thus giving official latitude for freedom of religion, although there are still clear limitations on religious gatherings and affiliation. The government does not officially favor any one religion or Church, but seems to be most tolerant of those Churches that maintain close ties to the state through the Cuban Council of Churches.[38] The Cuban Council of Churches (CCC), which is made up predominantly of historic Protestant churches, is generally friendly to the regime, although it is not a government-run organization.[39] In 1991, the Cuban Council of Churches along with several international ecumenical Protestant bodies held a meeting with Fidel Castro, which was broadcast on TV. This meeting helped pave the way for better relations between Protestants and the government and made it possible for the US-based National Council of Churches (NCC) to send humanitarian aid to Cuba, in open defiance of the nearly 50-year-long US embargo on Cuba, which the NCC pronounced as "morally wrong and politically ineffective."[40] Most important of all in the advance of public space for Christianity in Cuba was the visit of Pope John Paul II to the island in 1998, which "raised issue of growth of religion in Cuba for people of all faith backgrounds."[41] Castro's obvious enthusiasm for the visit seemed to many observers to signal an increasing place for Christianity within the political and social spaces created by the revolution, although this did not ultimately occur.[42]

By the end of 1998, the statistics that were available indicated that approximately 400,000 (roughly 4 percent) of Cuba's 11 million people were practicing Catholics[43] (i.e., baptized), but the current level of participation is low; the Cuban Catholic Church estimates that roughly 10 percent of baptized Catholics attend Mass regularly.[44] On the demand side of the equation, Protestantism has expanded rapidly in recent years. Estimates of the Protestant population fluctuate wildly, ranging from 150,000 to 300,000–650,000.[45]

Bearing out the pattern of expansion and contraction of religious rights, the end of the Special Period also brought a constriction in religious freedom after this period of expansion. In early 2001, the Communist Party produced a document warning that churches were inserting themselves into secular society and needed to be reined in. Since that time the government has issued a series of laws that reinforced restrictions on religious institutions: these include restrictions on construction permits, limits on charitable work, and serious restrictions on the number and types of foreign religious workers who may enter the country.[46] Since 2005, these restrictions have been made even more austere, resulting in limitations on the number of people who can gather to attend religious services in any one location, with close surveillance of local religious leaders, including the regular use of *orejas* (literally, ears) in religious services.

Protestantism in Cuba

Because the bulk of Christian expansion in Cuba is, rather unexpectedly, taking place in the Protestant sector, it is important to understand its context within the island nation. The history of Protestantism in Cuba is much like that in the rest of Latin America, but with a few key differences, including the close relationship between missionaries and the American occupation of the island. Perhaps because of the institutional weakness of the Catholic Church even before the revolution, Protestantism made relatively strong inroads in Cuba, especially in the east (*oriente*), to the extent that by the late 1940s they were able to cede some leadership to local people, many of whom had been trained in the mission schools.[47] Most of this came to an end in 1959, although the old missionary denominations have maintained work in Cuba on a somewhat limited basis until the present day.

Because it often took place somewhat prematurely or under duress, in many cases the nationalization of missions proved to be at best a mixed success. Cuba, after the triumph of Fidel Castro's revolution in 1959, provides a good example. As we have seen, Cuba had been widely evangelized after the 1898 Spanish–American War. The Cuban missions were unusually well supported, since many American policymakers and ordinary citizens considered missionaries to be a "third force" of US interests in Cuba, along with the military and business, a vanguard poised to provide Cubans with the religious and cultural components of what was considered to be an overall "civilizing mission."

By the mid-1930s – pressed by economic concerns, the new mandates of the Good Neighbor Policy, and, especially, by emerging Cuban nationalism – the missions began to adopt a program of "indigenization," in which they gradually turned the running of the schools over to educated Cuban leaders. As part of indigenization, the home mission boards continued to closely monitor, support, and, to some extent, control the Cuban Protestant institutions, but the churches nonetheless began to develop a local identity and leadership. By the late 1940s, Protestant work – including actual church attendance – had grown dramatically, especially in the eastern part of the country. By the early 1950s, Cuba had one of the largest Protestant populations and most indigenized Protestant Church establishment of any country in Latin America.[48]

Because they were already innovators and outside of the conventional venues of power, Cuban Protestants were among some of the early supporters of the revolution. Even today the government-sanctioned Cuban Council of Churches, a Protestant body, continues to endorse the regime. Yet what could, potentially, have been a symbiotic relationship between Protestant churches and the new communist government quickly soured, to the lasting detriment of the missionary churches, as the early revolution was not at all friendly to the cause of religion. The revolutionary government's early ideological opposition to religion resulted in the arrest and detention of active Christians (mainly Catholics, as there were relatively few Protestants at the time) in re-education camps. Between 1966 and 1967, the government sent many priests,

pastors, and others who "made religion a way of life" into Military Units to Aid Production (UMAPs), where they and other *lacra social* (social scum), such as homosexuals, pot smokers, and students who listened to banned foreign music, worked in involuntary servitude on sugar plantations and public works, until the system was abandoned in 1967.[49] Just as serious a problem was the loss of progressive members to revolutionary loyalty and conservative members to exile (the latter group included a majority of the clergy). The repression of religion, combined with the Cuban churches' isolation from their home denominations, has meant that even in Cuba, a former "success story," the mainline denominations have not faired well. In the early twenty-first century, Christianity is on the rise again in Cuba, but primarily among Pentecostals and Catholics, and only to a lesser extent within the historic Protestant churches.[50]

Nevertheless, during the revolution's heyday in the 1960s and 1970s, Protestants who stayed, represented largely by the CCC, tended to be sympathetic to the revolution, seeing in it a basic worldview that parallels Christian values. The CCC, along with the Protestant Theological Seminary – the largest of 11 seminaries in Cuba – champions the revolution and has developed a full theology to support it, stressing that progressive Christians share the social goals of the revolution. As a result, member churches of the CCC are not subject to the same level of restriction and monitoring as are non-member denominations.

The Cuban House Church movement

This brings us, finally, to the expansion of non-traditional types of churches, somewhat below the radar, which are congregations of believers who are (usually) not associated with the larger denominations and who meet, often secretly, outside of the recognized churches. These are Cuba's house churches, known as *casas cultos*. The house church movement is one of the most dynamic forces in Cuban Christianity today. The house church movement is by and large a Protestant phenomenon, although there are also at least 200 Catholic *casas de misiones* on the island that are homologues of the Protestant *casas cultos*.[51]

Casas cultos provide a way of working around a building problem (as religious organizations cannot own property in Cuba), but they are also a strategy of church growth. The house church movement originated as a way to circumvent the law that all churches, regardless of size or denomination, must officially register with the government, but which permitted the congregation of 12 or fewer people for religious services. (This restriction is widely ignored, as many *casas cultos* readily squeeze 40 or more people, for example, into a single one-bedroom apartment.)[52] In 2005, Cuban Protestant pastors placed the number of *casas cultos* in Cuba anywhere from 10,000–15,000, a figure that is only a rough estimate, given the semi-clandestine nature of the movement.[53]

As the house church movement has expanded, so have government restrictions upon it. According to new government regulations that went into effect in September of 2005, all house churches, even with fewer than 12 members, must register with local officials in order to obtain permission to operate.[54] House churches that do not have proper documentation are subject to closure by authorities, with the people who live in the house being evicted.[55] Directive 43 and Resolution 46 also stipulate that two house churches of the same denomination cannot be located within 2 km (1.25 miles) of each other and they must allow government officials to monitor worship services.[56]

As restrictions against the churches have expanded, so has surveillance of their members, whose identity as practicing Christians is regarded as potentially antithetical to the revolutionary project. While repression of Christians is nowhere near the level that it was during the days of the UMAP camps, *casa culto* members understand that fellow worshipers often serve as informants for the government, and that overstepping their bounds may result in penalties, ranging from subtle harassment to loss of the social privileges available in a socialist state (such as jobs and access to free healthcare and education) to outright arrest.

Under such constrained circumstances, then, why do Cubans bother to seek out house churches at all? At one level, it may have to do partly with a sparse institutional presence of both the Catholic Church, weakened by years of suppression, and mainline Protestant churches, which are somewhat compromised by their enthusiasm for the government, in the countryside. Most Cubans who convert to Protestant

Christianity are young and have grown up in a society that was officially atheist; their conversion, then, is not a rejection of one religion for another, but their first embrace of any religion at all, and under less than optimal circumstances. Or is this really so? Certainly, the dire exigencies of the Special Period, when grievous economic crisis posed not only a political challenge to the regime but also an existential crisis for the many Cubans who had grown up believing in the revolution's promises, accelerated the movement of Cubans into house churches. The influx of Cubans into the house church movement may represent a conversion from the secular religion of the revolution to the religion of *Jesucristo*. Like their Central American and historical counterparts, many modern Cubans, too, use religion to wrest a sense of order and meaning from a world that might otherwise threaten to overwhelm them.

Notes and References

[1] Ralph Lee Woodward, *Central America: A Nation Divided* (Oxford University Press, 2nd edn, 1985), 40.

[2] Miles Wortman, *Government and Society in Central America, 1680–1840* (New York: Columbia University Press, 1982), 42.

[3] See Francis Augustus MacNutt, *Bartolomew* [sic] *de las Casas: His Life, His Apostolate, and his Writings* (New York: G.P. Putnam's Sons, 1909), 188.

[4] Woodward, *Central America*, 40.

[5] See William Taylor, "Cofradias," chapter 12, *Magistrates of the Sacred: Priests and Parishioners in Eighteenth Century Mexico* (Stanford, CA: Stanford University Press, 1996), 301–23.

[6] Wortman, *Government and Society*, 43.

[7] See Martha Few, *Women Who Live Evil Lives: Gender, Religion, and the Politics of Power in Colonial Guatemala* (Austin, TX: University of Texas Press, 2002).

[8] John Lloyd Mecham, *Church and State in Latin America: A History of Politico-Ecclesiastical Relations* (Chapel Hill, NC: University of North Carolina Press, 1966 [1934]), 309.

[9] Ibid., 319.

[10] Ibid., 308.

[11] Ibid., 327.

[12] Robert C. Broderick, ed., *The Catholic Encyclopedia* (Nashville, TN: Thomas Nelson Publishers, 1987), 523.

[13] See Phillip Berryman, *The Religious Roots of Rebellion: Christians in the Central America Revolutions* (Maryknoll, NY: Orbis Books, 1984).

[14] Ernesto Cardenal, *El Evangelio en Solentiname* (Salamanca: Ediciones Sígueme, 1975–8).

[15] Michael Dodson, *Nicaragua's Other Revolution: Religious Faith and Political Struggle* (Chapel Hill, NC: University of North Carolina Press, 1990).

[16] Oficina de Derechos Humanos del Arzobispado de Guatemala, *Never Again: Recovery of the Historical Memory Project* (Maryknoll, NY: Orbis, 1999).

[17] Gonzalo Baez-Camargo, *Protestantes enjudiciados por la Inquisición en Iberoamerica* (Mexico: Casa Unida Publicaciones, 1960).

[18] Available online at: <http://www.lib.cam.ac.uk/deptserv/biblesociety/>.

[19] David Stoll, *Is Latin America Turning Protestant?* (Berkeley, CA: University of California Press, 1990).

[20] Enrique Domínguez and Deborah Huntington, "The Salvation Brokers: Conservative Evangelicals in Central America," *NACLA* 17/1 (1984): 2–36.

[21] See Virginia Garrard-Burnett, *Terror in the Land of the Holy Spirit: Guatemala Under General Efraín Ríos Montt, 1982–1983* (New York: Oxford University Press, 2010).

[22] Everett A. Wilson, "Sanguine Saints: Pentecostalism in El Salvador," *Church History* 52/2 (1983): 189, and especially 186–98.

[23] See Duncan Earle, "Authority, Social Conflict, and the Rise of Protestant Religious Conversion in a Mayan Village," *Social Compass* 39/3 (1992): 379–89.

[24] David Martin, *Tongues of Fire: The Explosion of Pentecostalism in Latin America* (Oxford: Blackwell, 1990), 285.

[25] Allan Anderson, *An Introduction to Pentecostalism: Global Charismatic Christianity* (Cambridge: Cambridge University Press, 2004), 77.

[26] John L. Allen, "Pentecostal Pastors Say Charismatic Movement Stems Catholic Losses," *National Catholic Reporter,* March 21, 2007, available online at: <http://ncronline.org/node/4990>.

[27] *The Catholic Encyclopedia,* available online at: <http://www.newadvent.org/cathen/04558c.htm>.

[28] Mecham, *Church and State in Latin America*, 299.

[29] Luis Martínez-Fernandez, *Protestantism and Political Conflict in the Nineteeth-Century Hispanic Caribbean* (New Brunswick, NJ: Rutgers University Press, 2002), 14.

[30] Louis Perez, Jr., *Essays on Cuban History: Historiography and Research* (Gainsville, FL: University of Florida Press, 1995), 65.

[31] Louis A. Perez, Jr., "Protestant Missionaries in Cuba: Archival Records, Manuscript Collections, and Research Prospects," *Latin American Research Review* 27/1 (1992): 105–20.

[32] "Table of Statistics on Religious Affiliation in the Americas Plus Spain and Portugal," at: <http://www.prolades.com/>.

[33] See Fidel Castro, *Fidel y la religion: Conversaciones con Frei Betto* (Quito: Manana, 1985).

[34] "International Religious Freedom Report, 2002," Bureau for Democracy, Human Rights, Labor, US Department of State, available online at: <http:www.state.gov/g/drl/rls/irf/2002/14039pf.htm>.

[35] Washington Office on Latin America, "Crossing the Divide: The Protestant Churches in Cuba," available online at: <http://www.ncccusa.org/news/cuba/wolaprotestant.html>.

[36] An estimated 70 percent of Cuban Catholics are also practitioners of Santería. See "International Religious Freedom Report, 2002," Bureau for Democracy, Human Rights, Labor, US Department of State, available online at: <http:www.state.gov/g/drl/rls/irf/2002/14039pf>. See also Thomas A. Tweed, *Our Lady of the Exile: Diasporic Religion at a Cuban Catholic Shrine in Miami* (New York: Oxford University Press, 1997).

[37] Ira Rifkin, "Cuba's Other Christians: Islands Protestant Population is Climbing," *Presbyterian News Service*, 22 January 1998, available online at: <http://www.pcusa.org/pcnews.oldnews/1998/98024.htm>.

[38] "International Religious Freedom Report, 2002," Bureau for Democracy, Human Rights, Labor, US Department of State, available online at: <http:www.state.gov/g/drl/rls/irf/2002/14039pf.htm>.

[39] "The Church in Cuba: A Brief History," 1–2. For more on ideological ties between the State and the CCC, see Sergio Arce Martínez, *The Church and Socialism: Reflections from a Cuban Context: Essays* (New York: Circus Productions, 1985).

[40] Washington Office on Latin America, "Crossing the Divide," 2.

[41] Ibid., "Crossing the Divide," 1.

[42] "The Visit of His Holiness Pope John Paul II to Cuba: An Assessment of its impact on Religious Freedom in Cuba," Hearing Before the Subcommittee on the Western Hemisphere of the Committee on International Relations, House of Representatives, One Hundred Fifth Congress, second session, March 4, 1998.

[43] Available online at: <http://www.pcusa.org/pcnews/oldnews.1998/98024.htm>.

[44] "International Religious Freedom Report, 2002," Bureau for Democracy, Human Rights, Labor, US Department of State, available online at: <http:www.state.gov/g/drl/rls/irf/2002/14039pf.htm>.

[45] Ira Rikin reports a figure of 300,000 Cuban Protestants for 1998; because this figure is nearly 10 years old and because the number of converts is apparently still increasing, this would appear to lend credence to the higher figure given here.

[46] "International Religious Freedom Report, 2002," Bureau for Democracy, Human Rights, Labor, US

Department of State, available online at: <http:www.state.gov/g/drl/rls/irf/2002/14039pf.htm>.

[47] See Jason M. Yaremko, *U.S. Protestant Missions in Cuba: From Independence to Castro* (Gainesville, FL: University of Florida Press, 2000).

[48] Ibid.

[49] Lily Cardamom, "God in Cuba," Master's thesis in Latin American Studies, Tulane University, May 1, 2006 (Lily Cardamom is a pseudonym).

[50] Ira Rifkin, "Cuba's Other Christians: Island's Protestant Population is Climbing," January 22, 1998, available online at: <http://www.pcusa.org/pcnews.oldnews/1998/98024.htm>.

[51] Ibid.

[52] Alter and Robles, 2006.

[53] Cardamom, "God in Cuba," 59.

[54] To receive a permit to conduct legal services, a congregation must provide the government with information on scheduling, the condition of the house, the property of the house with its papers, and verify that religious services cannot bother the neighbors. Available online at: <http://www.christiantoday.com/news/missions/christian.house.churches.in.cuba.facing.new.restriction.laws/494.htm>.

[55] Rose T. Caraway, "Tangible Hope: Cuban Protestantism in the Post-Soviet Era," Ph.D. dissertation, University of Florida, Dept. of Religious Studies, 2011, p. 78.

[56] Michelle Vu, "Christian House Churches in Cuba Facing New Restriction Laws," *Christian Today*, September 20, 2005, available online at: <http://www.christiantoday.com/article/christian.house.churches.in.cuba.facing.new.restriction.laws/4019.htm>.

Further Reading

Anderson, Allan. *An Introduction to Pentecostalism: Global Charismatic Christianity.* Cambridge: Cambridge University Press, 2004.

Cardenal, Ernesto. *El Evangelio en Solentiname.* Salamanca: Ediciones Sígueme, 1975–8.

Chesnut, R. Andrew. *Competitive Spirits: Latin America's New Religious Economy.* New York: Oxford University Press, 2003.

De la Torre, Miguel A. *La Lucha for Cuba: Religion and Politics on the Streets of Miami.* Berkeley, CA: University of California Press, 2003.

Jenkins, Phillip. *The Next Christendom: The Coming of Global Christianity.* New York: Oxford University Press, 2002.

Martin, David. *Tongues of Fire: The Explosion of Protestantism in Latin America.* Oxford: Blackwell, 1990.

Mecham, John Lloyd. *Church and State in Latin America: A History of Politico-Ecclesiastical Relations.* Chapel Hill, NC: University of North Carolina Press, 1966 [1934].

Steigenga, Timothy and Edward Cleary, eds. *The Conversion of a Continent.* New Brunswick, NJ: Rutgers University Press, 2007.

Stoll, David. *Is Latin America Turning Protestant?* Berkeley, CA: University of California Press, 1990.

Taylor, William. *Magistrates of the Sacred: Priests and Parishioners in Eighteenth Century Mexico.* Stanford, CA: Stanford University Press, 1996.

Treto, Raul Gómez. *La Iglesia Católica durante la construcción del socialismo en Cuba,* 3rd edn. Havana: CEHILA, 1994.

Tweed, Thomas A. *Our Lady of the Exile: Diasporic Religion at a Cuban Catholic Shrine in Miami.* New York: Oxford University Press, 1997.

Williams, Philip J., Timothy J. Steigenga, and Manuel A. Vásquez, *A Place to Be: Brazilian, Guatemalan, and Mexican Immigrants in Florida's New Destinations.* New Brunswick, NJ: Rutgers University Press, 2009.

12

Christianity in Latin America
Changing Churches in a Changing Continent

Samuel Escobar

Introduction

In 1892, at the commemoration of 400 years of Columbus's arrival in the Americas, Nicaraguan poet Ruben Darío wrote a poem that described the miserable state of the continent and he depicted Christ, who was walking the streets, as a thin, frail, and scared man in contrast with Barrabas who had slaves and golden decorations. Nothing could express better the perception that the Latin American intelligentsia had of Christianity in Latin America as a total failure, and its irrelevancy to the future. One hundred years later, in 1992, the mood of the intelligentsia had changed. That year liberation theologian Gustavo Gutiérrez published his book *Las Casas: In Search for the Poor of Jesus Christ*, a massive and thorough study of the work of Bartolomé de Las Casas and his struggle for justice on behalf of the Indians in the sixteenth century, pointing to its relevance as a model for the social struggles of the twentieth. As were other works of Gutiérrez, this book was favorably received by the intelligentsia. For Dario, "poor Christ" inspired compassion, while for the readers of Gutiérrez, "the Christ of the poor" was pointing the way to the struggle for justice in the twenty-first century.

The contrast in attitudes corresponds to the changes Christianity experienced during the past century in Latin America. Through intense and steady evangelism, evangelicals saw their numbers multiplied in Latin America. On the other hand, motivated in part by that growth, the dominant Roman Catholic Church was revitalized. However, these changes have brought about a seriously divided Christianity that could find itself engaged in religious in-fighting that will prevent the Churches from playing a significant social and political role in the new century.

Decades of Change

The term Latin America refers to those countries placed between the US–Mexico border and Patagonia, the southern tip of Chile and Argentina in South America. Thus it includes Mexico, Central America, and South America. The term describes the countries that received the Iberian cultural influence of Spain and Portugal referred to as "Latin," which incorporates the French influence in Haiti. It also includes the Spanish-speaking countries in the Caribbean, namely, Cuba and the Dominican Republic, as well as Puerto Rico. The background for the change of Christianity in these countries was the critical social transformation experienced by the continent throughout the twentieth century. During the colonial era, under the domination of Spain and Portugal (sixteenth to eighteenth centuries), the dominant Roman Catholic Church had provided the ideological justification for a system that enslaved the indigenous minorities and

Introducing World Christianity, First Edition. Edited by Charles E. Farhadian.
© 2012 Blackwell Publishing Ltd. Published 2012 by Blackwell Publishing Ltd.

Map 12.1   Latin America

Figure 12.1 Iglesia Sarhua, Peru. Photographer: Odelon Berrocal F. Used by permission of Sarhua Art Décor.

kept the dominant elites in power. After independence in the 1820s, modernizing groups and parties were opposed by the Church and consequently, at least sometimes, they welcomed the presence of Protestant missionaries who started to arrive when the colonial situation ended. During the initial decades of the twentieth century, before World War II, in most countries there were efforts toward modernization, trying to move ahead, away from the feudal social and economic systems inherited from Iberian colonialism. Industrialization and urbanization were the motors that brought accelerated cultural change. After World War II, a wave of movements struggled for democratization and modernization under the banners of either socialism or developmentalism, following American-style capitalism. These attempts had moderate success in some cases or were a complete failure in others, due to the deep-seated structural contradictions and the restrictions imposed by the global tensions of the Cold War.

The social turmoil accelerated with the coming of the Cuban Revolution (1959) and President Kennedy's response, called the Alliance for Progress, which in themselves exemplified dramatically the dilemmas of Latin America. At the end of the decade of 1960, few people would have expected the kind of painful transitions that Latin America experienced during the new globalization era of the last three decades of the twentieth century. By the mid-1960s, the dreams of social utopias that always follow popular revolutions filled the air with combative songs and the walls with Marxist slogans. By the year 2000, revolutionary poetry had given way to numbers and statistics, and in the twenty-first century the average citizen has become conversant with the economic lingo of the market: investments, interests, privatization, and stabilization. The cities look more crowded, there are more children begging in the streets, and in some countries the ideological terror of the guerrillas and the armed forces has been replaced by the armed violence of drug traffickers and common criminals. Against the background of such social and political change, there is an explosion of religious activity that has taken social scientists as well as Christian leaders by surprise. In almost every large city in Latin America you see theaters converted into worship places, and in many countries you find Catholic priests preaching in streets in the open air or holding healing services on TV, just like Pentecostal pastors. In radio stations all over the continent, Catholic and Protestant broadcasts are so much alike that it is difficult to distinguish one from the other. Additionally, Brazilian-born para-evangelical churches have burgeoned in Europe, Islam has expanded in Southern Mexico, Brazilian Spiritism has crossed borders with success, and there is a revival of native pre-Iberian religions.

The Crisis of Christendom

When we pay attention to the religious demographics we realize that Latin America holds significant influence for world Christianity. Almost half of all the Catholics in the world live in Latin America. Consequently, the Catholic hierarchies consider the region as a reservoir of human and material resources for their missionary work in the future but, during the most recent decades, more people have left Catholicism in order to become Protestant than at the time of the Protestant Reformation in the sixteenth century. Brazil, with its population of over 170 million, is considered the largest Catholic nation in the world, but the Catholic percentage of the population went down from 92.8 percent in 1970 to 88.4 percent in 1980, and to 73 percent in 2000. In fact, the 34 million Protestants (evangelical and Pentecostals) of Brazil might currently be a religious majority in comparison with the number of Catholics who actually practice their religion.

The most recent edition of *Operation World* – usually well informed – gives the figure of 55 million evangelicals in Latin America and the Caribbean.[1] More detailed and careful analysis shows steady growth in places such as Colombia, where evangelicals numbered 85,000 in 1968 (0.43 percent of the 19 million population) and had become close to 2 million

(5 percent of the 38 million population) in the year 2000. With the growing attention paid by sociologists and Roman Catholic hierarchies to this phenomenon, there is also a good amount of qualitative analysis of growth that gives ground for reflection. Take, for instance, the case of Chile, where Protestantism has been present for more than a century. A sociological study by the Catholic university in that country concludes that 13.9 percent of the population is evangelical. Research among the upper classes shows that while only 6.2 percent claim to be Protestant, 81.9 percent claim to be Roman Catholic. The same study reported that among the poorer sections of the population, 21 percent claim to be evangelical.[2] The study also points out that while the average Catholic priest has gone through a minimum of 10 years of rigorous formation, many of the evangelical pastors are self-taught. South America and Europe have similar numbers of Catholics (280 million in Europe compared to 297 million in South America, and a similarly sized land mass). However, while Europe has 1,342 Catholics per priest, South America has 7,112 Catholics per priest.[3]

The response to Protestant growth among some conservative sectors of Catholicism is to attribute it to a foreign conspiracy. In his opening address to the Latin American Bishops Conference at Santo Domingo (October 1992), Pope John Paul II challenged them to "defend" their flock from "rapacious wolves." This statement was a clear allusion to the growth of evangelical churches, usually described as "sects" in Catholic documents. The Pope added: "we should not underestimate a particular strategy aimed at weakening the bonds that unite Latin American countries and so to undermine the kinds of strength provided by unity. To that end, significant amounts of money are offered to subsidize proselytizing campaigns that try to shatter such Catholic unity."[4] Other Catholic leaders and scholars, especially foreigners with pastoral experience in Latin America, are openly critical of this "conspiracy theory" approach. Dominican Edward Cleary, commenting on the Pope's speech, wrote: "Ten years of study has convinced me that there is not a strong relation between money spent and results. The great advances seen in Protestant growth in Latin America are not the results of dollars from the United States."[5] Research and observation have led other Catholic specialists to agree with Cleary, because the churches that are growing faster are the ones that do not depend on connections outside their countries.[6]

Latin America has been the kind of laboratory in which a centuries-old Christendom that shows signs of decline and fatigue is confronted by the presence of vigorous minorities committed to evangelize. There are also other regions where established or "mainline" churches are facing the same situation. This is also the case for some of the state churches in Europe and for so-called historic or mainline denominations in places like North America and Australia. But the growth of Catholicism or new denominations in the United States and Australia, for instance, has not evoked the kind of passionate reaction that the growth of Protestantism in Latin America has produced among some Roman Catholics.

At a time of great spiritual confusion within an increasingly postmodern culture, and deep social disturbances caused by globalization, Protestants and Catholics in Latin America must converse and evaluate the facts and their attitudes from a perspective informed by history and theology. They have to respond to the cries of the urban masses living in expanding cities, and to the selfishness of multinationals and powerful elites that use every available means to maintain their privileges. Some of the most acute questions about the cooperation of Christians in mission, such as those concerning youth violence and disintegration of families, are being tested in these urban centers, but there are very few examples of cooperation. The present challenges for ecumenism and cooperation are rooted in a long religious and social history, and a first step in the direction of mutual understanding could be a critical understanding of mission history and a theologically based reflection that would clarify the perception of different Christian traditions. Let us take, for instance, the different ways that the forms of Christianity have been introduced in Latin America.

Figure 12.2 La Paz, Bolivia. Wayne McLean (http://commons.wikimedia.org/wiki/File:Central_La_Paz_Bolivia.jpg) used under the Creative Commons Attribution-Share Alike 3.0 Unported license

Contrasting Origins and Developments[7]

At the time of the Iberian conquest of the Americas, Europe was dominated by Christendom, the close alliance of religious, social, and economic power. The pattern was transported to the Americas by the colonial enterprise. Latin American Christianity was characterized by the fact that even after the colonial period, the dominant Roman Catholic Church came to depend for its survival on the material support and benefits received by it from the state. Ivan Vallier's hypothesis about the opposition of the Roman Catholic Church to modernization is based on analysis of the way in which the Catholic Church was implanted in Latin America. In the sixteenth century there was a close relationship between Iberian conquest and evangelization, and Church leaders tended to equate the growth of Christianity with the advance and establishment of the Spanish or Portuguese empire. Some of the missionary Orders struggled for a deeper work of evangelization but conquest became the dominant pattern. As Vallier says, "Colonization equalled Christianization. For this reason the Church did not have to be preoccupied about the strength of its religious life at the grassroots. Unwittingly this lack of concern for strong religious motivations locked the Church into a position of extreme dependency on the secular order."[8]

By contrast, the arrival and establishment of Protestantism in the nineteenth and twentieth centuries was marked by an emphasis on the call to personal conversion. Methodist theologian José Míguez Bonino has provided a socio-theological analysis of this individualistic emphasis that he argues was "in keeping with the theology and practice of the Anglo-American 'Evangelical Awakenings.' In comparison with Roman Catholic form and ritual, Protestant preaching stressed the need for personal encounter with Jesus Christ, a vivid experience of forgiveness and a new moral life."[9] For Míguez, the social impact of this religious process showed "clear signs of the transition from a traditional to a modern society, from the feudal to the bourgeois person," and he outlined a threefold set of social consequences. First, the individualistic personal conversion is the origin of voluntaristic communities formed by people who have left behind social mediations. Second, while in traditional religion "religious categories are projected in a supernatural screen," in the Protestant experience "the supernatural is projected on the screen of subjectivity." Third, religious conversion is related to a transition in the moral realm. "The focus now is on internalization of duty, a sense of responsibility, and the virtues of early capitalism – industry, honesty, moderation, frugality."[10] The social impact of this threefold direction of the Protestant conversion experience is summarized as follows, "Protestantism helps to create persons who correspond to and contribute to the change in social structures and mentality. It reinforces the liberal bourgeois utopia of the free moral agent."[11]

After the break away from the Iberian empire between 1810 and 1824, the nineteenth century was a time of nation-building for Latin America. Liberal elites were active both in the independence movement and in the process of nation-building. Jesuit historian Jeffrey Klaiber summarizes fittingly the conflict that Liberalism had with the Catholic Church during this process. "In the eighteenth and nineteenth centuries liberalism emerged as a new and powerful political force, and it constituted a new source of legitimacy. The church, which did not learn to change with the times, lost a measure of its own legitimacy in the eyes of liberals, positivists and other reformers of advanced thinking."[12] The search for a participatory exercise of citizenship thus takes an anti-clerical dimension with more similarities to what happened in the French Revolution than to developments in the Anglo-Saxon world. Modernizing elites were confronted by the opposition of the Catholic Church to democratic ideas and practices, all of which were seen with great suspicion. Moreover, in their struggles against the new liberalizing trends, conservative parties looked for legitimization in the Catholic Church and they usually found it.

Modernizing elites admired the Anglo-Saxon way of life and democratic ideas, and consequently they favored the coming of Protestant missionaries whose presence was seen as a source for democratic teaching and practices. One of the reasons the elite championed religious pluralism and freedom was in order to favor immigration from Anglo-Saxon and Protestant countries. In a study about Protestantism in Peru, for example, I have shown that though a modern, democratic, and pluralistic society was an ideal embraced by the liberal elites, it could well have remained as nothing more than an ideal. It only started to become a reality when there was a religiously motivated dissident community that was ready to stand in the face of legal discrimination and endure violent persecution.[13] The same happened in relation to the incorporation of indigenous peoples into national life. There were many literary and philosophical proponents of equality and human rights for aboriginals, but their writings remained as nothing more than interesting literature. Only when Protestant missionaries immersed themselves into the lives of indigenous people did Protestant communities rise up and start to demand a right to exist. As a result, the human rights of indigenous peoples became a matter of national concern. In addition, more democratic legislation was passed and new social actors appeared on the scene.[14] There is a growing body of scholarship studying the social impact of this type of historic Protestantism in Latin America. However the type of Protestantism that grew more significantly in the final decades of the twentieth century was what we could call "Popular Protestantism" of the Pentecostal type.

Changes in Roman Catholicism

During the second part of the twentieth century the Roman Catholic Church in Latin America went through a process of significant change. The growth of evangelical Protestantism was part of a larger phenomenon, the massive exodus of people from the dominant Church, a Church whose structure of religious life, religious institution, and pastoral practices had hardly changed for four centuries, making it unable to cope with the challenges of the fast pace of social change. Political movements of peasants and workers, based on populist or Marxist ideas, were attracting the potential leaders away from the Church. In 1955, the first Latin American Council of Bishops (CELAM I) met in Rio de Janeiro and concluded by asking Catholics from other parts of the world to come and help them avoid the impending catastrophe brought by the rise of both communists and Protestants. To everyone's surprise, the Catholic Church

changed. Jesuit historian Jeffrey Klaiber writes, "against all predictions to the contrary, including those of Max Weber himself, the Catholic Church changed; it ceased to be a bulwark of the established order and turned into a force for social change."[15]

During the Second Vatican Council (1962–5) the hierarchies of the Church acknowledged and officially approved the reforming and renewing of pastoral and theological trends that had been developing in different parts of the world. The impact of the Second Vatican Council was registered in Latin America during the second assembly of the Bishops Council (CELAM II) that met in the city of Medellín in Colombia (1968). Medellín became a symbol of the transformations that were shaking Catholicism in the region. The challenge of Protestant growth at the grass roots of society developed in spite of limitations and persecutions. Additionally, the new practice by Catholic missionaries from North America and Europe of immersing themselves in aiding the poorest segments of society clearly revealed the need for the Catholic Church to revise its stance. Liberation theology was the expression of that new awareness. Some influential theologians in Medellín, such as Gustavo Gutiérrez and Juan Luis Segundo, were not first and foremost political activists but as theologians they were concerned with the pastoral well-being of their Church. They proposed a new and critical reading of the social role their Church had historically played in Latin America, a new reading of Scripture, and a new definition of Christian praxis. The bishops agreed to adopt a new stance that was described as "a preferential option for the poor." The various sectors of the Church interpreted this option in different ways. The more radical sectors aligned with socialist political movements of the left, and some of them adopted Marxism as a way to interpret social reality. With the conviction that history was moving toward socialism, they threw their lot in with socialist and communist movements. Such an option was a key element in several forms of liberation theology. The more traditional sectors intensified efforts to provide assistance to the poor, channeling vast resources made available by Catholics from Europe and North America into relief and development assistance.[16]

The changes brought by Medellin were significant. Klaiber's historical study, published in 1998, has the advantage of a long-term perspective that allows for a sober and objective look at what actually was a controversial and polarized period. A key issue for Klaiber is the role of the Catholic Church in providing "legitimacy" to a particular socio-political regime. Using Weberian categories, Klaiber defines legitimacy as "the popular consent that undergirds power." He argues that in Latin America there has been a tension between authoritarian *caudillos* who offered charismatic and traditional legitimacy, on the one hand, and, on the other, the liberals who wanted a democratic type of legitimacy based on equality before the law. According to Klaiber, the Catholic Church enjoyed its own legitimacy based on religion, and could thus provide legitimacy to the social order through what could be called a religious sanction. In his overview of how the Catholic Church fulfilled this legitimizing role and how that changed during the second part of the twentieth century, Klaiber offers a valuable summary of the process. He writes:

> In Medellin the bishops made a dramatic call to create a new social order based on justice and human rights. With this change the Church legitimized many of the ideals of the old liberals – democracy and human rights . . . Most of all the church legitimized an entire popular movement that had been emerging since the end of the Second World War.[17]

A central component of the "entire popular movement" to which Klaiber refers is the existence of the Christian Base Communities (CBC). Some argue that CBCs are the most permanent and enduring result of the liberation theology movement. Theologians aware of the tight connection between theology and the practical Christian life realized the importance of the CBCs. Gustavo Gutiérrez thus said that these communities are "one of the most fruitful and significant events in the present day life of the Latin American church . . . their growth throughout our continent has helped to raise the hopes of the poor and oppressed."[18] And 11 years after Medellín, the document of the Third Bishops Council that met in Puebla, Mexico (CELAM III, 1979), referred to the CBCs as "the joy and hope of the Church." For the bishops, these communities "embody the Church's preferential love for the common people. In them their religiosity is expressed, valued and purified, and they are given a concrete opportunity to share in the task of the Church and to work commitedly for the transformation of the world."[19] There have been controversies among Catholics as to how that transformation takes place with some stressing the religious dimension, and others stressing political activism, but in several countries, the CBCs have been the means for Catholic participation in civil society movements.

There is a causal correlation between evangelical and Pentecostal growth in Latin America and the rise of the CBCs. This is especially evident in Brazil where a popular and indigenous kind of Protestantism existed that did not depend on an educated clergy, sophisticated methodologies, or funds from abroad, and this version of Protestantism motivated pioneers of the CBCs such as José Marins.[20] Pentecostalism was a movement coming "from below," with its own religious and social dynamism and a great expansive power. Today, scholars trying to understand the role of religion in the life of the urban poor, or the relationship between democracy and religion in Latin America, are naturally drawn to comparative studies of the CBCs and the Pentecostals.[21] The puzzling question for social scientists, Church historians, and bishops in the 1980s was to understand why it was that though the Catholic Church took a preferential option for the poor, the poor themselves were taking an option for the Pentecostal churches.

The Emergence of the Poor

The sudden and profound changes in Eastern Europe symbolized by the fall of the Berlin Wall in 1989 had strong repercussion in Latin America. Leftist intellectuals and political parties had been unable to understand the social dynamism boiling at the grass-roots level during the decade of the 1980s. Part of the unique social dynamics in Latin America was the relentless process of accumulation that turned cities into urban labyrinths. This brought to light the emergence of new segments of the population that in the past could be hidden in the distant rural areas but who have now invaded massively the streets of capitals like Lima, Mexico, Guatemala, São Paulo, Caracas, or Bogotá. These emerging popular sectors demonstrated their ability to become social and economic actors without the tutorial paternalism of Marxist parties and their outdated theories.[22] They constitute the appearance of *The Other Path* as economist Hernando de Soto has called it, in a clear contrasting allusion to the classic revolutionary way symbolized by the Maoism of the Shining Path group in Perú.[23] De Soto has demonstrated that the vastness of informal economies has proven that the poor have entrepreneurial abilities to survive and emerge in spite of oppressive bureaucratic control and inefficient socializing measures. There is also a religious dimension to this emergence. The expansion of popular Protestantism in the form of popular churches among these emerging masses has become a surprising phenomenon. These churches retain key elements of the Protestant message but they present and live them out within the context of the culture of poverty, which includes the dynamism to which De Soto refers.

The bulk of this growth corresponds to Pentecostal churches and some observers predict that this will become the predominant religious force in the twenty-first century. Pentecostal churches are indigenous in nature and inspired by a contagious proselytistic spirit. They show some of the marks of the early Pentecostal movement in North America that Hollenweger also associates with indigenous non-white churches in other parts of the world, namely: glossolalia, oral liturgy, a narrative style in the communication of their message, maximum participation of all the faithful in worship and prayers, inclusion of dreams and visions in public meetings, and a unique understanding of the body/mind relationship applied in healing by prayer.[24] These Pentecostal churches grew especially among the most marginalized social groups in the urban areas, usually unnoticed during their first decades. However, in some cases political circumstances brought them to public attention, especially when governments experienced tensions with the Roman Catholic Church and therefore saw Pentecostals as an alternative source of religious legitimation.

It could be said that these popular Protestant churches have become alternative societies that create a closed world where people are accepted and become actors, not on the basis of what gives them status in the world around but in terms of values that come from their vision of the kingdom of God. This fact has captured the attention of social scientists who by working at the micro level have brought to light the transforming nature of the spiritual experience offered by these churches.[25] British sociologist David Martin has summarized and interpreted a vast amount of data from the accumulated research of the two decades that preceded his study published in 1990. He finds that "The new society now emerging in Latin America has to do with movement, and evangelicals constitute a *movement*. Evangelical Christianity is a dramatic migration of the spirit matching and accompanying a dramatic migration of bodies."[26]

On the other hand, observers, scholars, and religious leaders have had to come to terms with the fact that in spite of all good theory and good intentions many actions in favor of the poor were tainted by a paternalistic approach. Social and political conscientization took the form of a struggle for the poor, trying to create a more just society *for* them rather than *with* them. Historical churches connected to world communities and denominational families had access to funds, foreign press, and even diplomatic ties that were used in an effort to help the victims of poverty or state terrorism. Many times the source for the emergence of these movements has been among the poor, but those seeking to aid them have failed in mobilizing the poor themselves. By contrast, the popular Protestant churches are popular movements in themselves. Their pastors and leaders do not have to identify with the poor; *they are the poor*. They do not have a social agenda but an intense spiritual agenda and it is through that agenda that they have been able to have a social impact. As Martin observes about the impact of the Pentecostal experience, "Above all it renews the innermost cell of the family and protects the woman from the ravages of male desertion and violence. A new faith is able to implant new disciplines, re-order priorities, counter corruption and destructive machismo, and reverse the indifferent and injurious hierarchies of the outside world."[27] This redemptive power of experience has worked at an individual level, but a key question for the future concerns what the possibilities are for its long-term social impact through political action and participation in civil society.

Mission from Below

Reflection upon the process that we have summarized here shows that mission in the future, within the frame of a post-Christendom situation, will follow a pattern that could be described as "mission from below." This will be in contrast with the pattern present during the days of Christendom, which could be described as mission "from above," from a position of military, financial, or technological power. Christian mission that begins "from below" will go back to the New Testament pattern that was seen in Jesus himself and the early Church. This is, for instance, the style of the new generations of Catholic missionaries associated with liberation theologies and coming from Spain. The six Jesuits who were killed by a rightist military squad in El Salvador in November of 1989 were university professors and theologians working among the poor. For decades, Bishop Casaldaliga, a defender of the Indians in Brazil, has been the subject of harassment and threats from wealthy landowners.[28] The pattern of mission from below will have to inform the practice of Latin American Christians who are now being sent to take part in the world mission of the Church.

The lesson is especially relevant for Latin American evangelicals whose traditional evangelistic zeal has also led them into a growing involvement in world mission. Since 1987 a measure of coordination of missionary activity from Latin America to other parts of the world has been provided by COMIBAM, a net of agencies and individuals that was formed after a missions congress held in Sao Paulo, Brazil. Progress in evangelical missionary work from Latin America has been significant. It is estimated that in 1982 some 92 Protestant organizations were sending a total of 1,120 Latin Americans as missionaries to other parts of the world. By 1988 there were 150 organisations and some 3,026 missionaries.[29] The most recent figures shown on the webpage of COMIBAM indicate that there are 9,625 Latin American missionaries sent by 641 mission agencies. Of this total of missionaries, 3,372 work in other regions of the world.[30] These figures, compiled by scholars who have specialized in the subject, are generally conservative estimates and do not include many spontaneous movements that are hard to document.

None of these figures include migrants who on their own do missionary work elsewhere in the world, though they are not related formally to established agencies. In most cases, the presence of migrants is marked by the precariousness of their situation that can only be understood as a presence "from below." It is estimated that in Europe alone there are 3 million legal or illegal Latin American immigrants. If even 10 percent of these immigrants are practicing Christians they constitute the potential of a new missionary presence, and, in fact, some of them are already acting as such, with a promise of renewal of a declining European Christianity. Peruvian missiologist Miguel Angel Palomino has studied some cases[31] and there is also a fascinating sociological study comparing the missionary dimensions of the African and Latin American diasporas in other parts of the world.[32]

Catholic Self–Evaluation and Agenda

As the end of the twentieth century approached, the leadership of the Roman Catholic Church worked at an evaluation of its status and ministry in Latin America. The Synod of the Americas (Rome, November to December of 1997) brought together 300 bishops and cardinals from Latin America, the United States, and Canada. Evidently the Vatican wanted to see greater official coordination between North and South. They emphasized a "new evangelization," acknowledging that "the church in the past had stressed sociological solutions to poverty whereas now the emphasis should be on conversion."[33] This new scheme means greater financial aid from North to South, and coordination of efforts to reach Hispanics in the United States, who have been converting to Protestantism at a rate that alarms Catholics.

The "Post-synodal Apostolic Exhortation" that Pope John Paul II presented in Mexico on January 22, 1999, is known as *Ecclesia in America*, an official summary of the agenda of the Church of Rome for the coming years. As is usual in official documents, a distinction is kept between the Protestant Churches that participate in the ecumenical dialogue led from Geneva by the World Council of Churches and the more dynamic evangelical and Pentecostal Churches, which are called "sects." *Ecclesia in America* states:

"The proselytizing activity of the sects and new religious groups in many parts of America is a grave hindrance to the work of evangelization." Although Catholics are encouraged to have ecumenical attitudes, "These attitudes, however, must not be such that they weaken the firm conviction that only in the Catholic Church is found the fullness of the means of salvation established by Jesus Christ."[34]

The agenda, in view of the advance of evangelicals, demands "a thorough study, to be carried out in each nation and at the international level, to ascertain why many Catholics leave the Church." A review of pastoral policies is required "so that each particular Church can offer the faithful more personalized religious care, strengthen the structures of communion and mission, make the most of the evangelizing possibilities of a purified popular religiosity, and thus give new life to every Catholic's faith in Jesus Christ." The review also includes a change of emphasis from the social to the spiritual. In a clear reference to a post-liberation theology stance, *Ecclesia in America* says, "it is necessary to ask whether a pastoral strategy directed almost exclusively to meeting people's material needs has not in the end left their hunger for God unsatisfied, making them vulnerable to anything which claims to be of spiritual benefit."

What is evident now to any attentive observer is that in Latin America Catholic priests and lay people are imitating many of the pastoral and evangelistic methods that were created and developed by Protestants from the historical or popular Protestant Churches. Many Catholic television programs have the same structure as evangelical or charismatic programs, popular evangelical hymns from the 1970s and 1980s have been included in Catholic songbooks, and there is now wide use of Bible study in small groups, meetings in homes with time for testimony, biblical meditation, and prayer. In some cases the methods have been modified and adapted, but in other cases it has become hard to distinguish what is Catholic from what is evangelical.

The tone of *Ecclesia in America* is evidence that though scholars and missiologists may acknowledge the positive role of the evangelical presence in the development of self-reform and changes in Latin American Catholicism, the official position of the bishops, with almost no exceptions, continues to be hostile toward evangelicals. The Roman Catholic claims of possession of absolute and full truth have not changed. In fact, the same intransigence colors the way official Roman Catholic teaching evaluates the historical role of Protestantism and its right to existence. Of course, the practical consequences of these claims are more evident in those places where Catholicism is still the predominant Church.

On the other hand, at the grass-roots level, there is an increasing number of projects in which Catholic and evangelical Christians cooperate without any concealment of their identity, regardless of what official documents may say. In critical areas of life where the state is insufficient or unwilling to help people in need, Christian compassion expressed in projects of service is frequently the only resource for the poor classes. This writer has witnessed how cooperation is happening in Bible translation and distribution, pastoral work in prisons, disaster relief, work with street children, and defense of human rights in several countries. There is no collected record of what is taking place but it surely may be a sign for the future.

Assessing Evangelical Growth

Although the growth of evangelical and Pentecostal churches could be considered a relatively recent phenomenon, there are some disturbing facts that have been uncovered by missiological studies. In some countries there are signs of decline and defection. Careful field research has provided data showing that a number of people from evangelical churches are returning to the Catholic Church or leaving Christianity entirely. The most disturbing of such studies was conducted by Jorge Gómez in Costa Rica, and it provides a factual account of these trends. Gómez's research was completed during 1994 and he could make use of other rigorous sociological samples of studies carried on between 1989 and 1991. Summarizing his study, Gómez concludes, "From the almost 20% of the population that in some moment of their lives have been or are Protestant, only 10% were Protestant at the time of the study."[35] Defection has been higher than what pastors and denominational leaders ever thought it would be. The groups in which defection is more frequent are young adults

(18–24 years of age), men, persons born in Protestant homes, and new believers (within the first or second year of their affiliation).

There is a direct relationship between intentional discipleship or catechetical process and retention of members. The churches that have lost more members are those that have no clear plan of discipleship and pastoral care. Among the top reasons for defection are the inability of defectors to live up to the standards required by the churches, and the financial and sexual scandals among pastors and leaders. These two factors are two faces of the same problem, what we could describe as a pastoral crisis among Protestants in Latin America. The predominance of independent missions, the extreme individualism of their theology and their missionary methods, and the competitive attitude that has prized numerical growth at any cost explain in part this pastoral crisis. Enthusiastic evangelism is not matched by a theologically based pastoral work to take care of the new believers. The social agenda that Latin American societies place before churches requires a better formative process of rank-and-file Christians.

One could also place here the lessons gained from the political participation of evangelicals in Latin America. Numerical growth raised expectations about what was going to be the social and political impact of the evangelical presence in Latin America. There has been a significant social impact in at least three forms.[36] First, within the worsening social conditions whose victims are specially children, youth, and those affected by terrorism and political violence, evangelical churches and missions have demonstrated an exceptional ability to mobilize resources and volunteers and to create networks to assist those in need. For instance, the "Viva network," an initiative of the Latin America Mission (LAM), has managed to connect a good number of agencies and persons that work with children at risk across the continent. Second, church growth among indigenous populations has proved to have a redemptive social effect, raising living standards and self-reliance. Anthropological and sociological work from non-partisan scientists has demonstrated this in countries such as Guatemala, Mexico, Ecuador, Peru, and Bolivia.[37] Third, Pentecostal growth among the urban poor has had the same redemptive effect, though on a less visible scale, which is more difficult to

measure. In any case, the evangelical presence has helped the urban poor in their survival strategies for "coping with poverty."[38]

For Protestants in Latin America, the great demands of the social agenda make it imperative to work for cooperation and union of different denominations and movements. Two organizations work in that direction. On the one hand, CLAI (*Consejo Latinoamericano de Iglesias*, Latin American Council of Churches) was established in Mexico in 1978 by an initiative of historical denominations, including Presbyterians, Methodists, some Baptists, or Anglicans, and this was related to the World Council of Churches. On the other hand, there is CONELA (*Confraternidad de Evangélicos Latinoamericanos*, Confraternity of Latin American Evangelicals), founded in 1982 as an initiative from agencies and churches related to conservative evangelical missions, and related to the World Evangelical Alliance. None of these organizations has been able to enlist the majority of Latin American Protestants, in spite of the fact that there are Pentecostals in both of them. However, for the purpose of theological reflection and production, the *Fraternidad Teológica Latinoamericana* (FTL) (Latin American Theological Fraternity) has been able to enlist persons that are active both in CONELA and CLAI.[39]

One would expect a logical progression from social transformation to political action, but after more than three decades of evangelical presence in Latin American politics there are serious doubts and disappointments, even to the point of embarrassment. Brazilian scholar Paul Freston has been following the subject and has gathered factual information about Protestant participation in politics, working with a team in different parts of Latin America.[40] There is a wide spectrum of experiences and some discernible patterns. In Guatemala, charismatic evangelicals achieved positions of power, as in the cases of Efrain Rios Montt, after a military coup, and Jorge Serrano Elías as a result of an election. Rios Montt had difficulties continuing his political career because of the accusations of genocide among the indigenous groups during military operations against guerrillas. Serrano Elías resigned under pressure due to the seriousness and depth of the proved corruption of his regime. In the case of Peru where for a time, under ousted-president Fujimori, there were several evangelicals in Congress, one cannot point to any significant contribution from one of them to legislation or political life that would be consistent with the experience of evangelicals in that country. None of these leaders showed in their public life any of the typical characteristics of the social Protestant ethics. In the absence of basic convictions and ethical clarity these politicians from the evangelical camp seemed to be guided by expediency and personal interest, in the same way as many other politicians. However, there is another trend that should not be overlooked. Members of traditional churches elected to political office, such as Methodist Jose Miguez Bonino in Argentina, Presbyterians Pedro Arana in Perú and Jaime Ortiz in Colombia, made important contributions, shaped by their evangelical faith, to the debate and legislation in their countries. As time goes on, inevitably more evangelicals will be elected to power in this new century. On October 6, 2002, more than 4 million people voted for Rosinha Garotinho as governor of the Rio de Janeiro state in Brazil. She is a well-known Presbyterian journalist, and was preceded in the governor's seat by Benedita de Silva, a popular Afro-Brazilian leader from the Assemblies of God.[41] These evangelical women enjoying success in politics as members of socialist parties are symbols of a departure from the traditional stereotypes about evangelicals in Latin America. Their stories show not only the reformation of *machismo* (male chauvinism) in Latin American life to which evangelicals are making a significant contribution, but also the new challenges that both historical Protestants as well as Pentecostals are facing as their churches grow numerically. These cases have to be understood within the frame of Brazil that has the longest tradition of evangelical presence in political life. Latin American evangelical churches are thus challenged to provide pastoral care for their politicians. Theologians and pastors have the task of articulating a contextual social and political Protestant ethics.

Post-Denominational Christianity?

The more recent figures of evangelical numerical growth include large numbers of people who are part of independent mega-churches, a new emerging religious force that could be described as para-evangelical. Its origins are among charismatic Catholics disaffected with Rome, independent missions from some US mega-churches, and groups that split from evangelical churches. Some of these mega-churches are connected to the so-called neo-Apostolic movement championed by Peter Wagner and others in the United States. These para-evangelical churches initially seek legitimization by connecting to evangelicalism. However, their numerical growth, their disregard for theological definition, and their ability to develop forms of church life relevant to the postmodern culture, as well as their claim to originality, may turn them into a new religious force different from both evangelicals and Roman Catholics.

Just like in North America there are signs of a post-denominational situation in which all kinds of ecclesiastical barriers are crossed, not so much through an intentional ecumenical effort but rather as a flux created by lack of permanent loyalties. In some of these mega-churches we see the sale of sacred objects such as blessed water and oil, the appointment of "apostles" with unlimited and unquestionable authority, and methods of fund-raising in which givers are promised 10 times what they give to their church. Some of these practices are much closer to those of traditional popular Catholicism than to those of Reformation churches. Could this be the Latin American equivalent of what Donald E. Miller has called "reinventing American Protestantism" in his study of three American mega-churches?[42] In any case, this reinvention of Protestantism is a denial of some of the key tenets of the Reformation that provided the means to renew Christianity in Europe during the sixteenth century and in Latin America during the twentieth.

Conclusion

There is in Latin American Christianity the potential to play a significant role in the twenty-first century. This is already happening in their own territory and abroad. Globalization has not brought significant social changes in Latin America to overcome the abysmal difference between the few rich and the important segments of the population who live in poverty and marginalization. The growth of democracy in the region is still threatened by failed socialist experiments and populist regimes. What Christians are already doing in terms of disaster relief, assistance to the poor, empowerment of marginalized people, education for the poor, social criticism in defense of human rights, and fostering the mobilization of civil society, as part of their mission agenda, is still indispensable for the survival and well-being of Latin American societies.

Notes and References

[1] Patrick Johnstone and Jason Mandryk, eds, *Operation World* (Carlisle: Paternoster, 2001), 33–4.

[2] ALC News Service, August 10, 2001.

[3] Bryan T. Froehle and Mary L. Gautier,"Latin American Catholicism," *International Bulletin of Missionary Research* 282, April 2004: 69.

[4] Alfred T. Hennelly, S.J. ed., *Santo Domingo and Beyond* (Maryknoll, NY: Orbis, 1993), 48.

[5] "John Paul Cries 'Wolf,'" *Commonweal*, 20 November 1992: 7.

[6] I have summarized pastoral observations from Catholic authors that follow this approach in *Changing Tides: Latin America and World Mission Today* (Maryknoll, NY: Orbis, 2002), ch. 8, 88–98.

[7] In this section and the next I am borrowing from my article "Religious Transitions and Civil Society in Latin America," in Roland Hoksbergen and Lowell M. Ewert, eds, *Local Ownership, Global Change: Will Civil Society Save the World?* (Monrovia, CA: World Vision, 2002), 162–82.

[8] Ivan Vallier, *Catholicism, Social Control and Modernization in Latin America* (Englewood Cliffs, NJ: Prentice Hall, 1970), 48.

[9] José Míguez Bonino, *Toward a Christian Political Ethics* (London: SCM Press, 1983), 60.

[10] Ibid., 61.

[11] Ibid., 61.

[12] Jeffrey Klaiber, SJ, *The Church, Dictatorships and Democracy in Latin America* (Maryknoll, NY: Orbis, 1998), 5.

[13] Samuel Escobar, *Metodistas y Adventistas: Dos Modelos de Proyecto Protestante en el Perú, 1877–1915* (Lima: Cátedra de Misiología, 1995–6).

[14] Samuel Escobar, "Religion and Social Change at the Grass Roots in Latin America," in *Annals of the American Academy of Political and Social Science* (November 1997): 81–103.

[15] Jeffrey Klaiber, SJ, *The Church, Dictatorships and Democracy*, 5.

[16] From a Liberation Theology perspective see Gustavo Gutierrez, "Expanding the View," an introduction to the fifteenth anniversary revised edition of his book *A Theology of Liberation* (Maryknoll, NY: Orbis, 1988); from an American academic perspective, Paul Sigmund, *Liberation Theology at the Crossroads* (New York: Oxford University Press, 1990); from an evangelical perspective, Samuel Escobar, *La fe evangélica y las teologías de la liberación* (El Paso: Casa Bautista de Publicaciones, 1987).

[17] Jeffrey Klaiber, SJ,*The Church, Dictatorships and Democracy*, 5.

[18] Sergio Torres and John Eagleson, eds, *The Challenge of Base Christian Communities* (Maryknoll, NY: Orbis, 1982), 115.

[19] *Puebla Document*, par. 213.

[20] Samuel Escobar,"Christian Base Communities: A Historical Perspective," *Transformation* 3 (July–September 1986): 1–4.

[21] Cecilia Loreto Mariz, *Coping With Poverty: Pentecostals and Christian Base Communities in Brazil* (Philadelphia, PA: Temple University Press, 1994); William H. Swatos, *Religion and Democracy in Latin America* (New Brunswick, NJ: Transaction Publishers, 1995).

[22] An excellent panorama of the process among indigenous peoples is offered in Edward L. Cleary and Timothy J. Steigenga, eds, *Resurgent Voices in Latin America: Indigenous Peoples, Political Mobilization and Religious Change* (New Brunswick, NJ: Rutgers University Press, 2004).

[23] Hernando de Soto *The Other Path* (London: I.B.Tauris, 1989).

[24] Walter J. Hollenweger,"After Twenty Years' Research on Pentecostalism," in *International Review of Mission* 75/297: 3–12.

[25] I have studied the conflicting approaches to popular Protestantism in "The Promise and Precariousness of Latin American Protestantism," in Daniel R. Miller, ed., *Coming of Age: Protestantism in Contemporary Latin America*, (Lanham, MD: University Press of America, 1994), 3–35.

[26] David Martin *Tongues of Fire* (Oxford: Blackwell, 1990), 284.

[27] Ibid., 284.

[28] Jeffrey Klaiber, SJ,*The Church, Dictatorships and Democracy*, 33–4 and 187–9.

[29] Data taken from Larry Pate, *From Every People: A Handbook of Two-Thirds World Missions with Directory/Histories/Analysis* (Monrovia: MARC, 1989).

[30] Available online at: <www.comibam.org>.

[31] Miguel Angel Palomino, "Latino Immigration in Europe: Challenge and Opportunity for Mission," *International Bulletin of Missionary Research,* April 2004: 55–8.

[32] Andre Corten and Ruth Marshall-Fratani, eds, *Between Babel and Pentecost: Transnational Pentecostalism in Africa and Latin America* (Bloomington, IN: Indiana University Press, 2001).

[33] Thomas J. Reese, "The Synod Points Out Needs," *America* (January 3, 1998): 3.

[34] John Paul II, *The Church in America: Ecclesia in America Post Synodal Apostolic Exhortation.* English text (Washington, DC: United States Catholic Conference, 1999), 125–8.

[35] Jorge I. Gómez, *El crecimiento y la deserción en la iglesia evangélica costarricense*, San José: INDEF, 1996, 133.

[36] More information about this point in chapter 5 of my book *Changing Tides* (Maryland, NY: Orbis, 2002), and in Tetsunao Yamamori et al., *Serving With the Poor in Latin America* (Monrovia: MARC, 1997).

[37] I offer a brief summary of findings in chapter 5 of my book *Changing Tides*.

[38] Cecilia Mariz, *Coping With Poverty*.

[39] FTL publishes a *Journal of Latin American Theology* twice a year, available online at: <www.fratela.org>.

[40] Paul Freston, *Evangelicals and Politics in Africa, Asia and Latin America* (Cambridge: Cambridge University Press, 2001).

[41] *Nuevo Siglo*, CLAI, Quito, Ecuador, November 2002.

[42] Donald E. Miller *Reinventing American Protestantism* (Berkeley, CA: University of California Press, 1997).

Further Reading

Cleary, Edward L. and Timothy J. Steigenga, eds. *Resurgent Voices in Latin America: Indigenous Peoples, Political Mobilization and Religious Change*. New Brunswick, NJ: Rutgers University Press, 2004.

Comblin, José. *Called For Freedom: The Changing Context of Liberation Theology*. Maryknoll, NY: Orbis, 1998.

Cook, Guillermo, ed. *New Face of the Church in Latin America*. Maryknoll, NY: Orbis, 1994.

Dussel, Enrique, ed. *The Church in Latin America 1492–1992*. Maryknoll, NY: Orbis, 1992.

Freston, Paul, ed. *Evangelical Christianity and Democracy in Latin America*. New York: Oxford University Press, 2008.

González, Ondina E. and Justo L. González. *Christianity in Latin America: A History*. New York: Cambridge University Press, 2007.

Gutiérrez, Gustavo. *Las Casas: In Search of the Poor of Jesus Christ*. Maryknoll, NY: Orbis, 1993.

Heaney, Sharon E. *Contextual Theology for Latin America*. Milton Keynes, UK: Paternoster, 2008.

Klaiber, Jeffrey S. J. *The Church, Dictatorships, and Democracy in Latin America*. Maryknoll, NY: Orbis, 1998.

Salinas, Daniel. *Latin American Evangelical Theology in the 1970's: The Golden Decade*. Leiden-Boston: Brill, 2009.

13

Brazilian Charisma
Pentecostalized Christianity in Latin America's Largest Nation

R. Andrew Chesnut

Historical Introduction

For most of its five centuries of history, Brazil, like Spanish America, has been Catholic. Like their Spanish cousins, the Portuguese at the beginning of the sixteenth century claimed the newly discovered land on behalf of their king and Catholic faith. Papal bulls granted the New World to the Iberian Crowns and charged them with evangelizing the indigenous peoples of the Americas. The evangelization of Brazil's indigenous population and African slaves was generally carried out in a more relaxed, laissez-faire manner than in much of Spanish America. The great sugar plantations of the Northeast were the center of Brazilian colonial life, and if there happened to be a resident priest on the plantation his pastoral activities were primarily focused on the owner and his family and not the African slaves. On the Amazonian frontier the Jesuits made heroic efforts to evangelize the native Amazonians and protect them from slave raiders, but their new faith afforded them little protections from the ravages of smallpox and other lethal diseases brought to the New Word by the Europeans. On the eve of independence from Portugal in 1822 Brazil was thoroughly Catholic, but the predominant type of faith practiced there was a folk Catholicism that syncretized elements of African religions, medieval Portuguese Christianity, and indigenous beliefs.

Catholicism remained the official state religion during the new nation's first six decades. Following the lead of Mexico, which had separated Church and state three decades earlier, Emperor Dom Pedro II disestablished the Catholic Church in 1888 and thus set the legal foundation for the growth of Protestantism. Mainline Protestant denominations from the US were the first to take advantage of the new religious liberty and sent missionaries to proselytize Brazilian Catholics at the end of the nineteenth century. In general, Brazilian Catholics showed little interest in the Gospel preached by North American Presbyterians and Methodists. The Pentecostal message of healing and spiritual rebirth, however, was received with such great enthusiasm from the moment it arrived on Brazilian shores in 1910 and 1911 that in less than a century it has become the predominant form of Christianity practiced in Latin America's most populous nation.

After a half-century of explosive growth, charismatic Christianity has attained hegemonic status in Brazil's religious economy. The great majority of church-attending Christians in the country worship at services in which the Holy Spirit takes center stage. Among Protestants, Pentecostalism has enjoyed such success that at least 75 percent of all *evangélicos* (the preferred term for Protestants in Brazil and throughout Latin America) belong to Pentecostal denominations

Introducing World Christianity, First Edition. Edited by Charles E. Farhadian.
© 2012 Blackwell Publishing Ltd. Published 2012 by Blackwell Publishing Ltd.

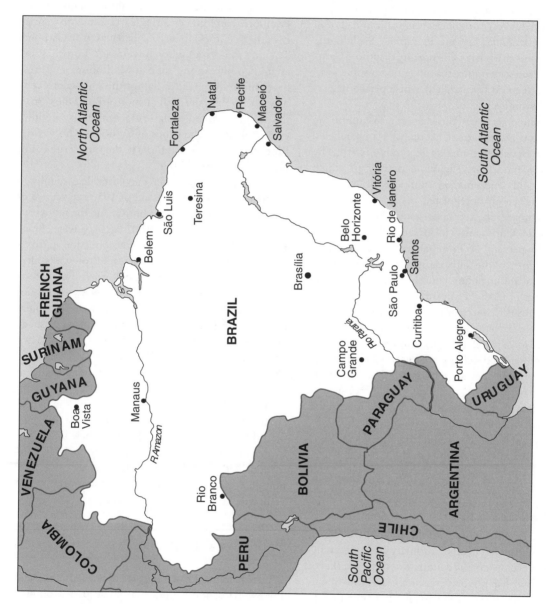

Map **13.1**   Brazil

such as the Universal Church of the Kingdom of God or Pentecostal-style charismatic mainline churches.[1] Across the Christian divide, the Catholic Charismatic Renewal (CCR) has mushroomed to the point that in just three decades since its arrival in Brazil, the largest Catholic nation on earth, it can claim at least half of all practicing Catholics among its ranks.[2] Such is the hegemony of charismatic Christianity that those Catholic and Protestant groups that do not offer some form of pneumacentric (spirit-filled) worship face stagnation and even decline.

The main objective of this chapter is to explore the reasons for charismatic Christianity's unparalleled success in Brazil's free-market economy of faith. The theoretical model of religious economy in which churches and denominations compete for "religious consumers" in an unregulated market of faith will help the reader better understand the success of charismatic Christianity in Brazil. In present-day Brazil 80 percent of Protestants practice a spirit-centered form of the faith, mostly in Pentecostal and pentecostalized mainline churches. Similarly, some 60 percent of Catholics in this, the largest Catholic nation on earth, are charismatics.[3] Through examination of the elements that determine the success or failure of any religious organization competing in an unregulated religious economy, charismatic Christianity's recipes for success will become clear. Analyses of products, marketing, and consumers will illuminate the determining factors in ecstatic Christianity's commanding position in the free religious market.[4] A few introductory remarks on Pentecostalism and a brief profile of the Catholic Charismatic Renewal (CCR), which has received scant academic attention, will allow for a better understanding of the two groups that dominate the Christian marketplace of Brazil.

As the premier non-Catholic religion in Brazil, Pentecostalism has been the primary religious architect and developer of the country's new free market of faith. If Brazilian popular consumers are now free to choose to consume the religious goods that best satisfy their spiritual and material needs, it is largely due to the unparalleled growth of Pentecostal churches since the 1950s. This charismatic branch of Protestantism single-handedly created religious and social space where Brazilians from the popular classes are free not

to be Catholic. Given Catholicism's historic role as one of the constituent elements of Latin American national identities, Pentecostalism's construction of an alternative religious identity for those unhappy with their inherited faith is no minor achievement. For more than four centuries (early sixteenth to mid-twentieth century) to be Brazilian was to be Catholic. The tiny minorities who converted to historic Protestant denominations, such as Methodism and Presbyterianism, in the latter half of the nineteenth century, and then to the faith missions around the turn of the century, risked social ostracism and sometimes even violence at the hands of Catholics who viewed Protestant converts as traitors to the One True Faith, if not to the nation itself.[5]

That not more than 5 percent of Brazilians identified themselves as Protestant as late as 1950 is evidence of the failure of historic Protestantism and the numerous faith missions to attract a critical mass of converts. Since Pentecostal churches currently account for approximately 80 percent of all Brazilian Protestants after almost a century of evangelization, the obvious conclusion is that Pentecostalism's predecessors did not offer attractive religious goods and services to popular religious consumers.[6] If the stigma attached to shedding one's Catholic identity had been the only factor impeding conversion to Protestantism, the historic churches and faith missions would be thriving at present. However, the only historic Protestant churches able to compete effectively with the Pentecostals are those that have pentecostalized and embraced spirit-filled worship. In Brazil these schismatic Protestant churches generally maintain their denominational title but distinguish themselves from their non-charismatic brethren by adding the term "renewed" (*renovada*) to their name.

Pentecostal Catholics

While mainline Protestants, such as Methodists and Presbyterians, and Catholic Base Christian Communities (CEBs) struggle to maintain a presence throughout Brazil, another Catholic movement easily fills soccer stadiums in the major cities with tens of thousands of fervent believers. At the beginning of the twenty-first century, the Catholic Charismatic

Renewal (CCR) stands as the largest and most dynamic movement in the Brazilian Catholic Church. Even leaders of the liberationist wing of the Catholic Church, who often view charismatics as alienated middle-class reactionaries, admit that no other ecclesial movement has the CCR's power to congregate and mobilize the faithful.

The nation's most vibrant Catholic lay movement nevertheless has received very little academic attention. If the CCR's popular appeal has yet to register among students of Brazilian religion, it is because liberation theology and CEBs have captured the hearts and minds of many North American and Brazilian social scientists during the past quarter-century. The notion of a "preferential option for the poor," and the attempts to build the Kingdom of Heaven on Brazilian soil through political and social transformation, proved far more appealing to many scholars than a socially disengaged movement dedicated to transforming individual lives through conversion. Academic sympathies aside, however, the Charismatic Renewal demands scholarly attention because of its extraordinary appeal among Catholic laity and its unanimous approval by the Brazilian Bishops' Conference. If the perennial shortage of priests has eased somewhat in the last two decades and if the Catholic Church is finally employing mass media, especially television, as a tool for evangelization, it is because of the charismatics, whose missionary zeal rivals that of their chief competitors in the religious marketplace, the Pentecostals.

Although the CCR manifests diverse local and national characteristics, it is generally a Catholic lay movement that seeks to revitalize the Church through the power of the third person of the Trinity, the Holy Spirit. That both US and Brazilian charismatics initially called themselves Pentecostal Catholics is revealing: Catholic charismatics share the same ecstatic spirituality as Protestant Pentecostals and, like Pentecostals, Catholic charismatics are pneumacentrists, that is, the Holy Spirit occupies center stage in believers' religious praxis.

Through baptism in the Holy Spirit, individual charismatics believe that they are endowed with gifts of the Spirit, such as glossolalia (speaking in tongues) and faith healing.[7] For charismatics and Pentecostals alike, these charismata are powerful and palpable proof of the presence of the Spirit in their lives. In addition to pneumacentrism, charismatics tend to share, though to a lesser degree, the biblical fundamentalism and asceticism of their Pentecostal progenitors. Of course, what most distinguishes charismatics from other Catholics is their special emphasis on the transformative power of the Holy Spirit.

The most recent figures from the International Catholic Charismatic Renewal Services (ICCRS), the CCR's international headquarters at the Vatican, estimate that some 120 million Catholics belong to the movement in over 200 countries. Latin American charismatics, according to the ICCRS, number around 74 million, accounting for almost two thirds of the global total.[8] A recent survey discovered that at least half of all Brazilian Catholics are charismatic.[9] Data for other Latin American countries are lacking, but the CCR is the largest and most active Catholic lay movement in most nations and in all likelihood can claim at least a third of the region's practicing Catholics.

Like Pentecostalism, its Protestant forbear, the Catholic Charismatic Renewal is a religious product imported from the United States. In the late 1960s, the same charismatic spirituality that had given birth to Pentecostalism in the first decade of the twentieth century and had led to the formation of charismatic communities among mainline Protestants, such as Episcopalians and Presbyterians, in the 1950s and 1960s finally penetrated the US Catholic Church. The CCR specifically traces this genesis to the "Duquesne Weekend" in February of 1967, when some 25 students at Duquesne University in Pittsburgh (a Catholic institution that, appropriately, was founded by members of the Congregation of the Holy Ghost) gathered for a spiritual retreat with two professors who had already been baptized under the direction of Presbyterian charismatics. Many of the students were baptized in the Holy Spirit and received charismata, marking the first event in which a group of Catholics experienced Pentecostal spirituality.

From Duquesne the nascent movement spread to other college campuses, foremost of which were Notre Dame and Michigan State Universities. During the next decade, the Renewal grew rapidly, spawning charismatic prayer groups and "covenant communities," in which members sought to develop their spiritual lives in a communal setting. By the mid-1970s, the CCR had expanded to the point that it could pack stadiums. In 1974, approximately 25,000 believers attended a CCR international conference at Notre Dame. Three years later in Kansas City, some 50,000 Protestant and Catholic charismatics participated in an ecumenical assembly, which drew extensive press coverage.[10]

These two events are significant not only for their size but also for two major themes that they underscored. At the Notre Dame Convention, a mass healing ritual led by Dominican priest Francis MacNutt propelled the spiritual gift of faith healing to the center of charismatic religious praxis. Father MacNutt, who already was a pioneer in exporting the CCR to Iberoamerica, consolidated his position as a leading proponent of faith healing in the movement with the publication that year of his book *Healing*.[11] At the Kansas City gathering it was the ecumenism of the assembly that took the most prominent position. From its inception, the CCR in the United States had been strongly ecumenical, particularly with mainline Protestant charismatics (known as neo-Pentecostals in the United States). Many CCR prayer groups included Protestants, and even some covenant communities counted "separated brethren" (a Catholic term meaning Protestants) among their ranks.[12] Although many, if not most, of the original CCR groups in Latin America were founded by ecumenical pastoral teams, faith healing has proven to be a much more attractive feature than ecumenism in Brazil.

Mirroring the pattern of Pentecostal expansion to Brazil more than a half-century earlier, the CCR was brought to the country by evangelists only a few years after its birth in the US city of steel, Pittsburgh. Jesuit priest Edward Dougherty and compatriot Father Harold Rahm were to serve as agents of the CCR's expansion to Brazil. Having been baptized in the Holy Spirit at a charismatic retreat in early 1969, Father Dougherty felt compelled to share his new-found charisma with fellow Catholics in Brazil, where he had previously served as a missionary. Returning to Brazil in 1969, Padre Dougherty shared his newfound spiritually with fellow Jesuit Father Rahm. By the end of the year Father Rahm was busy organizing charismatic retreats for Catholics in the university city of Campinas. Together the two charismatic Jesuits traveled throughout the country in the early 1970s, establishing prayer groups, the foundational base of the CCR.[13]

Fabiola Lopes, an Archetypical Pentecostal Consumer

Since the tastes and preferences of religious consumers largely determine the fate of any given religious enterprise in a competitive economy, consideration of the large class of popular religious consumers who have purchased the Pentecostal product is imperative. In other words, who are these millions of Cariocas, Paulistas, Recifenses, and Baianos, among others, who have converted to Pentecostalism since it first sank roots in Brazilian soil in the initial decades of the twentieth century? Sufficient research on Brazilian Pentecostalism has been conducted over the past decade to allow for a fairly accurate socio-economic profile of believers.

The archetypical Brazilian Pentecostal is Fabiola Lopes, a poor, married woman of color in her thirties or forties living on the urban periphery. She works as a domestic servant in the home of a privileged compatriot and was a nominal Catholic before converting to the Assemblies of God (AG) during a time of personal crisis related to her poverty. Of course, charismatic Protestantism is so widespread and differentiated now that there are hundreds of thousands of believers who possess none of these constituent elements of the Pentecostal archetype. For example, many of the members of the Foursquare Gospel Church are upper-middle-class professional men. Nonetheless, Fabiola Lopes personifies the most common socio-economic traits found among the vast population of believers.

Most salient among the socio-economic characteristics of *crentes* (or believers as they are often called in Brazil) are poverty, a nominal Catholic background, and gender. Historically, the great majority of Pentecostal converts have been poor, non-practicing Catholics. Numerous studies, including my own in Brazil, have shown that not only are Pentecostals poor, but also that they tend to have lower incomes and less education than the general population.[14] The largest study ever conducted of Latin American Protestantism, the 1996 ISER (Instituto Superior da Religião) survey of the Protestant population of Rio de Janeiro, found *crentes* to be considerably more likely to live in poverty and have less schooling than the *carioca* (resident of Rio de Janeiro) population at large.[15] Although Pentecostalism has ascended the steep socio-economic pyramid of Brazil, particularly since the 1980s, it continues to be predominantly a religion of the popular classes.

In addition to social class, most Brazilian Pentecostals share a common former religious identity. The majority of *crentes* had been nominal or cultural Catholics before converting.[16] Most would have been baptized in the Catholic Church and perhaps had even taken First Communion, but their contact with the institutional Church was minimal. However, their weak or non-existent ties to the Church in no way meant that their worldview had become secularized or disenchanted. In times of both need and celebration, nominal Catholics, like their practicing co-religionists, would send prayers of supplication or thanksgiving to the Virgin Mary or one of the many saints. Thus, due to their estrangement from the Church and the perennial shortage of clergy, no priest or pastoral agent would likely be present at the time of their poverty-related crisis, which so often leads afflicted individuals to the doors of a Pentecostal temple. It is among this vast field of nominal Catholics, who compose the majority of the Brazilian population, that Pentecostal evangelists have reaped such bountiful harvests of converts.

While the third conspicuous characteristic of the Pentecostal consumer market, the great female majority among believers, is not peculiar to the faith, it merits discussion because of the religion's status as the most widely practiced faith among women of the popular classes. Hence, product development and marketing strategies naturally must take into account the fact that women believers outnumber men by a ratio of two to one. In one of Brazil's largest and fastest-growing Pentecostal denominations, the Universal Church of the Kingdom of God (IURD), the ratio climbs to four to one.[17] Male believers, of course, continue to monopolize the pastorate and high-ranking Church offices, but Pentecostalism is largely sustained and spread by sisters in the faith.

Andrea Mariano, an Archetypical CCR Consumer

In contrast to the Pentecostals, the first adherents to the CCR were disproportionately middle-class, practicing Catholic women, and those who joined during the 1970s and well into the 1980s tended to share the characteristics of class, gender, and active religious practice. Although the CCR is now expanding among the first of these, the Brazilian popular classes, the movement during most of its short history has been solidly middle class. Thus the Catholic charismatic counterpart to Fabiola Lopes would be Andrea Mariano, a 40-something stay-at-home mom who was already a devout Catholic before joining a CCR prayer group during a marital crisis. In one of the first studies conducted on the CCR in Latin America, researcher Pedro Oliveira in the early 1970s found the majority of Brazilian Catholic charismatics to be middle and upper middle class, like Andrea Mariano. More than half the charismatics surveyed had at least a secondary education, and only 1 percent was illiterate.[18] Even 30 years later, Brazilians average only seven years of schooling.

After social class, gender also has been one of the marked demographic characteristics of the charismatic community in Brazil. Precise figures do not exist, but since the CCR's arrival, women have comprised approximately two thirds of the movement. Oliveira's study reported women as 71 percent of Brazilian CCR membership.[19] A 1994 Brazilian survey found the gender ratio had remained constant at 70 percent female. The same poll found that women also predominated in Brazil's Base Christian Communities, but at the significantly lower rate of 57 percent.[20] The third major characteristic that CCR members have in common is their prior status as active Catholics. Oliveira's study confirms that the great majority of Brazilian charismatics had been active Catholics before joining; furthermore, 80 percent had participated in other Church lay groups, particularly *cursillo*.[21] Thus, in its initial phase, the CCR rarely attracted nominal Catholics, much less Pentecostal converts.

Useful Products

The above profile of Pentecostal and CCR consumers in Brazil contributes to a better understanding of the religious products that pneumacentric Christians purchase and consume in churches and in their daily lives. Defining religious products as the doctrine and worship services of faith-based organizations, this section of the chapter considers the spiritual goods and services that have resulted in charismatic Christianity's unmatched success in Brazil's free market of faith. The task at hand, then, is not to identify every religious product but to scrutinize those whose popularity among consumers has led to spirit-centered Christianity's dramatic expansion in Brazil since the 1950s.

The utilitarian nature of Pentecostalism and popular religion in general means that the spiritual products offered to consumers of the divine must prove useful in their daily lives. Products that do not relate to believers' quotidian existence will find few purchasers in the popular religious marketplace. This does not mean that consumers of the popular classes are only religious instrumentalists who evaluate spiritual products solely on the basis of their capacity to provide relief from the afflictions of everyday poverty. Spiritual products that hold little relevance to the social reality of impoverished believers will collect dust on the lower shelves of the market. Since most Brazilian religious consumers are much better acquainted with Catholic products, rival spiritual firms, in order to compete, must offer goods that are simultaneously familiar and novel. That is, the non-Catholic product must provide sufficient continuity with Catholic doctrine or worship to maintain the potential consumer's comfort level. At the same time, the product must differentiate itself from the Catholic brand. Pentecostalism possesses exactly this type of product in its doctrine and practice of faith healing. More than any other of its products, it is the Pentecostal belief that Jesus and the Holy Spirit have the power to cure believers of their spiritual, somatic, and psychological ills that impels more Brazilians to affiliate with *crente* churches. All Catholics, whether practicing or nominal, are familiar, if not experienced, with the healing powers of the saints and the Virgin Mary. In fact, it is their status as powerful agents of divine healing that has won such world renown for Virgins such as Aparecida, Guadalupe, and Lourdes.

Pentecostal faith healing thus is really not a new product per se, but a greatly improved one. With the great exception of the Catholic Charismatic Renewal, divine healing had continued to exist on the fringes of the twentieth-century Brazilian Catholic Church. The curing of all types of ailments through promises and petitions to the Virgin and saints has customarily taken place beyond the pale of the institutional Church, and if any human mediators were involved at all, they were more likely to be *curandeiras* (folk healers) than priests. In striking contrast, Pentecostal preachers from the earliest days made *cura divina* a centerpiece of both doctrine and practice. Indeed, it was an act of faith healing in 1911 that led to the birth of the western hemisphere's largest Pentecostal denomination, the Brazilian Assemblies of God.[22] Whereas Catholic Masses offered little liturgical space for the healing of believers' everyday afflictions, Pentecostal worship services and revivals in which Jesus or the Holy Spirit failed to operate through the congregation to cure worshipers of their illnesses are almost unimaginable. Of such importance is faith healing to the mission of the Brazilian Universal Church of the Kingdom of God that two days of its weekly schedule of services are devoted to it. Hence Brazilian Pentecostalism took what had been a marginal product in institutional Catholicism and turned it into the *sine qua non* of its own religious production.

While faith healing, more than any other product, induces religious consumers to join the Pentecostal enterprise, it is still another benefit that facilitates the recovery and maintenance of believers' health over the long term, namely conversion, in which joining a Pentecostal church is conceptualized as part of a process of spiritual rebirth, allowing the believer to be born again into a healthy new environment where the demons of poverty can be neutralized. Conceived as a "positive transformation of the nature and value of a person," religious conversion appeals most to those individuals and groups who have been stigmatized or negatively evaluated by society.[23] A conversionist religion, then, which offers the possibility of a new life far removed from the afflictions of the old, would be understandably popular among those millions of Brazilians, especially women, seeking to turn away from family conflict, alcoholism, and illness.

This element of the conversion process is of such importance that two thirds of my male informants in

Brazil mentioned the repudiation of "vice" as the most important change in their life since conversion. And, not surprisingly, they cited worldly temptations as their second greatest problem after financial hardship.[24] Since the streets of Brazil, especially on the urban margins, are still largely a male domain, it follows that the rupture caused by conversion to Pentecostalism is greater for men. As practicing Pentecostals, men must leave the temptations of the street behind and focus on their home and family life. In short, this product of conversion allows believers to reclaim and maintain their health through their rebirth into a salutary new environment, largely devoid of the demons of the street.

If believers find themselves assailed by such demons, their religion offers them a specific brand of faith healing to exorcize them. Exorcism, usually referred to as liberation (*libertação* in Portuguese), has been practiced by Pentecostal preachers since its early days. But over the past two decades neo-Pentecostal churches have brought it from the fringes of religious practice to its present prominence. Indeed, in its weekly calendar of worship, the Universal Church of the Kingdom of God (IURD) devotes Fridays to *cultos de libertação* (exorcism services).

Pentecostalism shares its final salient product, ecstatic power, with its main religious rivals, African-Brazilian faiths, such as Umbanda, and charismatic Catholicism, but emphasizes it in greater measure. Just as the dialectic between illness and faith healing attracts millions of converts, so too does that between socioeconomic impotence and spiritual power. With direct access to the Holy Spirit through baptism in the Spirit and charismata, such as glossolalia (speaking in tongues) and prophecy, impoverished Brazilian Pentecostals experience intense spiritual power. Filled with the force of the Holy Spirit, impoverished believers are steeled to do battle with the demons of deprivation, which can make life for those on the urban and rural margins a living hell.

Figure 13.1 Deliverance from Demons. Roberto Filipe (http://commons.wikimedia.org/wiki/File:Libertacao.jpg) used under the Creative Commons Attribution-Share Alike 3.0 Unported license

The Catholic Charismatic Renewal (CCR) and Pentecostalism have multiplied exponentially in Brazil for similar reasons. A slight modification to the Pentecostal dialectic makes plain the mass appeal of the CCR. While the thesis of affliction or illness is the same for both the Renewal and Pentecostalism, the higher social class position of CCR adherents translates into a less direct relationship between misfortune and poverty. The afflictions that compel middle-class Brazilians to join the CCR may stem less directly from material deprivation and more often from psychological problems, such as those that may stem from early childhood trauma. It follows, then, that the distinct origins of the Pentecostal and CCR dialectical theses lead to different manifestations of the same antithesis of faith healing. Whereas the *cura divina* (faith healing) practiced in Pentecostal churches has tended to focus on healing the physical illnesses that plague the Brazilian poor, the *cura interior* (inner healing) offered at charismatic masses and assemblies in the 1980s more often involved the "inner healing" of painful memories and past psychological stresses.

Inner healing has been the predominant form practiced in the CCR, but, since the late 1980s, competition with Pentecostalism has led to the formation of a cadre of priests who specialize in "liberation" or exorcism ministries. So strong is current consumer demand for deliverance from demonic possession that some priests, such as the Brazilian charismatic superstar Marcelo Rossi, even celebrate weekly "liberation masses" (*missas de libertação*).[25] Acknowledging his pastoral debt to Pentecostal leader Bishop Edir Macedo, whose Universal Church of the Kingdom of God (IURD) brought exorcism to the fore of pneumacentric Christianity in Brazil, Padre Marcelo observed, "it was Bishop Edir Macedo who woke us up."[26] As the CCR proceeds down the Brazilian class scale, both exorcism and physical healing will continue their advance from the margins of charismatic practice to the center.

Figure 13.2   "Brazilian Export: The Universal Church of the Kingdom of God in Buenos Aires, Argentina." Roberto Fiadone (http://commons.wikimedia.org/wiki/File:Av_Corrientes_Iglesia_Evangélica_ex_Mercado_de_las_Flores.jpg) used under the Creative Commons Attribution-Share Alike 2.5 Generic license.

Aparecida as Advance Guard

To ensure the Catholic identity of the CCR, Brazilian bishops have emphasized the role of the Virgin as defender of the faith and guardian of orthodoxy. The Virgin, particularly the national patroness, Aparecida, is the most potent and visible symbol of Catholic identity in Brazil. For a movement rooted in Pentecostal spirituality, which has historically been radically anti-Catholic in Brazil, what better way to preserve the Catholic identity of the Renewal than through emphasis on the element that most distinguishes the Church from its Protestant competitors? Thus the Virgin, in both her national and myriad local incarnations, has, over the past decade and a half, come to constitute the dividing line that separates Catholic charismatics from Pentecostals.

Episcopal emphasis on the importance of the Virgin is a clear example of the marginal differentiation of an otherwise standardized religious product. In the figure of the Virgin, the Church's chief religious producers offer an appealing variant to the pneumacentric spirituality shared by both Catholic Charismatics and Pentecostals. Without the Mother of God to differentiate them, only the Pope is left to guard the bridge leading to Pentecostalism.

Marketing the Faith

As any business student knows, it is not sufficient for a firm to simply possess an appealing product. In modern consumer societies where prospective customers are presented with a dizzying array of goods and services, businesses must aggressively market their product to get their message to consumers. So important is marketing, particularly in affluent consumer societies such as the US, that a product's packaging and advertising often have greater bearing on sales than the quality of the product itself.

Admittedly, the science of marketing is not as developed in religious economies as commercial ones. But without a successful strategy of evangelization that offers doctrine and worship directly to prospective believers, spiritual firms operating in a free market of faith will find it hard to compete with these rivals who actively and creatively evangelize. And in the religious economy of present-day Brazil no religion has evangelized as successfully as charismatic Christianity. If in less than a century spirit-centered Christianity has become hegemonic in the region, it is in no small measure due to the skillful marketing of the faith. This section, then, considers the ways in which Pentecostal denominations and the CCR have successfully advertised and packaged their religious products to Brazilian spiritual consumers. In the evangelical idiom, the next section of this chapter examines the methods of evangelization that have won so many "souls for Jesus."

Like their Pentecostal brethren in the US, Brazilian *crentes* are the most skilled marketers in the region's new religious economy. They have utilized diverse media to deliver the simple but potent message to prospective converts that affiliation with Pentecostalism will imbue them with sufficient supernatural strength to vanquish the demons of poverty. It is the dynamic and controversial Universal Church of the Kingdom of God that has captured the essence of Pentecostal advertising in its evangelistic slogan, "stop suffering." The pithy phrase *"pare de sofrer,"* typically printed in bright red letters, calls out to the afflicted poor of Brazil from the church walls through pamphlets and newspapers of this innovative denomination. A combination of low- and high-tech media invite religious consumers, mainly nominal Catholics, to relieve their suffering by embracing Jesus and the Holy Spirit within the walls of the church that advertises its product.

One of the most effective means of marketing the Pentecostal product is the oldest method of *crente* evangelization in Brazil, home visits. The founders of the Assemblies of God in Brazil, the Swedish-American immigrants Gunnar Vingren and Daniel Berg, proselytized in early twentieth-century Belém through visits to victims of a yellow fever epidemic and other maladies.[27] Since then, hundreds of thousands of Pentecostal pastors and lay persons have knocked on flimsy doors throughout the nation's urban periphery and countryside to spread the good news of healing to those suffering from poverty-related afflictions. In the Assemblies of God, lay women evangelists, called *visitadoras* (visitors) proselytize not only door to door but also in hospitals filled with those who are especially predisposed to accept a prescription for divine healing. Until the Charismatic Renewal developed its own home visit campaign in the 1980s to target nominal Catholics, Pentecostals and neo-Christians, such as Mormons and Jehovah's Witnesses, were the only groups who brought their products directly to the homes of Brazilian spiritual consumers.

For those Brazilians who do not come into contact with Pentecostalism through low-tech marketing, evangelists have made it difficult to avoid exposure to their product through their advertisements in the mass media and on the Internet. Despite the rapid growth of Pentecostal tele-evangelism in the region since the early 1980s, it is the oldest form of electronic media, radio, that continues to account for the bulk of *crente* broadcasting. While Pentecostal-owned television stations, such as the IURD's Rede Record, transmit mostly commercial programs, many radio stations broadcast nothing but Pentecostal preaching, music, and conversion testimonials, 24 hours a day.

Radio has a twofold advantage over television as a marketing tool for the Pentecostal product. It is significantly cheaper than television. Only the largest denominations, such as the Assemblies of God, IURD, and Foursquare Gospel Church can afford the high costs associated with proprietorship of a station or production of programs. In contrast, some smaller churches that could never dream of appearing on television possess the funds to purchase small amounts of air time, particularly on the AM band of some of the many radio stations in Brazil that carry Protestant programming.[28] In addition, while TV antennae have become a growing fixture on the skyline of the urban periphery, radio is ubiquitous among the Brazilian popular classes.

Following in the footsteps of their North American brethren who dominate religious broadcasting in the US, a few large Brazilian Pentecostal denominations enjoy a commanding position in the transmission of spiritual programs. With the exception of the pioneering but short-lived programs of the nationalistic Brazil for Christ denomination in the 1960s and the IURD in the early 1980s, Brazilian owned and produced Pentecostal television did not take root until the late 1980s. Since the early part of that decade, US tele-evangelists, such as Assemblies of God members Jimmy Swaggart and Jim Bakker, had dominated Protestant broadcasting in the country. Given the superior resources of the North American tele-evangelists, it was only natural

that they served as the trailblazers in Brazilian Pentecostal television.

By the end of the 1980s, however, a few major *crente* churches, such as the Assemblies of God, Foursquare Gospel, IURD, and International Church of the Grace of God (Igreja Internacional da Graça de Deus) were producing their own programs, and in the case of the IURD, purchasing its own station. In November of 1989, the IURD made Brazilian and Latin American history when it bought the Rede Record television and radio stations for US$ 45 million. With Record now owned by the IURD and Globo, Latin America's largest broadcasting corporation, by a staunch Catholic impresario, the battle for Christian market share has played out on the small screens of Brazil. Both networks have aired *novelas* (evening soap operas) satirizing and even demonizing each other. And Padre Marcelo, the dashing young star of the Catholic Charismatic Renewal, has appeared frequently on Rede Globo's variety and talk shows.

Ever seeking novel ways to market their products, large Brazilian Pentecostal churches have joined the revolution in information technology and have developed Internet websites.[29] The IURD website even has its own chatroom in which members and the curious can discuss matters of faith in "real time." The small but increasing minority of Brazilian believers who have Internet access can take pride in the fact that their denominations have embraced the latest mass medium as a novel way to market their religious product to those in need of healing. The plethora of Internet cafes throughout the country has made it even easier for believers, especially technologically savvy youths, to go online even if they do not own a computer.

The Pentecostal product sold in the mass media is particularly appealing when packaged in the form of testimonials, music, and exorcism. Whether on television, radio, or at rallies in soccer stadiums, the conversion narrative of a Pentecostal convert is often a powerfully emotive account of how Jesus or the Holy Spirit restored the believer's health or saved her from one of the demons of deprivation. Listeners and viewers experiencing their own crises hear or see someone from the same or similar social class dramatically turn his life around through acceptance of Jesus and affiliation with the church broadcasting the program. Such advertising, of course, is ubiquitous among commercial firms. Dramatic before and after photos, along with testimony of consumers who supposedly used a particular diet product invite obese Brazilians and North Americans to remake themselves as slim and fit men and women.

Pentecostal sales representatives also package their product in the emotional form of music. In addition to worship services, romantic ballads, pop songs, and regional rhythms, all set to evangelical lyrics, blare from Pentecostal radio and television stations. The most musical of all the major branches of Christianity, Pentecostalism rouses its believers and attracts new converts through its melodic electric guitars, drums, tambourines, and synthesizers. Whether background mood music or moving hymns, melodic rhythms constitute such an integral part of *crente* worship services that in Brazil they are sung and played during at least two thirds of the typically two-hour long service.

Although not of the same caliber and sophistacion as Pentecostal marketing, CCR advertising puts the movement at the forefront of Catholic missionary activities. The CCR responded to the call made at the 1992 CELAM (Latin American Bishops' Conference) in Santo Domingo for more vigorous evangelization efforts by intensifying its proselytizing activities. Of course, faith healing in its multiple forms is probably the most effective form of evangelization, but beyond attracting nominal Catholics back to the ecclesial fold through the promise of restored health, the CCR has taken specific pastoral measures to win new adherents. At the grass-roots level, charismatics copy the Pentecostal competition by evangelizing through home visits and mass rallies. The "visitation ministry," as it is called in Brazil, sends lay missionaries, who are mostly charismatics, to the homes of the "target population" of vulnerable nominal Catholics to invite them to attend a prayer group or some other church function.

By the mid-1980s, rallies, revivals, and healing marathons, in which thousands of believers gathered at soccer stadiums and gymnasiums to receive the power of the Holy Spirit, were no longer peculiar to Pentecostalism. Annual national CCR assemblies, known as *cenacles* (*cenáculos*), filled stadiums throughout the country. The Brazilian Renewal attracted 150,000

on Pentecost Sunday of 1987 and again in May of 1991.[30] Renowned international CCR leaders, especially those who specialized in healing ministries, such as North American priest Robert DeGrandis and his Canadian colleague Emiliano Tardiff, attracted thousands of impoverished believers to rallies that were propelled by faith-healing sessions and much upbeat popular music.

The CCR also emulates its Pentecostal rivals in embracing mass media, particularly television and radio. Such is the Renewal's dominance of Catholic radio and television that there would be very little church programming without it. Most of the programming on the country's 181 Catholic radio stations is produced by CCR members.[31] The Brazilian Renewal has moved far beyond the simple broadcast of charismatic Masses to the production of religious dramas akin to Latin America's popular *telenovelas* (soap operas).

It is no coincidence that charismatic television is strongest in Brazil, the Latin American nation that has the greatest amount of Pentecostal programming. As previously mentioned, the Universal Church of Kingdom of God runs its own station, Rede Record. More than any other factor, it was Pentecostalism's dominance of religious broadcasting that compelled the Brazilian CCR to embrace television as a powerful evangelical medium. Father Edward Dougherty has made CCR history not only by importing the movement to Brazil but also by pioneering in Catholic TV. In 1983, his charismatic association, Associação do Senhor Jesus (Association of Lord Jesus), aired the country's first CCR program, *Anunciamos Jesus* (*We Announce Jesus*), which is currently the country's longest-running weekly charismatic program.

Over the past decade, "Padre Eduardo" has expanded his operation to include control of a large television production facility, O Centro de Produção Século XXI (Century 21 Production Center). Century 21, located in the small city of Valinhos, São Paulo, comprises three large studios, which employ the latest technology in video production and a spacious auditorium for hosting studio audiences. Its programs are shown on national television, covering 85 percent of Brazil's territory, and recently Century 21 has started to export its product to other Latin American nations, the United States, and Europe.[32]

Also a skilled fundraiser, Father Dougherty finances his enterprise through a combination of contributions from the 70,000 members of his Association of Lord Jesus, sales of television programs and religious articles, and occasional donations from wealthy Brazilian, North American, and European charismatics. Conspicuous among the latter is the Breninkmeyer family, which owns C&A, the international chain of department stores with a strong presence in Brazil.[33] In contrast to his initial efforts, which were spurned by the Conference of Brazilian Bishops under the influence of progressive bishops, Dougherty has won widespread episcopal support over the past decade for his starring role in bringing the Brazilian Church into the homes of millions of TV viewers. "The Catholic church went for a long time without investing in communication," commented Dougherty's local bishop, Monseñor Geraldo Azevedo of Campinas. "That's why we need an offensive to counterbalance the presence of Pentecostal churches in the mass media."[34] Beyond the world of Catholic television, the CCR has greatly benefited from increasing exposure on secular TV, especially on Latin America's largest network, Rede Globo.

Spirit of the Free Market

If at the beginning of the twenty-first century, Brazilian Christianity has pentecostalized to the extent that the Catholic Church's most dynamic movement is its own version of Pentecostalism, it is because charismatic Christianity has developed superior religious products and marketed them more successfully than its competitors in the free market of faith. Over the past five decades popular religious consumers in Brazil have exhibited a strong preference for pneumacentric spirituality in both its Christian and non-Christian forms.[35] It is no coincidence that the most successful Christian denominations in the country are those that revolve around direct contact with or even possession by the Holy Spirit. Charismatic Catholicism and Pentecostalism share the common element of pneumacentrism; and one of the primary functions of the Spirit is to heal individual believers of their earthly afflictions. In his study of the CCR in

Curacao, Armando Lampe makes the crucial point that religions of possession are also ones of healing; the two moments are inextricably intertwined.[36] Thus charismatic Christianity has prospered in Brazil's unregulated market of faith because its religious specialists produce the standardized products, faith healing and pneumacentric spirituality, that popular consumers demand. In contrast, organizations such as the Catholic Base Christian Communities (CEB) and mainline Protestantism, which offer neither supernatural healing nor direct contact with the Holy Spirit, have failed to thrive in the popular religious marketplace.

Notes and References

[1] Pentecostalism emerged from the Holiness movement of the nineteenth century. Literal interpretation of the Bible, ecstatic worship, and asceticism characterized the believers. Baptism in the Spirit is the central tenet and experience of Pentecostal religion.

[2] Available online at: <http://pewforum.org/world-affairs/countries/?CountryID=29>.

[3] Ibid. "Charismatic" is an umbrella term denoting those Christians who have adopted Pentecostal forms of beliefs and practices. Thus Pentecostals themselves, and both Protestants and Catholics who prefer a more Spirit-centered practice are considered charismatics.

[4] In their groundbreaking study of the historical winners and losers in the US religious economy, *The Churching of America, 1776–1990*, Finke and Stark demonstrate that the fate of religious organizations in a free-market economy depends on their products, marketing, sales representatives, and organizational structure. Translated into the ecclesiastical idiom, doctrine, evangelization techniques, clergy, and polity are the four factors that determine the success or failure of any given religious enterprise in a pluralistic environment. Broadening Finke and Stark's narrowing pairing of the religious product with doctrine, I include liturgy or forms of worship in my definition of the religious product.

[5] Faith missions were non-denominational evangelical Protestant organizations that sought to convert Latin American Catholics. They were often more theologically and culturally conservative than mainline Protestant churches.

[6] Available online at: <http://pewforum.org/world-affairs/countries/?CountryID=29>.

[7] Baptism in the Spirit is the central tenet and experience of Pentecostal religion. It is based on an event in the book of Acts in which the Holy Spirit descended on the Apostles in tongues of fire, causing them to preach in languages previously unknown to them. Pentecostals claim that the Holy Spirit possesses them similarly during the spiritual baptism.

[8] Available online at: <http://www.iccrs.org/CCR%20worldwide.htm>.

[9] Available online at: <http://pewforum.org/world-affairs/countries/?CountryID=29>.

[10] Abelardo Soneira, "La Renovación Carismática Católica en la Argentina," *Revista del Centro de Investigación y Acción Social* 477 (1998): 473–86.

[11] Richard Bord and Joseph Faulkner, *The Catholic Charismatics* (University Park, PA: Pennsylvania State University Press, 1983).

[12] Covenant communities are CCR groups that live communally and often take vows of poverty, chastity, and obedience.

[13] Father Edward Dougherty, personal communication, July 16, 1998.

[14] R. Andrew Chesnut, *Born Again in Brazil: The Pentecostal Boom and the Pathogens of Poverty* (New Brunswick, NJ: Rutgers, 1997).

[15] The ISER survey included mainline Protestants whose higher income and educational levels raised the mean. If only Pentecotals had been surveyed the gap between believers and the general population would have been substantially larger. Instituto Superior de Estudos da Religião, *Novo nascimento: Os evangélicos em casa, na igreja, e na política* (Rio de Janeiro: ISER, 1996).

[16] Daniel Míguez, "Exploring the Argentinian Case: Religious Motives in the Growth of Latin American Pentecostalism," in Christian Smith and Joshua Propoky, eds, *Latin American Religion in Motion* (New York: Routledge, 1999), 221–34.

[17] ISER.

[18] Pedro Oliveira et al., *Renovação Carismática Católica: Uma analise sociológica, interpretações teológicas* (Petropolis, Brazil: Vozes, 1978).

[19] Ibid.

[20] Reginaldo Prandi, *Um sopro do espirito* (São Paulo: Edusp, 1997).

[21] Pedro Oliveira et al., *Renovação Carismática Católica*. The Cursillo (little course) movement was founded in 1949 in Spain by Monseñor Juan Hervas. In Latin America, it sought to organize and train middle-class laity with the overaching goal of Catholicizing the workplace and society in general.

[22] Chesnut, *Born Again in Brazil*.

[23] Rodney Stark and William Bainbridge, *A Theory of Religion* (New York: Peter Lang, 1987).

[24] Chesnut, *Born Again in Brazil*.

[25] "Não sou artista, nem quero ser ídolo de ninguem: Meu sonho era jogar futebol," *CARAS*, December 4, 1998.

[26] Samarone Lima and Thais Oyama,"Católicos em transe" *Veja*, 1998. Available online at: <www2.uol.com.br/veja/080498/p_092.html>.

[27] Ibid.

[28] Pedro Moreno, "Evangelical Churches," in Paul Sigmund,ed., *Religious Freedom and Evangelization in Latin America* (Maryknoll, NY: Orbis, 1999), 49–69.

[29] A search in March of 2009 found the following Brazilian churches to be running their own websites: the IURD, the Assemblies of God, Igreja Pentecostal Deus é Amor-Brazil (God is Love), Igreja do Evangelho Quadrangular (Foursquare Gospel Church), Brasil para Cristo (Brazil for Christ), and Igreja Internacional da Graca de Deus (International Church of the Grace of God).

[30] Monique Hebrard, *Les Charismatiques* (Paris: Cerf-Fides, 1991). Luiz Roberto Benedetti, "Templo, Praça, Coração: A articulação do campo religioso católico," PhD diss., University of São Paulo, 1988.

[31] "Não sou milagreiro" *Isto É*, December 24, 1997.

[32] Brenda Carranza Dávila, "Renovação Carismática Católica: Origens, mudanças e tendências," Master's thesis, Campinas State University, Brazil, 1998.

[33] Ibid.

[34] Ibid.

[35] The religions of the African diaspora, such as Vodou and Candomble, are the main non-Christian pneumacentrists.

[36] Armando Lampe, "The Popular Use of the Charismatic Movement in Curaçao," *Social Compass* 45/3 (1998): 429–36.

Further Reading

Brown, Diana. Umbanda: *Religion and Politics in Urban Brazil*. Ann Arbor, MI: UMI Research Press, 1986.

Burdick, John. *Looking for God in Brazil*. Berkeley, CA: University of California Press, 1993.

Chesnut, R. Andrew. *Born Again in Brazil: The Pentecostal Boom and the Pathogens of Poverty*. New Brunswick, NJ: Rutgers, 1997.

Chesnut, R. Andrew. *Competitive Spirits: Latin America's New Religious Economy*. New York: Oxford University Press, 2003.

Finke, Roger, and Rodney Stark. *The Churching of America, 1776–1990*. New Brunswick, NJ: Rutgers University Press, 1992.

Gill, Anthony. *Rendering Unto Caesar: The Catholic Church and the State in Latin America.* Chicago, IL: University of Chicago Press, 1998.

Landes, Ruth. *A City of Women.* New York: Macmillan, 1947.

Mariz, Cecilia. *Religion and Coping With Poverty in Brazil.* Philadelphia, PA: Temple University Press, 1994.

Serbin, Kenneth. *Secret Dialogues.* Pittsburgh, PA: University of Pittsburgh Press, 2000.

Stark, Rodney, and William Bainbridge. *A Theory of Religion.* New York: Peter Lang, 1987.

Part V

The Pacific

14

Christianity in Australia and New Zealand
Faith and Politics in Secular Soil

Marion Maddox

Historical Introduction

Christianity first challenged the indigenous cultures in Australia and New Zealand just two centuries ago. The first Christian service on Australian soil was conducted on February 3, 1788, by Rev. Richard Johnson, chaplain to the First Fleet of convict settlers sent to found the penal colony of New South Wales, eight years after its coast was first charted by Captain James Cook. In New Zealand, missionaries to Māori were among the earliest European settlers.

Otherwise, the first Europeans tended to be whalers, rural settlers, and, in much of Australia, convicts. Sparse populations and harsh conditions meant religious practice was neither within the reach nor on the agenda of many. Moreover, clergy's authoritarian role in Australia's convict settlements undermined their credibility with a poor and often brutalized population. Rev. Samuel Marsden, appointed assistant chaplain to the penal colony of New South Wales in 1793, doubled as a magistrate; his sentences earned him the nickname of "the flogging parson."

Australian and New Zealand Christianity has grown out of a variety of intercultural, interdenominational, and interfaith encounters. The first peoples of both nations have contributed their own theological perspectives, although white churches have been slow to appreciate them. An array of immigrant cultures has contributed to the richness.

In the late twentieth and early twenty-first centuries, the proportions of Orthodox, Catholics, and Pentecostals grew in both places, while proportions of Anglicans and mainline Protestants declined. Eastern Orthodox churches benefited from large-scale migration after World War II. The same post-war wave brought Italians to boost the Catholics, whose first generations tended to be Irish (convict or free). From the 1970s, East Timorese, Vietnamese, South American, and Lebanese refugees brought further cultural diversity, while the turn of the twenty-first century brought more Catholics, again often as refugees, from Africa, the Balkans, and Iraq.

In both Australia and New Zealand, inhabitants of Anglo-Celtic origin, who tend to hold the culturally dominant positions, have been abandoning Christianity at increasing rates since the 1970s. In the 2006 census, 64 percent of Australians identified with some Christian tradition, while 19 percent chose "no religion." Fewer than 10 percent attended church weekly.

In 2006, 55 percent of New Zealanders chose a Christian affiliation, a significant drop compared to the over 60 percent who did so five years earlier. Religiosity is sharply divided on ethnic lines: more than 80 percent of New Zealand's substantial Pacific Island diaspora identified as Christian, and 57 percent of Māori nominated a Christian denomination. More than 34 percent of New Zealanders chose "no

Introducing World Christianity, First Edition. Edited by Charles E. Farhadian.
© 2012 Blackwell Publishing Ltd. Published 2012 by Blackwell Publishing Ltd.

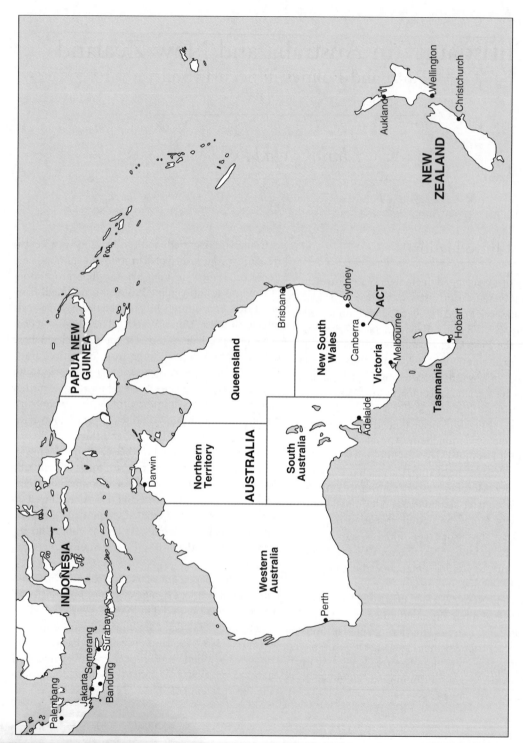

Map 14.1 Australia and New Zealand

religion," 73 percent of them of European descent. An exception is the trend toward large Pentecostal churches, whose success-oriented prosperity message and youthful, pop-music-fueled worship have proved attractive to middle-class and upwardly mobile Anglo congregants.

At New Zealand's Destiny Church, a similar message and style appeals to a largely Māori and Pacific Island membership. Destiny shares with many other prominent Pentecostal churches in Australia and New Zealand an alignment with conservative politics, even briefly launching a political party that shared its name. Destiny's founder's biography carries the blurb: "Never before have the forces of religious, political and social activism converged more powerfully."

Australia's Family First Party, founded in 2001 by members of the Australian Assemblies of God (renamed Australian Christian Churches in 2007), won a Senate seat in the 2004 Federal election. Australia's largest church, Hillsong, is also part of Australian Christian Churches, and attracted considerable publicity for its close association with parliamentarians and party officials from the conservative Liberal-National coalition.

Perhaps in response to this conservative realignment, politicians began urging Australians, and to a lesser extent New Zealanders, to see themselves as living in a "Christian country." Both countries' British colonial heritage has ensured Christianity a larger place in national culture than the numbers alone might suggest. While a "secularization thesis" of declining religious influence had become conventional wisdom in the 1970s and 1980s, the new century opened with Australian political leaders proclaiming their religiosity. This chapter focuses on the complicated relationship between Christianity and politics.

Church and State

Neither Australia nor New Zealand inherited a strong tradition of philosophical debate about Church and state, or secularist struggles. Both countries were colonized after the fires of Enlightenment fervor in Europe and the US had cooled. Their developing legal and political systems approached questions of religion pragmatically. In New Zealand, localized pro-establishment campaigns seemed dated from the outset, beginning just as Dissenters were gaining rights in England.

In 1901, the Commonwealth of Australia, formed out of a federation of former British colonies, adopted its Constitution, drafted in Australia and passed as an Act of the British Parliament. The Australian founders' deliberations reflect influences of both English establishment and American Church–state separation. They drafted a Constitution with a religiously framed Preamble (describing the federating colonies as "humbly relying on the blessing of Almighty God"), preceding a minimally separationist main text. Relations between religion and the Commonwealth are specified in Section 116 of the Constitution:

> The Commonwealth shall not make any law for establishing any religion, or for imposing any religious observance, or for prohibiting the free exercise of any religion, and no religious test shall be required as a qualification for any office or public trust under the Commonwealth.

In interpretation, it has proved considerably weaker than the US Constitution's free exercise and no establishment clauses, on which it was modeled. Australia's Constitution limits itself to a negative protection against Commonwealth interference, permits government support for religious institutions, and does not constrain the states.

New Zealand has no written constitution. In 1911 (*Carrigan* v. *Redwood*), the Supreme Court underlined that "there is no State Church here." In particular, "the Anglican Church in New Zealand is in no sense a State Church." In 1917 (*Doyle* v. *Whitehead*), Chief Justice Stout reiterated:

> As a nation, we have nothing to do with religion. Every religion has equal rights before the law. None are supported by the State, and our highest offices of state can be held by men not professing the Christian religion.

The Bill of Rights Act (1990) protects freedom of "thought, conscience, religion, and belief" (s. 13) and freedom of religious "worship, observance, practice or teaching, either individually or in community . . . and either in public or private" (s. 15). The Human Rights Act (1993) prohibits discrimination on grounds of "religious belief" and "ethical belief," including lack of religious belief (s. 21).

Of increasing constitutional importance since the 1970s has been New Zealand's founding document, the Treaty of Waitangi. It guarantees Māori the continued possession of their "Lands and Estates Forests Fisheries and other properties." In the Māori text, "other properties" is *taonga*, "treasures," which has been taken in Treaty interpretation to include cultural and religious heritage. Today, Christian belief and practice have been absorbed into much Māori ritual practice. Christian prayer in Māori language is the standard way to begin many public events. Rather than any potential violation of religious freedom, this practice is construed as honoring "Treaty principles."

Both countries incorporate Christian ritual in public and parliamentary life. Both national parliaments open each sitting day with prayer, fly the Union Jack and the Southern Cross on their flags, and, until 1984, invoked God in their respective national anthems. Australia then replaced "God Save the Queen" with the secular "Advance Australia Fair," but New Zealanders have two national anthems of equal standing, both invoking God: "God Save the Queen" and the far more frequently sung "God Defend New Zealand."

While definitive figures are difficult to obtain, parliamentarians appear to be significantly more likely to identify as Christian and to attend church than the general population.[1] As Christian practice has fallen, the kind of role played by public Christianity has changed, with a more overtly political dimension re-emerging.

In 1946, the Australian parliament launched its Parliamentary Christian Fellowship, made up of Members and Senators from all parties. The Fellowship's weekly breakfasts, visiting speakers, and annual church service for the opening of parliament were painstakingly bipartisan and apolitical. Australia's parliament has also seen more intimate prayer, Bible study, and support groups for Members and Senators. One such group in the late 1990s and early 2000s had between 25 and 30 members, almost all from the conservative side. In an interview with the author in February 2000, future prime minister Kevin Rudd described himself as "probably the only leftie there." The group emphasized personal faith rather than politics. Nevertheless, Rudd discerned political effects:

One of my Labor Party colleagues said to me, "Kevin, never pray with the bastards, because if you do it makes it harder to hate 'em" ... if you get to know these guys, they're just like me, flawed human beings. And while you will not resile from fundamental policy differences ... you have some respect for them, as opposed to people who are not restrained by anything. ... And does that have a political consequence? You're more likely to listen with some respect [when a group-member is speaking].[2]

From 1986, an annual National Prayer Breakfast aimed "to reach out to the 'unchurched' among Senators and Members and in all walks of life and from all parts of the country" and to "encourage Australians to recognise their privileges and responsibilities before God." The event brought Australia into an international network of national prayer breakfasts stemming from the US National Prayer Breakfast that was founded in 1953 and seeded worldwide.[3]

The Australian National Student Leadership Forum on Faith and Values was founded in 1997 and hosted by a group of Members and Senators from all parties. Its content and format mirror the Washington National Student Leadership Forum on Faith and Values, which, like the US National Prayer Breakfast, presents publicly as an initiative of Members of Congress, while being discreetly sponsored and organized by a secretive organization called "the Family" or "the Fellowship." Australia's student leaders study, as their main example, the "servant leadership" of "Jesus of Nazareth." The Forum's Sydney secretariat was instrumental in establishing New Zealand's "Aspiring Leaders' Forum on Faith and Values" in 2006. Its website promises participants will "talk at length with each other about their personal beliefs," including "the significance of faith and values," although the organizers "do not intend for it to be overly religious."

Neither country has been immune from recent global trends toward more polarized views about matters such as whether (some particular kind of) faith should be enshrined in the country's public life. Both countries debate the role that religious commitments should play in legislative responses to bioethical questions such as abortion, euthanasia, and infertility treatments, or social issues relating to sexuality and family life, with Christians prominent on both conservative and progressive sides. In Australia, Christians also weighed in on whether Australia should adopt a Bill of rights, the subject of a national consultation in 2009. Several conservative evangelical and Pentecostal organizations campaigned hard against it, fearing it might restrain them from preaching their own traditions' superiority. In New Zealand, civil unions available to both heterosexual and homosexual couples triggered a strong debate in 2004, while, in 2007, physical punishment of children was fiercely defended by some conservative evangelicals and Pentecostals, citing Proverbs 22:15, against a proposed change to the criminal code.

In Australia, Kevin Rudd heralded his accession to the leadership of the Australian Labor Party (ALP) in 2006 with an unprecedented (for Australian leaders) policy manifesto: a pair of articles in a national current affairs magazine about Dietrich Bonhoeffer. He drew attention to the Labor Party's Christian socialist roots and denounced any suggestion that Christian values were the prerogative of the conservative parties. His first act on assuming office as prime minister was to offer a national apology to the so-called "stolen generations" of indigenous Australians taken from their parents. The parliamentary ceremony marking the apology avoided overtly Christian references, but echoed many of the liturgical features of Christian confession.

In 2010, Julia Gillard became Australia's first female prime minister. The publicity attracted by her declaration of unbelief on taking office showed how entrenched religiously inflected politics had become in Australia since the early 1970s, when atheists and agnostics held high office with minimal public notice.

Christians and Social Justice

Christians have not just sided with a would-be establishment or with the recently resurgent Christian right. Church leaders in both Australia and New Zealand have just as long a tradition of supporting progressive causes. Australia's first Roman Catholic vicar-general, Rev. Dr William Ullathorne (1806–89), wrote tracts like *The Horrors of Transportation*, opposing transportation of criminals to Australia, and appeared before the House of Commons Select Committee on Transportation chaired by William Molesworth in 1838.

Figure 14.1 Rev. John Dunmore Lang, D.D., A.M., for upwards of 50 years minister of the Scots Church, Sydney. Published by the proprietor J. T. Gorus, November 1873. Courtesy of the National Library of Australia.

Then, as later, political agreement could unite doctrinal opponents, and Ullathorne's anti-transportation crusade found an ally in a staunchly anti-Catholic Presbyterian minister, Rev. Dr John Dunmore Lang (1799–1878). After a fiery relationship with his church, Lang eventually entered the New South Wales parliament. In addition to ending transportation, his platform included fairer elections, and wider voting rights. According to Lang, the Bible endorsed only one form of government: republicanism, underpinned by political equality, universal suffrage, and popular election. Critics insisted that "a professed minister of religion" should not "meddle" with politics but "mind your own proper business and leave these things to other people," labeling his ideas "Chartism, Communism, and Socialism." Lang retorted that in that case, those "isms" must stem from the same source as his own convictions, namely, "that Word of God which endureth for ever."

Nineteenth-century churchmen also risked controversy on matters of race. When Lang died, 500 Chinese mourners led his funeral procession, honoring his efforts at loosening restrictions on Chinese immigration. Congregationalist Rev. Dr James Jefferis argued in the 1870s for equal wages for Chinese and Australian workers. Some Australian and English evangelicals were central in attempts to protect indigenous peoples' rights. One, evangelical missionary George Augustus Robinson, complained in 1846 that expanding pastoral leases would soon leave Australia's indigenous peoples "no place for the soles of their feet." His reports moved another evangelical, British secretary of state Earl Grey, to insist that indigenous people retained rights to their land. Grey's interpretation laid the groundwork for the High Court of Australia's Wik decision exactly 150 years later, which found that native title persists on the large areas of Australia subject to pastoral leases.

One of the longest-standing strands of churches' public activity has been in social welfare services, which expanded further when the neoliberal ascendancy of the 1990s and early 2000s saw religious organizations encouraged to take up still more of the welfare load. In New Zealand, the policy extended as far as a self-contained residential "Faith-Based Unit" in the state-run Rimutaku prison, aimed, according to Prison Fellowship International, at "rebuilding and transforming inmates' values and character." In Australia, the conservative government of John Howard (1996–2007) increased involvement of Church organizations in delivering what had previously been government services – subsequently copied by US Republican President George W. Bush and British Labour Prime Minister Tony Blair.

As churches received increased government funds, they found it harder to criticize government policy. Fear of losing future contracts (perhaps to organizations with much less experience in the area) could restrain criticism. Moreover, the shift to Church rather than public welfare provision had the side effect of encouraging de-unionization of the welfare workforce. As not-for-profit organizations, relying heavily on volunteer labor and often paying their employees at the lower end of the salary scale, churches could provide cheaper services than either government or private enterprise.

John Howard's conservative coalition was replaced in 2007 by the Australian Labor Party (ALP), led by self-described Christian socialist Kevin Rudd. Rudd, a practicing Anglican who, as a backbencher, had once described the Churches' proper role as "an irritant on the body politic," addressed many of the former areas of contention between churches and government. In particular, his government softened the most punitive restrictions and penalties for jobseekers, accelerated processes for assessing claims for refugee status so that asylum-seekers were no longer held in detention for months or years, and ensured asylum-seeker families with children were no longer incarcerated.

However, it was not the fact of the leader's faith that made him more receptive to the Churches' critique. His opponent, Tony Abbott, a practicing Catholic and former seminarian, promised, if elected, to return to the Howard government's hard line on social issues, and to resume forcing asylum-seeker vessels back out to sea. Religious convictions interact with a leader's political ideology, but seldom trump it.

Catholics and Politics

New Zealand's first Catholics were French Marist missionaries led by Jean-Baptiste Pompallier. He took part in the negotiations leading to the Treaty of Waitangi, and asked Governor Hobson to ensure that the Treaty would protect religious freedom. Accordingly, a statement was read to the assembled chiefs before they signed:

> E mea ana te Kawana ko nga whakapono katoa o Ingarai, o nga Weteriana, o Roma, me te ritenga Māori hoki e tiakina ngatahitia e ia.
> [The Governor says that the several faiths of England, of the Wesleyans, of Rome, and also Māori custom shall alike be protected by him.]

This verbal guarantee is sometimes called the Treaty's unwritten "Fourth Article."

Catholics are New Zealand's second-largest religious group, after Anglicans. If census trends continue, the Catholic Church will soon be the largest. In 1986, Catholics overtook Anglicans as Australia's largest denomination. In the 2006 census, over 5 million of the nearly 20 million Australians identified as Catholic.

Arriving first as convicts or as working-class migrants fleeing poverty, Australian Catholics encountered discrimination in education and employment that entrenched their disadvantage. Their experience of colonial rule in Ireland predisposed them to republicanism, and Catholics remain prominent in the Australian republican movement. Together with trade unionists and feminists, Catholics spearheaded the successful "no" campaign in each of the referenda (1916 and 1917) that canvassed conscription for World War I.

Like other working-class voters, Catholics historically supported the Australian Labor Party. From 1940, the Catholic bishops issued annual Social Justice Statements aiming to shape public attitudes and policy, as well as to inform lay Catholics about social issues of the day. Catholic Action groups provided a non-political channel for lay people to work for social betterment. The *Catholic Worker* newspaper (established 1936) opposed both capitalism and communism, inspired by Catholic social teaching, in particular the encyclical *Rerum Novarum* (1891). The *Catholic Worker*'s second editorial (February 1936) announced:

> We do not regard the Communist Party as our chief opponent . . . Communism will sink under the weight of its own falsity, its own materialism, and its own consistent betrayal of the interests of the working classes. Communism is not our great adversary. The exalted position of Public Enemy number one is reserved for Capitalism, not because it is . . . intrinsically more evil than Communism . . . but because today it dominates the world. Capitalism, that is the enemy!

However, during World War II, fears of a communist takeover of Australia prompted one of the *Catholic Worker* founders, B. A. ("Bob") Santamaria, to initiate a new, secret lay organization called the Catholic Social Studies Movement, or simply "the Movement," devoted to anti-communist activity. From its inception in 1942, the movement enjoyed moral and financial support from Melbourne's Archbishop Mannix and, from 1945, was overseen by a committee in which Mannix was joined by Archbishop Gilroy (Sydney) and Bishop O'Collins (Ballarat). It maintained parish lists of trade union members, whom priests encouraged to attend union meetings to organize opposition to communist officials. The movement also sought influence in ALP branches. Its existence remained unknown even to many Catholics until 1954, when Labor leader H. V. Evatt publicly denounced the group, blaming its destabilizing influence for his party's loss of that year's federal election.

The revelation led to a crisis, known as the "Split," from which the ALP took two decades to recover. Movement-aligned party members, including most of the Victorian branch, were expelled, forming a breakaway party. Initially named Australian Labor Party (Anti-Communist), it is mostly remembered by its later title, the Democratic Labour Party (DLP). It won Senate seats from 1955 until 1974, and was dissolved in 1978, although a new party of the same name won a seat in the Victorian parliament in 2006.

The Split had longlasting consequences for the Catholic Church and for Australian politics. First, the public crisis ended the movement's official Church standing. During 1956 and 1957, parts of the Catholic hierarchy, particularly in Sydney, became increasingly concerned about the movement's influence and potential to embroil the Church in party politics. A delegation of Australian bishops appealed to the Vatican. In three letters during 1957, the Vatican made increasingly clear that bishops could veto movement activities in their own dioceses; that it expected the movement to leave "aside all direct action upon unions and political parties"; and that the movement could not claim to be acting in the Church's name. In December of 1957, Santamaria founded a new organization, the National Civic Council, to continue the movement's aims.

Second, by splitting the traditional Labor vote, the DLP was instrumental in keeping the ALP out of office federally until 1972. Australia's electoral system uses a combination of preferential voting and proportional representation, and the DLP directed preferences to the conservative parties. In turn, this eroded the traditional association between Catholics and Labor. As Catholics became increasingly well educated and middle class, and discrimination against them decreased, some Catholics felt increasingly at home in the conservative parties. The DLP's dissolution translated into increased first preferences for the Liberal and National Parties. Several commentators trace the "Catholicization of the Liberal Party" to this point.

Sir Robert Menzies, the Liberal Party's founder and its first prime minister (1949–66), added an attraction for newly middle-class Catholics to support his conservative side of politics. Since the 1880s, most colonies (states from 1901) had allowed government funding only to free, secular state schools. Catholics, who feared the secular or Protestant slant of such schools, had responded by establishing their own schools. These could, however, be overcrowded and staffed by sometimes minimally trained religious, whose vocation was expected to make up for any gaps in formal education. In 1956, the Menzies-Fadden government opened the door to government aid for Catholic schools in the Australian Capital Territory (ACT) (then directly controlled by the federal government). Menzies entered the 1963 election with a proposal to introduce federal government aid for Church schools beyond the ACT. Though the ALP added state aid to its platform three years later, the fact that Menzies had made the first move won him a measure of Catholic support.

In 1964, a group called the Council for the Defence of Government Schools (known as DOGS) formed to challenge the constitutionality of state aid to Church schools under the "no establishment" provision of s. 116. After numerous legal and practical hurdles, their case was finally heard in the High Court in 1980. The full court concluded, six to one, that state aid to religious schools did not amount to "establishing" a religion and so did not breach s. 116. The majority decision further entrenched the minimalist reading of s. 116 that has remained dominant in Australian discussions of religion–state relations, but which the decision's critics maintain is far from the founders' intentions.

Under John Howard, federal support for non-government schools grew much faster than for government schools. Regulation changes encouraged growth in Church schools, and their share of students greatly increased. During the 2004 election, then ALP leader Mark Latham was badly damaged by accusations that he had a secret "hit list" of wealthy Church schools targeted for funding cuts. By 2007, according to the Australian Bureau of Statistics, private enrolments had increased 21.9 percent over 1997 numbers, compared to a 1.7 increase in public school enrolments; barely two thirds of Australian school students attended state schools. The Labor government elected in November of 2007 maintained the Howard funding model for private schools, including the wealthiest elite schools. Some commentators feared the state system was being run down to the point where it would be merely a second-rate safety net for those unable to pay for private education.

While the Catholic system had made the beachhead into state aid, the most dramatic growth under the Howard government was in non-denominational and fundamentalist Protestant schools. Their social and, especially, economic message is often much more directly aligned with those of Australia's conservative parties than is the Catholic system. While congenial to political conservatives on sex and so-called "family" issues, Catholic social teaching can be highly critical of social inequality and of neoliberal economic and international relations priorities.

Indeed, denominational differences now divide Australian Christians less than political ideology. Conservative Catholics find common ground with conservative Protestants in opposing abortion, euthanasia, and homosexuality. Disagreements remained as strong as ever over veneration of the saints or the real presence in the Eucharist, but such matters have lost priority. Similarly, progressive Catholics find common cause with progressive Protestants in denouncing the effects of a capitalist market on the poor or advocating greater gay and lesbian rights within their churches.

Around the turn of the twenty-first century, still more Australian Catholics moved away from their Labor traditions. A bitter struggle in the conservative, and historically anti-Catholic, Liberal Party during 2009 saw four practicing Catholics, spanning the party's left–right spectrum, contest the leadership. One, the prominent moderate Joe Hockey, launched his bid with a public lecture entitled "In Defence of God." He was beaten in a party ballot by the hard-right former seminarian, Tony Abbott, whose religious commitments had always formed a highly visible component of his political persona.

Indigenous Australians, Māori, and Christianity

At different times, missionary churches took different lines on whether converts had to abandon traditional ways in order to become Christian. Especially once the Gospel went out into the world, backed by the military, economic, and technical might of empire, missions played an ambiguous role in the process of colonization. On the one hand, some of the earliest advocates for indigenous peoples' rights were missionaries. Missionaries were among the first colonists to learn and record indigenous languages, to protest at massacres and mistreatment, and to advocate appropriate recognition of indigenous land ownership. Missions also provided a physical space within which indigenous communities could maintain and pass on aspects of their culture, though this was often achieved clandestinely and in the face of missionary disapproval.

On the other hand, missions were central in the effort to "civilize" and "Christianize" native peoples – which, in effect, meant hastening the collapse of already traumatized cultures. In Australia, Rev. William Walker (1800–55) was the first missionary charged with evangelizing the indigenous population. He arrived in the colony of New South Wales 33 years after the First Fleet. In the meantime, indigenous impressions of Europeans had been formed through a generation of dispossession and violence. Evangelism was further hampered by several recurring factors. First, the missionaries and government universally assumed that conversion must start with abandoning traditional, nomadic lifestyles. The establishment of a mission was often accompanied by a grant of land; but semi-nomadic people often saw little point in remaining on it.

Moreover, the government placed high expectations on the missionaries: they were to atone for the damage done to indigenous societies by the depredations of white settlement, to educate the children and convert the adults, and to persuade indigenous communities to live in peace with white colonists, who had done little to deserve trust.

Both government and missionary societies persevered. Catholic, Anglican, Methodist, Congregationalist, and Lutheran missions continued to be established in various parts of New South Wales (which then included most Australian colonies). But, by 1848, all had been abandoned, having achieved a total of just one adult baptism.

In the 1950s, the Bandjalang people, in northeastern New South Wales, experienced a Pentecostal revival with elements of traditional religion. The Elcho Island Revival of 1979 similarly gave birth to an indigenous-led Christian movement, in which indigenous tradition was not disowned, but incorporated into a theology emphasizing the importance of land and justice for Aboriginal peoples. In contrast to the first-generation missionaries, who insisted that knowledge and

wisdom flowed in only one direction, the Elcho Island movement, and the Uniting Aboriginal and Islander Christian Congress that eventually grew out of it, have drawn attention to indigenous spiritual and theological insights. In the words of Rev. Dr Djiniyini Gondarra, a leader of the Congress and former Moderator of the Uniting Church's Northern Synod, indigenous culture and spirituality offer "blessings" that Christian churches should be readier to receive. Today, around 70 percent of indigenous Australians identify on the census as Christian.

In New Zealand, early European missionaries were likely to complain not that Māori were indifferent to Christianity, but that they took it up too enthusiastically, taking literally its messages of liberation and millennial vindication. Three lay missionaries went to New Zealand in 1809, five years ahead of the first permanent European settlers. By 1835, more than 1,000 Māori attended worship regularly. Ten years later, George Clarke, the Chief Protector of Aborigines (and himself a missionary) estimated that, of a Māori population of 110,000, nearly 64,000 were in church regularly.

Māori adroitly adapted Christianity to fit their religious and cultural needs, as their society suffered repeated traumas of disease, dispossession, and repression. In the early years of colonization, Māori eagerness to gain access to the Bible meant that literacy, and knowledge of English, spread to communities who had had no contact with Europeans. So close was the apparent connection between the Bible and European power that a copy, or even single pages, came to be treated as potent charms.

The second half of the nineteenth century saw the rise of Māori prophets, who were teaching that Māori were the chosen people whose liberation and vindication would come as surely as had that of the Hebrews in Egypt. Some advocated armed resistance to Europeans; others, like Te Whiti o Rongomai and Tohu Kākahi, preached non-violence. During the early 1880s they led a stunning, though unsuccessful, demonstration against land confiscation. As government surveyors, working under armed guard, attempted to mark out the confiscated lands for settlement, Māori men ploughed up the land, sowed it with wheat, and fenced it off, ploughing and sowing over roads and any other structures that might lie in their way. As fast as the ploughmen and fencers were arrested, more took their places, some having traveled great distances to take part. Eventually, a settler army numbering several thousand arrived to take Te Whiti's village of Parihaka. The army's way was blocked by singing children and parties of girls playing with skipping ropes. Once the soldiers had pushed their way through to the village center, they found 2,500 villagers sitting in total silence. Thus they remained, while scores, including Te Whiti, were arrested. Over the following three weeks, villagers continued peaceful resistance as their crops were burned and village ruined.[4]

A common theme among Māori prophets was that of overcoming tribal differences in the name of pan-Māori unity, a particular concern of Tahupotiki Ratana. Ratana began a Christian healing ministry in 1918, which established itself as a separate church in 1925. According to the 2006 census, the Ratana Church claimed over 50,000 adherents out of New

Zealand's roughly 4 million people. Of those who identified as Māori in the 2006 census, 11 percent nominated one of the Māori churches that developed out of the prophetic movements of the nineteenth and early twentieth centuries.

Ratana was deeply interested in politics and his movement remained influential on elections, particularly in relation to parliament's designated Māori seats. The Church's historic alliance with the Labor Party has, on at least two occasions, delivered Labor the seats to form government. This association began to break down in 2004, when MP Tariana Turia split from Labor to form the Māori Party. After the 2008 election, it entered a confidence and supply agreement with the conservative National Party government.

In Australia, the relationship between non-indigenous and indigenous peoples can form a rare overlap between the concerns of conservative and progressive Christians. At times, it has cut across the alignment

Figure 14.2   Armed Constabulary Field Force, Parihaka. Photographer unknown. Source: James Cowan, *The New Zealand Wars: A History of the Maori Campaigns and the Pioneering Period: Volume II: The Hauhau Wars, 1864–72.* Wellington: R.E. Owen, 1956.

between conservative churches and conservative political movements, in contrast to areas of consensus like free-market economics and sexuality. John Bradford held the federal seat of McPherson for the Liberals from 1990 until he resigned from the party in 1998 to become, briefly, the only Christian Democrat in federal parliament. He stood unsuccessfully for the Senate in the 1998 election, sharing his ticket with an indigenous businessman, Kerry Blackman. Mainly famous as an ultra-conservative Christian morals campaigner, Bradford resigned from the Liberals over disagreements with the Howard government, including its amendments to the Native Title Act 1993 that disadvantaged indigenous communities and benefited mining and pastoral interests.

The Native Title amendments drew substantial Church attention. Anglican Bishop of Canberra-Goulburn George Browning observed:

> I can't remember any other issue in recent times which has gained such a broad consensus of opinion amongst church leaders ... We argue about ... a host of other issues, but on this one the unanimity of mind is quite extraordinary.

Christian Parties

No mainstream political party in Australia or New Zealand has adopted an explicitly Christian identity, in the manner of a European-style Christian democrat party. Nonetheless, the two countries' political systems elicit different forms of Christian party politics.

Since 1996, when New Zealand adopted a European-style Multi-Member Proportional (MMP) system, groups seeking parliamentary influence have an incentive to join that country's proliferation of minor parties, in the hope of being in a position to provide coalition numbers for a major party, in return for policy concessions. However, that prize has eluded successive Christian parties. Several openly Christian groupings (Christian Heritage, Christian Democrat, Future New Zealand, Destiny Party, Kiwi Party, New Zealand Pacific Party) have failed to gain the threshold for parliamentary representation (either 5 percent of the vote or an electorate MP). The highest profile of any self-described Christian party to date was achieved by Destiny Party, offspring of the Pentecostal, Māori-led Destiny Church. When the New Zealand parliament debated a Bill to introduce civil unions (a legal union equivalent to marriage, available to same-sex and heterosexual couples), the sight of 5,000 black-shirted Destiny supporters marching down Wellington's main street in protest reportedly prompted a number of wavering MPs to support the Bill. Destiny never achieved parliamentary representation, and dissolved in 2007.

The nearest that MMP has produced to a successful Christian party was when Future NZ merged with a secular party, United, to form United Future NZ. While UFNZ Leader Peter Dunne routinely denied it was a Christian party, six of the seven MPs elected in its 2002 high tide had close connections to conservative Christian movements. The party split in 2007, returning United to its secular roots, while its Christian faction formed the Kiwi Party. In the 2008 election, it lost its only seat.

In Australia, the robust two-party system has discouraged minor party proliferation. Government is formed by whichever party holds a majority in the House of Representatives, where the electorate-based single-member preferential system makes it all but impossible for a minor party to gain sufficient numbers to wield significant influence. Consequently, Christian groups seeking influence in the House of Representatives have found most success by aligning themselves with one or other of the major parties.

By contrast, minor parties have enjoyed some success in the Senate, which is elected by proportional representation, with 12 Senators per state. The Senate's function as a house of review means that a party without a majority can nevertheless have a major effect in blocking or passing legislation. It was here that the DLP (discussed under Catholics and politics, above) was able to exert its influence until 1974. After its dissolution, former DLP Senator and outspoken Catholic, Brian Harradine, sat as an independent, often exercising a deciding vote, particularly in relation to questions of sexual morality and indigenous rights.

Since the early 1990s, conservative religious alignments have played a formative role in the Liberal Party. One, called the Lyons Forum, was instrumental in the party's early 1990s reorientation towards the socially conservative positions that laid the groundwork for

John Howard's 1995 return to the Liberal leadership, and for his moving the party to the right.

The Forum defined itself as "pro-family," declaring: "The family is the God-ordained foundation of our society." A series of Howard government initiatives originated in the Lyons Forum, such as tax arrangements favoring single-breadwinner, two-parent families; defining marriage as between a man and a woman; and the unsuccessful Sex Discrimination Amendment Bill 2001 and 2002 to allow the States to make fertility services available only to heterosexual couples. In 1996, Forum founding member Kevin Andrews moved a private member's Bill that overturned the Northern Territory's short-lived euthanasia law, the Rights of the Terminally Ill Act (1995).

From at least the mid-1970s, with its rise of secular nationalism with republican undertones, the kind of civil religion that characterizes American politics seemed thoroughly alien to Australian public life until the late 1990s. Prime ministers tended either to claim no particular religious beliefs (Whitlam, Hawke) or to practice a subdued, establishment-style faith that did not form a prominent part of their public persona. Australia's second-longest serving prime minister, John Howard (1996–2007), described himself as only an occasional churchgoer and played down questions about his spiritual life. Nevertheless, he made what he called "Christian values" a significant part of his electoral appeal. He, and his senior ministers, visited conservative mega-churches, made public appeals for more Christian celebrations at Christmas, upbraided schools for not teaching "values," and talked up Australia's "Judeo-Christian culture."

The puzzle for political analysts is why Australia's very secular electorate should respond to such religious prompts. Australia lacks a significant demographic analogous to the evangelical base associated with the US Republican right. However, the electoral appeal in Australia was not primarily to the relatively small numbers of practicing Christians. Under Australia's compulsory voting system, conservatively inclined Christians would be voting for the Coalition parties already. Church-based get-out-the-vote campaigns, of the kind seen in the USA, are redundant in Australia, where the vote comes out by law. Instead, the appeal was mainly to the much larger part of the Australian electorate that, while remaining personally uncommitted with respect to religion, regards Christianity as a benign force for social good. Such voters made their presence felt electorally by supporting social policies like outsourcing welfare services to Church agencies, following then treasurer Peter Costello's assessment that those on society's margins need not only material help but also moral uplift. Many nominal Christian or uncommitted parents send their children to conservative Christian schools, seemingly undeterred by the fact that many require their teachers to sign a statement of belief that asserts that non-Christians cannot be saved. The attraction of such schools to minimally or non-religious parents was often that they imparted "values," something children were perceived to need and the wider society to lack.

Minor Groups, Major Influence

Particularly during the decade from the mid-1990s, a large number of parachurch and non-denominational organizations gained prominence, together creating the impression of an evangelical activist base on the political right. In practice small and often comprising some few individuals, they held well-publicized conferences, in Parliament House or other prominent sites, heard addresses from high-profile politicians, published proceedings, and had their pronouncements read into the official parliamentary record. A sample of such organizations includes the Australian Prayer Network, Parliamentary Prayer Network, Fatherhood Foundation, Australian Heart Ministries, National Marriage Forum, Christian Heritage Forum, Australian Families Association, National Day of Thanksgiving, National Alliance of Christian Leaders, and the Australian Christian Lobby.

The 2007 and 2010 federal election campaigns were preceded by an event called "Make It Count," organized by the Australian Christian Lobby (ACL), in which the two major party leaders addressed a Christian live audience, broadcast over the Internet to church groups, who were required to register with the organization beforehand. A privately funded incorporated body, ACL's website declares it is not "denominationally or politically aligned." ACL is funded by donations from individuals, businesses, and congregations and is not accountable to any church structure. Yet it established itself in media and government eyes as a source of Christian opinion as it lobbied against, for example, same-sex couples' right to marry or adopt children; euthanasia; abortion; and religious freedom legislation.

Secular right-wing think tanks such as the Centre for Independent Studies, Institute of Public Affairs, and others have endorsed the theological right's social and economic stances, while attacking the mainline Churches' more progressive social policy. A conservative "family" agenda proved a crucial component of the right's economic activism, providing a readily graspable justification for Christian political involvement.

Unlike its more intensively studied US cousin, Australia's Christian right managed to achieve considerable political effect without large numbers of adherents, acting instead as a highly motivated and well-organized vanguard. In 2004, Australians became aware of an even smaller, more insular group, which had nevertheless arguably affected the results of elections both in Australia and New Zealand and as far afield as the USA, Canada, and Europe.

The Exclusive Brethren is a branch of a British movement formed in the 1820s. In 2002, Sydney businessman Bruce Hales succeeded his father as the group's world leader, known as the Man of God or Elect Vessel. The group rejects government by the people, traditionally eschewing politics. Since government properly belongs to God, they do not vote.

But, for decades, Exclusive Brethren have been enthusiastic lobbyists of government, achieving exemption from labor laws for their businesses (because they oppose trade unions as a matter of conscience) and extraordinary government subsidies for their schools. In recent years, the group's political concerns extended well beyond matters affecting their own community.

Exclusive Brethren in Australia number about 15,000 (out of a national population of 21 million). Its worldwide membership is estimated at around 40,000. Yet this tiny, non-voting group has wielded considerable political clout.

During the 2004 federal election campaign, with Howard polling badly, the Exclusive Brethren leadership exhorted members to support the Liberal campaign – which they did, to the tune of A$370,000 of electoral advertising in the final weeks, plus extensive

in-kind support. In one rural electorate, the conservative candidate reported that the Brethren had offered a contribution "more than twice our current campaign budget" for advertising and "an army of 500 + people ready to walk the streets delivering material for my campaign," while insisting that their contribution not be made public.[5] Within weeks of the Australian election, in which the Exclusive Brethren contribution had remained almost entirely undetected by political commentators, the Thanksgiving 2004 Committee, a front group for the Australia-based sect, was registered with the American Internal Revenue Service. Thanksgiving 2004 spent over US$500,000 on newspaper advertisements supporting George Bush and the Florida Republican Senate candidate, Mel Martinez, known for opposing gay marriage, hate crimes legislation, and abortion (even after rape or incest), and whose office was linked to a Republican strategy memo describing Florida woman Terri Schiavo's 15-year coma as a "great political issue" that would "excite" the party's "pro-life base." In March of 2005, another Exclusive Brethren front group, called Concerned Canadian Parents, operating out of a short-lived post-box address, launched a campaign against same-sex civil marriage. According to the *Vancouver Sun* (July 15, 2005) "tens of thousands" of direct mail letters targeted constituents of MPs who supported the Bill.

Six months later New Zealand's Labour government, which had outraged fundamentalist Christians by legislating for civil unions for same-sex couples, and enjoyed minor party support from the New Zealand Greens, faced a general election in which, initially, the prospect of a change of government seemed remote. But an intensive advertising campaign, including newspaper spreads and letterbox drops across the country, attacked Labour and the Greens and advocated policies similar to the conservative National Party's, though none of the advertising bore National Party authorization. In the campaign's final days, the blitz was revealed as the work of New Zealand Exclusive Brethren. After the election, journalist Nicky Hager found that the NZ$1.2 million contribution had been negotiated with then National leader Don Brash and then finance spokesman (subsequently prime minister) John Key. Almost exactly a year after the NZ election, Swedish newspaper *Aftonbladet* revealed "millions" of crowns support for the conservative Alliance for Sweden coalition. The finance turned out to come from UK Brethren.

The Exclusive Brethren's founder, John Darby, was a key figure in the birth of pre-millennial dispensationalism, the idea that human history is passing through a series of biblically foretold "dispensations" that will culminate in Jesus's physical return, when he will reign on earth for 1,000 years. Like other pre-millennialists, Exclusive Brethren expect the rapture and, like many, have recently given it a political interpretation. In 2004, as Australia and the US were approaching their respective elections, several newspapers quoted a former member recalling the sect's international leader, Bruce Hales, linking the election result to the rapture's timing. The Australian-based sect's irruption into successive election campaigns around the world demonstrates the effect a tiny religious group, whose aspirations are far different from those of the majority, can wield in secular societies, where religious incursions tend, for the most part, to pass unnoticed.

Conclusion

In both Australia and New Zealand, Christianity is the historically dominant religious tradition, now practiced actively by only a minority of the population. Yet its political and cultural importance far outweighs its demographic standing. Politically, the fact that a large part of the population today respects Christianity as a source of "traditional values," even if having only a vague idea of what those might be, has proved both an advantage to politicians and parties seeking to align themselves with a "values agenda" and a problem when Churches have become outspoken critics of government policy.

Both countries' histories of immigration have brought waves of different Christian traditions. For example, Australian Catholicism was first shaped by Irish convicts and working-class settlers; then, after World War II, Southern European migrants brought a different set of Catholic traditions. Significant numbers of Vietnamese refugees and immigrants in the late twentieth century again changed the country's Catholic profile. In New Zealand, the predominance of Anglicans in the North Island and Canterbury area,

and of Presbyterians in the south of the South Island, has contributed to this small nation developing distinctive regional characteristics. The rise of Māori denominations and the vibrant religious life of Polynesian immigrant Christians has further contributed to the diverse national culture.

Christianity arrived in Australia and New Zealand as a consequence of, and pretty much simultaneously with, the conquest of the traditional cultures by Western, especially British, invaders. The ensuing social, environmental, and political upheavals make it impossible to assess Christianity's impact in isolation from the impact of the other, simultaneous changes. In both countries' public spheres, Christianity has at times reinforced the political and cultural status quo, while at other times (or even at the same time) providing a powerful discourse of dissent. Its churches and other institutions have provided vulnerable people with both abuse and succor, and marginalized groups with both safe havens and oppression. Its public spokespeople have at once comforted and discomfited the powerful, both uplifted and berated the downtrodden. For both better and worse, these two very secular societies are nevertheless now unimaginable without their sometimes forgotten Christian roots.

Notes and References

[1] Marion Maddox, *For God and Country: Religious Dynamics in Australian Federal Politics* (Canberra: Department of the Parliamentary Library, 2001), 13–15.
[2] Ibid., 127.
[3] Jeffrey Sharlet, *The Family: The Secret Fundamentalism at the Heart of American Power* (New York: Harper 2008).
[4] Te Miringa Hohaia and Gregory O'Brien, eds *Parihaka: The Art of Passive Resistance* (Wellington: Victoria University Press, 2002).
[5] Michael Bachelard, *Behind the Exclusive Brethren* (Melbourne: Scribe Publishing, 2008), 193–5.

Further Reading

Bachelard, Michael. *Behind the Exclusive Brethren.* Melbourne: Scribe Publishing, 2008.

Hohaia, Te Miringa and Gregory O'Brien, eds. *Parihaka: The Art of Passive Resistance*. Wellington: Victoria University Press, 2002.

Maddox, Marion. *For God and Country: Religious Dynamics in Australian Federal Politics*. Canberra: Department of the Parliamentary Library, 2001.

Maddox, Marion. *God Under Howard: The Rise of the Religious Right in Australian Politics*. Sydney: Allen & Unwin, 2005.

Sharlet, Jeffrey. *The Family: The Secret Fundamentalism at the Heart of American Power*. New York: Harper, 2008.

15

Christianity in Polynesia
Transforming the Islands

Ian Breward

Beginnings

Polynesia covers the islands of the Eastern Pacific south of the equator, with the exception of the Fiji group. When Polynesians and European explorers encountered one another in the eighteenth century, there was mutual incomprehension and fascination. Categories of explanation needed to change on both sides. Polynesians surmised that European gods must be more powerful than their own. Although there were traditions of Tangaloa, a high God, they did not often impinge on daily life. A host of deities needed to be propitiated by prayers, offerings, and sacrifice to bring success and avert disasters. Religious festivities were frequent, including singing, dancing, gift giving, and sexual activities to ensure that fertility and food gathering were bountiful. Encounters with the gods in dreams, trances, and visions gave Polynesian religion a different quality from Christianity.[1]

Tahitian Foundations

The first missionaries, by assuming the superiority of European culture, lost opportunities to make connections between Polynesian religion and Christianity. Nor did they have even the beginnings of analysis of primal religion. They assumed it would be simple to learn Polynesian languages and that the natives would speedily convert from witchcraft, infanticide, cannibalism, slavery, and endemic warfare. Knowledge of the complex positive dynamics of tribal societies, including generosity, hospitality, oratory, and care for the environment, was only slowly acquired. Development of relationships and understanding was often complicated by hostile Europeans, who rejected missionary values and resented their influence.

The London Missionary Society (LMS) workers, who arrived on the ship *Duff* in 1797, included ministers, as well as tradesmen.[2] They came from differing denominations, shared popular misunderstandings of Polynesian culture as reported by Captain Cook and had none of the expertise needed to reduce other languages to writing. They did, however, possess technical skills useful to the Tahitians. The islanders were puzzled by the new arrivals' failure to understand the rules of reciprocity, let alone that the land granted for occupation was for use, not ownership. The missionaries' hope to establish a church in accord with local culture was not to be realized for many years. It took time to realize that the agreement of chiefs to accept the new religion was essential. Only then would their community accept and be prepared for education into a new way of life. That involved a major change from preaching for individual conversion.

Missionaries were landed on Tahiti, the Marquesas, and Tongatapu, but after a year a number of them were

Introducing World Christianity, First Edition. Edited by Charles E. Farhadian.
© 2012 Blackwell Publishing Ltd. Published 2012 by Blackwell Publishing Ltd.

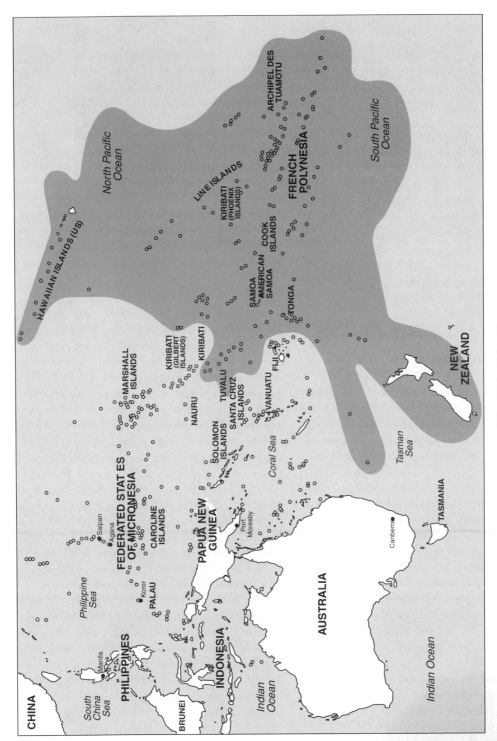

Map 15.1 Polynesia

so discouraged that they went to Sydney. Those who stayed began to use the Maohi language and worked with chiefs such as Pomare. He began to see advantages in Christianity, such as literacy, and unsuccessfully requested baptism in 1812. Other missionaries had worked in the Leeward Islands and found support by chiefs, such as Paofai, and had encouraged some to join praying societies, and to keep the Sabbath. By late 1815, Pomare had defeated his opponents and returned to Tahiti. He was baptized on May 16, 1819.[3]

Few missionaries saw that adoption of Christianity was on Polynesian terms, not a surrender to European models of Christianity. They did not always understand that some chiefs were using the new religion to enhance their power, or that "teachers," as Christian workers were called, inherited some of the sacred status of primal priests, alongside the sacred power of chiefs. Traditional religion was by no means defeated.

Indigenous Pioneers

Rapid expansion of Christian influence on the Leeward Islands led to the development of Christian legal codes, the formation of congregations, the introduction of Christian celebrations in May, recruitment of Christian teachers to commend the new faith, and acceptance of the value of peace, over against the destructive consequences of constant war. Even more important was the purchase of a ship that Williams and Threkeld used to carry missionaries to the southern Cooks in 1823. Papeiha and Vahapata, deacons from Raiatea, had been already landed on Aitutaki in 1821 and had been successful in transmitting Christianity, building a church, persuading people to keep the Sabbath, and follow some basic Christian moral teachings. Papeiha was moved to Rarotonga, where he won the confidence of Makea, the high chief, married another chief's daughter, acquired land, and ministered in chiefly style.[4]

Ta'unga, one of the most outstanding Polynesian missionaries, who worked in New Caledonia and then in Samoa, emerged in this context. Takamoa College was founded to train ministers in 1839. By 1857, 61 missionaries from the Cook Islands were serving

Figure 15.1 Papeiha – Cook Islands missionary from J. Williams, *A Narrative of Missionary Enterprises in the South Seas*, London: Snow, 1837, p. 574.

elsewhere, though 36 had died and 7 had been martyred. While some failed, they made remarkable contributions to the development of Polynesian and Melanesian Christianity. Maretu's journal gives a vivid account of this missionary experience. He vividly described the feasts that accompanied the building of the church at Avarua, when 700 pigs were killed to mark the completion of the frame, as well as giving examples of how people translated Christianity into their own culture. Chiefs who attended worship were much impressed and said, "the pages of the Bible were God himself jumping about."[5] Although British missionaries were influential and sometimes were disappointed by the lives of Christians, they encouraged Cook Islanders to value their culture in the light of the teaching of the Scriptures and did not inhibit islanders' love of singing, dancing, and feasting, or diminish gift exchanges. Christian prayers before any significant activity replaced those from the primal religion.

John Williams's visits back to Britain made him a missionary hero. His *Narrative of Missionary Enterprise* remains a classic, as does William Ellis's *Polynesian Researches*. Sending indigenous teachers as missionaries to other islands built on the tradition of Polynesian navigation. Language and culture were very similar in Polynesian islands and Polynesian missionaries were self-supporting, unlike their British colleagues. Even more importantly there was no period of cultural adjustment.

Catholic Origins

Roman Catholic missionaries followed different priorities.[6] The Picpus Fathers arrived in the Gambier Islands in 1834. Caret, Laval, and Brother Murphy came from an ultra-montane French Catholicism with strong monarchical convictions. The first adult baptisms occurred during Lent, 1835. The *marae* (the place where a tribe's religious and communal celebrations were held) were destroyed, because of their religious associations. Chiefs had their hair cut, indicating that their head, the most sacred part of their body, now was under a new authority. Churches, schools, and simple hospitals were built, and a traditional French-style Catholic community created. A French Protectorate had been established after a French naval vessel came to Tahiti after Laval and Caret were expelled in 1836. Queen Pomare was forced to apologize and guarantee religious freedom for Roman Catholics.[7] The Re-organised Latter Day Saints, later known as the Sanitos, introduced a further variety of Protestant Christianity in 1841 to the Tuamotu and Austral Islands. They only slowly made an impact.

Another strand of French Catholicism came through the Marists, led by Bishop Pompallier. He stopped briefly in Mangareva in September 1837, before dropping priests in Wallis and Futuna and then going on to New Zealand. He hoped also to commence work in Samoa and Tonga, to prevent the spread of Protestant heresy. By early 1841, many of the Wallisians were converted. Futuna was more resistant and Fr Chanel was opposed by some influential chiefs. He was murdered on April 28, 1841. In 1954, Fr. Chanel became patron saint of Oceania. A huge church in Alofi honors his memory. Bataillon was made Vicar Apostolic of Central Oceania in 1842, commencing missionary work in Fiji, Samoa, and Tonga, as well as consolidating French-style Catholicism on Wallis and Futuna.[8]

Tongan Methodism

Following the LMS failure to plant Christianity in Tonga, the Wesleyan Walter Lawry began work at Mu'a on Tongatapu, under the protection of the important chief Fatu. He lasted a year before returning to Sydney. Tahitian teachers had arrived from Bora Bora to work in Vava'u and Tongatapu. In 1826, J. Thomas and J. Hutchinson began work at Hifohifo. Thomas stayed till 1859 and became revered as the founder of Tongan Methodism. Moving to Ha'apai, he was protected by Taufa'ahau. In early 1829, he baptized the chief, Peter Vi, who persuaded Taufa'ahau of the virtues of Christianity, so that he defiled symbols of traditional gods and was baptized early in 1830. He put away all but one wife and became a local preacher. By 1834, a mass movement into Christianity followed the conversion of all three major titleholders. The music and singing of Methodism and its emotional warmth gave a new form to the boundaries between the sacred and the common, replacing the singing and dancing of the fertility cults with Christian celebrations. The Sabbath became sacred. Taufa'ahau also cooperated militarily with his cousin Ma'afu to help establish a significant Tongan presence in Eastern Fiji. Tongan preachers, such as Joeli Bulu, served in Samoa, Fiji, and then in Melanesia.[9]

One of Tauf'ahau's previous wives was the daughter of the high chief of Manono, Samoa. She took the Lotu Tonga home in 1832. (Lotu was the term given to an act of worship, or a church.) By 1835, over 60 villages had adopted it. That was consolidated by the arrival of Peter Turner in 1835. This was yet another example of the spread of Christianity with no British missionary involvement. Tauf'ahau and the Samoans linked with him rejected the comity agreement with the LMS and continued to cooperate in building Samoan Methodism.[10]

Although Taufa'ahau ruled the two northern groups and had set up a Christian law code in 1839, he was resisted on Tongatapu, especially around Pea. To complicate matters, the chiefs there had invited Fr Chevron to minister, seeing in this the possibility of French support. A small Roman Catholic community emerged. Then in 1845 Taufa'ahau inherited the last of the three great titles. He was crowned King George Tupou on December 4, 1845. Taufa'ahau drew up a Constitution and modified noble privilege, concentrating his own authority.[11]

With the help of J. G. Moulton, who arrived in 1865, Tupou College was founded. With high academic standards, it educated a Christian governing elite, grounded in Methodism. Moulton's translations

Figure 15.2 "King George of Tonga" from George Brown, *An Autobiography*, London: Hodder & Stoughton, 1908, p. 456.

of the Bible and hymns were very influential, because of their language, which enriched everyday speech, as well as worship. The king wanted the Church to be more independent of the Australasian Wesleyan Conference and appointed Shirley Baker as prime minister in 1880 to achieve this end. For a variety of reasons, this process ended in Tongan dissociation and the formation of the Free Wesleyan Church. A minority, led by Moulton, remained part of the Australasian Conference and was brutally persecuted. Tonga was the only Polynesian territory not to be colonized. The royal family was also unique in the authority it exercised in both spiritual and political matters.

In Samoa, awareness of Christianity in Tahiti and Tonga was focused by the arrival of Tahitian teachers and kinship between Manono and Tonga.[12] Support from Malietoa, who held major titles, led to rapid observance of the Lotu Tahiti, especially keeping the Sabbath and a passion for literacy, which was believed to be a key to European superiority. Schools were another important sign of Christian allegiance. The absence of a strong priesthood led to a family-centered Christianity within village patterns of authority, with evening prayers and singing, a pattern still flourishing.

Marists, with Samoan teachers, went to Samoa in 1845, supplemented later by priests provided by Bishop Bataillon.[13] The support provided by Mata'afa, holder of a major title, at Mulinu'u was enhanced by his conversion. Titles in Tonga and Samoa conferred status and authority in families and regions. Samoans were attracted by the ceremonies of Catholicism, the dignity of priestly vestments, and the sense that they could link with an international Church. Development of an indigenous priesthood, comparable to the ministries of the LMS and Wesleyans, remained a dream till late in the twentieth century. Nevertheless, French priests localized effectively in Polynesian societies, creating closely knit communities and offering opportunities for education that diminished the foreignness of worship in Latin and governance from French bishops.

Local Governance

LMS missionaries, prodded by London, gradually extended the authority of teachers, ordaining them, creating a Council of Elders, and Fono Tele (Great Council). Increasingly, Samoans expected missionaries to implement their advice in the Samoan District Committee. Wesleyans were part of the Australasian General Conference. Both denominations established influential theological colleges at Malua and Piula respectively, as well as developing a network of village schools. LMS leaders, such as J. E. Newell, adapted skillfully to the establishment of a German Protectorate in 1900, welcoming the end of internecine wars. Partnership with German missions made possible the sending of Samoan missionaries to New Guinea.[14] Mormons and Seventh-day Adventists struggled to survive, for they did not engage with Samoan culture, remaining separated enclaves.

The LMS extended their reach to Polynesian outliers, such as Niue, Tokelau, and Tuvalu (formerly Ellice Islands). Niue, unlike other parts of Polynesia, had no hereditary chiefs. Its 5,000 people were fiercely resistant to the introduction of Christianity, but Peniamina, a Niuean, broke down some opposition. Paulo, from Samoa, finally persuaded many islanders that peace inspired by the new religion was better than constant war. By 1852, there was a significant group of worshipers. W. G. Lawes and his brother Frank encouraged the Niueans to express their faith in traditional ways. After all, they had become Christians for Polynesian reasons.

The same processes can be observed in Tuvalu, a group of eight atolls, to which Samoan teachers came in 1865. Chiefs' and pastors' authority combined to establish a new sacred order. For church and other purposes, Samoan replaced the local language. The Samoan Bible was used, until finally replaced by a Tuvaluan version in the twentieth century. Tuvalu was a Christian micro-society with no resident missionary until 1958. Polynesian love of singing, dancing, and oratory flourished, along with careful Sabbath observance and some adaptation of Polynesian values to the codes of the Old Testament. The Tokelau Group, spread over 200 kilometres, was also closely related to Samoa.

Reactions to Colonialism

That interaction was underscored by the emergence of Polynesian variants of missionary Christianity, in which the boundaries between the primal sacred and the common were redrawn on Polynesian terms. The Mamaia movement emerged on Tahiti and the Leewards, led by Teao and Hue, between 1826 and 1841. It included reversion to polygamy and extramarital relations, as well as aspects of Millenarianism. Some chiefs supported it, for they resented the way their status and authority had been affected. In Samoa, the Siovili cult had different dynamics, emerging before significant missionary influence, but reflected Siovili's contact with Christianity.[15]

The interaction between European colonialism and Polynesian Christianity can best be illustrated by changes that occurred in Tahiti, following the establishment of the French Protectorate. Some LMS missionaries were willing to work on French terms, but others believed that the Paris Mission should take over superintendence of the churches. The handover began in 1863. The French missionary families, such as the Vienots and Verniers, provided outstanding leadership. They developed an appropriate Constitution, avoided involvement in politics, and skillfully navigated the increasingly anti-clerical policies of French governments, which were disastrous for the Picpus Fathers. In other ways they were influential leaders in education, in founding the Blue Cross to counter alcohol abuse, and contributing to civic bodies. Some British LMS missionaries were willing to work with the French colonial regime, but others felt that this would marginalize the indigenous Church. Handing

over their work to the Paris Mission was therefore the best long-term solution, because they could deal directly with the French government in Paris.

The French missionaries fostered vigorous congregational life along Polynesian cultural lines. They enhanced the Maohi ethos of the Church, ensuring that the language survived at the congregational level, even though it was forbidden in schools. *Himene* (hymns) retained pre-Christian elements, *tuaroi* were popular debates on the meaning of the Bible, and the Me celebrations provided opportunity for cultivating unity. They were not significantly affected by French separation of Church and state in 1905, for that did not apply in French Polynesia. Although Catholic parishes lacked the cultural integration of Protestant congregations, expansion continued steadily, especially among the migrant Chinese community. Marquesans remained largely Catholic. A Catholic Bible was published in 1914. The Sanitos, or Reorganised Latter-day Saints, had become the third largest church by the beginning of the twentieth century.

Wallis, Futuna, and parts of French Polynesia were mini-kingdoms, integrated around monarchical Catholicism. Here too, there were important adjustments to Polynesian priorities, especially where clergy and bishops were alert to these. The French separation of Church and state in 1905 dramatically reduced financial support and the supply of clergy, for all religious houses were closed. Locals had not been educated to support their clergy.

In the twentieth century, the churches were less led by missionaries, for the colonial context had changed. New Zealand assumed rule in the Cook Islands, Tokelau, and Niue, as well as taking over Samoa from the Germans after their defeat in 1918. Missionary authority was weakened by the expansion of government functions, even though the missionaries remained influential, when they had served for long periods. The life of Polynesian Christians and their patterns of worship did not change significantly, but their role in governance began to widen.

Samoan Devolution

That was especially the case in Western Samoa. New Zealand rule aroused increasing opposition from

Samoans, who were angered by the dismissive way some of the administrators dealt with their culture. The influenza pandemic had a huge impact on Church leaders, making it harder to deal with the problems of the 1920s, because so many had died. The rejection of colonial authority through the movement named the Mau was badly handled and affected the LMS Church very seriously. Offerings were cut off because some missionaries were seen as opponents of the Mau's plea for political independence. Civil war was averted through the work of R. Bartlett, a specially chosen LMS worker. His capacity for negotiations with both sides led to Samoans laying down their arms. Similar tensions in American Samoa were firmly dealt with by the authorities.

In addition, newly arrived LMS missionaries were alarmed by Samoan demands for more than an advisory role. Matters reached a crisis when the Samoan District Committee in 1928 needlessly dismissed the Fono Tele, or Great Council, which was a vital meeting time for Christians from all over Samoa. The London office sent two retired missionaries, Hough and Parker, to deal with the situation. They recommended that consultation needed to be significantly widened.[16] Bishop Darnand and E. Shinkfield, a Methodist, also played a similar mediating role within their communities. Increased responsibility for senior ministers and their partnership with chiefs led eventually to the LMS Church playing an important part in discussions that led to independence in 1962.

Tongan Reunion

In Tonga important changes occurred through Queen Salote's initiative in reuniting the Free Church, founded in 1885, and the Wesleyan Church in 1924. Although some in the Free Church stayed out and attempted to claim all the property of the Free Church, they lost the legal battle. Chiefly and island rivalries led to the formation of the Church of Tonga, strongest on Vava'u. Although R. Page became President of the Free Wesleyan Conference in 1925 and held office until he left Tonga, he was very careful to advise, rather than dominate. He and his colleague A. H. Wood at Tupou College did a great deal to bring unity to the

new Church, working closely with the Queen, who highly valued their work. She retained considerable authority over the conference and appointments, as well as enhancing work amongst women.[17]

Although the new Church was a conference within the General Conference in Australia, that relationship was handled carefully and did not lead to domination, as some Tongans had feared. The survival of traditional convictions about healing indicated that there were areas of Tongan Christianity where missionary influence had been slight. Although there was revival in the 1920s, which replicated some of the early features of Tongan Methodism, there was still a strong strand of legalism. The establishment of a Free Wesleyan theological college in 1933 was an important forward move. Catholicism under Bishop Blanc showed little sign of growth and priestly vocations were rare. The most effective Catholic work was through the schools of the Sisters of the Third Order of Mary and their pastoral influence.

In the Cook Islands, close relations with the Church in French Polynesia remained. The centenary of missionary contact was joyfully celebrated in 1923. Apathy in congregations was growing, indulgence in bush beer was a serious problem, and sexual behavior did not always conform to missionary expectations. The colonial authorities refused to enforce some of the historic LMS laws, supported by some chiefs, restive about the decline in their status and authority. Takamoa continued to train pastors and missionaries, secondary schools were established, with Marists and Seventh-day Adventists also seeking a foothold through the founding of schools. Few islanders joined them as members.[18]

Moving to Political Independence

World War II did not lead to a Japanese invasion of Polynesia. The American troops, who came in their tens of thousands, brought massive injections of cash and infrastructure into subsistence economies, as well as anti-colonial ideas, new hymns, and wider denominational horizons. French Polynesians opted for the Free French government and fought in their forces, for they had become loyal to France. In turn, that brought fresh perspectives to both Protestant and Catholic Churches.

Tongans contributed to the British war effort, just as Samoans and Cook Islanders did to New Zealand's. In the immediate post-war years, Cook Islanders in increasing numbers migrated to New Zealand for education and employment. People from Tokelau, Niue, and Samoa followed the same pattern, providing income for their relatives at home and for the churches there. Catholics from Wallis and Futuna traveled in increasing numbers to New Caledonia, undermining the close links between ecclesiastical and chiefly authority and developing closer links with mainstream French culture.

Post-war Changes

All the Polynesian churches, from the 1950s, faced the challenge of new religious ideas, the stirrings of demand for political independence and economic changes toward a cash economy. Mormons poured huge sums of money into the building of schools and churches. Increasing membership led to the formation of stakes, wards, and growing numbers entering the priesthood. Control from Salt Lake City was still all-embracing and little attention was given to becoming more indigenous. Yet the largest Tongan Free Wesleyan congregation is found in Salt Lake City, indicating that practical educational and employment advantages can outweigh indigenization. In Tuvalu, social and political change led to the emergence of a politically and religiously independent micro-state in 1978. Niue and Tokelau continued in association with New Zealand, but their Churches remained politically as well as culturally influential. Pitcairn Island, still linked with Britain, is a religious anomaly. Its tiny population is Seventh-day Adventist. Other Polynesian outliers, such as Tikopia, are part of Melanesian Churches.

Pressures from the United Nations grew for New Zealand to move from trusteeship to the grant of independence for Samoa, achieved in 1962. The Congregational Christian Church of Samoa was created. Its college at Malua was upgraded by Dr John Bradshaw, who served there from 1954 until 1965. It has become an outstanding educational institution under the leadership of Dr O. Perelini. Bradshaw also was crucial in fostering new forms of worship, contemporary hymns, and helping the transition to an independent Church, as was B. Thorogood in the Cook Islands, semi-independent from New Zealand in 1965, even though the fundamental ethos changed little in both countries.

Outward Migration

By the 1970s, the number of Cook Island congregations linked with the Congregational Church at home had begun to grow steadily because that provided a familiar religious context, even though many migrants joined the Presbyterian Church of New Zealand in 1969. Samoan Methodists were slower to follow into church self-government, for they still valued their ties with the Australian Conference, but a separate conference was set up in 1964. Staff at Piula is now all Samoan, most with overseas postgraduate degrees. Most Island theological colleges now teach for undergraduate degrees, leaving postgraduate teaching to the colleges in Suva, Fiji. In American Samoa, links with American Methodism were strengthened. The LMS churches there separated with some animosity from those in Western Samoa in 1980, associating with the United Church of Christ, though family and cultural ties remained strong.[19] Mormons built a temple at Pesega in 1985.

French Developments

In French Polynesia, the possibilities of political independence were slender because such colonies were regarded as constitutionally part of France. Nevertheless, atomic testing between 1966 and 1995 and the granting of independence to French colonies elsewhere led to discussions about politics, which the French authorities found difficult. In 1958, a referendum was held on continuing association with France. Pressure grew for the use of Maohi in schools and the media. Pouvanaa Oopa, once a deacon, moved into politics, advocating Tahiti for Tahitians. He was tried for subversion and exiled to France from 1959 until

1968, but became a Senator in 1971, as well as founding his own church.[20] In 2004, French Polynesia was made an overseas country of France.

The French authorities regarded the Protestant Church as simply an association for worship, without recognizing that it was fundamental to French Polynesian identity. In 1963, it became independent of the Paris Mission. Its leaders also became active in the Pacific Conference of Churches, founded in 1966, after a groundbreaking Pacific-wide conference in Samoa in 1961. John Doom, for example, became a leading opponent of French and American atomic testing in this ecumenical body, which has mediated new directions. In 2006, he became a member of the Central Committee of the World Council of Churches and in 2009 a vice president. This was an example of the modest way in which a small Pacific Church could contribute to world Christianity, despite distance from centers of power.

Growing numbers of French atomic staff and increasing tourism challenged traditional Christianity. The Evangelical Church changed its name to the Ma'ohi Protestant Church in 2004, symbolizing its role in sustaining Maohi identity when new religious groups, such as Pentecostals, were challenging the traditional Churches' ways of being Christian. Changes in worship, governance, and mission were essential if young people were to be retained. Conservative members needed to be won over to accept changes to historic relationships between the Gospel and Maohi culture.

Recent leaders of the Ma'ohi Protestant Church have taken important initiatives, which have had no counterpart elsewhere in Polynesia. It was established that 50 percent of the Church's executive must be young people. Serving for five years gives them an opportunity to become future leaders. The general secretary, Seline Hoiore, is a lay woman, who is also deputy moderator of the Pacific Conference of Churches. Her senior leadership role in Tahiti has no parallel in other Polynesian Churches. With Pastor Maraea, the forward-looking President of the Protestant Church, giving leadership with spiritual depth, significant attempts are being made to arrest the declining influence of the Church and to heal some debilitating splits. Ministry as mediation is being explored. Catholics had successfully incorporated char-

ismatic renewal since the 1980s and also welcomed a major movement of Chinese Tahitians into the Church.

Educational Advances

Advanced theological education was provided in Suva, Fiji, through the Pacific Theological College (1966) and the Pacific Theological Seminary (1972), which aimed to teach students in both French and English, in order to equip future ministers and priests to lead their local Melanesian and Polynesian churches in a rapidly changing world. The staff had become largely indigenous by the twenty-first century and some have made valuable contributions to Pacific theological scholarship. Some graduates studied for doctorates elsewhere and returned to their local colleges and churches with perspectives that alarmed older clergy, who were poorly prepared to deal with theological challenges and pleas for new styles of ministry. Frustrated with the tension between tradition and desire to create new forms of Church, some Pacific Theological College graduates split from their mother Churches. If current challenges are to be met, scholarly leadership, however, will be important in both anglophone and francophone churches.

Resisting change was not a viable strategy, for tens of thousands of Polynesians were migrating. They had to adapt to new contexts. Their views inevitably affected their families and villages, especially because they sent remittances home, which became increasingly important to Polynesian Churches. Initially, migrants joined related Churches in their new homes, but increasingly the island Churches set up branches in Australia, New Zealand, and the United States, partly because they have a surplus of ministers. The Cook Islands Christian Church, for instance, aims to double its New Zealand congregations from 16 to 32. Adaptations and family rivalries affected home Churches, for migrants were not content simply to replicate historic patterns of worship and governance.

Ecumenism and Renewal

Another major set of changes came through the Second Vatican Council. Its emphasis on ecumenism and increased responsibility for mission churches led to the appointment of indigenous bishops, such as Pio Taofinu'u of Samoa in 1968, later appointed a cardinal. Relationships with Protestants slowly changed, leading to shared Bible translations, common statements on significant public questions, and some joint activities in ministry. In 1976, Catholics joined the Pacific Conference of Churches, much earlier than some Catholic Churches elsewhere. Charismatic emphases and the emergence of Pentecostal churches brought further variety. Young people in particular welcomed their music, more spontaneous worship, and the challenge to more dedicated discipleship.

In Tonga, a local renewal group emerged, the Tokaikolo Christian Fellowship, led by Senituli Koloi. His spiritual passion and healing ministry resonated with many Tongans who were looking for more than conventional piety. He separated from the Free Wesleyan Church in 1976. Nor did leaders, such as Dr S. A. Havea, persuade many Tongan Methodists that "coconut theology" (an attempt to restate Christianity in Polynesian categories) was an adequate substitute for traditional belief, formed in the missionary era. Its integration of the Gospel and Polynesian culture is still the dominant paradigm, unlikely to be changed in less than a generation, even with Methodist leaders of the scholarly stature of the current President and General Secretary of the Tongan Methodist Conference, Drs F. Ahio, and T. Havea.

Catholicism developed a sharper edge under the leadership of Bishop Finau, consecrated in 1972, whose concern for social justice led to the king accusing him of being a communist.[21] Catholics dealt more adequately than Methodists with the social and political challenges facing their nation, as well as indigenizing worship. The creation of a Pastoral Council in 1992 brought welcome consultation into decision-making. A Mormon temple was built in 1983 in recognition of the rapidly growing Tongan membership. Some Mormons even spoke hopefully of Tonga becoming the first Mormon nation.

Urbanization brought new relationships, charismatic renewal and tensions between denominations, challenges to pastors and congregations to develop new forms of religious education, and the need to recognize the changing roles of women, who slowly were being included in governance, both religious and political.

Their ordination is still not possible in most Churches. In Samoa, a Bible School was established in 2007, alongside Malua College, to give lay members opportunities for religious education.

Political independence meant that the Churches had to think in new ways about how to share in nation-building and economic development, instead of focusing on village life. Tongan Methodists and Catholics have found it hard to agree about the boundaries of democracy, though that changed in 2010, when all members of parliament became popularly elected. Another problem has been how to deal with Tongans convicted overseas and deported back to Tonga. Church relationships with Polynesian governments are close. The current General Secretary of the Cook Islands Christian Church is also Minister of Agriculture. The present king of Tonga is a lay preacher.

The churches are largely self-supporting, with talented, well-educated indigenous leaders. Many, such as Dr. U. Salavau, Secretary of the Congregational Christian Church in Samoa, have overseas education and professional experience. In another respect, knowledge of developments in other parts of the Pacific has declined because island missionaries have largely stopped working in Melanesia. Changes in worship and ministry are slow, but unavoidable because of the alternatives offered by new groups, mainly from the United States, often brought in by returning nationals.[22] Yet there have been signs that many Polynesian Churches sideline difficult issues, rather than working through them or welcoming initiatives by younger clergy, because senior ministers still exercise such authority.

A Distinctive Christianity

A Pacific identity was emerging, overlaying historic cultural divisions, because of increased opportunities for travel overcoming geographical isolation, alongside the effects of the impact of migration, ecumenism, and tourism. Limited economic resources, government inefficiency, some corruption, environmental degradation, over-population, and new social problems pose serious challenges, as does the growing gap between the wealthy and disadvantaged. Some churches are overweighted with administrative costs, lack adequate auditing, and are increasingly dependent on overseas grants for initiatives needed to cope with rapidly changing societies. There are sharp divisions about how best to cope with change and how to minister to members overseas without jeopardizing relations with partner churches, especially in Australia and New Zealand.

Nevertheless, Polynesia is one of the most strongly Christian regions in the world; despite the impact that religious pluralism has had in the last 50 years. Christianity was rapidly and successfully incorporated into Polynesian culture. War and slavery disappeared. Remarkable numbers of indigenous missionaries worked in both Polynesia and Melanesia. Governance of the churches was shaped by British and French missionaries, but Polynesian patterns of authority remained influential. Since the 1940s, American influence has grown and political independence has changed the churches' environment. They still, however, retain their strong communal base in meeting the challenge of translating their historic heritage in a rapidly changing context. Their small size and distance from other churches has meant that their international influence has been small, compared with the impact of Asian and African churches.

Notes and References

[1] T. Swainson and G. Trompf, eds *The Religions of Oceania* (London: Routledge, 1995); I. Goldman, *Ancient Polynesian Society* (Chicago, IL: University of Chicago Press, 1970).

[2] J. Wilson, *Missionary Voyage* (New York: Praeger, n.d.).

[3] J. Garrett, *To Live among the Stars* (Suva, Fiji: Institute of Pacific Studies, 1982), 13–42; H. Vernier, *Au vent des cyclones,* Papeete: Église évangélique de Polynésie Française, 1985.

[4] Garrett, *To Live among the Stars,* 81–7, 116–21.

[5] R. G. Crocombe, ed., *The Works of Ta'unga* (Canberra: Australian National University, 1987); P. Buck, *Mangaia and the Mission* (Suva, Fiji: Institute of Pacific Studies, 1993); M. Crocombe, ed., *Cannibals and Converts* (Suva, Fiji: Institute of Pacific Studies, 1983), 62ff.; A. Greiler, ed., *Catholic Beginnings in Oceania,* (Adelaide: Australian Theological Foundation, 2009).

[6] R. Wiltgen, *The Founding of the Catholic Church in Oceania* (Canberra: Australian National University, 1979); P. Gallagher, *The Marist Brothers in NZ, Fiji and Samoa* (Tuakau: Marist Bros Trust Board, 1976).

[7] Garrett, *To Live among the Stars,* 88–96; P. Hodee, *Tahiti 1834–1984* (Paris: Archveche de Papaeete, 1983).

[8] F. Angleviel, *Les Missions a Wallis et Futuna* (Bourdeaux: Michel de Montaigne University, 1994).

[9] S. Latukefu, *Church and State in Tonga* (Canberra: Australian National University, 1974); E. Wood-Ellem, ed., *Tonga and the Tongans* (Melbourne: Tongan Research Association, 2007), 47–59, 87–102.

[10] M. Dyson, *My Story of Samoan Methodism* (Melbourne: Ferguson & Moore, 1875), 29–37.

[11] Latukefu, *Church and State in Tonga,* 22–51.

[12] Garrett, *To Live among the Stars,* 121–35.

[13] J. Heslin, *History of the Roman Catholic Church in Samoa* (Apia, Western Samoa: J. Heslin, 1995), 24–30.

[14] J. Garrett, *Footsteps in the Sea* (Suva, Fiji: Institute of Pacific Studies, 1992), 197–9.

[15] J. D. Freeman and W. R. Geddes, eds *Anthropology in the South Seas* (New Plymouth: Thomas Avery, 1959).

[16] I. Breward, *History of the Churches in Australasia* (Oxford: Oxford University Press, 2001), 276–8.

[17] E. Wood-Ellem, *Queen Salote of Tonga* (Auckland: Auckland University, 1999), 276–8.

[18] J. Garrett, *Footsteps in the Sea,* 424–5.

[19] J. Garrett, *Where Nets were Cast* (Suva, Fiji: Institute of Pacific Studies, 1997), 245–53; R. Allardice, *The Methodist Story in Samoa* (Apia, Western Samoa: Methodist Church, 1984).

[20] J. Garrett, *Where nets were cast,* 413–17; B. Saura, *Politique et Religion à la Tahiti* (Papaeete: Polymages-Scoop, 1993).

[21] D. Mullins, *Bishop Pateliso Finau* (Auckland: Catholic Publications Centre, 1974), and *He Spoke the Truth in Love* (Auckland: Catholic Publications Centre, 1994).

[22] Indispensable sources on recent developments include M. Ernst, *The Role of Social Change in the Rise and Development of New Religious Groups in the Pacific Islands* (Hamburg: Lit, 1996), and *Globalization and the Reshaping of Christianity in the Pacific Islands* (Suva, Fiji: Pacific Theological College, 2006).

Further Reading

Britsch, R. L. *Unto the Islands of the Sea.* Salt Lake City: Deseret, 1986.

Crocombe, R. G. et al. *Polynesian Missions in the Pacific.* Suva, Fiji: Institute for Pacific Studies, 1992.

Ernst, M. and Nokise F., eds. *The Pacific Islands.* Suva, Fiji: Pacific Theological College, 2009.

Fer, Y. *Pentecostisme en Polynesie Francaise.* Geneva: Labor et Fides, 2005.

Garrett, J. *To Live among the Stars*. Suva, Fiji: Institute for Pacific Studies, 1982.

Garrett, J. *Footsteps in the Sea*, Suva, Fiji: Institute for Pacific Studies, 1992.

Garrett, J. *Where Nets were Cast*, Suva, Fiji: Institute for Pacific Studies, 1997.

Herda, P. et al. *Vision and Reality in Pacific Religion*. Canberra: Pandanus, 2005.

Lange, R. *Island Ministers*. Canberra: Pandanus, 2005.

Saura, B. *La Société Tahitienne au Miroir d'Israel*. Paris: CRNS, 2005.

16

Christianity in Micronesia
The Interplay between Church and Culture

Francis X. Hezel

Historical Overview

In June of 1668, six Jesuit priests, together with lay mission helpers and a force of Spanish troops, landed on Guam to begin evangelizing the people of the Mariana Islands. Guam is by far the largest of the islands scattered throughout the Western Pacific north of the equator, an extensive area that is known as Micronesia. The area includes what today are known as the island nations of Palau, Federated States of Micronesia, Republic of the Marshall Islands, Kiribati and Nauru, as well as the US territory of Guam and the Commonwealth of the Northern Mariana Islands. The arrival of this missionary band marked the beginning of evangelization in Micronesia, indeed the earliest sustained attempt at evangelization anywhere in the Pacific. The arrival of Catholic priests was followed by a period of intermittent hostilities between the Spanish and local people and a disastrous loss of life resulting from diseases that the Europeans introduced. By the turn of the century, both the flag and the faith were planted, and the Spanish kept Guam and the rest of the Marianas as a colony for the next 200 years. Two Jesuit attempts to introduce Catholicism to the neighboring Western Carolines in the beginning of the eighteenth century were unsuccessful, however.

It was only in the mid-nineteenth century that Christianity was first introduced to the rest of Micronesia. Not long after American whalers had discovered the attractions of Pohnpei and Kosrae as refreshment ports, reportedly "deepening the shadows of heathenism" with the corrupting influence of their own conduct, the American Board of Commissioners for Foreign Missions (ABCFM) missionaries and their Hawaiian co-workers founded a mission in the Eastern Carolines in 1852. Over the course of the next two or three decades, they established growing Congregational churches on Pohnpei, Kosrae, the Marshalls, and the Gilberts (Kiribati). By the early 1870s, the American Board missionaries had trained a group of Pohnpeian mission teachers, a few of whom were deployed to Chuuk to the west to bring the Church to the Mortlocks. Within a short time some of these men and their wives had made their way from these atolls to the high islands of Chuuk where, aided by American missionaries, they quickly established the faith throughout the entire island group. By the end of the century, the Congregational Church was solidly established throughout the eastern part of Micronesia: the Eastern Carolines (Pohnpei, Kosrae, and Chuuk), along with the Marshall Islands, Nauru, and Kiribati.

When Spain pressed its claim for title to the Caroline Islands in 1885, against the counter-claims of Germany, the islands were awarded to Spain by papal arbitration. Within a year or two, Spanish Capuchin missionaries were landed on most major island groups to establish Catholicism there. In the Western Carolines (Yap and Palau) this was to be the initial contact

Introducing World Christianity, First Edition. Edited by Charles E. Farhadian.
© 2012 Blackwell Publishing Ltd. Published 2012 by Blackwell Publishing Ltd.

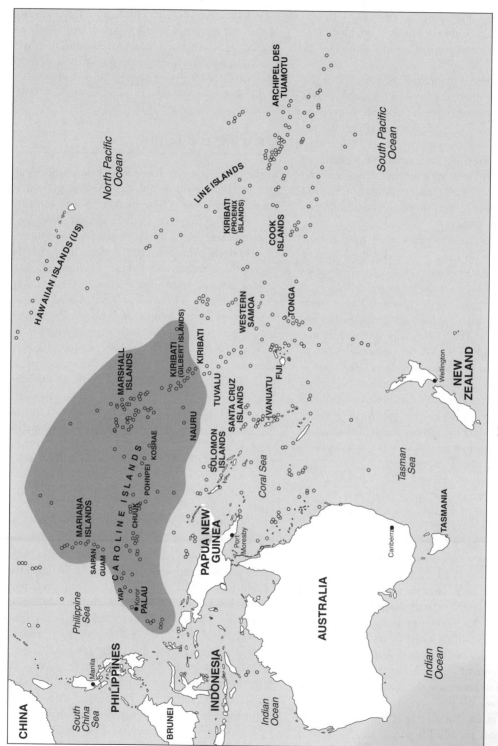

Map 16.1 Micronesia

of islanders with Christianity. In the east, Catholic missionaries would contest the fields in which American Protestant missionaries had already labored for 20 or 30 years.

In 1899, as Germany acquired the islands that the Spanish had once ruled, the German Capuchin priests and brothers who replaced the Spanish Capuchins continued to extend Catholicism throughout the region. In 1911, priests were sent to Chuuk, where they rapidly gained adherents. Meanwhile, Missionaries of the Sacred Heart took up work in Nauru and the Marshalls, focusing chiefly on the islands of Jaluit and Likiep, while their French-speaking colleagues concentrated on the Gilberts.

The Congregational churches were by this time operating largely on their own under local pastors. The number of American and Hawaiian missionaries had dropped sharply over the years and fell off even more in the early twentieth century. On the other hand, German evangelical Liebenzell missionaries entered the scene in 1907. Originally destined for the China Inland Mission (CIM), the missionaries had to be reassigned after the Boxer Rebellion (1900) put an end, temporarily at least, to the influx of foreign missionaries in China. In 1929, Liebenzell missionaries expanded their work to include the Western Carolines, soon spreading throughout the area from Palau to the outer islands of Chuuk to serve as a counterbalance to the Catholic efforts there.

Catholic missionary efforts continued throughout the twentieth century, for the development of local church leadership in Catholicism has always lagged behind the Protestant churches, in good part because of the demands of priestly celibacy and the long seminary training requirements. Spanish Capuchins on Guam were replaced by Americans until, after World War II, local vocations to the priesthood multiplied sufficiently to staff the parishes. Spanish Jesuits provided the manpower needed to build the churches in the Northern Marianas and Carolines and Marshalls until the end of World War II. Thereafter, American Capuchins staffed the Marianas, while American Jesuits continued the work of their Spanish brothers through the post-war era up to the present. Missionaries of the Sacred Heart only recently resumed the work they had begun in the Marshalls a century earlier, even as they continued their pastoral

aid in Kiribati and Nauru. Throughout the second half of the century, the Catholic Church was finally beginning to be entrusted, slowly at first and then with increasing rapidity, to the leadership of those islanders who had for so long been hearers rather than preachers of the Word.

Drawing the Line

In the early stages of their work, missionaries established markers to distinguish their neophytes from the general population. These markers, which served to offer Christian followers a public identity, were more often than not determined in opposition to features of the traditional culture that the missionaries regarded as pagan. On Pohnpei and Kosrae, for instance, those seeking admission into the Protestant Church were expected to abstain from *sakau* (kava), a drink that was widely used by the people on both islands on ceremonial occasions. Kava, which was employed in the ancient religious rites and taken as preparation for communicating with the spirits, symbolized adherence to the old ways. Rejection of the drink, on the other hand, signified that a person was ready to make a definitive break with everything in the culture that the missionaries judged to be idolatrous or superstitious. In the Marshalls, where tattooing was invested with religious significance, those who wished to become members of the Congregational Church were enjoined to refuse to submit to tattooing when they came of age.

In Chuuk and the central Carolines, as in many other parts of the Pacific, participation in local dances often became the shibboleth. Local dances were judged to be licentious, not just because of suggestive bodily movements, but because of the context in which they were held. Even into the early twentieth century local dances were a carnival-style event, often lasting several days and accompanied by feasting, a setting that was calculated to create a frenzied sense of abandon among the island population. Sexual excesses were an expected outcome of such events. The German colonial authorities in Chuuk, who initially encouraged a revival of traditional dancing, were forced to impose strict limits on the duration of island dances following the turn of the twentieth century after one of the atolls hosted its neighbors for a dancing display that lasted two and a half months. At the end of it all, the atoll's food supplies had been depleted, and the exhausted population faced near starvation for the next several months. In Ulithi, as in some of the other atolls, the sexual abandon associated with dances continued periodically until well into the twentieth century. It is not surprising, then, that dancing was near the top of most missionaries' prohibition list.

In islands where women traditionally went bare-breasted and men often wore little more than a loincloth, Western clothing soon came to be a distinguishing feature of Protestant converts. Islanders everywhere happily donned trousers and shirts or calico dresses at the missionaries' injunction, if only because they considered foreign clothing a stylish advance rather than an imposition. Marshallese chiefs, who had the money to do so, outfitted themselves in suits and vests and beamed from under top hats, despite the heat and humidity.

Even Catholic missionaries, generally more accepting of cultural differences, insisted on conformity at times. A Franciscan nun who had just arrived in Yap in 1905 described, in an unintended but striking allegory of local reaction to cultural imposition, how the young school-girls would gather on Sunday afternoon preparing to begin the new school week, discard the grass skirts they customarily wore in their own villages and don the dresses required of them in the classroom. In Catholic schools of that day as well as Protestant, what was acceptable in the village did not meet acceptable dress standards in school. The same nun noted that at meal times the nuns would watch to make sure that the girls were using their knives and forks rather than their fingers.

In its initial phase at least, Christianity in all its denominational forms tended to define itself in opposition to the culture. Even today we witness some of the more recent Christian arrivals – Pentecostal churches and small evangelical groups – doing much the same thing, as they thunder against select cultural practices, denouncing them as the deceits of darkness. Older denominations, on the other hand, have had to come to terms with the culture and its practices. In doing so, they tend to eschew the simple dichotomies that once served to demarcate the light of Christ from the darkness of the traditional culture.

Backlash to Christianity

Whatever the feelings of Micronesian islanders toward Christianity, island people normally accorded a status of immunity to the missionaries themselves. Thus, Robert Logan, the well-known Congregational pastor working in Chuuk in the early 1880s, could sally into the thick of battle unharmed, his trademark black umbrella in hand. More often than not, he could report that after his appearance the hostilities came to a quick end. The early Protestant missionaries to the Marshalls, an island group noted for its violence against visiting ships in the early nineteenth century, were protected by Kaibuke, the very chief who had sworn to avenge the death of his brother some years earlier by attacking every ship that anchored off Ebon. However adverse the effects of the religion they brought to the islands may have been judged, the person of the missionaries was protected.

Only in the Marianas in the late seventeenth century and during the first missionary sorties into the Western Carolines a few decades later were missionaries attacked and killed. Twelve Jesuit priests and brothers in the Marianas, together with perhaps two dozen lay catechists, and another three Jesuits in the Carolines died violent deaths. But they were accompanied by Spanish troops, whose rapaciousness and hauteur often made them more of a hindrance than a help to the missionaries they were supposed to protect. Had the missionaries undertaken their work without the protection of the state, they probably would have fared no worse than those who first brought the Gospel to Polynesia a century later.

Even so, the new religion faced severe struggles for legitimacy. At times its emissaries were pitted against priests of the local deities in contests that might have recalled the encounter of Aaron and Pharaoh's sorcerers.[1] The power of the Christian God was tested repeatedly by chiefs and adherents of traditional religious beliefs, although not always in confrontational fashion. As unsubstantial as the old religious systems might have seemed to foreign missionaries, it was unthinkable that local devotees would let them perish without a struggle.

When Benjamin Snow, the earliest Congregational missionary on Kosrae, first ventured into the more remote part of the island to preach the Gospel in 1856, he met stiff opposition from the priests of Sinlaka, one of the major deities there. Offended at Snow's intrusion, the priests threatened their people that any who attended Christian church services could expect swift punishment from the gods, perhaps in the form of another flu epidemic similar to the one that had claimed 100 lives the year before. When Snow's most devoted disciple was injured by a swordfish while out fishing one day, this was understood as a sign of Sinlaka's anger at those who espoused the new religion. Accordingly, most of the people kept their distance from the missionary, who watched his congregation dwindle to no more than two or three. The tables were turned a few years later, however, when the paramount chief, who was hostile to Christianity, suddenly dropped dead while he was inspecting the land he had just seized from one of Snow's church members. The power of the Christian God was not to be trifled with after all, Kosraeans realized.

In the nearby Marshall Islands, the reaction of island chiefs to Christianity soon changed from mild interest to decided coolness. With the death of Kaibuke, the paramount chief who had protected the missionaries during their first five years, resentment deepened and chiefs began to retaliate against those who had defected to the new religion. For the first time they began terrorizing new converts, in some cases even burning down their houses and threatening their lives. But this proved to be the final flailing of a traditional belief system that was soon to be dead.

Yap, an island known for its resistance to change, saw the rise of a cult movement in 1889, just three years after the arrival of the first Capuchin missionaries. The movement was led by seven local priests who prophesied that all foreign missionaries would be driven from Yap. They revived an old fertility cult in honor of the ancient Yapese spirits, promising that women who attended the religious dances held in the sacred site would become pregnant. For a time, the site was a gathering spot for all those who protested the arrival of Christianity. The Catholic priests reported with some self-satisfaction that the movement waned after the wives of five of the seven cult leaders died and several of the women devotees who had attended in the hope that they might have children either suffered miscarriages or died in childbirth.

The reversion to nativism that appeared in the Mortlock Islands, southeast of Chuuk, and in Palau was undoubtedly as much a reaction to government policies and other forces for change as it was to Christianity. A "wave of heathenism," as the Protestant missionaries called it, flared up intermittently in Mortlocks between 1903 and 1908. Besides the revival of old dances, it featured a return to traditional dress and the use of turmeric as adornment, reversion to mediums for contact with the spirits of the dead, and other forms of the shamanism associated with old deities. The movement, which never spread widely through Chuuk, seemed to burn itself out after a few years.

A few years later, in 1917, another nativistic movement sprang up in Palau when Temedad, a former policeman during the German administration, began undergoing seizures that were attributed to the god of his village. As a spirit medium and prophet, Temedad claimed healing powers and the ability to foresee the future. Gathering a group of close followers, he traveled the length of Palau predicting the day in which Palau would be free of foreign ways and their proponents. Although he was jailed by government authorities, Temedad's disciples carried on the Modekngei movement that he had founded. Long since stripped of its millenarian thrust while incorporating certain features of Christianity, the religion has retained followers up to the very present.

Church Contributions: Education and Healthcare

The first formal educational institution anywhere in the Pacific was San Juan de Letran on Guam, opened in 1669, the year after the missionaries arrived in the Marianas. A few years later another mission school was opened for girls. The schools, which operated throughout the next century, were the beginning of a long tradition of Christian involvement in education. The Congregational missionaries in the Carolines operated small schools throughout the region in the mid-nineteenth century, long before a public school system existed. A small printing press was standard mission equipment in those years, when pastors were heavily involved in translating scripture into the local languages for their flock. Catholics, by contrast, would invest their energy into translating devotional manuals, catechisms, and prayer books for their faithful. Edward Doane, an American Board missionary in the Marshalls, wrote in 1861 that eager schoolchildren milled around the handpress and snatched the broadsheets to read even before the ink was dry. Reading was all the rage in the islands the missionaries served, as he happily noted, and yearly mission summaries of the day tallied "readers" as well as converts.

As their flocks grew, American Protestant missionaries founded training schools, roughly the equivalent of high schools, where they could prepare the local men who would replace them as pastors and teachers and the women who would become their wives and supervise lessons for village children. The two most famous of these were the training school in Ohwa, Pohnpei, and an even larger one in Mwot, Kosrae.

From these schools would issue the first local missionaries to be sent to other islands in the region.

Catholics, especially during the twentieth century, opened some excellent schools. The German Missionaries of the Sacred Heart operated a full elementary school on Jaluit, in the Marshalls, that soon became the premiere school in all of Micronesia. After World War II, when American Jesuits assumed authority over the mission, they set up elementary schools and later high schools throughout the Caroline and Marshall Islands. The best-known and most highly regarded were Xavier High School in Chuuk, which was founded in 1952, and Pohnpei Agriculture and Trade School, opened in 1965. Both accepted students from every island group throughout the region. Meanwhile, the Capuchins established Mt Carmel School on Saipan and a network of parish elementary schools on Guam. Other religious Orders opened Father Duenas, a boys' high school, and two superior girls' schools, Our Lady

Figure 16.1 Fr. Edwin McManus with students at Maris Stella Elementary School, a Catholic school in Palau, 1965. Photo: Micronesian Seminar, Pohnpei. Used by permission.

of Mercy Academy and Notre Dame Academy. St John's Academy, arguably the best school in the region, was founded by the Episcopalian Church during the same period.

In Micronesia, as in many other places throughout the world, Christianity introduced education where there had been none. Because of the value the Church placed on Scripture, it played a pioneering role in the development of literacy. Even when public school systems were finally established, church-run schools, generally known for their superior quality, lifted educational standards. Today, private church-run schools enroll only about 10 percent of all schoolchildren in the region, perhaps half of the percentage that they educated during the early 1960s, the heyday of mission schooling. Nonetheless, the private schools have preserved their reputation for academic excellence up to the present.

Christian missions are not as well known for their efforts in providing healthcare to people who had none, but there are notable examples in the region. A little-known Jesuit brother, Jacopo Chavarri, assigned to the Marianas in 1693, served for 50 years as the pharmacist for a people decimated by a host of Western illnesses. Luther Gulick, the Congregational pastor-physician serving on Pohnpei during the dreadful smallpox epidemic in 1854 that wiped out nearly half the population, inoculated hundreds on the island, thus saving their lives. Fr Gebhard Rüdell, the German Capuchin who began the Catholic mission in the Mortlocks in 1911, found the people reeling from the shock of a major typhoon that had devastated their islands four years earlier and suffering from a virulent typhus epidemic that had taken many lives. Summoning medical supplies and a physician from Pohnpei, the priest began instructing people on how to improve the quality of their drinking water.

Long before dispensaries were opened in the villages, church pastors dispensed medicines, bandaged wounds, administered shots, and sometimes transported the sick to the nearest hospital. Medical supplies were routed to the churches from charitable organizations as well as from the government itself. The pastor, after all, was the best-educated and often the best-provisioned individual in the village, and so was expected to care for the bodily needs of his parishioners in the fashion of the Good Shepherd. Generations of

pastors did so during all those years when the sick had no one else, other than the local herbalist or healer, to whom they might turn.

Local Church Leadership

From the very outset of its missionary activity, the American Board set as its goal the establishment of local churches in the islands that would be "self-financing, self-governing, and self-propagating." While the Congregational churches were in no rush to make converts – it was six years before the first islanders were received into the Church on Pohnpei, and eight years on Kosrae – members were soon after elevated to leadership positions in the Church. By the early 1870s, just 20 years after the first American missionaries landed, a training school was in operation on Pohnpei to prepare local pastors, teachers, and deacons. If anything, the process was accelerated for the Marshalls and Gilberts. By 1880, when the training school for these island groups was relocated to Kosrae, the Church in these two archipelagos had been left to the care of a few Hawaiian teachers and a dozen or two Micronesians trained in the mission school.

The training school produced dozens of committed men and women to bring the faith to those islands in eastern Micronesia not yet evangelized. The second generation of Protestant missionaries consisted more often than not of islanders themselves, recent converts who had been elevated to leadership roles in their Church. By the turn of the century there were 20 ordained native pastors and 80 more preachers and teachers serving a total Church membership of over 6,000. In addition, the churches were well on the way to becoming self-supporting with their annual collections of about $7,000.

Catholics found it impossible to match this achievement, partly because there were no intermediate offices in those days to help screen those who would become pastors. Leadership in the Catholic Church required one long, arduous leap from the pew to the pulpit that demanded commitment to the priesthood from the beginning. Other obstacles included long years of study abroad, severance of the priest from his own community, and a life of celibacy among a people for whom this was all but unthinkable.

As time went on, Catholics could and did serve as catechists, or village prayer leaders, but they could not preside at the Eucharistic celebration on Sunday. Only in the 1970s were married deacons incorporated into the Catholic Church leadership system – at first on Pohnpei, then in Chuuk, in Yap, and in the Marshalls. In recent years, deacons have provided the day-to-day leadership in many of the parishes throughout these island groups. Meanwhile, the development of local priests to replace foreign missionaries lagged for a long time. In the Marianas only two Chamorros had been ordained before the war, although there are now 21 local priests active on Guam and another four in the Northern Marianas. Progress was even slower in the Carolines and Kiribati where, apart from a single Pohnpeian Jesuit priest ordained in 1940, the first generation of priests appeared in the 1960s and 1970s. There are now 14 local priests working in the diocese of the Carolines, including two priests from Kiribati. In recent years Kiribati has been blessed with such an abundance of local clergy that they have not only staffed all the parishes there but also assisted in neighboring dioceses. The Marshalls and Nauru, on the other hand, still do not have a single local priest. Today the Catholic dioceses of the Northern Marianas, Guam, the Caroline Islands, and Kiribati all have local bishops at their head; only the Marshall Islands does not.

Inculturation of the Church

If, as we have seen, the Church initially defined itself in contrast to the culture, it follows that it eventually came to terms with the culture in which it was embedded. As this happened, it assimilated some of the cultural forms and began to reflect the values of the society that surrounded it. This slow process, which varied in manner and degree from place to place as the Gospel was digested by local congregations, may be called inculturation.

Changes in Church leadership may provide one example. While Congregational churches remained under the general supervision of American overseers until the early 1960s or so, the number of island pastors was limited. In 1965, for instance, Pohnpei Island had no more than two or three full pastors, with Church

teachers leading the weekly services in most of the island churches. On Kosrae two pastors served the entire population. After the American supervisors were withdrawn, the number of pastors, teachers, and deacons multiplied. Today Pohnpei has 20 or 30 ordained pastors, while Kosrae has 14. The number of pastors in Chuuk and the Marshalls increased in much the same way, so that a single congregation may well have had three or four ordained pastors at its head. The Church titles – deacons and teachers as well as pastors – have proliferated not so much because they are needed for the Church's smooth functioning, but so that they can be bestowed on distinguished members of the congregation in recognition of their contribution just as traditional titles were passed out in the old chiefly systems. The Catholic Church, as it has inculturated, has shown the same tendency in recent years. In Chuuk, for instance, there are now more than 40 ordained deacons, with as many as four or five on a small island in the lagoon. Today Church titles, besides being a call to service, are undeniably a path to prestige for those who hold them.

Even the way island churches support themselves is distinctive. At fund-raising events in Congregational churches individuals usually file up to a table in the front of the church and put down their contributions while the congregation sings lively hymns. More often than not, these events reflect the islanders' love of song and display. Kava plants and pigs may be raffled off at Catholic Church fundraising events on Pohnpei. A Catholic gathering to raise funds for a new church in Palau featured bands, take-out food, and other sales – all in a party atmosphere. In Chuuk, an old cultural form known as the *tëëchap* is frequently used, with each clan presenting in turn an envelope containing the money it has raised in advance, as the amount is marked on a board. Those who wish to add to their own clan's tally are encouraged to do so publicly. The competitive gift-giving contributes to the festivity while also encouraging more lavish generosity on the part of the congregation.

Church worship, too, eventually has taken on a distinctive island flavor. For decades after the arrival of the Church, religious services in the islands were almost indistinguishable from those held in other parts of the world. Then, following the Second Vatican Council (1962–5), Catholics consciously began to make liturgical adaptations aimed at making use of cultural symbols. Flower leis were placed on the heads of the newly baptized to signify the title they were receiving with the sacrament, and they were presented to the one presiding at the liturgy along with the gifts of bread and wine. During special liturgies in some churches, large feasting bowls were carried up, in time with traditional dance steps, at the presentation of gifts. Dances and chants were incorporated into various parts of the services. In a ritual evocative of the Pohnpeian ceremony conducted when forgiveness was being asked of a chief, *sakau* (kava) was symbolically offered to the Lord in communal reconciliation services held on Pohnpei. In Yap, famous for its dignified dances, distinctive island wailing and stately women's dances were introduced into the Holy Week services.

Church music, in the meantime, had undergone changes of its own. At first it was a cappella congregational singing of numbers translated from the standard European or American hymnals. It was not long, however, before islanders themselves began composing hymns with a distinctive island sound. Instrumental music, absent at first, was eventually supplied by organs, guitars, and often enough today by keyboards. The richness and variety of religious music today represents Church inculturation at its best.

Celebrations of major Church feast days have taken on the exuberance of island life. During the week before Easter, Congregational churches in eastern Micronesia – Pohnpei, Kosrae, Chuuk, and the Marshalls – have adopted the custom of rotating pastors. The visiting pastors are feted during the week and sent off at its end with furniture, household furnishings, and other gifts from the community they visited. Christmas celebrations are distinctive in each island group. In Kosrae, the congregation practices months ahead of time for a glittering marching display that is offered in the main church by various subgroups, all performed in beautifully tailored uniforms and dresses. In the

Figure 16.2   Women dressed in uniform for presentation of songs at the Christmas celebration in the Kosrae Protestant Church (Marshalls), c.1977. Photo: Micronesian Seminar, Pohnpei. Used by permission.

Marshalls, uniformed youth groups perform line-dancing routines known as *jeptas* (originally from the word "chapter," suggesting its biblical origins), with the whole performance sometimes lasting as long as an entire day and night. Catholics in Chuuk are more likely to celebrate feasts like Christmas and Easter with a long gathering, or *mwiich*, in the parish meeting house following church services. There, young people will present dramatizations of the events of these feasts, which are interspersed with short talks and hymns, many composed especially for the celebration.

In Guam and the Marianas, islands that remain strongly Catholic, villages celebrate the feast day of their patron saint with a fiesta even to the present day. The fiesta, with its Mass, procession behind the statue of their patron, and the feast afterwards, bears all the outward signs of Spanish influence during the long period of that country's colonial rule. Yet these fiestas reflect in equal measure something much older – the Micronesian partiality to a party, especially one that celebrates their locality and offers people the opportunity to show off their capacity to host guests in great number.

Impact of the Church on Society

If the evolving Church was clearly stamped with marks of the culture into which it had been introduced, the reverse was also true. In time, the island cultures began to exhibit the imprint of the Church.

Once the initial resistance to Christianity ended, the islands on which the new religion had taken root were pacified, and the overt hostilities that had periodically broken out between rival villages were terminated. It is true that the colonial authorities encouraged, even demanded, the cessation of warfare. Still, the churches contributed immeasurably to maintaining the peace simply through the presence of a local pastor who could serve as something of an ombudsman and mediate in intra-village tensions. The Church made perhaps an even greater contribution through the Gospel ethic of forgiveness that it preached. Missionary letters abound in stories of individuals who showed a heroic readiness to turn the other cheek even after suffering an injury that would have been a *causa belli* just a few years before. Some 30 years ago, a Chuukese man, holding the office of teacher in his church, gathered his family together after his daughter had been killed in a sexual assault and admonished his sons not to revenge themselves on the offender and his kin. Such heroic forbearance may not be the normal response even today, but it would have been unthinkable in the pre-Christian past.

Even beyond this, the Church offered a large banner under which smaller social and political units could unite. This was especially important on those islands in which there was no paramount chief. Belief in Christ provided a bond between people of different locales just as membership in the same clan had in the traditional times and continues to do today in many places. A shared faith embraced a far larger portion of the population than clan ties, however, while providing an ideological basis for regarding even the stranger with sympathy. Denominational differences within Christianity led to wariness and even recriminations at times, but except in parts of Kiribati for a short time there were no violent eruptions among Christians of different denominations.

The Church had a strong hand in abolishing the clubhouse prostitution that was a traditional feature of village life in the Marianas, Palau, and Yap. Christianity took a strong ethical stand, and a decidedly counter-cultural one, when it asserted that extramarital sexual relationships were wrong. As difficult as this teaching must have been for their converts, the early Jesuit priests in the Marianas recounted one story after another of women who were prepared to surrender everything, even their lives, to avoid transgressing this law. Even if the Church did not put an end to youthful sexual escapades as such, it did engender a sense that such adventures were not as harmless as they were once thought to be. In a day in which sexually transmitted diseases, including HIV, have cast a dark shadow over what may have once been regarded as natural self-expression, and when high teenage pregnancy rates, sexual assault, and incest have become serious problems, the Church's message was prophetic.

Observance of the Sabbath by abstaining from work and by attending church services was another gift from the Church to society. So successfully was this practice grafted on to society at large that up to the present day the common word for Saturday can be literally translated as "Day of Preparation" in the Chuukese,

FRANCIS X. HEZEL

240

Pohnpeian, and Marshallese languages since food was prepared on this day for the entire weekend. On those islands where Catholics, who were never as rigorous as Protestants in enforcing the Sabbath ban on work, arrived first, Saturday is simply called *Sabado*, the Spanish loanword for that day of the week. The strictness with which Sunday rest is observed today varies considerably from place to place, but everywhere the day is special.

Meetings of any sort in the islands today begin with a prayer even before the formal welcome. As secular-minded as they might otherwise be, international organizations and foreign groups are always advised to select a pastor from one of the local churches to handle this obligatory formality. It would be tempting to suggest that Christianity has had some influence on the agenda of many of these meetings, particularly those that deal in the currency of human rights, but that question may lie outside the scope of this chapter. Let it suffice to say that the impact of the Church has gone well beyond insuring that society makes time for religious activity, whether at the start of meetings or on the first day of the week. The Church has worked its way into the soul and heart of the society in a variety of other ways so that island society and the Church are closely intertwined today, for better or for worse.

Other Church Contributions

Neither missionaries nor the local pastors who followed them have ever been exclusively taken up with the care of souls, for they have recognized from the outset the link that exists between the body and soul – the material and spiritual dimensions in humans. The education that Christian churches have provided is just one aspect of the development work in which these churches have been engaged from the start. Just as they taught people to read and write, and dispensed medicine when they were sick, the churches have instructed people in new techniques of building and farming, improved sanitation, and even defended their people from the depredations of foreigners. What we today call human development has always been an integral part of church work in Micronesia, as in so many other parts of the world. Whatever theology it has used to justify such efforts, the Church has worked

tirelessly to build a new society, one founded on the love of Christ.

In the 1960s some of the Catholic missionaries in the Caroline Islands were engaged in promoting credit unions and cooperatives, the most notable of which were a housing coop on Pohnpei and a fishing coop in Chuuk. A German Liebenzell missionary on Yap started up a private airline that offered regular service to the outer islands of that area. Protestants and Catholics alike were a vital force in producing radio programs for broadcast on development themes, with some of the smaller Protestant groups eventually starting their own FM radio stations. Churches of all denominations had a large stake in youth work; most organized youth groups met regularly for religious instruction and recreational activities. In doing so, they also initiated programs for young people who wished to give up alcohol, tobacco, or any other "addiction" that they felt was harmful to their lives. These programs, situated squarely within a religious framework and offering group support from other like-minded youth, were an island alternative to the better-known but less culturally appropriate Twelve Step programs.

Churches have also made a significant contribution in scholarship. Early Protestant missionaries generally showed little interest in the traditional culture and took a purely functional view of the language, while Catholics, especially the German Capuchin and MSC missionaries, brought to their work a strong interest in anthropological and linguistic scholarship that issued in an impressive list of publications. The early linguistic contributions included August Erdland's dictionary and grammar of Marshallese, Callistus Lopinot's book on the Chamorro language, and Salvador Walleser's work on Palauan. Their contribution to the anthropological literature was even more impressive. Erdland produced a volume on Marshallese culture, Salesius Haas did a book on Yap, and Lorenz Bollig wrote what remains a classic work on Chuuk, not to mention the articles that were published in the German *Anthropos* series. In more recent years, German Liebenzell missionaries Klaus Müller and Lothar Käser have added to the flow of anthropological scholarship on the islands with their books on Chuuk. Ernest Sabatier wrote with rare insight on Kiribati and Nauru, while Edwin McManus later authored works on the Palauan language, and Elden Buck produced a Church history of Kosrae that was tantamount to an island history. Francis Hezel has written several historical works on the region in an attempt to fill the void that once existed in this discipline.

Many of the churches have expanded their educational sights to include the entire community. Perhaps the most reliable news outlet on Pohnpei today is the Baptist-run FM radio station. Other churches are engaged in the production of video programs that can be broadcast on local television channels. Micronesian Seminar, a research-education center established by the Jesuits in 1972, has become one of the outstanding resource centers for print and photographic materials on the area, while producing a large body of video programs and written papers on social issues. Micronesian Seminar also hosts a popular website (<www.micsem.org>) that offers its products to the thousands of Micronesians living abroad.

Possibly one of the most significant services rendered by the churches goes largely unrecognized, however. Church ministers, whether expatriate or local, have always been in an especially favorable position to broker in the conversation between local societies and the powers of the West. Dwight Heine, a Marshallese Protestant Church official, did this in the 1950s when he appeared before the UN Trusteeship Council to testify on the damage done to his people in the nuclear testing in the northern Marshall Islands. Some years later, other representatives from the United Church of Christ and the Catholic Church were weighing in on the effects of US political and economic policies on the local population. The ministers and priests who have been party to this dialogue do not simply serve as advocates, but as cultural interpreters between one conversation partner and the other.

Characteristics of the Micronesian Church

To state that the Church has become a significant part of the social landscape in the islands is to understate the fact. Indeed, in many places it is the dominant institution in the daily life of the people. There are parallels in other parts of the world, of course, but to find a suitable analogy in the West we would probably have to recall the importance of the Church in the late Middle Ages. In Europe then as in Micronesia today, the Church was so closely linked to the local community that they were all but indistinguishable. The Church calendar regulates much of the life of villagers; its choirs perform at community events; its pastors call down blessings at the onset of projects and the dedication of buildings; its policies are invoked as norms for community behavior.

This is not to say that government and Church have been fused; they remain institutionally distinct, even though their mutual influence on one another is great. If society and Church have developed a symbiotic relationship, it is less through institutional links as such than through personal ties. In small island societies government and traditional leaders more often than not also hold important positions in the churches. Johnny Hadley, who died not long ago on Pohnpei, is a good example: he served as a pastor in the Congregational Church, while he also held the second highest chiefly role in his large section of Pohnpei, and headed an important government office for years. Hence, this single individual combined leadership roles in what are viewed as the three distinct sectors of life on Pohnpei: government, Church, and custom.

The Church has also incorporated many of the features of traditional belief and practice, even some of those that might have been regarded as "heathenish" by early missionaries. Traditional island societies everywhere were populated by a host of spirits – nature spirits, patron deities, and guardian spirits of those who have died, to name but a few kinds. Spirit possession, which was a common occurrence in pre-Christian days, still appears to happen today, although often in reaction to some upsetting event within the family or community. The belief in spirits has survived the introduction of Christianity, but in our day most people go to the Church rather than to traditional healers for help in neutralizing their harmful influence. Priests are regularly summoned to exorcize "demons" from young women undergoing trance-like seizures, and blessed water is used to ward off such evil from other family members. In fact, crowds of people turn up at Catholic churches after the Easter Vigil services to fill their containers from the fonts of holy water blessed that evening. Sacred objects like religious medals and blessed palm leaves, as well as rituals and blessings, are as important today as they were in earlier times – and for the same reason. They are seen as protections from illness and other harm that is often attributed to sorcery worked by another person.

Micronesian churches, reflecting the spirit of the people, are strongly grounded in the concrete reality of island life. Hence, the churches put much heavier emphasis on behavior than on belief (which is taken for granted, in any case). It is hard to imagine island churches waging war with one another over the finer points of theology. On the other hand, discipline is a critical matter in determining who is in and who is out of the Church. Depending on the denomination, smoking, drinking, an adulterous affair, or a second marriage can distinguish the true member from the outsider in a way that interpretations of Christology never could. Likewise, when Churches split from one another, their differences invariably have far more to do with decisions affecting Church order – for example, on whether to ordain a certain person as pastor – than on doctrinal matters.

Overall, the words of Charles Forman's depiction of the Pacific Church – "a folk church representing the society and reflecting its standards rather than a prophetic church" – ring as true today as ever.[2]

Challenges of the Church Today

The Church in Micronesia has made great progress in meeting the challenge of inculturation; today it is tightly woven into the fabric of society. The danger, however, is that the Church may have become too domesticated – that fitting comfortably into the large niche that has been carved for it, the Church might be a little too accommodating to society. If the risk of the past was that the Church might overlook the value of island culture, the danger in our own time is that the Church might become a prisoner to culture. The Church is called to be a prophetic voice calling whole peoples, not just individuals, to the service of the Lord. It is tempting for local churches to abandon their prophetic role on the grounds that the Pacific way is non-confrontational.

The Church in Micronesia also faces the danger of becoming too inward-looking. It can easily become absorbed in institutional glitter or the increase of its

membership at the expense of its broader evangelizing mission. Just as fundraising is competitive in the Pacific, so is the design and construction of churches, with each local community eager to outdo the others. Someone once stated, with some justice, that competitive church-building is the national sport in Micronesia. It is tempting to bask in its pride of place in the community rather than risk walking the alleyways of Babylon. It is safer to tend its flock exclusively instead of offering outreach to the broader community, to restrict its message to narrowly defined religious topics rather than attempt its larger task of providing healing service to the world.

Finally, the Church is called on to respond to the new religious groups that have begun work in the islands in the last 20 or 30 years. Many of these new groups are mistrusted and even feared for their aggressive evangelism. The new spirit of understanding and collaboration among older denominations, a hard-won achievement after a century or more of suspicion, seems to be threatened by these new hard-line religious groups. The challenge for the Micronesian Church here is not only to preserve the ecumenism that has been achieved but also to extend it to these groups as well, while stoutly refusing to revert to a simplistic spiritualism in order to protect its membership.

Conclusion

Since those first missionaries arrived in the islands – over three centuries ago in the Marianas and more than a century and a half ago in the rest of the area – Christianity has carried on a deep engagement with the island cultures of Micronesia. At times, the new religion was enthusiastically embraced by the peoples it hoped to transform, while on other occasions it provoked resentment and even open hostility. Over the years the churches have made singular contributions to island life, perhaps none more valued than their pioneering work in formal education and their contributions to basic healthcare. What's more, in translating the Bible into local languages, they have given the island cultures a body of written material – often the only one in island tongues. In recent years, churches have sponsored community development projects of different kinds, even as they have contributed to research on island cultures and languages.

In their encounter with local peoples, the churches themselves have been transformed, as we have seen. Church worship, church life, and church leadership have all taken on many of the features of the societies in which Christianity has been transplanted. To call Christianity a foreign-born institution is to tell only half the story; it is to omit mention of the ways in which Christian churches have been adapted to the socio-cultural environments in which they have been introduced.

Christianity, of course, brings a belief system and a set of values that has been embedded in the island cultures of Micronesia. Indeed, the beliefs and values, along with the practices that accompany them and the institutions that support them, have been woven so tightly into the culture that in some places, especially the Marianas and Kosrae, the churches can be barely distinguished from the general social landscape. Throughout Micronesia, as in other parts of the Pacific, Christianity has become so fundamental to social life that it is difficult to imagine the islands without the Church.

Notes and References

[1] Exodus 7.8–12.
[2] Charles Forman, *The Island Churches of the South Pacific* (Maryknoll, NY: Orbis, 1982), 103.

Further Reading

Bliss, Theodora Crosby. *Micronesia, Fifty Years in the Island World: A History of the American Board*. Boston, MA: American Board of Commissioners for Foreign Missions, 1906.

Crawford, David and Leona. *Missionary Adventures in the South Pacific*. Tokyo: Tuttle, 1967.

Forman, Charles. *The Island Churches of the South Pacific: Emergence in the Twentieth Century*. Maryknoll, NY: Orbis Books, 1982.

Garrett, John. *To Live among the Stars: Christian Origins in Oceania*. Suva, Fiji: Institute of Pacific Studies, 1982.

Hezel, Francis X. "The Catholic Missions in the Caroline and Marshall Islands: A Survey of Historical Materials," *Journal of Pacific History* 5 (1970): 213–27.

Hezel, Francis X. *The First Taint of Civilization: A History of the Caroline and Marshall Islands in Pre-colonial Days, 1521–1885*. Honolulu: University of Hawaii, 1983.

Hezel, Francis X. *The Catholic Church in Micronesia: Historical Essays on the Catholic Church in the Caroline-Marshall Islands*. Chicago, IL: Loyola University Press, 1991.

Scopes, Barrie. *Nauru Congregational Church, 1887–1987*. London: Council for World Mission (World Council of Churches), 1987.

Strong, William E. *The Story of the American Board: An Account of the First Hundred Years of the American Board of Commissioners for Foreign Missions*. Boston, MA: Pilgrim Press, 1910.

Sullivan, Julius. *The Phoenix Rises: A Mission History of Guam*. New York: Seraphic Mass Association, 1957.

Zimmermann, Anna R. *Sixty Years Liebenzell Mission*. Morris County, NJ: Schooley's Mountain, 1960.

17

Christianity in Melanesia
Transforming the Warrior Spirit

Garry W. Trompf

How hard it is to generalize about "Christianities" among one quarter of the known discrete cultures on the planet! Over a thousand religio-linguistic complexes comprise traditional Melanesia (Oceania's "black islands"), from Vogelkop in West Papua (in Indonesia) across to Fiji's Vanua Levu (near the edges of Polynesia). That over 90 percent of the inhabitants of the Melanesian region admit connection with some Christian institution or another at least enhances our confidence that some historical "patterns" have stamped themselves upon the region's "pre-Christian diversity." Different missions have carved out spaces of foundation, settled operation, and expansion (often enjoying protection of colonial governments), and their operations have left characteristic marks on the contemporary scene.

Missionary and Cultural Background

The first of the Melanesian island groups to experience missionaries was Fiji (from 1835), and following the conversion of the great chief Cakobau in 1854, Wesleyan Methodism has had an immense impact on all levels of indigenous social life. After the Great Council of Chiefs ceded the islands to Britain (1874), indentured Indian immigrants were brought in to work on sugar plantations, so that by independence (1970), Fiji was divided ethnically, and one half has become defensively Melanesian Christian vis-à-vis Indian Hindus and Muslims.[1]

Chronologically, the other end of "the Melanesian arc" should come next. The Dutch laid formal claim over the western half of the great New Guinea island, or West Irian, from 1828, but most infrastructural work was left to missions, until serious preparations were made for independence (1958–63). After a poorly monitored 1969 plebiscite, though, the United Nations confirmed the territory as Indonesia's (now comprising her twin Provinces of West Papua and Papua). Against this background, we find that Dutch Reformed missionary activity has had lasting effects along the northern seaboard (starting from Doreh Bay in 1852) and Dutch Catholic work along the southern one. With gradual accessibility to the highly populated highland valleys (especially from 1954), the presence of lesser-known Australian and American missions – the Christian and Missionary Alliance, Unevangelized Fields Mission (UFM), and Baptist missionary societies most noticeable among them – brought greater denominational diversity there. More recently, however, non-Melanesian and Muslim migration has undermined indigenous hopes for black "Christian" nationhood.[2]

On the other side of the artificial border dividing the great New Guinea Island, the history of colonial intrusions differed significantly. There, admittedly, Catholic missions (especially the Marists) had been

Introducing World Christianity, First Edition. Edited by Charles E. Farhadian.
© 2012 Blackwell Publishing Ltd. Published 2012 by Blackwell Publishing Ltd.

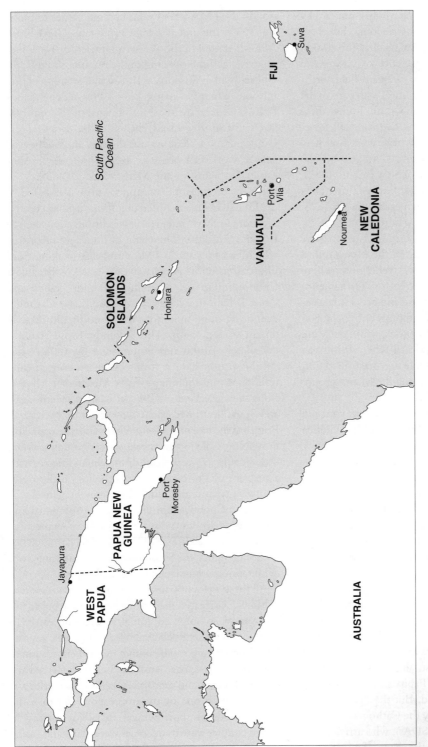

Map 17.1 Melanesia

trying their hand as early as the late 1840s, just as they had in the Solomons and New Caledonia, but these efforts all ended in sad failure, and security for mission work came with a stronger presence of traders and colonial authorities.[3] After 1885, Germany held north-eastern New Guinea ("Neu-Guinea") with parts of the Western Solomons and, despite soon losing these possessions in World War I, the Germans left long-term marks because their missionaries were later permitted to return to their stations. German Catholic work began on the northern tip of New Britain (1882), although the Australian Methodist George Brown had already established his mission nearby before 1875. Methodism's spread was mainly northwest (to New Ireland and New Hanover), and Catholicism's to New Britain and then along the coast of the New Guinea mainland (especially in the Sepik River regions, where the Divine Word Mission Society (SVD) gained a foothold in 1896 under Eberhard Limbrock's leadership).[4] The Lutherans became famously entrenched on the Huon Peninsula (from 1886 onwards), and were joined by the non-denominational Rhenish Mission in the Madang area (a comparable organization to this, the Liebenzeller, later evangelizing the Manus group, alongside the Catholics).[5]

Queensland and soon after Great Britain annexed Papua (the southeastern part of the great New Guinea island), which was for a time called British New Guinea (1886–1906). The Australians took responsibility for both the Territories of Papua and New Guinea until they attained independence as Papua New Guinea (PNG) in 1975. Both Dutch and Australian hegemonies were under serious threat during World War II (1942–5) with the invasion of the Japanese (who triggered Indonesia's independence before they retreated), but much of the Church life that persisted was remarkably protected by indigenous personnel. After World War I mission operations in Papua had been affected by the kind of Spheres of Influence policy known elsewhere in British domains in the 1890s. The Anglicans were assigned the northeast, Methodists the southeast, and the London Missionary Society (LMS) – in Papua since 1874 – the southern coast and hinterland. But the "gentleman's agreement" was not signed by the Catholics, let alone the Seventh-day Adventists (SDAs), who arrived surprisingly early (in 1908), and the shape of missioniza-

tion in the LMS sphere soon became harder to plot.[6] By 1939, the independent Protestant UFM (later APCM) started in the Western District (or Fly River region)[7]; and the opening of the populous highlands, especially after World War II, saw a huge influx of tiny missions alongside major ones.[8] Post-independence PNG is perhaps the most missionized of all countries.

Of the smaller island chains to the east of New Guinea, New Caledonia was the one in which evangelistic work first had any sizeable outcomes. After earlier problems for the Marist Order, Catholics secured the backing of France on the main island (1853), the French being interested in it first as a penal colony, then for its nickel, and in time as a curious equivalent to Britain's Australia. The chain of the New Hebrides, which had Polynesian LMS evangelists making fitful impressions on its peoples as early as 1839, became a Condominium (or co-ruling) of both France and Great Britain in 1906, with Anglicans and Catholics eventually more numerous in the north and Presbyterians to the south. The Solomon Islands were a completely British-run protectorate by 1898–9 and for this reason have a strong Anglican constituency (following the founding of the Melanesian Mission from New Zealand, 1849), yet Marists, Methodists, and SDAs flourished in the west (the former as far as Bougainville and more centrally on Guadalcanal).[9] By now, New Caledonian *kanaks* are very much second-class citizens in a veritable *Département* of France, with a mixture of Protestants and Catholics on the outer ("Lifu") group under much less cultural strain. As for the current political condition of the Solomons and the New Hebrides (now Vanuatu), they secured independence in 1978 and 1980 respectively, though not without conflict, the Solomons recently suffering from debilitating post-independence civil strife.

All these styles of Christianity arrived in a region so culturally variegated that we have no choice but to call it the most complex ethnological scene on earth. In terms of prevenient beliefs about spirit beings, a sprinkling of high gods can be found; monotheism was rare (God in one case, near Australia, being conceived as a cosmic serpent), and more often a cluster of deities was honored, with one or two more powerful than the others. Gods or spirit-beings crucial for victory in armed conflict were frequent, as were many and varied place-spirits protective of impressive or dangerous locales. As for the dead, sometimes with special differentiation between the recently or longer departed, or between problematic ghosts and more favorable ancestors, they evoked constant concern across the whole Melanesian canvas.[10] Traditional social organization was far from uniform, with high chiefs of Viti Levu (Fiji) virtually approximating to kings, and successful big-men in the central highlands of the great New Guinea island attaining leadership through a more democratic-looking process of competition. Pre-Christian ritual life typically entailed the colorful array of decorated dancers, but could differ considerably in scale; the mass killing of pigs or their displaying for exchange exemplify obvious cases of magnificence; altar systems on North Malaita in the Solomons give an air of "classic sacrificial cults"; while food prestations (of yams or bananas, for instance) are common among lowland peoples.[11] The laws, rules, taboos, customary regulations, and general mores of Melanesia make up a vast panoply of special, if often minor, diversities, as did the means of contacting and cajoling the spirit world, through dreams and altered states, so-called "magical" techniques and sorcery, and artistic representations of "the formidable" that involved specialist roles and disciplined lives. Such intricacies could not but be contextually important upon the arrival of evangelists; and in each and every case there is a story to be told about which institutions presented matters of tension to the bearers of high Christian ideals.

The dominant theme of Melanesian "socio-religious life," however, was the ethos of "payback." One may fairly characterize Melanesian traditional religions as "warrior religions," in that top priority was set on masculine participation in armed engagement against enemies and on female support of the "security circle."[12] It is simply impossible to divest warfare activity from religion in "pre-contact" Melanesia, considering inter alia the investment of time and energy put into warrior prowess, the ritual content of military actions, alongside the common nocturnal separation of husbands from their families so as to plan strategies and share defense from the "men's house." The initiations of youths, however varied in form, were uniformly to test male strength and endurance, and in certain societies initiates only became men through participating in raids – bringing back a victim's head to the elders, for instance, as the West

Papuan Waropen expected.[13] The typical warrior attitude was that he was defending his tribe (as the equivalent to a "nation"), or fighting alongside allies who had supported his tribe over generations, and thus there were heavy sanctions against those who hot-headedly took matters into their own hands and did not heed the elders.[14] The language of punition and revenge was often the same.

On the other hand, paying back had its concessive side. In festivities on a grand scale, pigs (sometimes killed and lined up in the hundreds) or harvested foodstuffs were given away by the host tribe to invitee groups with extraordinary magnanimity, the major intents being to increase prestige, consolidate or forge alliances, and create a celebratory space for match-making. When massive slaughter and prestations occurred they typically entailed an element of ritual sacrifice, humans offering gifts to please the deities and/or ancestors so that they would continue to bless their own people.[15] More humdrum give-and-take, moreover, had its own excitements in a whole "religious way of life," because the pressure to maintain obligations was forever present, and in any case there were life-cycle events (such as marriages and deaths) and special transactions in rounds of negotiation (such as in the Kula Ring island trade cycle of eastern Papua) in which ritualization was patent.[16] Gender relations were integrally wrapped in the pay-back arena. Typically, marriage involved bride price and women were often tokens of alliance – they came to live with the husband's family from another tribe (exogamy) and so had to prove themselves as trustworthy and productive, and not "the enemy within." As everywhere, male–female relations were always one node of the conflictual, and male fear of the deleterious effects of female (especially menstrual) fluids was forever high; while on the other hand successful marriages empowered members of both sexes.[17]

A crucial part of this chief "thematic" of payback in traditional Melanesian religions was cognitive and explanatory. The ongoing play of everyday events and "significant outcomes" affecting group relations demanded constant assessment, a calculation of "scores" in battle, or "registrations" of met and unmet obligations, and a mental reckoning in terms of praise and blame or rewards and punishments in each indigenous "logic of retribution." When somebody died it was rarely put down to "natural causes." Almost invariably sickness unto death resulted from sorcery, mostly from an enemy "out-group" for which the victim's people had no spirit or healing power to avert, and death on the battlefield or in raids ultimately came either from superior magico-spiritual techniques or neglect of protective measures.[18] Breaking a taboo or overstepping the accepted mark was usually taken to result in a weakening of the relationships supported by "non-empirical agents," especially dead relatives – the coastal Papuan people, the Motu, saw ideal relations symbolized by the strong central posts (*irutahuna*) of their chiefs' houses – so that trouble, sickness, and even death would result, and specialists would be asked to divine what had gone wrong.[19] Much explanation of day-to-day problems centered on divining (via specialists' séances, dreams, etc.) whose neglects or delicts had made the dead angry. With predominantly male-dominated societies many "immediate reactions" to troubles involved blaming women, and those who had "married in" and were not liked could be accused of witchcraft and exiled.

Much material culture was developed in association with revenge-reciprocity issues. Male hunting was akin to raiding (sometimes "headhunting"); women carried garden produce and babies in the same sorts of string-bags (*bilums*). Apart from the craftsmanship put into weapons (often decorated), the creation of effigies of spirit beings or the dead were characteristically formidable rather than endearing because they were shown as warnings, especially at times of some initiatory or cultic disclosure. Some might argue that "flashbulb"-type (or indelible) memories of such revealings, let alone of initiatory ordeals, are the most central features of Melanesian religiosity, thus considering it an essentially non-discursive modality that has had to face the barrage of wordy preaching borne by introduced Christianities.[20] But discursive "materials" were fundamental to Melanesian traditions: the traumas of initiations were followed by "teaching the rules" (albeit still in an atmosphere of dread); myths were told, retold, and invoked to legitimate values, and explanatory repertoires were applied to show how event-outcomes reflected blessings or hostile influences, contributing a conceptually energetic, philosophical side to Melanesian *Weltanschauungen*. In their quests for good results in terms of security and fertility,

Melanesians' fundamental concerns were comparable to those of primal or First Peoples the world over, although they were more characteristically concerned with the material benefits of their lifeways (rather than with all-round health, as among Africans), and even gods could be dispensed with if they were no longer expected to bring concrete aid.[21]

Melanesian Christianities

The process toward the "Christianization" of indigenous Melanesia makes up one of the world's most dramatic religious shifts of the last hundred years.[22] Because this change is relatively recent, in many inland cases within the present generation, "first encounter" scenarios are still fresh in group memories and have generated distinctive responses about the coming of "light" to "darkness," the true way as against wrong road, or the time of "living in peace together" (neo-Melanesian: *sindaun gut*) rather than of fighting (*taim bilong pait*). Thus every year, to illustrate, Goodenough Islanders (East Papua) celebrate the 1898 arrival of the Methodist missionary William Bromilow when charging warriors nearly dispatched the man of peace on their beach.[23] Traditions have often circulated that even before the first evangelists appeared, someone saw a vision or dreamt that extraordinary change would soon occur. Something in prior cultural heritage was often seen foreshadowing the Christian message: immediately the Catholic priests told about the Annunciation to the (central Papuan) Roro, for instance, listeners responded that they already knew of Mary as a mythic lady carrying her *bilum* and by implication pregnant with gifts and blessings. As in other contexts around the world, the Christian message was first received through the local lens, so that such corresponding motifs became the basis for heightening the significance of the new message for social transformation. Talk of Christ's sacrifice was easier to understand, of course, when there were parallels. The Toa[m]baita of north Malaita (Solomons) erected altars and offered a burnt holocaust like that in Leviticus 8, so the proclamation of Jesus as a final sacrifice for sin quickly made sense.[24] Among the treacherous Sawi (southeast West Papua), Regions Beyond Missionary Union worker Don Richardson famously picked out the practice of one tribe that offered another a boy child to make peace, and announced Jesus as the final Peace Child – an end to all enmity (cf. Tit. 2:14).[25] Notice how these illustrations, chosen judiciously, connect either to warrior prowess or to a more positive reciprocity, whether between people and gods or in interpersonal gift-giving.

Early conversions in the region often had to do with the failure of traditional retributive logic and thus with the acceptance of a Christian frame as a superior alternative. Clement Marau, an early Banks Islander Anglican evangelist on Ulawa (eastern Solomons) in the late 1880s, reminisced how, because nothing bad happened after he led a wedding procession through sacred groves, the local people sensed he brought a greater power than they possessed. Comparable reactions occurred when Christian predictions outdid pagan ones, or missionary medicines worked where traditional ones failed.[26] In many like scenarios that followed, if no punishment followed the destruction of sacred objects, then old fears and objects of worship were reckoned false. However, it was not as if the spirits would be thought incapable of paying back the bearers of change: Fr Joseph Knoebel, SVD, remembers how, when a Lake Kopiago tribe (Southern Highlands, PNG) brought sacred stones to be ceremoniously smashed and discarded to mark their new life, a splinter of one stone he dashed down bounced back and hit him straight between the eyes. For one crucial second he knew that any faltering or moaning would put the whole exercise in jeopardy![27] The trouble with this whole approach, in any case, was that in time old specialists who lost in status, or families disgruntled for not acquiring the prominence they sought, could eventually point to mishaps that provided reason for turning back to "custom" or "ancestral fashion" (or alternatively, for changing missions).[28]

What happened in early Church life as a result of such significant cultural intersections is variegated and follows no general rule, but they set the tone for the contemporary scene. There are basic matters to do with locales and objects entailed here. Sometimes places of cultic importance before contact were chosen as the very spots to erect new churches, thus honoring former spiritual activity as *praeparatio evangelicae* while dissipating the powers that backed inter-tribal ferocity

(as among the Daga, Milne Bay Province, Papua). On Mbau Islet, off the west coast of Viti Levu, Fiji, there is a curious black stone standing upright in the main church; it has a scallop to hold baptismal water carved into it, but it is the only traditional object in the place, previously used for beheading hundreds of sacrificial victims. A fixture associated with the time of cannibal darkness in Methodist imaging now designates a new and enlightened life. Naturally, it was very rare for churches to be built in the same style as traditional temples, but time allows for more daring contextualizations on these matters. To take Catholic cases, at Ambunti in the Sepik the main church carries a great ancestral "cloud of witnesses," in traditional mask-like style, as a mural behind the altar; in Port Moresby, PNG's capital, a prominent church replicates a great Mekeo *ufu* (or house of chiefs' ceremonial objects), a reminder of the first indigenous Papuan priest and bishop who served there – Louis Vangeke, who announced he had become "God's sorcerer."[29] Close to first exposures to the outside world, of course, any new material novelty brought by the "whitemen" signified access to superior power: even a prefabricated toilet, as many West Papuan Highlands Dani believed in early contact days (1950s), was a place where whites were secretly empowered by spirit helpers! In such settings, converts have a much shorter time and much pressure on them to catch up to other people in the nation with a longer history of engagement with Christianity.[30]

Another factor conditioning the subsequent profile of Church life had to do with the agents of change. The attitude of pre-existing leadership toward introducers of the new Way was often determinative. If old wielders of power saw it in their interests to convert, then group conversions were likely to occur, this being accepted as a way to avoid alienating old senses of community in the Lutheran mission policy of Christian Keysser (1930s). Religious change could come very slowly if individual conversion was insisted upon, although the danger in collective conversion was nominalism or the long leftover task of inculcating all the dimensions to being Christian.[31] In some cases the agents of change were unexpected. In Wain country (Huon Peninsula, Papua New Guinea), male hunters would bring back game to share with the women, but barely had eating started when a chosen man would

Figure 17.1 Catholic Church, Ambunti, Sepik River region, with ceiling decorations of ancestral figures. *Source*: Garry Trompf. Used by permission of the author.

suddenly appear in a mask as a spirit to chase the females off! "Women in the know" about these deceptions first welcomed the missionaries, women's social condition being bettered thereafter. Of course everywhere it was always males who had the best opportunities to train for the ministry, and they would lay the foundation for new elites in their countries (like the LMS pastors, serving like little "kings" in their Papuan villages). Yet

we are not to forget how clergy rising from lowly beginnings could serve to inspire a general sense of confessional loyalty. Lutheran leader Zuruwe Zurenuoc of New Guinea, for one, was disowned straight after birth by his mother and thrown over a riverbank. His mother's sister, noticing his absence, found him at the water's edge, his sticky body covered with ants. How powerful was this story, as one of providential redemption, when Zurewe became head bishop of his Church in 1973![32] And of course persons who died for the faith, foreign or indigenous, would be locally commemorated or given national significance – such as Catholic catechist Peter ToRot, a Tolai (of New Britain) who kept the Church alive during Japan's invasion and is the only indigenous Melanesian martyr to be declared Blessed (1995).[33]

Whatever the details, however, and yet helping to explain Melanesian "Christianities" in their diversity,[34] it is important to grasp the general patterns of religious change. There has been uniform missionary opposition to inter-tribal violence and homicidal payback, and the "primary effects" of Christianity across the region can be read in terms of the degrees to which these "negative reciprocities" have dissolved. Today only pockets of traditional (or near-traditional) tribal fighting remain, all in the highlands, and there men will travel armed to church and be asked to leave their weapons with an attendant at the door (as among the western Enga, Papua New Guinea). But what are deemed breakages of the Fifth Commandment for the churches, and murders under new national laws, are now often individual homicides motivated by persisting inter-tribal (and by now inter-district, even inter-regional) hostilities, and can re-erupt anywhere given enough pretexts. Because of the cultural context, and the use of inter-clan compensation ceremonies to pay for loss of life (especially in the highlands), penalties for killing are comparatively less severe than in most Euro-American or Muslim settings.[35] It cannot be too highly stressed that the political suppression of warriorhood activity, though, and the preached call to repress and transform it into something life-affirming, has actually eviscerated a good half of the "vital organs" of traditional religious life.

Because many colorful events of "positive reciprocity," or the other half of payback in the form of grand feasts or dramatic exchanges, were occasions of generosity and mirth, Christian evangelizers often felt persuaded to encourage their continuance. What happened depended on relative willingness to compromise. Very often key rituals carried intimations of warrior energy, invocations of gods and the dead, and sexual (or "generative") elements that missionaries considered unworthy of a Christianizing society, and they would explain their opposition. Compromises

might allow old festivals to take place with believers and traditionalists co-celebrating but able to put different meanings on the performances. Under such a rapprochement, the Motu people carried on their harvest festivals within the LMS sphere, with the centerpiece of the joyful time being the wearing of exceptionally tall spirit masks. Missionaries desisted from bringing this to an end, but when Japanese planes bombed Port Moresby in 1942, it "spontaneously" ceased for somehow being utterly irrelevant in a changed world.[36] Somewhat earlier, in the Gulf District (now Province) to the west (1937), the Elema of Orokolo Village put on their great *Hevehe* rite in the presence of the resident missionary, Ben Butcher, seeking his approval. He deemed it all quite magnificent, including the use of bull-roarers to voice the fearsome Ma-Hevehe spirit's arrival on the beach and the climactic discarding of ritual objects into the sea as a placation. He objected only to the short time permitting free sexual activity; and – probably because this was an unstated highlight! – the villagers decided to abandon the whole thing.[37] In general terms, traditional celebrations were encouraged more and lasted longer in Catholic areas, where natural revelation was more developed missiologically. Mainline Protestant areas produced more obvious forms of compromise, with sexual innuendos taken out of dancing, for example, and graceful styles of Polynesian (or *peroveta*) dance encouraged instead; while sectarian Protestant and Fundamentalist churches have attempted to eliminate anything with a mere whiff of "Satan's work" from the past. What has happened in the case of the largest pig-killing ritual in the highlands – among the Wahgi (central New Guinea Highlands) – is indicative. At the beginning, a Catholic priest would be invited to open the whole three-day festivity with prayer, "baptizing" it, as it were, whereas Lutherans would be encouraged to stay at home even if still fulfilling their exchange obligations, and Swiss Brethren adherents might protest, lining up to glare at visitors arriving to engage in such "follies." Nowadays inflation (much more than religious pressure) has caught up with the matter: it is too time-consuming to raise so many pigs, and making money dominates all (rather than magnanimously giving all one's pigs away to guests who might no longer be prepared to reciprocate and do what you have done).[38]

The missionary endeavor in Melanesia to cultivate positivities, however, has been much more concerned with rearrangements of traditional societies for peaceful coexistence than accommodating old practices. Thus, once the days of solemn peacemaking were over – with missionaries sponsoring "the burning of spears" – a widespread procedure for creating new societies was to encourage previously separated hamlets or house-lines into bigger villages. Seaboard hamleters who had secured themselves against enemies in isolated inland places were encouraged to come down to dwell within larger seaside communities, a pattern well documented for the Solomons.[39] The trouble with such moves is that they generated new frictions and with them a new and insidious phenomenon of negative payback – *intra*-group sorcery. In pre-contact days sorcery sometimes operated as a means of control and punishment within a clan, but in the torrid days of inter-tribal war few groups could afford to have a sorcerer undermining much needed warrior unity. Sorcerers, then, traditionally diverted their energies outwards against enemies, operating "the spear by night," as the Sepik River Abelam called it, to keep up the killing while the men were not at battle.[40] The typical "Christian village," however, now fell susceptible to internal dissensions, and, with the proscription of war and open murder, payment for sorcery or some form of witchcraft to weaken or dispense with one's antagonists became the predominant expression of negativities. It became the more insidious for infecting new local quests to unify Christian communities, although it formed a recognizably universal problem because the remnant of pagan beliefs that lasts longest in Christianizing societies has always been the working of malevolent spirit-power. Surprisingly, however, despite countless sermons directed against such "vestiges of dark times," there have only been a few Christian "drives" to stamp out sorcery (e.g., on Ambrym, Vanuatu, in 1973, and on Santa Isabel, Solomons, in 1984) like the anti-sorcery campaigns of Africa.[41] In spite of all the fear and frustration, too, commonly held views still circulate – noticeably in the Anglican sphere of Papua – that sorcery might be a necessary institution for holding greedy and arrogant people from destroying village "equalities"; and there are some outwardly Christian contexts, the large Massim village of Kalauna for one (in eastern Papua), where Church leaders are knowledgeable in sorcery.[42]

With the formation of Christian villages, most men's or long-houses have been dismantled, and cohabitation of nuclear (or minimally extended) families has been encouraged. Old fears about male contact with occasions of female "uncleanness" die hard, so that women are expected to go into seclusion just outside the village during their periods (and in Adventist villages this accords with albeit non-mandatory Levitical laws). In village and small-town church worship, therefore, one can expect women to sit in separate groups in the "pews" (almost always low benches), whereas city congregations are noted for freer mixing. Where families have access to money, naturally, the worldwide fashion of "brushing and dressing up" for church pertains; in rural and town settings celebrants will put on their fine (if often unironed) attire, but lay people make do with what they have, and the collective smell of smoking fires from family houses can linger over congregations, especially when packed for such occasions as Christmas! It can be expected that literacy will be better in urban areas, yet nowhere in the world do the Wycliffe Bible Translators and the Summer Institute of Linguistics possess more representatives than in Melanesia. Thus local communities increasingly acquire vernacular Bibles, and along with biblical materials and service books in *lingue franche* (neo-Melanesian varieties, Malayo-Indonesian *bahasas*, Hiri Motu, Kota, etc.), and the slowly increasing effect of national school systems, Melanesian Christianity is becoming more literate, with vernaculars conserved even if with newly injected meanings. Educational change, initiated by missionary work across the region and taken up by national governments, has given new advantages for women, some places being of longstanding interest where Christian women have showed remarkable leadership in defiance of general inequalities – the Massim in the Kwato Mission area, coastal Papua, and Presbyterians in and around Port Vila, Vanuatu.

Over the last hundred years, peoples living in areas historically assigned to well-established missions have developed a collective, even competitive, loyalty to their denomination. Until the early 1950s, fierce rivalry and occasional outbursts of animosity (even brawls) existed between Catholics and Protestants, who branded each other heretics and image worshipers respectively. Yet even before the Second Vatican

Council fraternization between the mainline Churches had laid foundations for the Pacific and Melanesian Councils of Churches (1961–; 1965–), pioneering exercises in ecumenism that have fully included the Catholics (though with prejudices against Adventists as "not fully Christian" dying hard).[43] By the 1970s, nonetheless, a congealing of Church patterns of life into virtual "neo-traditionalisms" prevailed, especially in the Reformed Protestant Churches. Problems were partly offset for Catholics through the vernacularization of the Mass; and the bigger churches had impetuses for rejuvenation as foreign mission bodies relinquished control into "autonomous" indigenous churches.[44] Through the United Church in Papua New Guinea and the Solomon Islands, the coastal Papuan LMS congregations and the Papuan, New Guinean, and Solomonese Methodists joined in an episcopal system (1968), yet certain stubborn conformities made matters hard. The Tolais were reluctant to give up their magnificent hymn-singing in the Kuanua tongue, often holding separate services in urban settings; and the Solomons component eventually went its own way in 1996.[45] More to the point, in village areas where Church (usually indigenous) leadership was less well trained, the mainline Churches became susceptible to calls for new life. In opposition to old routines – because Church life could appear more boring and less colorful as traditional celebrations died out – came charismatic and Pentecostal incursions. Largely confined to towns in the 1970s, their enthusiastic adherents returned to outlying places to press for change and renewal and processes of village worship bifurcation came into play.[46]

As in Africa, charismatico-Pentecostal vogues appeal to many people because they are outwardly vital (as against steady), spontaneous, and spiritistic (rather than circumscribed by introduced form), and engage more bodily movement (rather than up-and-down liturgical "good order"). Some older Church molds have been more resilient to these changes than others. The UFM (now the Pacific Christian Church) is relatively impervious, having cultivated an ethos of "masculine Christianity" among the powerful Gogodala people, a kind of transference of warrior energy into fearless evangelism, that has directed energies to missionize isolated Southern Highlands areas (oftimes

eagerly attacking pre-Christian culture).[47] Anglicans, and also Lutherans of the Morobe and Huon regions, have been less threatened (even despite local Lutheran schismatic activity, mainly in the highlands), but the United Church has been especially buffeted. Even the previously sturdy Methodist establishment on Fiji has experienced leaky cracks, knocked about by Fundamentalists as well as Pentecostals. Fundamentalism is a factor when dissatisfied preachers and newly arrived smaller (often American-originated) missions complain of "creeping modernization and secularization" (money-making, greater freedom for women, liberalized socio-sexual relations, with new music, magazines, party-type celebrations, and so on). The Bible, on a characteristic Fundamentalist analysis, has to be returned and adhered to more strictly, and churches too tolerant of liberal tendencies are to be abandoned. Fundamentalism has limited effect in Melanesia unless grafted into charismatico-Penetecostal churches;[48] in these the message for moral purity and personal transformation can be so electrifying when, apart from prayer in tongues, sermons are given "in the Spirit." The author vividly remembers (actually while seated beside the last of the famous von Trapp singers!) an indigenous Pentecostal pastor's sermon in the fastest yet most dynamic "pidgin English" he has ever heard. But unless there are means of gentle accommodation (as when Catholic charismatics hold their own special meeting after Mass), the new surge of enthusiasms often brings the worst out of small communities who thought they were spiritually unified.

With all these spiritistic developments, admittedly, come signs that Melanesians feel better able to respond to God "in their own way," experiencing new *rites de passage* with new spiritual waves.[49] Sometimes remarkable revivals have resulted. Various Solomonese preachers, fired by charismatic upsurges of outbursts, healing, and holiness among evangelicals on North Malaita, made their presence felt in the New Guinea Highlands. From their evangelizing, starting at Baiyer River Baptist Mission, the Kyaka Enga were stirred into remarkable collective acts of devotion, building, for instance, a huge palisade that was to represent the Jerusalem temple for a purified life, without hankering after pre-Christian ways or falling into bad personal habits, including stale or secretly uncommitted worship.[50] The continuing inroads of such newer

"Christianities" into older ones, though, should remind us of the previous expressions of adverse reaction
to "colonially tainted" missionary activity. Melanesia
has been the world's major host to the by now fabled
"cargo cults," new religious movements that derived
from the widespread assumption that European-style
goods, of the cargo of the foreign "masters," originated
from the spirit world. All aspects of fecundity, in
traditional understanding, came from the aid of deities
and/or the dead, and, in the absence of any knowledge
of modern factories, grass-roots ideologies disseminat-
ed that whites received their treasured items from their
heaven, and even that new goods were really made by
the ancestors for the blacks but were magically blocked
by the whites.[51] Going to church might be seen as the
"road to the cargo," and Christ's Second Coming
linked to its arrival; yet after disillusion set in with
this approach, indignant prophets and agitants relayed
their dreams and organized preparations of makeshift
wharves and airstrips to wait for the dead and/or Jesus
to bring ships or planes full of the desired wares. In any
case, such expectations had everything to do with
payback (or retributive) logic. On the one hand, they
expressed resentment for being deprived of new possibilities (though resistance was usually without arms
because of the governments' superior weaponry); on
the other hand, they indicated hopes for reciprocally
participating in the (at first astounding) imported order
of things.[52]

So-called cargo cultism was not the only form of
adjustment movement reacting to colonial pressures in
the Melanesian region. Some rebellions or revolts, let
alone nativistic revivals of pre-contact tradition, have
sought a measure of support from Christian beliefs.
Most social experiments hold high hopes of an eschatological kind, for the coincidence of biblical apocalyptic and the raft of new material changes lends itself
to this. Even cargo cults have slowly sought to put on a
"church front" to appear as competing denominations,
including cargo in the promise of Salvation.[53] Some
may now be ranked among the 30-odd Independent
Churches emergent in this part of the southwest
Pacific. A few such Churches are reminiscent of
renowned African models. The Christian Fellowship
Church (CFC), for example, broke away from the
Methodists on New Georgia (Western Solomons)
under Silas Eto, who, acclaimed as Holy Mama (or

"Father") and as an extra member of the godhead (like
Simon Kimbangu), conducted services in special white
robes and headgear. The members of the Congregation of the Poor on Fiji's Viti Levu, another defection
from Methodism, all wear special white robes as marks
of sectarian identity, and baptize under lightning, not
just with water, as their healer-prophet Loaniceva
instructed (cf. Matt, 3:11b). Such independencies,
opposed by mainline Churches, pay back their critics
by righteous indignation, as in the cases of the CFC and
Paliau Maloat's Church, with model villages, schools,
and gardens to outdo other churches.[54] Their founders, along with other religious leaders with agendas of
protest and reform, created precedents for charismatic
leadership and clerical involvement in modern
Melanesian politics.[55]

Threats to the very existence of Christianity in
Melanesia only exist as yet in the far west. Indian-
originated Hindu, Muslim, and Sikh communities in
bi-ethnic Fiji currently have drawn very little interest
from indigenes, and a widely proselytizing Baha'ism
attracts marginal response. With eastward (largely
spontaneous) transmigration into West Papua, however, the demographic shift is toward the (Malayo-)
Indonesian and mainly Muslim population outnumbering the blacks (Papuans). With Indonesia's Department of Religious Affairs giving more resources to
the nation's majority confession of Islam, the Churches
are increasingly vulnerable to religious conversion,
particularly in cities like Jayapura and Manokwari
where Muslim "protagonist groups" are strong. Even
in Wamena, a center in Dani country touted as the
frontier town for "the most primitive place" on earth,
the call of the muezzin sounds out intermittently from
a new Saudi-funded mosque (next to the main, albeit
recently built, Dutch Reformed Church), and two
Dani Christian hamlets have already converted.
Among menaces to the normal operations of Church
life and Christianity's service to national unity (as
invoked in Constitutions of the region's independent
states) are civil wars, which have wracked Bougainville
(PNG's easternmost, now autonomous, component)
(1989–2001) and the Solomons (1998–2003). Paradoxically, though, the stories of Christian civilians'
survival and also peace-building efforts in the horror of
these conflicts have provided some of the most inspi-
rational stories of faith commitment in Melanesia. The

West Papuan liberation movement (*Organisasi Papua Merdeka*) recently chose Christian pacifism rather than violence to handle the political domination of the Indonesian government (which has been accused of genocidal acts against indigenous opponents of its neo-colonial rule, particularly near the huge Freeport mine); while in New Caledonia, where resistance to massive colonialism was spearheaded by *kanak* priest Jean-Marie Tjibaiou (killed in 1989), the newest challenge is to counter the tragic ennui, the indigenes being bought off with good conditions and a soulless existence as the manipulated objects of French tourism and business interests.[56]

In various sectors prophetic black theology has manifested, with Benny Giay championing strong grass roots, including practical spirituality as a foil to imposed ideologies in West Papua; PNG philosopher-jurist Bernard Narokobi advocating the "Melanesian Way," not foreignness, in matters of justice, social relations, and religious life; and Rev. Sevati Tuwere celebrating multiculturalism in Fiji, not the "racial divide" that produces one coup after another.[57] Different calls for liturgical innovation are heard, such as the suggestions to use sago and coconut juice instead of bread and wine, to "show" betel-nut as a symbol of peace and friendship in the Mass, even, in one high Anglican Torres Strait peace ceremony, to place a pig's head on a church altar![58] Yet the key theological problematic, barely addressed in indigenous reflection, remains the persistence of payback mentalities.

Handling culture-specific payback matters will always require a very contextual discernment from Christians, but one can detect a general drift whereby endemic assumptions about reciprocity become embedded in practiced Christianity to produce distinctly Melanesian expressions of it. At least signifying a living dialogue,[59] "normative payback paradigms" encourage readings of the faith as a new, if better, legal regimen, or as a way of "exchanging" (perhaps even bargaining) with God (and with material ends or "cargo opportunities" in view).[60] "Do not payback us for our bad deeds, and we will not payback others for theirs," runs the Lord's Prayer in Loboda (Normanby Island, Papua), to epitomize the issue, putting emphasis on retributive principles rather than on the forgiveness in the Gospel that transcends them, or on "becoming sinners" than on receiving grace.[61] When trouble, sickness, and death occur, old ideas of sorcery compete with biblical talk of divine retribution, and the transference of payback thinking from tradition to indigenous Church life calls for theological vigilance.[62] There are strong, well-established seminaries and training centers to warn about such "cultural hangovers," with the brightest generators of theologico-missiological reflection being the Melanesian Institute at Goroka and the Pacific Theological College, Suva, although intellectual vitality suffers from the lessening involvement of expatriate academia. The *Melanesian Journal of Theology* (1985–) allows for voices on one theological edge of the Christian world to reach the wider Church. For the moment, however, urgent attention in the region is for strong pastoral care, with serious social problems (including "rascal" gangs, drugs, and HIV/AIDs) filling the horizon.

In summary, the impact of missionary Christianity in Melanesia has been incalculably immense, especially in calming local hostilities and creating conditions for new, healthier, and better-educated communities. Now that indigenous Christian leadership has rapidly been taking responsibility into its own hands, the greatest challenges for this region are to overcome old divisive tendencies and new denominational competitiveness, to translate the Gospel message into less foreign modes of thought, and keep up the momentum of struggle against modern forces of secularism and individual self-interest.

Notes and References

[1] See J. Garrett, *To Live among the Stars* (Geneva and Suva: World Council of Churches and Institute of Pacific Studies, 1982), 103–15.

[2] F. C. Kamma, "*Dit wonderlijk werk*" (Oegstgeest: Zending der Nederlandse Hervormde Kerk, 1977), vol. 1, chs 5–11; J. H. M. C. Boelaars, *Met Papoea's samen op weg* (Kampen: J.H. Kok, 1992-7), vol. 1.

[3] F. Tomasetti and Trompf, eds, *White on Black* (Sydney: University of Sydney Press [also online] 2010), docs 3–5.

[4] R. M. Wiltgen, "Oceania: The Youngest Mission (1825–1922)," in *Sacrae Congregationis de Propaganda Fide Memoria Rerum: 1825–1922*, 3, 1 (Freiburg: Sacra Congregatio de Propaganda Fide, 1975), ch. 15; N. Threllfall, *One Hundred Years in the Islands* (New Guinea Islands Region: Rabaul: United Church, 1975); M. T. Huber, *The Bishops' Progress* (Washington, DC: Smithsonian Institution Press, 1988).

[5] H. Wagner and H. Reiner, eds, *The Lutheran Church in Papua New Guinea* (Adelaide: Lutheran Publishing House, 1986), chs 2–3; and p. 350.

[6] N. Lutton, "Murray and the Spheres of Influence," in Lutton Nelson and S. Robertson, eds, *Select Topics in the History of Papua New Guinea* (Port Moresby: University of Papua New Guinea, 1969), 2–10.

[7] R. Weymouth, "The Unevangelized Fields Mission, 1931–1981," *Journal of Pacific History* 23/2 (1988): 179–90.

[8] H. Nelson, *Taim belong Masta* (Sydney: Australian Broadcasting Commission, 1982), 159.

[9] D. Hilliard, *God's Gentlemen* (Brisbane: University of Queensland Press, 1978); H. Laracy, *Marists and Melanesians* (Canberra: ANU Press, 1976); A. Tippett, *Solomon Islands Christianity* (London: Lutterworth, 1967), chs 12–14, 18–22; E. Were, *No Devil Strings* (Mountain View, CA: Pacific Press, 1970.

[10] G. W. Trompf, *Melanesian Religion* (Cambridge: Cambridge University Press, 2004 edn), esp. 9, 12–16.

[11] T. Swain and G. W. Trompf, *Religions of Oceania* (London: Routledge, 1995), 136–9, 140–6.

[12] For example, B. M. Knauft, "Melanesian Warfare: A Theoretical History," *Oceania* 60/4 (1990): 250–311.

[13] G. W. Trompf, *Payback* (Cambridge: Cambridge University Press, 2008 edn), 26–7.

[14] For example, L. Pospisil, *The Kapauku Papuans and their Law* (New Haven, CT: Yale University Press, 1958), esp. 236–8.

[15] G. W. Trompf, *Payback*, esp. 99–105, 121–3.

[16] Esp. B. Malinowski, *Argonauts of the Pacific* (New York: Dutton, 1961 edn), ch. 3.

[17] S. Hylkma, *Mannen in het dragnet* (The Hague: Martinus Nijhoff, 1974).

[18] M. Patterson. "Sorcery and Witchcraft in Melanesia," *Oceania* 45/2 (1974): esp. 132–60.

[19] S. Kopi, "Traditional Beliefs, Illness and Health among the Motuan People of Papua New Guinea, " Doctoral diss. (Sydney: University of Sydney, 1997), ch. 4.

[20] H. Whitehouse, *Arguments and Icons: Divergent Modes of Religiosity* (Oxford: Oxford University Press, 2000); F. Barth, *Ritual and Knowledge among the Baktaman of New Guinea* (Oslo: Universitetsforlaget, 1975).

[21] P. Lawrence and M. J. Meggitt, eds, *Gods, Ghosts and Men in Melanesia* (Melbourne: Oxford University Press, 1965), 12–22; R. Fortune, *Manus Religion* (Lincoln, NB: University of Nebraska Press, 1965 edn), 228–9.

[22] D. Barrett, ed., *World Christian Encyclopedia* (Nairobi: Oxford University Press, 2001 edn).

[23] M. W. Young, "Doctor Bromilow and Bwaidoka Wars," *Journal of Pacific History* 12/3–4 (1977): 130–3.

[24] On the above cases, see G. W. Trompf, *Melanesian Religion*, 66, 147.

[25] Richardson, *Peace Child* (Glendale, CA: G/L Publications, 1976), esp. 200–13.

[26] [Marau] *Story of a Melanesian Deacon,* trans. R. H. Codrington (London: SPCK, 1874), 68; D. O. Spencer, *Disease, Religion and Society in the Fiji Islands* (New York: J.J. Augustin, 1941).

[27] Cf. J. Knoebel, "Missionary Penetration," *The Word in the World* (1966): 186–7.

[28] P. Gibbs, *Bountiful Harvest* (Goroka: Melanesian Institute, 2007), 59–85.

[29] For these examples, G. W. Trompf, *Payback,* 359, 429; on Melanesian Christian art, esp. Aerts, *Christianity in Melanesia* (Port Moresby: University of Papua New Guinea Press, 1998), chs 2–3.

[30] [Anon., Australian Baptist Missionary Society]. "A Report on Dani Thinking" (unpublished mimeog., Tiom, December 18, 1962), 1, pt. c; cf. D. J. Hayward, *Vernacular Christianity among the Mulia* (Pasadena: University Press of America, 1997).

[31] See esp. C. Keysser, "Group Conversion among the Papuans," *International Review of Missions* 27 (1938): 403–14; idem, *Eine Papuagemeinde* (Neuendettelsau: Freimund-Verlag, 1950 edn); T. Farnbacher, *Gemeinde verantworten* (Hamburg: LIT, 1990), ch. 4–5.

[32] G. W. Trompf, *Payback,* 295, 454; N. D. Oram, "The London Missionary Society Pastorate and the Emergence of an Educated Papuan Elite," *Journal of Pacific History* 6 (1971): 115–32.

[33] C. G. ToVaninara, *The Life of Peter ToRot* (Vunapope: Missionaries of the Sacred Heart, 1975).

[34] See esp. J. Barker, ed, *Christianity in Oceania* (Lanham, MD: University Press of America, 1990), 22–3, 258–63.

[35] D. W. Young, *Our Land is Green and Black* (Goroka: Melanesian Institute, 2004), ch. 4.

[36] G. W. Trompf, "Oral Sources and the Study of Religious History on Papua New Guinea," in D. Denoon and R. J. Lacey, eds, *Oral Tradition in Melanesia* (Port Moresby: Institute of Papua New Guinea Studies, 1981), 162.

[37] T. Swain and G. W. Trompf, *Religions of Oceania*, 212, cf. 149–50; cf. F. E. Williams, *The Drama of Orokolo* (Oxford: Oxford University Press, 1940).

[38] See the J. Nilles/G. W. Trompf debate, "Simbu Ancestors and Christian Worship," *Catalyst* 7/3 (1977): 163–90; 8/2 (1978): 123–7.

[39] M. W. Scott, *The Severed Snake* (Durham, NC: Carolina Academic Press, 2007), chs 1–3 (Makira).

[40] A. Forge, "Prestige, Influence and Sorcery," in M. Douglas, ed., *Witchcraft Confessions and Accusations* (London: Tavistock, 1970), 259.

[41] See M. Zelenietz and S. Lindenbaum, eds, *Sorcery and Social Change in Melanesia* (spec. issue), *Social Analysis* 8

(1981): 81; G. M. White, *Identity through History* (Cambridge: Cambridge University Press, 1991), 111, 246.

[42] Cf. J. Barker, "Encounters with Evil: Christianity and the Response to Sorcery among the Maisin of Papua New Guinea," *Oceania* 61/2 (1990): 139–55; M. Young, *Fighting with Food* (Cambridge: Cambridge University Press, 1971), 126–7.

[43] K. James and A. Yabaki, eds, *Religious Cooperation in the Pacific* (Suva: Institute of Pacific Studies, 1989), esp. chs 1–4.

[44] F. Zocca, *Melanesia and its Churches*, trans. M. McCallum (Goroka: Melanesian Institute, 2007), 155–63.

[45] L. Boseto, "The Inheritance of the United Church in Papua New Guinea and the Solomon Islands," in S. Latukefu, with F. Tomasetti and G. W. Trompf, eds, *Integral Work* (Goroka: Melanesian Institute, forthcoming), ch. 9.

[46] M. Ernst, *Globalization and the Re-shaping of Christianity in the Pacific Islands* (Suva: Pacific Theological College, 2006), pts. 2–3.

[47] C. Wilde, "Acts of Faith: Muscular Christianity and Masculinity among the Gogodala," *Oceania* 75/1 (2004): 32–48.

[48] Note here J. Barr, "Pentecostal and Fundamentalist Missions and Churches," in S. Latukefu et al., eds, *Integral Work,* ch. 15.

[49] Start with M. Mailiau, "Searching for a Melanesian Way of Worship," in G. W. Trompf, ed., *The Gospel is Not Western* (Maryknoll, NY: Orbis, 1987), 119–27; cf. D. Tuzin, "Visions, Prophecies, and the Rise of Christian Con-sciousness," in G. Herdt and M. Stephen, eds, *The Religious Imagination in New Guinea* (Brunswick, NJ: Rutgers University Press, 1989), 187–210.

[50] J. Kale, "The Religious Movement among the Kyaka Enga," in C. Loeliger and G. W. Trompf, eds, *New Religious Movements in Melanesia* (Suva: Institute for Pacific Studies, 1985), 45–74. For West Papua, C. Farhadian, "Worship as Mission: The Personal and Social Ends of Papuan Worship in the Glory Hut," in idem, ed., *Christian Worship Worldwide* (Grand Rapids: W.B. Eerdmans, 2007), 171–95.

[51] P. Lawrence, *Road belong Cargo* (Manchester: Manchester University Press, 1964).

[52] Esp. P. F. Gesch, *Initiative and Initiation* (St August in: Anthropos-Institut, 1985).

[53] G. W. Trompf, "Pacific Movements," in C. Wessinger, ed., *Oxford Handbook of Millennialism* (Oxford: Oxford University Press, 2010), pt. 4, ch. 22.

[54] G. W. Trompf, "Independent Churches in Melanesia," *Oceania* 54/1 (1983): 51–72.

[55] For example, Jimmy Stevens, "Nagriamel," in C. Plant, ed., *New Hebrides: The Road to Independence* (Suva: Institute for Pacific Studies, 1977), 35–41.

[56] For the above, J. Bieniek and G. W. Trompf, eds, *Plight of Papua* (spec. issue), *Mi-cha-el* 9 (2003): chs 2–3; P. Howley, *Burning Spears and Mending Hearts* (London: Zed Books, 2002); P. Wete, *"Agis ou meurs": L'église évangelique de Calédonie vers Kanaky* (Suva: Lotu Pasifika Publications, 1991).

[57] B. Giay, *Zakheus Pakage and his Communities* (Amsterdam: Vrije Universiteit Amsterdam, 1995); B. Narokobi, *The Melanesian Way* (Port Moresby: Institute of Papua New Guinea Studies, 1980); I. Tuwere, *Vanua* (Suva: Institute of South Pacific Studies, 2002).

[58] R. Weymouth and K. Yandit, "Unevangelized Fields Mission," in Latukefu et al., eds, *Integral Work,* ch. 12; C. G. ToVaninara, "The Incorporation of Traditional Elements into the Liturgy," in G. W. Trompf, ed., *Melanesian Religion and Christianity* (Goroka: Melanesian Institute, 2008), ch. 5; T. Ama'analele, "The Pig of Christ," *Pacific Journal of Theology* 11 (2005): 33.

[59] See P. F. Gesch, ed., *Gospel Transformations* (Madang: Divine Word Institute, 1994).

[60] J. G. Strelan, *Search for Salvation* (Adelaide: Lutheran Publishing House, 1977).

[61] C. E. Thune, "Fathers, Aliens, and Brothers: Building a Social World in Loboda Village Church Services," in J. Barker, ed., *Christianity in Oceania,* 111; J. Robbins, *Becoming Sinners* (Berkeley, CA: University of California Press, 2004), 121–54; cf. T. Ahrens, *Grace and Reciprocity* (Goroka: Melanesian Institute, 2002).

[62] For example, K. J. Brison, "Giving Sorrow New Words: Politics of Bereavement in a Papua New Guinea Village," *Ethos* 26/4 (1998): 366, 376–81; C. Toren, "The Effectiveness of Ritual," in F. Cannell, ed., *The Anthropology of Christianity* (Durham, NC: Duke University Press, 2006), 185–209; M. Tomlinson, "Publicity, Privacy and 'Happy Deaths' in Fiji," *American Ethnologist* 34/4 (2007): 706–20.

Further Reading

Barker, John, ed., *Christianity in Oceania: Ethnographic Perspectives* (ASAO Monograph, 12). Lanham, MD: University Press of America, 1990.

Ernst, M. *Globalization and the Re-shaping of Christianity in the Pacific Islands.* Suva: Pacific Theological College, 2006.

Farhadian, Charles. *Christianity, Islam and Nationalism in Indonesia.* London: Routledge, 2005.

Garrett, John. *To Live among the Stars: Christian Origins in Oceania.* Geneva and Suva: World Council of Churches and Institute of Pacific Studies, 1982.

Jebens, Holger. *Pathways to Heaven: Contesting Mainline and Fundamentalist Christianity in Papua New Guinea.* New York: Berghahn, 2005.

Robbins, Joel. *Becoming Sinners: Christianity and Moral Torment in a Papua New Guinean Society* (Ethnographic Studies in Subjectivity, 4). Berkeley, CA: University of California Press, 2004.

Scott, Michael W. *The Severed Snake: Matrilineages, Making Place, and a Melanesian Christianity in Southeast Solomon Islands.* Durham, NC: Carolina Academic Press, 2007.

Trompf, Garry, ed., *The Gospel is Not Western: Black Theologies from the Southwest Pacific.* Maryknoll, NY: Orbis, 1987.

Trompf, Garry. *Melanesian Religion.* Cambridge: Cambridge University Press, 2004 edn.

Trompf, Garry. *Payback: The Logic of Retribution in Melanesian Religions.* Cambridge: Cambridge University Press, 2008.

Conclusion: World Christianity
Its History, Spread, and Social Influence

Robert D. Woodberry

In recent years, Europeans and North Americans have begun to realize the importance of world Christianity. This realization is transforming our understanding of Christian history, the future of Christianity, and the role it has played in shaping the world.

Ancient African and Asian Christianity and Its Social Impact

Increasingly, scholars recognize that African and Asian Christianity is ancient – beginning either before or concurrently with European Christianity (see chapters 1, 7, and 9). Much of what is now the Muslim world was once Christian. In fact four of the five patriarchates are now in predominantly Muslim/Jewish countries (Alexandria, Jerusalem, Antioch, and Constantinople/Istanbul). Only Rome is now in a predominantly Christian area.

Historically, Christians predominated in North Africa, the Middle East, and Turkey, and the Christian Fathers – Tertullian, Cyprian, Cyril of Alexandria, Athanasius, and Augustine – were North African. Even Christian monasticism began in Egypt. Christians also had significant presence in Iran, Afghanistan, Yemen, Saudi Arabia, and most central Asian countries. By the second century, Christians were in Afghanistan, and by 424 Afghanistan had over 12 metropolitan bishops. Thus, before there were Christians in Lithuania, there had been over 1,000 years of continuous Christian presence in Afghanistan.[2] Yet now Christianity is considered indigenous in Lithuania and foreign in Afghanistan.

Early Christianity also spread to parts of Asia that are not predominantly Muslim. South Indian Christians claim the Apostle Thomas spread Christianity there. This is hard to prove, but some non-Indian sources suggest the same thing and Christianity arrived very early. Ancient Christianity also spread to Sri Lanka, China, Mongolia, Tibet, and possibly to Indonesia and Malaysia (see chapters 7 and 9).[3] There are Christian inscriptions in Tibet/Xizang from before the start of Tibetan Buddhism.[4] Important segments of the Mongols were Christian (including Kublai Khan's mother and two brothers),[5] as were many Turkic peoples (e.g., many Uighers).[6] This Christian influence is still visible in the written languages of Mongol peoples – which are primarily based on Syriac, the language of the Eastern Church.[7]

Early Asian Christianity shaped other religious traditions (and was shaped by them as well). The prophet Muhammad interacted with both Jews and Christians and most Islamic rituals mirror earlier Jewish and Christian ones.[8] Some scholars even suggest that parts of the Qur'an copy Syriac Christian liturgical texts.[9] Sufism (i.e., Islamic mysticism) also contains many Christian elements.[10] Even in central Asia where Christianity was wiped out, artistic evidence remains: for example, Christian symbols are common in oriental carpets.[11]

Christianity seems to have shaped Mahayana Buddhism as well. When Kanishka (a Greek-speaking,

Introducing World Christianity, First Edition. Edited by Charles E. Farhadian.
© 2012 Blackwell Publishing Ltd. Published 2012 by Blackwell Publishing Ltd.

central Asian ruler, circa 127–44 AD) convened the council that established Mahayana Buddhism, Jews and possibly Christians were in his kingdom. Moreover, as Mahayana Buddhism developed, Christians and Buddhists seem to have interacted closely.[12] Most early Christian texts discovered in central Asia come from ancient Buddhist pagodas and monasteries (e.g., Dunhuang). The architecture of some early Eastern churches and the structure of Buddhist mandalas mirror each other (both represent the mystical structure of the universe in similar ways).[13] Moreover, a Christian monk named Adam who lived in Xian China circa 782 CE was an important translator of Buddhist scriptures into Chinese.[14] Thus, while Buddhism shaped central Asian Christianity, Christianity seems to have shaped Mahayana Buddhism as well, particularly the Pure Land form popular in Japan and Korea.[15]

However, violence, conversion, and emigration wiped out most Asian and African Christianity, though some ancient Christian minorities remain in India and the Middle East (see chapters 1 and 7).[16] Even in Ethiopia, Islamic invasions (1527–42 CE) decimated Christianity. Without the military intervention of the Portuguese, it is unlikely Ethiopian Christianity would have survived.[17]

Christianity during the European Colonial Period and Its Social Consequences

Over time, people forgot both this early Christian presence and that Islam and Buddhism were once imported through either force or missions. In the wake of European colonialism, nationalist movements often developed along religious lines, defining Christians and other minorities outside the realm of the nation.[18] Thus, many perceive Christianity as a "European religion, introduced in conjunction with colonization" even in India and the Middle East, which have almost 2,000 years of continuous Christian presence, far longer than most of Europe. This introduces two important themes: the association of Christianity with Western missions and the association of missions with colonialism.

However, the relationship between missions and colonialism was quite complex (see, for example, chapters 2, 4, and 9). Missionaries could not avoid association with European colonization. Colonizers could restrict missions and thus missionaries had to negotiate with them. Moreover, local people often associated missionaries and colonizers regardless of missionary attitudes or behavior. Of course, some missionaries were closely connected to the colonial state, but this was not universal.

Nonconformists and evangelical Protestant missionaries consistently pressed for separation between religion and state.[19] For example, the British East India Company (BEIC)[20] originally financed Hindu and Muslim festivals, banned Indian Christians from military or government service, and prevented Christian missionaries from entering their territory.[21] Evangelicals blocked the BEIC Charter in 1813 and forced them to allow missionaries. Through similar political action, missionaries gained legal permission to work with slaves in the Caribbean.[22] But missionaries had to fight for these rights.

In fact, even after Protestant missionaries forced greater religious liberty, colonial officials often gave hiring preference to non-Christians and kept missionaries out of Muslim regions – indirectly fostering the spread of Islam (see chapters 3 and 8).[23] Thus, easy generalizations about missions as the handmaiden of colonialism cannot be sustained.

During Europe's scramble for colonies most missionaries believed colonization was inevitable for most societies; the only question was who the colonizer would be. Thus Catholic missionaries typically wanted colonization by "Catholic" powers, which usually meant Catholic missions were subsidized and Protestants restricted (see chapter 12). Protestant missionaries typically wanted colonization by "Protestant" powers, which meant missionaries would be free to work with limited government interference. Protestants' concerns were heightened after France colonized Tahiti and Madagascar, expelled Protestant missionaries, and gave Protestant schools to Catholic religious Orders.[24]

However, in contexts where missionaries (1) believed colonization was avoidable and (2) were free to do mission work (e.g., Thailand and Ethiopia), many missionaries actively fought colonization. In other cases they pressured the British to create protectorates to prevent white settlers from confiscating indigenous land (e.g., Botswana) and worked hard to keep colonial officials from changing the rules after the fact.[25]

Social Consequences of Missions during the European Colonial Period

The social impact of Christian missions was also complex. Where the state financed and chose missionaries (e.g., Spanish and Portuguese colonies), missionaries often functioned like government officials and seldom challenged colonial or settler interests (see chapter 12). Even when priests and brothers protested abuses, it generally had little long-term effect. They did not have *independent* organizations they could mobilize (they appealed to the conscience of friends in the aristocracy). Moreover, white settlers and aristocrats could too easily punish and silence them (the Spanish and Portuguese Crowns controlled the Patronage of the Church).[26]

However, where the state did not finance or choose missionaries (i.e., British and American colonies), missionaries were more likely to critique both the colonial state and white settlers. Thus missionaries mobilized campaigns against slavery, forced labor, and the opium trade, and for indigenous land rights, and punishment of settlers and officials who abused indigenous peoples (see chapters 2, 3, 4, 9, and 14).[27] That said, most missionaries were not political activists. They thought their primary role was to convert people. Most backed into political agitation reluctantly and primarily when abuses interfered with their ability to convert people.[28]

Missionaries also tried to reform behaviors they considered immoral in their host societies (e.g., foot binding, sati,[29] female infanticide, female genital cutting, child marriage, polygamy, and indigenous slavery) (see chapters 2, 4, 8, 14, 15, and 16).[30] In the process they introduced many of the organizational forms and tactics that are prominent in modern social movements.[31] These mission-led campaigns created powerful reactions (see chapter 2).[32]

However, the British (and other religious liberty colonizers) needed the cooperation of local elites to run their colonies; thus these colonizers were forced to allow local elites to mobilize both against mission conversion attempts and for or against mission-sponsored reform movements. In the process Hindu, Buddhist, Muslim, and other elites created nation-wide organizations, newspapers, and recognized leaders that later became important in the anti-colonial movement and in the rise of political parties. In British colonies, this colonial civil society helped lay the foundation for postcolonial democracy. But because most organizations developed along religious lines, it also laid the foundation for interreligious violence (e.g., India, Pakistan, Sri Lanka, Burma, and Egypt).[33]

Missionaries were also important in transferring ideas, technology, and foodstuffs between "European" and "non-European" societies. Early Catholic missionaries (1500s–1700s) stand out in this regard. Jesuit artists influenced the art and architecture of India, Persia, China, and Japan, introduced more accurate world maps, astronomy, and mathematics to Asia, and transferred information about Asian religion, philosophy, arts, and technology back to Europe (see chapter 9).[34] These early Catholic missions were far more culturally sensitive than most subsequent missionary activity (either Protestant or Catholic) – at least in areas not under the Spanish or Portuguese Crowns.[35] Not until the twentieth century do we see such *widespread* attempts to respect and draw on indigenous cultures.

Missionaries of the nineteenth and twentieth centuries also had a transformative role on mass education, mass printing, public health, nationalism, democracy, and religious transformations.

(1) *Education.* Protestants believed people needed to be able to read the Bible in their own language. Thus, wherever they went, they quickly began mass education (including for women and the poor) (see chapters 1, 2, 3, 4, 5, 8, 14, 15, and 16). Prior to Protestant missions, economic, political, and religious elites in many societies had good educations, but did not transfer these skills to others. After initially resisting Protestant mission education, other groups invested in mass education to compete with them. But Protestants developed techniques for mass classroom education, produced early textbooks, and trained teachers who worked in other schools. Thus societies, regions, and ethnic groups with more exposure to Protestant missionaries still have higher educational enrollments and literacy rates.[36]

Missionaries were also crucial in teaching foreign languages, Western sciences, medicine, public health, and agricultural techniques, and in founding most early universities. Throughout Asia, investment in university education by the state and by non-Protestant religious groups consistently followed Protestant initiatives. States nationalized many mission-sponsored universities and cut their religious ties, but they remain among the best universities in Asia and the Middle East (see chapters 1 and 9).[37]

(2) *Printing and newspapers.* Protestant missionaries (and those who worked with them) also generally initiated mass printing and newspapers. Of course, printing skills were developed in East Asian societies hundreds of years before Europe, and they were first to discover metal, movable-font type. But until the arrival of Protestant missionaries, printing did not lead to newspapers or a radical transformation of who owned texts. Manuscripts continued to be a common form of communication well into the nineteenth century. Similarly, the Muslim, Theravada Buddhists, Sikh, and Hindu societies of Asia and North Africa were repeatedly exposed to printed material and printing technology over several hundred years, but did not print until they faced Protestant missionary competition.[38]

(3) *Western medicine and public health.* Missionaries were also important transmitters of Western medical ideas, through providing doctors and nurses, female literacy, public-health training, and creating medical schools in societies around the world (see chapters 8 and 16). This seems to have had a significant impact on life expectancies and infant mortality.[39]

(4) *Nationalism and democracy.* Missionaries also transferred ideas about democracy and self-determination, even if they did not fully apply them (see chapter 16).[40] Throughout Africa and Asia (including the Middle East), the first generation of nationalist leaders were almost universally graduates of missionary schools or had close contact with missionaries – even if some of them reacted strongly against Christianity (see chapters 1, 2, 8, and 9).[41] In statistical analysis, the historic prevalence of Protestant missionaries is a powerful predictor of democracy.[42]

(5) *Religious transformations.* All major world faiths were shaped by the encounter with Christian missions of the nineteenth and twentieth centuries. In reaction to Christian missions, Buddhism and "Hinduism"

became more textbased.[43] The Hindu Vedas (which were mostly transmitted orally) were compiled and codified into an "Ur-text." Versions of the *Mahabharata* and *Ramayana* were compared to create a standardized form – although these varied by as many as 26,000 lines.[44]

Hindus, Buddhists, and Muslims created social reform organizations and vernacular education systems to compete with missionaries, and reformulated doctrines to make them "more scientific," palatable to Westerners, and effective in challenging missionary critiques. Reformers framed Hinduism and Buddhism as more spiritual than the "materialistic" West, more tolerant and open to gender equality than monotheism, more rational and scientific than Christianity. They presented "Eastern" religion as the spiritual source from which all other religions flow. European and North American radicals (particularly Theosophists) helped foster these developments. The Theosophist Annie Besant was briefly head of the Indian National Congress Party and helped develop Hindu university education. Similarly, the Theosophist Coronel Olcott wrote the Buddhist catechism used in Sri Lankan schools for much of the twentieth century.[45]

In turn, these reformulated traditions shaped Europe and North America. They were used to critique Christianity, created impetus for religious universalism, and fostered interest in mysticism and meditation (neglected in Christianity since the Enlightenment).[46] During the early twentieth century, particular versions of these reformulated traditions were also used in Aryan racial ideology.[47]

Religious Consequences of Missions during the European Colonial Period

The spread of Christianity in Africa, Asia, Latin America, and Oceania has been primarily through the agency of local Christians, not missionaries (see chapters 2, 3, 9, 12, 13, 15, and 16). But foreign missionaries were important in initiating the introduction (or reintroduction) of Christianity into these regions of the world. Many assume that European colonialism spurred conversions, but the relationship between colonization and conversions seems to depend on how long colonization lasted, how much restriction colonizers put on religious alternatives, and whether the pre-colonial religion(s) had a written language.

Christians did use conquests and forced conversion in Europe and sometimes in Spanish and Portuguese colonies. But colonization and "incentivized" conversion are not only, or predominantly, a Christian/ European phenomena. Muslims "colonized" the Middle East, North Africa, Central Asia, and parts of Europe, sometimes for hundreds of years, before the majority became Muslim. Discriminatory laws against non-Muslims were not the only reason for conversions and differential fertility/survival, but they were important (see chapter 1).[48] Similarly, Arians invaded the Indian subcontinent and spread Vedic religion (part of what we now call Hinduism).[49] Asoka and Menander were military conquers who spread Buddhism, and Buddhist priests actively persecuted minority religions like Christianity in East Asia (see chapter 9);[50] Zoroastrians persecuted religious minorities in Persia;[51] Jews attempted forced conversions when they controlled Yemen.[52] Confucians and Taoists initially banned and persecuted both Christianity and Buddhism as foreign religions; though later Chinese rulers promoted Buddhism (see chapter 9).[53] The areas where different religions currently predominate is heavily influenced by military conquests and state imposition – even if these impositions are ancient enough that people have forgotten them.

Among European colonizers, the Spanish and Portuguese controlled Latin America and the Philippines for hundreds of years and severely restricted religious alternatives. Eventually conversion to Catholicism was almost universal (see chapter 12). However, other European colonial regimes were shorter and usually less religiously restrictive. This "weaker" colonization seems to have hampered conversions because it (1) associated Christianity with colonial oppression; (2) provided few material and social incentives to convert; (3) restricted polygamy, concubinage, and cross-racial marriage, thus limiting the number of children raised in the "colonial religion"; and (4) remained in power too briefly for discriminatory policies and emotional links to previous religious traditions to be forgotten.

If European colonialism fostered conversions, we would expect to find most conversions during the colonial period and among the people most subject to European domination, but we do not – at least outside Spanish and Portuguese colonies. Elsewhere, most conversions happened either before or after colonization and disproportionately among those most threatened by non-European domination.

In Polynesia, Christianity spread widely prior to colonization – mostly through Polynesian missionaries (see chapter 15). In China and Japan, Catholic Christianity spread widely in the 1500s and 1600s (prior to any significant colonial threat), but was then crushed. Later, when European colonialism was a threat, Christianity made little headway.[54] However, recently (well after any colonial threat), Christianity has spread rapidly in China again (see chapter 9). Most conversions in Africa came after the end of colonization – although a high rate of conversion started earlier.[55]

Conversely, domination by non-European, non-Christians seems to foster conversion to Christianity. For example, Japan colonized Korea and sponsored Buddhism and Shinto in an attempt to control and Japanize Koreans. Instead Christianity spread rapidly. Now about a third of Koreans are Christian. In Korea it was easy to be both a Christian and a nationalist (see chapter 9).[56] In most other Asian societies it was not.

Ethnic minorities and despised castes are also more likely to convert to Christianity (e.g., in China, Southeast Asia, and India) (see chapters 7 and 8)[57] and in Latin America, poor, marginalized people are more likely to convert to Protestantism (see chapters 12 and 13). Similarly, recent impositions of Islamic law (Sharia) and violent Islamist movements have spurred conversions from Islam to Christianity, although they have also caused existing Christian minorities to flee (see chapter 1).[58] In all these cases, when the major threat of oppression was from non-Christian (or non-Protestant) elites, conversions increased.

"Postcolonial" Christianity and Its Social Consequences

In the twentieth and twenty-first centuries Christianity has become increasingly a non-Western religion. Christianity has grown in Africa and Asia, and both Protestantism and church attendance have increased in

Latin America, but Christianity and church attendance have declined in Europe (see chapter 5). This raises several important questions: (1) what are the social implications of Christianity's spread outside Europe; (2) what are the social implications of Christianity's decline in Europe; and (3) are these two movements connected (e.g., will the European pattern of secularization inevitably spread to other societies as they "develop")?

Good statistical data about religion in Africa, Asia, Latin America, and Oceania are rare and recent, making it difficult to access the social impact of Christian growth. However, cross-national statistical literature consistently finds a positive association between the percent of Protestants in a society and both the level of democracy and the stability of democratic transitions.[59] There is also a strong positive association between the prevalence of Protestant missionaries and democracy.[60] However, qualitative and historical research suggests Protestant groups do not inevitably support democracy and can become as mired in corruption and abuse as anyone else (see chapters 4 and 12).[61] Thus any association between Protestantism and democracy is probabilistic, not deterministic. Moreover, the Catholic Church has been important for many post-1989 democratic transitions. Thus the statistical patterns may change over time.[62]

Protestantism generally also has a positive association with longer life-expectancies, lower infant mortality, lower corruption, more voluntarism, and greater education,[63] but again these relationships are complex; for example, some Protestant religious groups have been heavily involved in corrupt behavior. Moreover, there is substantial variation in the types of Protestantism that have spread (from "health and wealth" Pentecostalism[64] to high-Church Anglicanism) and it is unclear if the social impact of these different traditions is similar (see chapter 12).

Catholicism is not positively associated with these outcomes in cross-national statistical analysis (longer life-expectancies, lower infant mortality, lower corruption, more voluntarism, and greater education), but this may be a legacy of the close connection between Church and state in most Catholic societies prior to 1965 (rather than something inherent in the tradition).[65] In societies with greater separation

between Church and state, and thus greater religious competition (e.g., Ireland, Canada, and the US), the Catholic Church invested heavily in education and social services. Thus in the US, Catholics do not lag in education or other indicators of well-being.[66]

Moreover, Catholicism has also transformed substantially during the twentieth century. At the Second Vatican Council (1962–5) the Catholic Church officially recognized the validity of religious liberty, separation of Church and state, democracy, and vernacular Bible reading by the laity. Liberation theology and then counter-movements spread through the Catholic clergy. The charismatic renewal (often under lay leadership) became a powerful force among Catholics – particularly in Africa, Asia, and Latin America (see chapter 12).

Thus the social impact of Catholicism may be changing as well. Certainly the Catholic hierarchy has played an important role in many peace and democratization movements,[67] and both Catholics and Protestants report high levels of life satisfaction.[68] Moreover, in some countries (e.g., Korea) where Protestants have sullied their reputation through aggressive proselytization and association with authoritarian leaders, Catholicism has recently spread rapidly and Protestantism declined (see chapter 9).

The social consequences of Christian decline in Europe have also received little scholarly attention. Marriage and fertility rates have declined precipitously – falling well below replacement levels. Many scholars partially attribute this decline to secularization.[69] The economic historian Niall Ferguson suggests secularization may have fostered declining emphasis on work and slower economic growth.[70] However, this view is not widely held and life expectancies and quality of life in Europe remain high by world standards. A substantial popular literature suggests secularization has benefited European society, but most of these arguments have not been tested rigorously.[71]

Western scholars traditionally argued that as other societies modernized they would follow the European pattern and become more secular. However, many scholars now view Europe as the exception – not the rule (see chapter 5).[72] In Europe, the close historic connection between Church and state made the Church a target when secular elites wanted to take control of the state. State regulation of conversionary groups allowed state churches to be lazy, and pushed religiously active minorities to leave. The state paid clergy salaries, which undermined clergy's need to recruit congregants. State officials and landed elites often chose clergy who would maintain the status quo. Finally, for instance, Germany imposes a religious tax on people who attend church or claim a religious identity. The state decides how the money is used, not the tax payer. This creates financial incentives not to be religious (it is cheaper to be secular).

Interestingly, in the wake of European secularization, a wave of reverse missionaries from Africa, Asia, and Latin America are coming to Europe and North America (see chapters 5 and 12). Some of these missionaries are Hindu, Buddhist, Bahai, and Muslim, but many are Christian. Moreover, the members and clergy of European-based, hierarchical denominations like the Catholic and Anglican Churches are increasingly non-European and more theologically conservative. Over time more theologically conservative, non-Europeans will probably assume leadership in these Churches, with unknown implications.

Contextualization and Indigenization

Academics often critique missionaries and world Christianity for lack of contextualization (i.e., adaption to the local context). But missionaries often debated the best ways to contextualize Christianity well before the rise of modern anthropology.[73]

Historically, contextualization of religious traditions developed naturally through isolation. Japanese Buddhists were not trying to be different from Chinese Buddhists, but they had little regular contact, and Japanese versions of Chinese temples ended up looking different. East Asian Buddhist temples often copy Indian forms (e.g., images of elephants and lions), even though these animals do not exist in East Asia. Similarly, the "St Thomas" Christians of Southern India integrated rituals and architectural elements from Hinduism (see chapter 7), but this reflects long isolation.[74] Similarly, as Christianity spread in Europe (often through mass conversions), converts integrated pre-Christian forms into it (e.g., Christmas trees, Easter eggs – both of which are fertility symbols).

Now, contact between societies is much greater, and music, pictures, speakers, and books travel freely, creating greater potential for homogenization, but also spurring resistance. Some contextualization happens inevitably. People always interpret ideas and practices from their own cultural tradition, and meanings inevitably change as they cross cultures and languages. Translating the Bible into a local language requires contextualizing the meanings of Hebrew and Greek words and symbols into the language and symbolic vocabulary of a local people – which necessitates some meaning shift.[75] Other contextualization happens through popular movements (e.g., African Initiated Churches or AICs). Yet AICs thrived during the late-colonial period when anti-colonial and anti-European resentments were high, but have faltered since (e.g., see chapters 2 and 4).

Other contextualization has happened through academic theologians, missionaries, artists, and musicians. However, this type of contextualization has typically been more popular with missionaries and educated elites than ordinary local people. Missionaries have financed contextualized versions of Church architecture,[76] and there are several examples of attempts by missionaries at contextualization (e.g., see chapters 2 and 4). But local Christians have seldom copied and spread these approaches elsewhere. A market for world Christian art has also developed, but much of it is purchased by people in Europe and North America. Most self-conscious attempts to contextualize by intellectuals have not gained many adherents.

Why this resistance? Some may be inevitable distinctions between the tastes of elites and ordinary people. But converts are often distancing themselves from the dominant religion of their society and do not want to copy symbols from the tradition they are leaving. Thus they may not want a church that looks like a Hindu temple or rituals that mirror Islamic prayers. This is true in reverse. Europeans and North Americans who convert to Buddhism and Hinduism usually do not want temples that look like churches or monks who look like Protestant ministers; they enjoy the "exotic" and "authentic" feel of temples that imitate South Indian or Thai architecture and monks who wear saffron robes. Contextualization of Eastern religions in the West happens more through emphases on sexual liberation, gender equality, environmental-ism, and social action than in visual representation. Similarly, the types of Christianity that have spread outside Europe and North America focus heavily on local felt needs, such as dealing with demonic spirits, removing curses, and imparting spiritual healing (see chapters 3, 4, 7, 8, 12, 13, 16, and 17).

However, some self-conscious contextualization has been effective among Muslims and Hindus where social and legal restrictions on conversion are high. Here some movements avoid the label "Christian" and draw on Muslim or Hindu ritual practices. These contextualizations allow new adherents to stay in relationship with friends and family and therefore spread. However, these movements are very controversial with missionaries and other Christians.[77]

Accommodations that remove political, social, and economic barriers to conversion have often been effective, but also extremely controversial: for instance, allowing churches to organize by caste or race or allowing polygamy, female genital cutting, and slavery. These allowances have been made both in Europe and North America (race- and class-based organization, and moderating critiques of slavery) and elsewhere. Deciding which are morally justified contextualizations and which are morally reprehensible accommodations is difficult to define in the abstract. Who has the power and authority to decide these questions is also tricky.

Religious Persecution and Violence

Another important issue is religious persecution and violence. Christianity spread to parts of Europe through conquest (e.g., Lithuania) and Spanish and Portuguese colonizers often imposed Christianity on indigenous people. However, minority Protestant groups (e.g., Baptists and Quakers) became convinced that state-imposed religious conformity did not save anyone. Thus these minorities advocated religious liberty on religious grounds.[78] Even when they came to power and could have imposed a state religion (e.g., Rhode Island, Pennsylvania, and Delaware), they refused (see chapter 10). Over time religious liberty spread more broadly; for instance, after the Second Vatican Council (1965) religious liberty was accepted by the Catholic Church.

However, religious persecution is still common in many societies (see chapters 1, 6, and 8); thus any discussion of world Christianity must consider the role of persecution and violence in the spread of the religion. While many claim that monotheistic religions are more likely to initiate religious persecution,[79] the empirical evidence for this is weak. Measures of religious liberty in the twentieth and twenty-first centuries consistently suggest predominantly Protestant societies have the greatest religious liberty and predominantly Muslim countries the least.[80] Both are monotheistic.

Historically, "non-monotheistic" and secular societies have not been very tolerant either – at least not toward religions whose absolute moral claims limit rulers' power (e.g., Christianity). Authoritarian rulers have either tried to co-opt Christianity or destroy it. The Roman Empire allowed most religious traditions, but persecuted Christians. In Persia, Zoroastrians persecuted Christians. In Tang dynasty China, Taoist/Confucian rulers banned both Buddhism and Christianity as foreign religions, and persecuted Christians out of existence. In Ming dynasty China, Christians were annihilated once again (see chapter 9).[81]

When Christianity first entered Korea, Japan, and Vietnam it initially spread rapidly and was then severely persecuted by Buddhist and Confucian elites.[82] In fact, in Japan every family was forced to register with a Buddhist temple and Japanese were required to step on a picture of Jesus or Mary every year to insure that they were not Christian. Those who refused were tortured or killed.[83] Significant conversions to Christianity in Hindu India also spurred violent persecution, and interreligious violence continues to be a problem.[84]

Secular Enlightenment and Marxist governments have not been better (see chapters 5, 6, 8, and 12). In Europe, the French Revolution led to extreme violence against Catholics. In Latin America, Enlightenment revolutions in Mexico and Uruguay persecuted Catholics as well (and often continued restrictions on Protestants). Marxist regimes in Russia, China, Cambodia, Vietnam, Cuba, Ethiopia, Mozambique, and elsewhere have directly targeted Christians and killed millions. Thus religious violence is not inherently monotheistic or even religious. The point here is not to designate which group is the worst violator of religious freedom, but to suggest that most groups are capable of persecuting others. In fact, careful empirical work suggests that religious violence is often strategic, a means for political elites to maintain power.[85]

Conclusion

Christianity has interacted with other religious traditions throughout its history. The isolation of European "Christendom" is the exception rather than the rule. The long interactions between Christianity and other traditions have profoundly influenced all involved. Moreover, the religious geography of the world has been in regular flux for thousands of years. For example, the religions that predominated in Afghanistan, Egypt, and Korea have changed radically over time. But because we view so much history through the lens of European colonialism, we tend to overlook this, with important political and theoretical consequences. Currently Christianity and Islam are spreading in Africa and Asia, while Buddhism, Hinduism, Islam, and other religious traditions are spreading in Europe and North America, and Protestantism is spreading in Latin America. Thus, this long-term interaction is being renewed and revitalized. While some interactions between religions may be violent, history suggests that many interactions will be peaceful and engender creative religious and social transformations.

Notes and References

[1] I thank the Templeton Foundation for generous support that helped me complete this work.

[2] Philip Jenkins, *The Lost History of Christianity* (New York: HarperOne, 2008).

[3] Samuel Hugh Moffett, *A History of Christianity in Asia (Vol. I)* (Maryknoll, NY: Orbis, 1992); Adolf Heuken, SJ, "Christianity in Pre-Colonial Indonesia," in Jan S. Aritonang and Karel A. Steenbrink, eds, *A History of Christianity in Indonesia* (Leiden: Brill, 2008), 3–7.

[4] Christoph Baumer, *The Church of the East* (London: I.B. Tauris, 2006), 174–6.

[5] Kublai Khan (grandson of Genghis Khan) founded the Yuan dynasty in China (1271–1368 CE).

[6] Philip Jenkins, *The Lost History of Christianity*.

[7] Richard. C. Foltz, *Religions of the Silk Road* (New York: St Martin's Griffin, 1999), 69.

[8] J. Dudley Woodberry, "Contextualization among Muslims: Reusing Common Pillars," *International Journal of Frontier Missions* 13 (1996): 171–86.

[9] Christoph Luxenberg. *The Syro-Aramaic Reading of the Koran* (Berlin: Hans Schiler, 2007).

[10] Philip Jenkins, *The Lost History of Christianity*, 177.

[11] Volkmar Gantzhorn, *The Christian Oriental Carpet* (Köln: Benedikt Taschen, 1991).

[12] Richard. C. Foltz, *Religions of the Silk Road*, 45–7, 64–87.

[13] Volkmar Gantzhorn, *The Christian Oriental Carpet*, 39–42.

[14] Samuel Hugh Moffett, *A History of Christianity in Asia (Vol. I)* (Maryknoll, NY: Orbis, 1992), 301–2.

[15] For example, Masses for the dead. The story of Buddha's life also seems to contain Jewish and Christian elements and Maitreya (the future Buddha) mirrors the Jewish and Christian Messiah. Richard. C. Foltz, *Religions of the Silk Road*, 46; Etienne Lamotte, *History of Indian Buddhism* (Louvain: Peters Press, 1988), 668–75; Ralph R. Covell, *Confucius, the Buddha, and Christ* (Maryknoll, NY: Orbis, 1986), 30–1; Samuel Hugh Moffett, *A History of Christianity in Asia (Vol. I)*, 301–2; Philip Jenkins, *The Lost History of Christianity*, 14–6, 91–3.

[16] Philip Jenkins, *The Lost History of Christianity*. Jenkins claims that religious violence was the main reason for Christianity's decline in Africa and Asia (p. 141).

[17] Deborah E. Horowitz, ed., *Ethiopian Art* (Baltimore, MD: Trustees of the Walters Art Gallery, 2001), 57–8.

[18] Peter Van der Veer, *Imperial Encounters* (Princeton, NJ: Princeton University Press, 2001); Richard Gombrich and Gananath Obeyesekere, *Buddhism Transformed* (Princeton, NJ: Princeton University Press, 1988).

[19] Nonconformists were *not* members of the state Church (e.g., non-Anglicanism in England). Evangelicals were Trinitarian Protestants who emphasized evangelism and scriptural authority.

[20] The BEIC was a monopoly trade company given permission by the British to govern territories in Asia. After 1858, the British Crown took over administration of their colonies.

[21] Kenneth Ingham, *Reformers in India 1793–1833* (Cambridge: Cambridge University Press, 1956), 15; Robert Eric Frykenberg, *Christianity in India* (New York: Oxford University Press, 2009).

[22] Paul Knaplund, *James Stephen and the British Colonial System: 1813–1847* (Madison, WI, University of Wisconsin Press, 1953); Mary Turner, *Slaves and Missionaries* (Barbados: The Press University of the West Indies, 1998).

[23] Bengt Sundkler and Christopher Steed, *A History of the Church in Africa* (New York: Cambridge University Press,

2000), 650–4; Kenneth Ingham, *Reformers in India 1793–1833*, 15; Andrew E. Barnes, *Making Headway: The Introduction of Western Civilization in Colonial Northern Nigeria* (Rochester, NY: University of Rochester Press, 2009).

[24] James G. Greenlee and Charles M. Johnston, *Good Citizens: British Missionaries and Imperial States, 1870–1918* (Montreal: McGill-Queen's University Press, 1999).

[25] Neil Parson, *King Khama, Emperor Joe and the Great White Queen* (Chicago, IL: University of Chicago Press, 1998); Matthew Lange, *Lineages of Despotism and Development* (Chicago, IL: University of Chicago Press, 2009), 143–8.

[26] Robert D. Woodberry, "The Shadow of Empire: Christian Missions, Colonial Policy and Democracy in Postcolonial Societies," PhD diss. (Chapel Hill, NC: University of North Carolina, 2004). Catholic religious who protested colonial abuses include Bartolome de las Casas, Francesco Ingoli, Julián Garcés, Bernadino de Minaya, Epifanio de Moirans, Francisco José de Jaca, Miguel Garcia, and Gonçalo Leite.

[27] Robert D. Woodberry, "The Shadow of Empire"; Robert D. Woodberry, "Reclaiming the M-Word: The Consequences of Missions for Nonwestern Societies," *The Review of Faith and International Affairs* 4 (2006): 3–12; Norman Etherington, *Missions and Empire* (New York: Oxford University Press, 2005).

[28] Jon Miller and Gregory Stanczak, "Redeeming, Ruling, and Reaping: British Missionary Societies, the East India Company and the India-to-China Opium Trade," *Journal for the Scientific Study of Religion* 48 (2009): 332–52.

[29] In parts of India, when a high caste "Hindu" man died his wife(s) was expected to burn herself to death on his funeral pyre.

[30] Robert D. Woodberry, "The Shadow of Empire."

[31] For example, voluntary organizations with boards of directors, traveling speakers and newsletters, petition campaigns, marchers, signed pledges to boycott product, and so on.

[32] Peter Van der Veer, *Imperial Encounters*; Robert D. Woodberry, "The Shadow of Empire."

[33] Robert D. Woodberry, "The Shadow of Empire."

[34] Samuel Hugh Moffett, *A History of Christianity in Asia (Vols. II)*; Gauvin Alexander Bailey, *The Jesuits and the Grand Mogul* (Washington, DC: Smithsonian Institution, 1998); Gauvin Alexander Bailey, *Art on the Jesuit Missions in Asia and Latin America: 1542–1773* (Toronto: University of Toronto Press, 1999).

[35] In 1659 the Propaganda Fide (the congregation that oversaw most Catholic missions) instructed its missionaries:

> do not bring any pressure to bear on the peoples to change their manners, customs, and uses unless they are evidently contrary to religion and sound morals. . . . there is no stronger cause for alienation and hate than an attack on local custom, especially . . . when an attempt is made to introduce the customs of another people in the place of those which have been abolished. . . . do your utmost to adapt yourselves to them.

Cited in Stephen Neill, *A History of Christian Missions* (London: Penguin, 1986), 153.

[36] Robert D. Woodberry, "The Shadow of Empire"; Francesco Gallego and Robert D. Woodberry, "Christian Missions and Education in Former African Colonies: How Competition Mattered," *Journal of African Economies* 19 (2010): 294–319. In Europe, see Egil Johansson, *The History of Literacy in Sweden in Comparison with Some Other Countries* (Umeå, Sweden: Umeå University and Umeå School of Education, 1977).

[37] Robert D. Woodberry, "The Shadow of Empire"; Jessie Gregory Lutz, *China and the Christian Colleges: 1850–1950.* (Ithaca, NY: Cornell University Press, 1971); Eleanor H. Tejirian and Reeva Spector Simon, eds, *Altruism and Imperialism* (New York: Middle East Institute, Columbia University, 2002).

[38] With the possible exceptions of Egypt and Turkey, Robert D. Woodberry, "Religion and the Spread of Human Capital and Political Institutions: Christian Missions as a Quasi-Natural Experiment," in Rachel McCleary, ed., *Oxford Handbook of the Economics of Religion* (Oxford: Oxford University Press, forthcoming).

[39] Robert D. Woodberry, "The Medical Impact of Missions," paper presented at the winter meetings of the *American Society for Church History*, Atlanta, Georgia, January 5, 2007; Charles H. Wood, Philip Williams, and Kuniko Chijiwa, "Protestantism and Child Mortality in Northeast Brazil, 2000," *Journal for the Scientific Study of Religion* 46 (2007): 405–16.

[40] Robert D. Woodberry, "The Shadow of Empire."

[41] Dana Robert, "The First Globalization; The Internationalization of the Protestant Missionary Movement between the World Wars," *International Bulletin of Missionary Research* 26 (2002): 50–66; Robert D. Woodberry, "The Shadow of Empire."

[42] Statistically Protestant missions "explains" about half the variation in democracy in Africa, Asia, Latin America, and Oceania and removes the factors that dominate current cross-national research. Robert D. Woodberry, "Weber through the Back Door: Protestant Competition, Elite Dispersion, and the Global Spread of Democracy," paper presented at the National Bureau of Economic Research, Cambridge, MA, October 15, 2009.

[43] Many scholars argue that "Hinduism" is an amalgam of different traditions that came to be viewed as unified through the encounter with European colonization and missions. Unifying "Hinduism" was particularly important for unifying the nationalist movement. Peter Van der Veer, *Imperial Encounters*; Geoffrey A. Oddie, *Imagined Hinduism* (New Delhi: SAGE Publications, 2006).

[44] Peter Van der Veer, *Imperial Encounters*, 106–33.

[45] Ibid., especially pages 75–7, 143; Richard Gombrich and Gananath Obeyesekere, *Buddhism Transformed*.

[46] Peter Van der Veer, *Imperial Encounters*; Bradford Verter, "Spiritual Capital: Theorizing Religion with Bourdieu against Bourdieu," *Sociological Theory* 21 (2003): 150–74.

[47] Peter Van der Veer, *Imperial Encounters, 134–57*; Nicholas Goodrick-Clarke, *The Occult Roots of Nazism* (New York: New York University Press, 1992); Nicholas Goodrick-Clarke, *Hitler's Priestess* (New York: New York University Press, 1998).

[48] Richard W. Bulliet, *Conversion to Islam in the Medieval Period* (Cambridge, MA: Harvard University Press, 1979); Philip Jenkins, *The Lost History of Christianity*.

[49] Robert Eric. Frykenberg, *Christianity in India*.

[50] Samuel Hugh Moffett, *A History of Christianity in Asia (Vols. I & II)* (Maryknoll, NY: Orbis, 1992, 2005); Mikael S. Adolphson, *The Teeth and Claws of the Buddha* (Honolulu: University of Hawai'i Press, 2007).

[51] Richard. C. Foltz, *Religions of the Silk Road*, 64–7.

[52] Luce Boulnois, *Silk Road,* transl. Helen Loveday (Hong Kong: Odyssey, 2005), 236; Philip Jenkins, *The Lost History of Christianity,* 189.

[53] Samuel Hugh Moffett, *A History of Christianity in Asia (Vol. I)*, 293–314, 471–5.

[54] Samuel Hugh Moffett, *A History of Christianity in Asia (Vols. I & II)*; Robert L. Montgomery, *The Diffusion of Religions: A Sociological Perspective* (Lanham, MD: University Press of America, 1996).

[55] Philip Jenkins, *The Next Christendom* (New York: Oxford University Press, 2002); David Maxwell, "Post-colonial Christianity in Africa," in Hugh McLeod, ed., *The Cambridge History of Christianity (Vol. 9): World Christianities c.1914–c.2000* (New York: Cambrige University Press, 2006), 401–21.

[56] James Huntley Grayson. *Korea: A Religious History* (London: RoutledgeCurzon, 2002).

[57] Philip Jenkins, *The Next Christendom* (New York: Oxford University Press, 2002); Robert L. Montgomery, *The Diffusion of Religions,* 113–18, 142–8.

[58] J. Dudley Woodberry, ed., *From Seed to Fruit: Global Trends, Fruitful Practices, and Emerging Issues among Muslims* (Pasadena, CA: William Carey Library, 2008).

[59] Kenneth A. Bollen and Robert W. Jackman, "Political Democracy and the Size Distribution of Income," *American Sociological Review* 50 (1985): 438–57; Robert D. Woodberry and Timothy Samuel Shah, "Christianity and Democracy: The Pioneering Protestants," *Journal of Democracy* 15 (2004): 47–61; Rollin F. Tusalem, "The Role of Protestantism in Democratic Consolidation among Transitional States," *Comparative Political Studies* 42 (2009): 882–915.

[60] Robert D. Woodberry, "The Shadow of Empire."

[61] Paul Freston, *Evangelicals and Politics in Asia, Africa, and Latin America* (New York: Cambridge University Press, 2001).

[62] Daniel Philpott, "The Catholic Wave," *Journal of Democracy* 15 (2004): 32–46.

[63] Robin Grier, "The Effect of Religion on Economic Development: A Cross National Study of 63 Former Colonies," *Kyklos* 50 (1997): 47–62; Daniel Treisman, "The Causes of Corruption: A Cross-national Study," *Journal of Public Economics* 76 (2000): 399–457; Robert D. Woodberry, "Pentecostalism and Economic Development," in Jonathan B. Imber, ed., *Markets, Morals, and Religion* (New Brunswick, NJ: Transaction Publishers, 2008), 157–77; Robert D. Woodberry, "Religion and the Spread of Human Capital and Political Institutions: Christian Missions as a Quasi-Natural Experiment," in Rachel McCleary, ed., *Oxford Handbook of the Economics of Religion* (Oxford: Oxford University Press, 2011), 111–31. Charles H. Wood, Philip Williams, and Kuniko Chijiwa, "Protestantism and Child Mortality in Northeast Brazil, 2000," *Journal for the Scientific Study of Religion* 46 (2007): 405–16.

[64] "Health and wealth" Pentecostalism (or Word of Faith Pentecostalism) teaches that God will reward those who follow him well with health and wealth in this life.

[65] The social impact of Eastern Orthodox Christianity is seldom studied quantitatively.

[66] Lehrer, Evelyn L, "Religion as a Determinant of Economic and Demographic Behavior," *Population and Development Review* 30 (2004): 707ff.

[67] Daniel Philpott, "The Catholic Wave," *Journal of Democracy* 15 (2004): 32–46.

[68] Bjørnskov, Christian, Axel Dreher, and Justina A. V. Fischer, "Cross-Country Determinants of Life Satisfaction; Exploring Differenty Determinants across Groups in Society," *Social Choice and Welfare* 30 (2008): 119–73.

[69] Ron Lesthaeghe and Johan Surkyn, "When History Moves on: The Foundations and Diffusion of the Second Demographic Transition," in Rukmalie Jayakody, Arland Thornton, and William G. Axinn, eds, *International Family Change: Ideational Perspectives* (Mahwah, NJ: Erlbaum, 2007), 81–118.

[70] Niall Ferguson, "Economics, Religion and the Decline of Europe," *Economic Affairs* 24 (2004): 37–40.

[71] For example, Christopher Hitchens, *God is Not Great: How Religion Poisons Everything* (New York: Twelve, 2007).

[72] For example, Grace Davie, *Europe, the Exceptional Case* (London: Darton, Longman & Todd, 2002); Peter L. Berger, Grace Davie, and Effie Fokas, *Religious America, Secular Europe?* (Burlington, VT: Ashgate, 2008); Rodney Stark and Roger Finke, *Acts of Faith.* (Berkeley, CA: University of California Press, 2000).

[73] William R. Hutchison, *Errand to the World* (Chicago, IL: University of Chicago Press, 1987); Robert D. Woodberry, "Reclaiming the M-Word: The Consequences of Missions for Nonwestern Societies," *The Review of Faith and International Affairs* 4 (2006): 3–12.

[74] Eastern Orthodox traditions typically emphasize preserving tradition, not innovation and contextualization, e.g., Coptic Christians use of images is not "contextualized' to Muslim societies in which images are forbidden.

[75] Lamin Sanneh, *Translating the Message* (Maryknoll, NY: Orbis, 1999).

[76] Daniel Johnson Fleming, *Heritage of Beauty: Pictorial Studies of Modern Christian Architecture in Asia and Africa Illustrating the Influence of Indigenous Cultures* (New York: Friendship Press, 1937).

[77] J. Dudley Woodberry, ed., *From Seed to Fruit: Global Trends, Fruitful Practices, and Emerging Issues among Muslims* (Pasadena, CA: William Carey Library, 2008).

[78] Philip Hamburger, *Separation of Church and State* (Cambridge, MA: Harvard University Press, 2002); Robert D. Woodberry, "The Shadow of Empire."

[79] Barrington Moor, E., Jr. *Moral Purity and Persecution in History* (Princeton, NJ: Princeton University Press, 2000); Christopher Hitchens, *God is Not Great.*

[80] Freedom House, *Religious Freedom by Religious Background* (Washington, DC: Freedom House, Center for Religious Freedom, 2004); Brian J. Grim and Roger Finke, *The Price of Freedom Denied: Religious Persecution in the 21st Century* (Cambridge: Cambridge University Press, 2010). Prior to the 1700s, Muslims were sometimes more tolerant of religious minorities than Christians, although discrimination remained widespread. Jane I. Smith, "Islam and Christendom," in John L. Esposito, ed., *The Oxford History of Islam* (New York: Oxford University Press, 1999), 305–45; Marshall G. S. Hodgson, *The Venture of Islam* (Chicago, IL: University of Chicago Press, 1974).

[81] Philip Jenkins, *The Lost History of Christianity.*

[82] Samuel Hugh Moffett, *A History of Christianity in Asia* (Vol. II); Peter C. Phan, "Christianity in Indochina," in Sheridan Gilley and Brian Stanley, eds, *The Cambridge History of Christianity (Vol. 8): World Christianities c.1815–c.1914* (New York: Cambrige University Press, 2006), 513–27.

[83] Richard H. Drummond, *A History of Christianity in Japan* (Grand Rapids, MI: Eerdmans, 1971).

[84] Robert Eric. Frykenberg, *Christianity in India*; Steven Wilkinson, *Votes and Violence* (New York: Cambridge University Press, 2004). Although violence against converts is often blamed on reactions to European colonization (and the colonial encounter may have accentuated it), religious violence also occurred in areas and periods with little colonial influence. For example, a major persecution of Christian converts began in 1799 in Tirunelveli (1) before the area was annexed by the British East India Company; (2) even though the leaders of the movement (Sathyanathan Pillai, Rasa Clorinda, and Chinnamutta Sundaranandam David) were indigenous; and (3) the missionaries who trained the evangelists were Germans who worked in a Danish trading post. However, mass conversion of Dalits threatened high-caste Hindus' power (pp. 209–11).

[85] Steven Wilkinson, *Votes and Violence.*

Further Reading

Baumer, Christoph. *The Church of the East: An Illustrated History of Assyrian Christianity.* London: I.B. Tauris, 2006.

Covell, Ralph R. *Confucius, the Buddha, and Christ.* Maryknoll, NY: Orbis, 1986.

Etherington, Norman. *Missions and Empire.* New York: Oxford University Press, 2005.

Foltz, Richard. C. *Religions of the Silk Road.* New York: St Martin's Griffin, 1999.

Freston, Paul. *Evangelicals and Politics in Asia, Africa, and Latin America.* New York: Cambridge University Press, 2001.

Greenlee, James G. and Charles M. Johnston. *Good Citizens: British Missionaries and Imperial States, 1870–1918.* Montreal: McGill-Queen's University Press, 1999.

Grim, Brian J. and Roger Finke. *The Price of Freedom Denied: Religious Persecution in the 21st Century.* Cambridge: Cambridge University Press, 2010.

Jenkins, Philip. *The Lost History of Christianity: The Thousand-Year Golden Age of the Church in the Middle East, Africa, and Asia and How It Died.* New York: HarperOne, 2008.

Luxenberg, Christoph. *The Syro-Aramaic Reading of the Koran: A Contribution to the Decoding of the Language of the Koran.* Berlin: Hans Schiler, 2007.

Moffett, Samuel Hugh. *A History of Christianity in Asia*, vols I and II. Maryknoll, NY: Orbis, 1992, 2005.

Sanneh, Lamin. *Translating the Message: The Missionary Impact on Culture*. Maryknoll, NY: Orbis, 1999.

Turner, Mary. *Slaves and Missionaries: The Disintegration of Jamaican Slave Society, 1787–1834*. Barbados: The Press University of the West Indies, 1998.

Van der Veer, Peter. *Imperial Encounters: Religion and Modernity in India and Britain*. Princeton, NJ: Princeton University Press, 2001.

Woodberry, Robert D. "*The Shadow of Empire: Christian Missions, Colonial Policy and Democracy in Postcolonial Societies*," PhD diss. Chapel Hill, NC: University of North Carolina, 2004.

Woodberry, Robert D. "Reclaiming the M-Word: The Consequences of Missions for Nonwestern Societies," *The Review of Faith and International Affairs* 4 (2006): 3–12.

Index

Abbasid (Caliphate)   11
abolition   40–2
Abyssinia   38, 44
adaptations   24–5, 43, 101, 103–4, 121, 157, 223, 236, 238
Adogame, Afe   74,
Adventists   85, 222, 224, 246, 253
   see also Seventh-day Adventists
Afghanistan   19, 259
African Inland Mission (AIM)   27
African Instituted Churches (AIC)   23, 27–8, 46, 48, 53, 265
Afrikaners   54
Aladura   47
Albania   77, 79, 81, 84
Alberta   145
alcohol   192, 223, 240
Algeria (Algerians)   7, 12–13, 16–17
Allen, Horace N.   125, 127
Amaladoss, Michael   96
Amazon   186
American Bible Society   17
American Board of Commissioners for Foreign Missions (ABCFM)   16, 228, 230, 235–6
American Colonization Society   46
American University
   of Beirut   17
   of Cairo   17
Amin, Idi   28
ancestors   54–5, 58, 110, 120–1, 247, 254
Anderson, Rufus   41
Anglican (Episcopal; Church of England)   23–4, 26, 28, *29*, 30, 41, 42–3, 46, 49, 53, 55, 59, 67–8, 72, 89, 126, 142, *143*, 144–5, 164, 182, 189. 195, 198, 203, 208, 211, 213, 216, 236, 246, 249, 252–3, 255, 264, 265
Anglican Church Missionary Society (CMS)   16
Angola   38, 42
Annan, Kofi   30

anthropologists (anthropology)   54, 56, 58, 99, 182, 240, 265
anti-apartheid   51, 55
anti-imperialism   162
Antioch   119, 259
apartheid   59
apostasy   10, 17
apostle   36, 39, 58, 80–1, 119, 183
   Bartholomew   93
   Paul   77
   Thomas   259
Apostolics (Apostles, AIC)   48, 53, 55–8
Appenzeller, Henry G.   126, 132
Arabic   9, 12–13, 15–16, 18
   Bible   17
Arabs (Arab, Arabia)   9–18, 21, 38, 259
Aramaic   12
Argentina   171, 183, 194
Arians   263
Armenians (Armenia, Armenian Orthodox Church)   9, 11, 13–14, 16, 80
   genocide   13–14
Assemblies of God (AG)   32, 48, 53, 118–19, 183, 190, 192, 195–6, 205
Athanasius   7, 259
Augustine of Hippo   7
Australia   7, 19, 124, 175, 203, 205–16, 224–6, 244, 246
Australian Christian Lobby (ACL)   214
Azusa Street Revival   55

Babalola, Joseph   47
Baghdad   11, 18
Bakker, Jim   196
Bangladesh   95–6, 99, 103
baptism   21, 46, 55–6, 69, 103–4, 111–12, 114, 117, 120, 125, 164, 189, 193, 211, 220–1, 249
Baptist (church)   41–2, 46–7, 49, 58, 84, 85, 87, 95, 104–5, 111, 119, 142, *143*, 161–2, 164, 182, 241–2, 253, 266

Barrett, David   21, 28, *29*
Bartholomew, Saint   93
Base Christian Communities   188, 198
Basel Mission (German Missionary Society)   16, 42
Batak (people)   114, 120
Batemi (people)   26
Beirut   16
Belorussia   79, 81
Benin   39, 48–9
Berlin Conference   43
Bible   17, 23, 47, 53, 58–9, 67, 71, 119, 129, 142, 150, 181, 206, 207, 211, 220, 222, 253
    adaptation   24–5
    Arabic   17
    Catholic   223
    distribution   161, 181
    emphasis on reading   159
    Indonesian   118
    Karen   111
    Maohi   223
    Samoan   223
    schools   31, 72, 227
    Septuagint   44
    Society   17, 161
    translation   23, 44, 55, 67, 181, 227, 242, 252, 265
    vernacular   252, 261, 264
    women   16, 126
bishops   2, 11, 23–4, 26, 30, 32, 39, 42–3, 45, 55–6, 59, 80, 82–3, 89, 93, 116, 154, 156, 159, 164, 174, 177–8, 180–1, 189, 194–5, 197–8, 209, 213, 221–4, 227, 237, 249, 251, 259
Black Death   12
Blair, Tony   69, 208
Blyden, Edward Wilmot   43, 45–6
Bolivia   175, 182
Bonhoeffer, Dietrich   207
Botswana   53, 56–7, 59, 60, 261
Boxer Uprising (Movement, Rebellion)   124, 232
Brahmins   95, 100
Braide, Garrick   47
Brazil   39, 73, 159, 174, 178, 180, 182–3, 186, 188–98
British East India Company   104, 260
Buddhism (Buddhist)   *29*, 70, 96, 101, 106, 108, 110, 112, 114, 131, 133, 149, 259–63, 265–7
Burma (Myanmar)   114, 261
burqa   73
Bush, George W.   69, 208, 215
Byzantine (Byzantium)   7, 9. 11, 80–2, 84

Calvin, John (Calvinism)   67–8, 104, 118
Cambodia   108, 266

Canada   142–5, 149, 215, 264
Cape Verde Islands   38–9
capitalism   40–1, 51, 87, 173, 176, 209
Carey, William   41, 95
cargoism (cargo cultism)   254–5
Caribbean   73, 149, 154, 161, 171, 174, 260
Carthage   9, 11
Casanova, Jose   69
Castro, Fidel   164–7
catechisms   112, 150, 235, 262
Catholic Action (movement)   159, 209
Catholic Charismatic Renewal (CCR)   188–9, 192, 194, 196
Catholicism (Roman Catholic)   7, 9–11, 13, 16–18, 24–6, *29*, 30–1, 38–9, 42–3, 48–9, 53, 55, 59, 67–72, 77, 79–81, 87, 89, 93, 95–6, 100–4, 108, 110–22, 124–7, 133, 142, *143*, 145–7, 154, 156–7, 159–68, 171, 174–83, 186, 188–98, 203, 207–11, 213, 216, 221–7, 230, 232–41, 244, 246, 248–53, 260–1, 263–7
celibacy   24, 232, 236
Central Africa   38
Central America   154–7, 159–63, 168, 171
Chahine, Youssef   15
Chalcedon (Council of)   9, 80
Charismatic Christianity (worship)   28, *29*, 32, 41–2, 46, 48–9, 55, 59, 72–3, 87, 101–3, 118–19, 178, 181–3, 186, 188–98, 226–7, 253–4, 264
children   10, 15, 32, 38, 42, 83, 85, 97, 111, 112, 115, 173, 181–2, 207–8, 211–12, 214–15, 234–6, 263
Chile   171, 174
Chiluba, Frederick   59
China   11, 17, 86, 110, 122, 124–5, 128–30, 133–4, 149, 162, 232
China Inland Mission (CIM)   232
Christendom   2–3, 77, 80, 87, 145, 174–6, 180, 267
Christian and Missionary Alliance   244
Christians by region   *29*, *143*
Church Missionary Society (CMS)   16, 24, 41
civilization   9, 19, 25, 41, 43–4, 46, 61, 67, 70, 74, 79, 80, 113–14, 139
Clapham Sect   41
Codrington College   42
Cold War   79, 85, 147, 173
colonialism   45, 51, 113, 116, 129, 173, 223, 255, 260–1, 262–3, 267
Columbus, Christopher   164, 171
communism   68, 83, 85–7, 116, 127, 147, 159, 162, 207, 209
Confucianism   110, 125, 263, 266
Congo, Republic of   27, 42, 47–8, 51

Congregationalist (Congregational Church)   16, 32, 53,
     55, 145, 164, 207, 211, 230, 232–4, 237–8, 241
Conspiracy Case (Korea)   130
Constantine, Emperor   65, 81, 142
Constantinople   9, 11, 18, 80–2, 259
contextualization   45, 249, 265–6
Conversion   7, 9, 10, 11, 12, 14, 17, 21, 23, 33, 49, 54, 57,
     65, 72, 110, 112, 114, 124, 141, 156, 163, 164, 168,
     176, 180, 188, 189, 192, 193, 196, 211, 218, 221, 222,
     244, 249, 254, 260, 261, 262–3, 265, 266
Cook, Albert   23
Cook, Captain James   203, 218
Coptic   18
   Coptic Evangelical Organization   14
   Coptic Orthodox Church   9, 11, 12, 16, 19, 80
Costa Rica   154, 162, 181
Council of Chalcedon   9, 80
Council of Churches
   Cuban   166–7
   Latin American   182
   Melanesian   253
   Middle East   18
   National (Kenya)   30
   National (USA)   166
   Near East   18
   Pacific   253
   World see World Council of Churches
Council of European Bishops' Conferences (CCEE)
     89
Crete   11
Crowther, Samuel Adjai   42
Crusades   7, 11, 13, 16, 18, 31, 45, 65, 80, 85
Cuba (Cuba)   159, 164–8
   Cuban Revolution   159, 162
Cultural Revolution (China)   124
Cyril of Alexandria   7
Cyril, missionary to the Slavic nations   80
Cyrus   11, 13–14, 17

dalit (untouchable)   100, 105
Dani (people, West Papua)   249, 254
Davie, Grace   69–72
Debayle, Anastasio Samoza   160
decolonization   17
democracy   59, 74, 89, 127, 147, 157, 178, 183, 227, 261,
     262, 264
Destiny Church (New Zealand)   205, 213
dhimmi   7, 9, 10, 11, 13, 17
diaspora   14, 16–17, 19,
   African   165
   American   180

   Muslim   17
   Pacific Island   203
diviner   47, 54, 56
Dominicans   154, 156, 174, 190, 248, 254
Donovan, Vincent   25
Dougherty, Edward   191, 197–8
dreams and visions   56, 179, 218, 247
Dubai   10
Dutch East India Company (VOC)   108, 110, 112
Dutch Reformed Church   53, 244, 254

East Africa   21, 23–7, 29, 30–2
East African Revival   23–4
Eastern Orthodox Church   7, 10–11, 13–14, 18, 29, 77,
     79–82, 85, 87–9, 126, 203
   Antiochan   18
   Coptic   9, 19
   Ethiopian   80
   Georgian   81
   Greek   12, 15–16
   Oriental   80
   Russian   80–1
   Syrian   80, 97–8
ecology   150
Ecuador   182
ecumenism (ecumenical)   18, 23, 43, 53, 59, 71, 80–2, 87,
     89, 105, 118, 159, 166, 175, 180–1, 183, 190, 226–7,
     242, 253
Edinburgh Missionary Conference   21, 42–4
education   13–17, 21, 23–4, 26, 28, 32, 44, 46, 48–9,
     55, 66, 83, 100, 103, 106, 112–15, 119, 124, 130,
     133–4, 150, 156–7, 161, 167, 168, 184, 190–1, 208,
     210, 218, 222–3, 225–6, 227, 234, 236, 240–2, 252,
     261–2, 264
Egypt   7, 9–18, 42, 44–6, 211, 259, 261, 267
Ekuphakameni   58
Eliot, T. S.   43
El Salvador   156–7, 159–60, 163–4, 180
England   40–1, 48, 54, 67–8, 106, 142, 144, 145, 205
Enlightenment   44, 205, 262, 266
Estonia   79
Ethiopia (Ethiopians)   42, 44, 80, 260, 266
Ethiopianism   44–6, 48
Eucharist   26, 97, 101, 210, 237
European Union (EU)   68
Evangelical Awakenings   176
evangelize (evangelization)   10, 16, 17, 28, 31, 36, 38,
     42–4, 45, 47–8, 49, 77, 80, 87, 89, 95, 108, 110,
     124, 125–6, 161–2, 167, 175, 176, 180, 181, 186,
     188, 189, 195, 197, 198, 211, 230, 236, 242, 246,
     251, 253

Fairouz (Christian Lebanese singer)   15
Farabundo Martí Liberación Nacional (FMLN)   160
fascism   68, 146
Female Genital Cutting (FGC)   23, 27, 266
Ferguson, Samuel   43
Fiji   118, 221, 225, 228, 244, 247, 249, 253–5
Filipe, Roberto   193
Florovsky, Georges   82
foot binding   261
Foucauld, Charles de   16
Foursquare Gospel Church   48, 55, 190, 196, 224, 226,
    246, 260
France   7, 11, 13, 17, 49, 68–9, 71–2, 77, 108, 125
Francis, Carey   23
Franciscans   95, 154, 156, 233
French Revolution   176, 266
Fritze, Georg   25

genocide   14, 182
Gereja Kristen Indonesia   114
German (Germany)   16, 21, 25, 30, 65, 68, 74, 77, 79,
    146–7, 222–3, 230, 232, 235–6, 240, 246, 265
    Democratic Republic   79
    evangelical Liebenzell missionaries   232, 240
    Protectorate   222
German Missionary Society (also Basel Mission)   16
Ghana   40, 46, 48–9, 73
Giay, Benny   255
Gifford, Paul   59
Gikuyu (people)   27, 30, 32
Giriama (people)   26
Gitari, David   30
globalization   49, 117, 173, 175, 183
Goa   95–6, 99
Gospel Missionary Society (GMS)   27
Graham, Billy   147–8
Greeks (Greece, Greek Orthodox Church)   9, 13–16, 44,
    77, 79, 81–2, 259–60, 265
Grey, Earl   208
Guatemala   154, 156–7, 160, 162–4, 178, 182
Gutiérrez, Gustavo   171, 177–8
Gutmann, Bruno   25

Habash, George   15
Habermas, Jürgen   74
Harris, William Wadé   47
Hawaii   230, 232, 236
Healey, Joseph   25
healing   51, 53–8, 60, 67, 71, 101–3, 111–12, 118–19, 149,
    174, 179, 188–90, 192–8, 212, 224, 227, 234, 242, 248,
    253, 266

healthcare   13, 51, 56, 59, 112, 150, 169, 235–6, 242,
    262, 264
hegemony (Western)   44–5, 159, 161, 188
Hillmann, Eugene   25
Hillsong (Australian Christian Churches)   205
Hinduism (Hindu)   29, 53, 70, 95–7, 99–103, 105, 147,
    149, 244, 254, 260–3, 265–7
HIV/AIDS   58, 255
holiness movement   48, 55, 58, 163–4, 253
Holy Ghost Fathers   42
Holy Land   7, 65
Holy Roman Empire   77
Holy Spirit   42, 48, 53, 55–6, 58–9, 119, 150, 164, 186,
    189, 190, 192–3, 195–8
homosexuals   167, 207, 210
Honduras   154, 161, 163
hospitals   17, 42, 55, 112, 126, 128, 161–2, 195, 221, 226
Howard, John   208, 210, 214
human rights   17–18, 59, 74, 87, 89, 150, 154, 177–8, 181,
    184, 205, 240
Hussein, Saddam   15

Iberian (Iberia)   36, 39, 41–3, 45, 47, 49, 171, 173–4,
    176, 186
identity   13, 32, 42, 44, 71, 81, 86, 96–7, 99, 104, 106,
    115–16, 146, 163, 167–8, 181
    Christian   70, 96–7, 101–2, 105, 188, 195, 213, 226–7,
        254
    cultural   106
    ethnic   35, 106, 114, 118, 120
    multilingual   11
    Muslim   15
    national   81, 87, 126
    public   232
    religious   69–70, 87, 96, 154, 156, 181, 191, 265
immigration (immigrant)   11, 85, 145, 147, 149, 157, 161,
    176, 207, 216
imperialism (Western)   16, 96, 124–5, 134, 161
India (Indians)   9–11, 13, 19, 39, 41, 53, 93, 95–6, 99–101,
    103–6, 149, 254, 259–63, 265–6
Indies
    Netherland Indies   113
    West Indies   41–2, 44, 114, 154
indigenization   23–4, 45, 110, 127, 167, 225, 265, 259
Indonesia (Indonesians)   108, 110–12, 114–20, 244, 246,
    252, 254–5
International Bible Society   23
Internet   2, 117, 196, 214
Iran   9–14, 16, 259
Iraq   7, 9, 11, 12, 19, 203
Ireland (Irish)   69, 146, 208, 216, 246, 264

Iron Curtain   79, 87
Islam   7, 9, 10, 11, 13, 15, 17–19, 28, 31, 36, 38, 43, 45,
    48–9, 70, 73, 79–80, 83, 85, 96–7, 106, 108, 111,
    115–18, 149, 174, 254, 259, 263, 265, 267
Israel   7, 14, 17, 19, 142, 249
Istanbul   12, 14, 259
Italy   68, 77, 146

Jamaica   42, 161
James, Saint   65
Japan (Japanese)   122, 124–34, 146–7, 224, 246, 251,
    260, 261, 263, 265, 266
  Japanese Occupation   110, 119, 130
Jehovah's Witnesses   196
Jerusalem   11, 17, 46, 253, 259
  Jerusalem Council   77
Jesuits   16, 25, 38–9, 95, 112, 122, 124, 125, 141, 156,
    160, 176–7, 180, 186, 190, 230, 232–3, 235–7, 239,
    241, 261
Jesus (Jesus Christ)   9, 16, 25, 28, 31, 36, 45–6, 53–5, 59, 77,
    83, 86, 93, 101–2, 105, 119, 150, 176, 180–1, 192,
    195–8, 206, 216, 248–9, 254, 266
Jews (Jewish)   9, 10, 12–14, 16–17, 28, 85, 97, 141, 143,
    145–7, 259, 263
jizya   9, 11
John XXIII, Pope   159
John Paul II, Pope   89, 126, 160, 165, 167, 174, 180
Johnson, James   45
Johnson, Richard   203

Kampala   32
Kanamai Statement (1993)   26
Karamonjong (people)   26
Karen (people)   111, 114, 117
Karen National Union   117
Kenya   21, 23–4, 26–8, 29, 30–1
Kerala   96–7, 99–100, 105
Keysser, Christian   249
Khrist Panthis   101–2
Kimbangu, Simon   47, 254
Kongo (people, kingdom)   38–9

Lang, John Dunmore   207
las Casas, Bartolomé   154, 156, 171
Latin   65, 67, 70, 79, 144, 157, 159, 162, 222
  liturgy   16
Latin America   149, 154, 156, 159–62, 164–7, 173–84,
    189, 190–1, 196–8, 262, 265–7
Latin American Bishops' Conference (CELAM)   159,
    177–8, 197, 186
Latin American Mission (LAM)   162

Latvia   79
law   40, 83, 86, 87, 116, 118, 124, 125, 139, 143, 144, 149,
    156, 157, 165, 166, 168, 178, 205, 214, 215, 247, 251,
    263
  Christian (also canon law)   26, 31, 221, 224, 239, 252
  Islamic (also shariah)   10, 263
League of Nations   17
Lebanon (Lebanese)   13–15, 17–18
  Christians   14
  Maronites   13
  refugees   203
Lerner, Max   139
Levant   9, 36
liberation theology   59, 116, 159–60, 162, 165, 177–9,
    181, 189, 264
Liberia   38, 41–2, 45, 47, 49
literacy   18, 21, 28, 54–5, 67, 112, 161, 211, 220, 222, 236,
    252, 262
Lithuania   77, 79, 259, 266
liturgy   25, 44, 46, 48, 65, 71, 81–3, 87, 93, 97, 114,
    179, 238,
London Missionary Society (LMS)   41, 54–5, 218, 221–5,
    246, 250–1, 253
Luther, Martin   65, 77
Lutherans   41, 68, 72, 80, 95, 143, 211, 246, 249–51, 253
Luwum, Janani   30

Maasai (people)   25, 27
Macedo, Edir   194
Macedonia   77, 79, 81
McLoughlin, William, G.   139
Madurai   95
Malawi   54, 59
Malaysia   108, 115, 117, 121, 259
Mali   39, 48–9
Maluku   117–18
Mamluk Dynasty   11
Manila   111, 115
Māori   213
Maoist Revolution (China)   162
Maranke, John   57
March First Movement (Korea)   122, 130, 132
Marists   221–2, 244, 246
Maronites   13, 16, 18
marriage   7, 14, 25, 58, 69, 97, 110, 114, 213–15, 242,
    247, 264
  child   261
  intermarriage   11–12, 263
Martin, David   163, 179
martyrs   11–12, 30, 65, 82, 85, 124, 160, 220, 251
Marxism   83, 177

Mary (Virgin) 101, 111, 191–2, 248, 266
Maryknoll 25, 157, 159–60
Masowe, Johane 58
Mau Mau 27
Meghalaya 96, 103
Mehmet 11
Melanesia 220–1, 225–8, 244, 246–55
  Christianities 248
Mennonites 84–5
Menzies, Sir Robert 209
Methodist 17, 42–3, 43, 49, 68, 104, 126–7, 131–2, 145, 161–2, 164, 176, 182–3, 186, 188, 211, 221, 224–5, 227, 244, 246, 248–9, 253–4
Methodius, missionary to the slavs 80
Mexico 111, 141, 149, 156–7, 171, 174, 178, 180, 182, 186, 266
Michigan State University 189
Micronesia 230, 233, 236, 238–43
Middle East 7, 9–10, 12–14, 16–19, 93, 259, 260, 262–3
military 11, 13–14, 27, 30, 67, 79, 83, 104, 112, 117, 119, 133, 141, 146, 160, 164, 167, 180, 247, 260, 263
Miller, Donald E. 150, 183
millet 12–13
missionaries 9, 11, 16–17, 19, 21, 23, 25–6, 36, 38–9, 41–5, 47–50, 53–6, 65, 67, 80, 95, 100, 104, 110–12, 114–15, 117, 119, 122, 124–34, 157, 161–4, 167, 173, 176–7, 180, 186, 197, 205, 208, 210–11, 220–4, 227–8, 230, 232–7, 240–2, 244, 46, 250–2, 260–6
Mizoram 96, 103–4
modernization 32, 87, 118, 125, 134, 161, 173–4, 176, 253, 264
Moffat, Robert 54
monasticism 82, 259
Mongolia 103, 122, 259
Monotheists (monotheism, monotheistic) 7, 43, 49, 246, 262, 266
Montt, Efrain Rios 163, 182
Moravians 16, 25
Mormons (Latter-day Saints) 17, *143*, 196, 222, 225, 227
Mozambique 42, 266
Mugabe, Robert 59
Museveni, Yoweri 30
Muslims 7, 9–19, 28, *29*, 30–1, 36, 42–3, 48–9, 53, 65, 80, 95, 97, 99, 101–3, 108, 112, 116–17, 149, 244, 251, 254, 259–63, 265, 266

Nagaland 96, 103
Nairobi 24, 26, 31–2
Narokobi, Bernard 255
nationalism 13, 43–4, 46, 87, 104, 122, 125, 127, 129–34, 162, 167, 261, 262

National Student Leadership Forum on Faith and Values
  Australia 206
  US 206
Native Pastorate (West Africa) 45
Nazarites (AIC) 53, 57–8
Nazism 146
Ncube, Pius 59
Nepal 96, 99
Nestorians (Church of the East) 9, 11, 14, 19, 93, 122
Netherlands 69, 108, 113–14
Newbigin, Lesslie 2
New Guinea 222, 244, 246, 249–50, 253
New Testament 28, 45, 180
New Zealand 203, 205–9, 211–13, 215, 217, 223, 225, 246
Nicaragua 154, 156, 159–60, 163, 171
Nicea (Council) 80–1
Nigeria 42–3, 45–6, 48–9, 73
de Nobili, Roberto 95
North Africa 7, 9, 12, 16–19, 259, 262–3
North America 14, 19, 31, 38, 40, 95, 124, 139, 141–2, 145, 147, 149–50, 161–2, 175, 177, 179, 183, 186, 189, 196–8, 259, 262, 265–7
Notre Dame University 190
Nova Scotia 41

Oberlin College 42
Oceania 221, 244, 264
Ojo-Cole, Julius 46
Olang, Festo 23
Old Testament 28, 45, 47, 223
Oman 17
Oosthuizen, G. C. 56
Ottoman 11–14, 19, 77, 79, 83

Pacific 77, 141, 203, 205, 218, 227, 230, 232, 234, 242–3, 254
  Canadian Railroad 145
Pacific Conference of Churches 226
Pacific Theological College 226, 255
Pacific War 110
pacification 43
Pact of Umar 9
Pakistan 7, 95–6, 99, 101, 104, 261
Palestine 7, 13, 14, 15, 17
Panama 154
Papua New Guinea 246, 249, 251, 253
paternalism 132, 163, 179,
Paul, Saint 45, 77, 97
payback 247–8, 251–2, 254–5

Pentecostal (Pentecostalism)   17, 23, 27–8, *29*, 30–2, 36, 47–50, 53, 55–6, 58–9, 68, 72–3, 84–5, 87, 101, 118–19, 163–5, 167, 174, 177–83, 186, 188–98, 203, 205, 207, 211, 213, 226–7, 233, 253, 264
Pentecostal Association of Tanzania   32
People of the Book   9
persecution   9, 11, 77, 83–4, 87, 93, 117, 124–5, 142, 161, 177, 266
Persian (Persia)   7, 9, 93, 106, 261, 263, 266
Persian Gulf   17
Peru   173, 176, 179–80, 182–3
Philip, John   55
Philippines   95, 108, 111–16, 118–19, 221, 249, 263
pietism   41, 44, 46, 71, 85, 118, 139, 147, 227
Pluralism
   Christian   9, 95
   Islam   9
   Religious   95, 105, 139, 144, 147, 149, 176, 228
polygamy   114, 223, 261, 263, 266
Popular Front for the Liberation of Palestine (PFLP)   15
Portugal   38–9, 108, 124, 154, 171, 186
praeparatio evangelicae   249
pre-millennialists   216
Presbyterian   9, 16, 42, 49, 104–5, 125–7, 142, *143,* 145, 161–2, 164, 182–3, 186, 188–9, 207, 216, 225, 246, 252
prophet (prophetic movements)   27, 31, 36, 46–7, 56–8, 71, 119, 121, 211–12, 234, 240, 242, 254–5, 260
prostitution (prostitutes)   41, 239

Quakers   40, 67–8, 161, 164, 266
Québec   141, 144,
Qur'an   9, 10, 43, 259

Rahm, Harold   190
railroad   143, 145
Redeemed Christian Church   73–4
Reformation   65, 67–8, 70, 79, 159, 161, 174, 183
Reorganized Latter-day Saints   223
revival   15, 23–4, 40, 42, 46–9, 53, 55, 70–1, 73, 104, 112, 119, 126, 128–9, 142, 145, 174, 191, 197, 211, 224, 232, 234, 253–4
Rhenish Missionary Society (RMG)   114, 246
Ricci, Matteo   122
rites controversy   122
Roman Empire   65, 77, 81, 93, 266
Romero, Oscar Arnulfo   160
Ross, John   125
Rossi, Marcelo   194
Royal Institute for Inter-Faith Studies (RIIFS)   18

Rudd, Kevin   207–8
Russia   7, 13–14, 77, 79–82, 87, 125, 126, 128, 266

sacraments   111, 159
Sadrach, Kiai   119
salvation   21, 25–8, 55, 129, 141, 161, 164, 181, 254
Samoa   220–7
Sandinista   160
Sarawak   115, 121
Saudi Arabia   10, 259
Scandinavia   65, 69, 72
science   44, 68, 89, 127
Scotland   26, 68, 122, 195, 262
secularization   68–71, 157, 205, 253, 264–5
self-determination   262
Septuagint   44
Serbia   79, 81–2, 87
Seventh-day Adventists   222, 224, 238, 259
sex slavery   32
shariah   7
Sheen, Fulton J.   147
Shembe, Isaiah   57–8
Shorter, Aylward   25–6
Sidang Injil Borneo   121
Sierra Leone   36, 38, 40, 42–6, 49
Sikhism (Sikh)   *29*, 95, 149, 254, 262
Sisters of Cluny   42
slavery   10, 32, 40, 42, 44, 45, 54, 55, 146, 150, 218, 228, 261, 266
Society for African Mission   42
Society for the Propagation of the Gospel (SPG)   161
sociologists (sociology)   67–8, 93, 97, 99, 147, 149–50, 174, 179–80, 181–2
South Africa   17, 21, 27, 53–7, 59
Soviet Union *see* USSR
Spain   38, 69, 71, 77, 108, 116, 154, 156, 164–5, 171, 180, 230
Sri Lanka   93, 95–6, 99, 259, 261, 262
Sudan   10, 16, 17
   Northern   11
Swaggart, Jimmy   196
Sweden   19, 67, 72, 216
Swedish Free Mission   32
Switzerland   77
Syria (Syriac)   9, 97, 259
Syrian Christians   97, 99–100, 104

Tahiti   208, 218, 220–3, 205, 225–6, 260
Taiwan   122, 124, 149
Takamoa College   220, 224
Tamil   95

Tamil Nadu 96
Tanzania 24–8, *29*, 30–2, 51
Taoism 263
Tauf'ahau 221
Ta'unga 220
teachers 27, 46, 102, 110, 112, 115, 214, 230, 235–7, 239, 261
Temple, William 83
Tertullian 7, 259
Thai 265
Thailand 108, 110–11, 114, 260
Thomas, Saint 93, 259, 265
Three-Self Patriotic Movement 124
Tibet 19, 103, 259
Timor Leste 108, 116
Tokugawa (Shogunate) 124
Tokyo 133
Tonga 211, 221–2, 224, 227
torture 30, 130, 266
totalitarianism 82, 87
Tranquebar 95, 189
Translation (of the Bible) 23, 42, 44–5, 55, 67, 112, 115, 118, 181, 221, 227
Trappist monks 16, 144
Treaty of Waitangi 206, 208
Trinity 47
Turks (Turkish) 14, 77, 79, 82–3
Turkey 9, 11, 14, 82, 259
Tuskegee Institute 42
Tutu, Archbishop Desmond 59
Tuwere, Sevati 255

Uganda 23–4, 26–8, *29*, 30–1
Ukraine 13, 79, 81, 87–8
Underwood, Horace G. 126
Unevangelized Fields Missions (UFM) 244
United Bible Society 23
United Church of Japan 125
United Methodist Church *143*
United Nations 17, 225, 244
United States (US) 18–19, 23, 55, 72, 161–2, 166–7, 171, 183, 186, 189–90, 195–6, 205–6, 208, 214–16, 230, 241, 264
Universal Church of the Kingdom of God (IURD) 191, 193–4, 196
Universal Declaration of Human Rights (UDHR) 18
Université Saint-Joseph (Beruit) 16
university 18, 35, 60, 174, 180, 190, 262
University of Balamand 18
Urban II, Pope 11
urbanization 159, 162, 173

USSR (Soviet Union) 79, 80–1, 83–5, 87, 147, 165
Uttar Pradesh 100

Vanuatu 246, 252
Vatican II (Second Vatican Council) 25, 70, 120, 127, 159, 162, 177, 226, 237, 252, 264, 266
Veda 262
veneration
    ancestors 54, 60, 110
    holy images 110
    Host 102
    Maria 114
    mountain spirits 121
    saints 210
Venn, Henry 24, 41, 44–5
vernacular
    Bible 252
    church 27
    church music 120
    education system 262
    languages 2, 159, 161, 252
    literature 55
    Mass 253
    translation 23, 42
    version of Christ's life 116
Vietnam 108, 110–11, 116–17, 121, 149, 205, 216, 266
violence 260
    against Armenians 13
    against Christian converts 188
    against women 179
    Christian initiated 116
    Crusades 11
    dalits (outcastes) 99
    drug trafficking 174
    El Salvador 160, 163
    ethnic 117
    Europe 211
    Guatemala 163
    Hanoi 117
    interreligious 31, 261
    inter-tribal 251
    Japanese 132
    Kenya 30–1
    Maluku (Indonesia) 31, 118
    Marshalls (islands) 233
    Mizo 105
    and monotheism 266
    Muslim 116
    Palestinian struggle 15
    religious persecution 266
    terrorism 182

violence (*cont'd*)
  West Papua   255
  youth   175
virgin (virginity)   58, 110
  "The Queen Virgin"   77
Virgin Mary   111, 191–2, 195
voluntarism   72, 264

Wales   203, 207, 211
Weissköppel, Cordula   73
Wesleyans (Wesleyan Church)   41, 208, 221–2, 224–5,
    227, 244
West Africa   16, 27, 36, 38, 39, 41–9, 53
West Indies   41–2, 45
West Papua (Western New Guinea)   114, 115, 118, 244,
    247–8, 250, 254–5
Wilberforce, Willliam   41
Williams, John   220
Wilson, Woodrow   131
witchcraft   32, 47, 51, 56, 59, 156, 218, 248, 252
Wolof (people)   38
women   45, 53–4, 56, 100, 106, 110, 115, 119, 156, 191,
    192, 197, 224, 233–9, 241, 247–50, 252–3, 261
  African   24, 48
  Apostolic Church (Africa)   57
  Bible study group   126
  "Bible Women"   16
  Catholic   191
  Christian   10, 15
  dancing   238
  European churches   71
  evangelical laywomen   59, 60, 183, 195
  India   100–1
  Jewish   10

Korean   130–1
Maryknoll   160
menstruation   252
mission   42
Muslim   10, 15, 73
  ordination of   81, 115
  priests   70
Protestant missionaries   17, 110
Redeemed Christian Church of God   74
South Africa   54, 58
Southeast Asia   111, 112, 115
urbanization   227
World Christianity   7, 9, 80, 174, 226, 260, 265–6
World Council of Churches (WCC)   80, 180, 182, 226
World Evangelical Alliance   182
World Vision   53
World War I   14, 17, 43, 46–7, 114, 145, 209, 246
World War II   68, 73, 79, 83, 125–6, 146, 159, 173, 178,
    203, 209, 216, 224, 232, 235, 246
Wycliffe Bible Translators   252

Xavier, Francis   115, 124

Yoachim III (Orthodox Patriarch)   18
Yoruba (Yorubaland)   41, 46–7
Young Turks   14

Zambia   59–60
Zimbabwe   53, 57–9
Zionist (AIC)   47, 53, 55–8
Zoroastrians   9, 29, 263, 266
Zulu   56–7
  Zionists   56
Zurenuoc, Zuruwe   250–1